The BELTWAY BIBLE

A Totally Serious A–Z Guide to
Our No-Good, Corrupt, Incompetent,
Terrible, Depressing, and Sometimes
Hilarious Government

Eliot Nelson

St. Martin's Griffin
New York

 For information, address St. Martin's Press, 175 Fifth Avenue, New York, N.Y. 10010.

www.stmartins.com

Designed by Jonathan Bennett

Library of Congress Cataloging-in-Publication Data

Names: Nelson, Eliot, author.
Title: The Beltway Bible : a totally serious A–Z guide to our no-good, corrupt, incompetent, terrible, depressing, and sometimes hilarious government / Eliot Nelson.
Description: First edition. | New York : St. Martin's Griffin, 2016.
Identifiers: LCCN 2016012743| ISBN 9781250099259 (paperback) | ISBN 9781250099266 (e-book)
Subjects: LCSH: United States Politics and government—Humor. | Political culture—United States—Humor. | BISAC: HUMOR / Topic / Political. | POLITICAL SCIENCE / Government / General.
Classification: LCC PN6231.P6 N38 2016 | DDC 320.97302/07—dc23
LC record available at https://lccn.loc.gov/2016012743

First Edition: September 2016

10 9 8 7 6 5 4 3 2 1

To Betty and Freck, for decades of faithful service atop the Nelson Oversight Committee

We were born of risen apes, not fallen angels . . .
—Robert Ardrey

INTRODUCTION

Are you on the toilet?

Sorry, I don't mean to be crude. You see, my publisher tells me this is a "gift title," that is, a book that will be given to news junkies as birthday presents, left under Christmas trees for poli-sci majors, and purchased on a whim for especially disgruntled NPR listeners. That got me thinking: *What kind of book do people typically gift?*

1. Cookbooks
2. David McCullough books
3. Coffee-table books
4. Books you read on the toilet

You're not going to find any stir-fry tips in here. I'm not a nationally beloved chronicler of the Founding Fathers and this isn't a glossy compendium of Man Ray photographs. So it's a bathroom book, which mean you're more than likely to be, er . . .

. . . well I'm just glad you're here! My humble offering may live in a little wicker basket beside your toilet, sandwiched between a decade-old *Elle* and a jaundiced, water-warped collection of crossword puzzles, but I'm OK with that.[1]

[1] Or perhaps you're in a bookstore pretending to read this in hopes that an attractive stranger is drawn to your intellectual curiosity. If so, PUT DOWN THIS BOOK *IMMEDIATELY.* No one *ever* got laid by conspicuously reading something with "A to Z" in the title. You might as well be

You might well be wondering: *Why is this guy rambling about the toilet? Isn't this a book about politics? Where are the juicy tidbits about interns and tales of wanton corruption and malfeasance? And what is an omnibus bill?* Three things:

1. Be patient, that'll come later.
2. "Juicy tidbits." *Heh.*
3. Hear me out.

As far as associations go, you could do worse than politics and excrement. Given the political arena's near perpetual state of dysfunction, linking feces and government just *feels* right, y'know? Like, on a *visceral level*. I'm not saying the next time you mention politics while playing Taboo or Catch Phrase a friend will exuberantly blurt out, "fecal matter!," but considering human waste is regularly used as an adjective to describe our leaders, and since we're on the topic already, let's run with it. Also, a lot of very respectable and important people I interviewed for this book suggested I do an entry on the best places in Washington to use the bathroom. I didn't, but it came up a lot.

A lot.

We don't think of politicians on the toilet, do we?[2] Then again, we don't usually think of *anyone* on the toilet. But as with Santa Claus, Oprah, and your mother, we ascribe a kind of Barbie and Ken quality to our legislators. You may be surprised to learn that legislators are actual human beings. *Very flawed* human beings, sure, but human beings nonetheless.

---

flashing bedroom eyes at hotties while perusing *Thyroids for Dummies* or the dalmatian calendar on sale by the cash register.

Or maybe you're an industrial pulp mill, slowly grinding unsold copies of my hard work into a soupy mix of de-inking chemicals, soggy paper, and my unrealized dreams. My only hope is that this is reincarnated into something pleasant like a poster for a Meryl Streep movie or one of those arrow-shaped signs that stoners in gorilla costumes spin outside of car washes.

[2] Well, LBJ, maybe.

We do ourselves a disservice when we dehumanize Washington and reduce its processes and people to a few superficial talking points. *Checks and balances, lobbyists, pork barrel spending, the electoral college, filibusters, Dick Cheney's bimonthly virgin sacrifice upon a marble altar in the Heritage Foundation's basement to placate the icy god of darkness and ward off the eternal sleep of death for another moonturn, yadda yadda yadda.* The more entrenched this view becomes, the less able we are to grasp the complexities of the situation and perhaps even start to do something about it. *Yes,* there is corruption and *yes* there are systemic issues that can probably be fixed if we removed our heads from our asses—they'll come up often enough in this book.

If there's one thing to keep in mind as you read *The Beltway Bible,* it's this: the problems affecting our government are more complicated, more muddled, more difficult to pinpoint, more . . . *human* than your civics textbook or favorite cable news show might make them out to be. Understanding cases of unapologetic wrongdoing and learning the basic systems of government are the easy parts. If Washington's only problems were a surplus of Jack Abramoffs or our ignorance about quorum calls, our problems would be much more readily identifiable and fixable. Not only is the government infinitely complex, but so, too, are the people in and around it, and when you combine the complexity and vagaries of human nature with the complexity and vagaries of a government overseeing 300-plus million people, things don't always go as planned.

Washington isn't a nest of vipers. Really. It's a city of mostly well-intentioned people who, like the rest of us, sometimes cut corners out of expedience, self-interest, or, quite possibly, the greater good. It's a city defined not by its cardinal sins, but by its venal ones. For every bug-eyed backbencher who insists Mexican immigrants are all al-Qaeda sleeper agents, or every slick lobbyist clamoring to sign an energy company that drenched half of Puget Sound in unrefined crude, there are thousands of far more relatable individuals committing much less conspicuous, and more ethically muddled, offenses: the congressman who votes for a discriminatory bill that won't go anywhere to earn political capital so he or she can defeat their challenger who would bring a much more harmful agenda to Washington; the reporter who holds off on a story about a senator's special interest fundraiser to stay in the lawmaker's good graces for a larger piece about malfeasance among congressional leadership; the political staffer who holds their tongue when a colleague cashes out at a lobbying firm because they, too, might one day want to stop working eighty hours a week while making $45,000 a year.

All these people, I might add, use toilets.

It's the ubiquity of these minor-to-moderate transgressions that both perpetuates some of our government's deeper problems but also, in an odd way, keeps Washington from becoming a den of unbridled corruption—Babylon with flag pins, if you will. On the one hand, such behavior generates a feedback loop, making it more and more normal as the years roll by. On the other hand, the latticework formed by these networks of noble-minded but ethically imperfect politicos creates a kind of moral safety net, allowing some of the ethical give that most of us accord ourselves, but serving to keep people from plunging themselves into the proverbial muck and mud of the Washington swamp.

Of course, there are countless people who crash through that net. You've likely read a lot about them: amoral members of Congress, lawbreaking lobbyists, and so forth. This isn't to excuse them, and this book is by no means an establishmentarian treatise. Yet there's a yawning gap between what constitutes the *status quo* and what constitutes *human behavior*. Understanding how our very human government officials and advocates navigate our institutions and the rules governing them is the first step toward fixing the status quo. Anyone who insists that throwing the bums out will solve all our problems is doing themselves and you a great disservice.

This mentality is illustrated, literally and figuratively, by two incredibly heinous paintings by the artist Andy Thomas, *Callin' the Blue* and *Callin' the Red*.[3]

They're great: both paintings depict groups of presidents, living and dead, playing pool. In one, a smiling Barack Obama prepares to sink a ball into the side pocket as former Democratic presidents including Andrew Jackson, JFK, and Bill Clinton look on, sporting shit-eating grins and sipping bourbon.[4] A similar scene is represented in the Republican painting, with Abraham Lincoln slyly grinning beside Teddy Roosevelt while Richard Nixon, Ronald Reagan, both Bushes, and Gerald Ford share laughs.

Both paintings make *Dogs Playing Poker* look as abstract as a Miró canvas, and if it weren't for an absence of happy little trees, you'd think the things were dreamed up by Bob Ross. Also, not for nothing, it's remarkable that Andrew Jackson walked into his presidential bro hang, saw a black guy, and didn't immediately drop dead again.

Also, who invited *Gerald Ford*?

Aesthetic judgments aside, the paintings' awfulness really derives from what they represent: a two-dimensional understanding of Washington, not only of our leaders, but how they deal (or should deal) with one another. Depending on whom you ask, Washington is either too chummy, or not chummy enough. Whatever the case, and the truth is a little of both, the two sentiments are ably represented, albeit in comic exaggeration. It speaks to the images that flicker into our minds when we hear phrases like "Beltway insiders" and "the political class," or when we read that all of Washington is abuzz over something, or consider the city's entrenched clubbiness that obscure House candidates vow to single-handedly dislodge. Somewhere, the thinking goes, the entire political class—those Beltway insiders, those people "familiar with the situation"—are all crammed into a

[3] If you're ever in Washington, you can see them hanging at Clyde's, an ersatz pub/clubhouse that serves tourists overpriced burgers and artichoke dip (a thinking man's TGI Friday's, if you will).

[4] I'm guessing it's bourbon.

pool room somewhere, guffawing, slapping backs, and plotting to line their pockets and destroy your life.

Of course, few people actually believe that a freshman congressman will change Washington, and most of us have a sense that Washington's power base is too diffused to fit into a single wood-paneled lounge. However, there's a small part of us that nevertheless buys into the idea that Washington's ills and the people who perpetrate them are two-dimensional, easily identifiable, and eminently fixable. If only. Mario Cuomo famously said that we campaign in poetry and govern in prose. We also critique the government in poetry—angsty, adolescent poetry, but poetry nonetheless.

The hundreds of thousands of people who scurry about our federal offices are flesh-and-blood humans with mortgages, families, nagging blood pressure problems, hidden caches of porn, and the countless other challenges and personal blemishes that characterize modern white-collar life. These are overstressed boomers trying to balance the rigors of work, life, and family; heartbroken twenty-somethings rebounding from breakups by numbing their brain with booze and their thumbs with Tinder; untold numbers of people counting down the hours until they can get home and watch television in their underpants; aging office workers who long ago stopped removing their security badge from their neck for the train home.

There are moments of acute unreality, to be sure—a senator striding across Constitution Avenue while wolfing down a Starbucks breakfast sandwich; the Lincoln Memorial coming into view as you whiz down Rock Creek Parkway; the mind-boggling poverty that exists in Washington mere blocks from the National Mall and the imposing Beaux Arts federal offices that encircle it. And, in a certain way, that's what this book is. Not just an overview of how the government works and classifications of the people tethered to it, but how those people and those institutions metabolize the amazing realities and unrealities of power. While I hope *The Beltway Bible* provides you with information that may have been omitted from CNN, I also hope much of it is recognizable. There isn't much distinguishing the kabuki theater of political spin from the kabuki theater of your company's community service day, when your boss and the head of HR pretend your employer's mission statement, "Growing Opportunity, Growing Communities," is anything other than PR-derived bunk.

Political books tend to be divided into two camps. On one side, you have your *serious* books: the policy proposals, the probing biographies of lawmakers, the deeply researched histories of legislative battles. These are the books that earn people endowed chairs at prestigious universities and appearances on the *PBS NewsHour,* that allow *Times* reporters to go on book leave, and that solemnly collect dust on bookshelves in austerely furnished and rarely used living rooms. On the other side, you have your *juicier* books: the tell-alls, the gossipy campaign ticktocks, the D.C. social diaries, the autobiographies from iconic movers and shakers with titles like *A Good Run: My Life At the Center of It All.* These are the books that titillate political observers, that prompt endless speculation, and that undoubtedly have the best book parties.

Practitioners of both genres turn up their noses at each other. The serious author scoffs at the philistine fluff peddled by their counterparts; and, from the cramped confines of their think-tank office or newsroom cubicle, comforts himself with the fact that he is truly doing God's work. Across town in his Georgetown rowhouse den, the mover and shaker grins, reclines in his Eames chair, and sips his bourbon.[5]

However, like most anything else in life, politics is a mixture of the high and low, the academic and the unquantifiable reality of life on the ground. This book won't cover every last thing about Washington—a person could spend their entire life trying to chronicle and alphabetize every Senate rule or campaign trail fixture and still not get past "John Roberts's Coffee Breath." It will, though, contain introductions to most of the basic stuff: how bills are passed,

---

[5] I'm guessing it's bourbon.

how the White House and federal agencies are structured, how the Supreme Court works, yadda yadda yadda. Mixed into that will be entries on the people who pull the levers and twist the gears, and (hopefully) vivid and humanizing accounts of the people who try to influence them.

I didn't follow a formula in choosing what to include, or how many column inches to dedicate to each issue. Are super PACs as significant as Jumbo Slice, the drunk food political staffers wolf down in the wee small hours? Of course not. But since warts-and-all depictions of Washington's denizens so rarely accompany descriptions of governmental mechanics, I felt compelled to give extra attention to some seemingly frivolous things in the hopes of creating a more resonant account. Also, I had *a lot* of fun with the Jumbo Slice entry. My account might sometimes be overly raw, a little messy, and perhaps a little mean, but so, too, is Washington.

So to those of you on the toilet, I hope this book makes your future digestive endeavors more enjoyable and informative.

ACCENTS

Albatross for politicians who have struggled for centuries to reconcile their regional pronunciations with the prejudices of whomever they were trying to please. If lawmakers could dress their vocal chords up in camo gear and have them spray ducks with buckshot for the press, they probably would.

The recent trend has been for pols to play up, if not outright feign, a folksy drawl. Take, for example, Joe Biden's 2012 sermon-like warning to an African American audience that Mitt Romney's economic agenda would "put y'all back in chains" or then-Minnesota governor Tim Pawlenty's brief 2012 presidential campaign, when he shed his Midwestern prosodies for something that sounded like Captain from *Cool Hand Luke* having a stroke.

However, that trend has run against the historical norm. YouTube clips of antebellum politicians aren't easy to come by, but with only a few exceptions, the rhetoric of the day, even the political attacks, was remarkably haughty. "I cannot believe that killing 2,500 Englishmen at New Orleans qualifies for the various, difficult and complicated duties of the Chief Magistracy," Henry Clay snipped about his 1824 presidential campaign opponent, Andrew Jackson. *Me-ow!*

The proliferation of radio in the twentieth century further highlighted the preference for bland or aristocratic accents. Al Smith, the

Democrats' 1928 nominee for president and the first Catholic presidential candidate, alarmed the public with his gravelly brogue, which recalled, to put it kindly, a blender filled with thumbtacks. Conversely, Franklin Roosevelt spent twelve years telling Americans, in his distinctly nonrhotic way, that the only thing they had to *feah* was *feah* itself—yet no one seemed to mind.

If there was a turning point, at least nationally, it may well have been Harry Truman's 1948 presidential campaign. Truman spent his first term trying to stifle his nasally Midwestern intonations, but abandoned that effort for the "give 'em hell, Harry" phase of his reelection campaign and let 'er rip. And by "'er," I mean his diphthongs.[6] Sixteen years later, LBJ won the largest landslide in American presidential history, despite having an accent typically found at an Abilene cattle auction.

In the wake of the conservative revolution of the 1980s and 1990s and the bifurcation of the country into "real" and "fake" America, the onus has been on coastal, big-city politicians to deep-fry their accents whenever possible. Sure, George W. Bush was the son of a Northeastern political dynasty and attended Phillips Academy, Yale, and Harvard, but he liked to clear brush from his Texas ranch and sounded like someone who did.

Accent fluctuations, however, aren't always conscious—linguists attribute some shifts to a phenomenon known as "code-switching," where a person alternates between the vocal norms of the groups to which they belong. Barack Obama famously adopted a "blacker" voice when speaking to African American audiences, a result likely of the time he spent in Chicago's South Side as a community organizer. Hillary Clinton's voice has run the gamut during her life as a child of the Midwest, Arkansas's first lady, Washington fixture, and New York senator. This isn't to say that some of these instances are totally natural—during a 2007 campaign stop at an African Ameri-

---

[6] Free Advice to Political Operators: Careless workplace chatter about your favorite political diphthongs might land you in the middle of a sex scandal.

can church in Selma, Alabama, Clinton sounded like she was doing a bad impression of a small-town, suspender-snapping country lawyer ("Ahhh've come too faaahhh from where ahhhh stahhted frommm")—but not all are inherently Machiavellian.

See also, *"America," "American People," "Constituent," "'Democrat Party,'" "'-ghazi' vs. '-gate,'" "Main Street"*

ACCESS

Both a means and an end to power. To be in the know. To have someone's ear. To be a somebody. To have a seat at the table. To be in the room. To be an onion ring in the french-fry container of the Beltway.

The most obvious form of access is the professional kind, which includes all the boldfaced names who yell at you on TV: the agency chiefs, the newspaper columnists, the senators, the interest group directors—all the folks whose jobs provide access. But this kind of access is not only enjoyed by famous people who pretend to care about you, it's enjoyed by literally *thousands* of people you've never heard of who pretend to care about you. Examples include a congressman's scheduler; the political editor tasked with directing his outlet's coverage; the union activist who doles out money to homeless people to appear at a protest; the twenty-two-year-old social media director who decides how the president will express his support for on Twitter with a goat meme.

Then there's the unofficial kind of access, the social kind of access—the access where the real magic happens. A person can hold no official title or have no real responsibilities of note, but because they once worked at the Senate Banking Committee and still have brunch regularly with its legislative director, because their son is in the same Hebrew school as an FCC commissioner's, because they cohosted Golf Bros and Tennis Hoes night with the current White House director of legislative affairs while AEPi brothers at Dartmouth, they have influence. The partner at a lobbying firm doesn't care if a job applicant has a master's in public policy and can say with certainty that there is a .05 correlation—with a margin of error of +/–.002—between a divided Congress and budget agreements. The partner cares that the applicant works for the House Transportation Committee and is sleeping with its staff director.

Shameless exploitation of access has catapulted some of Washington's most famous figures to their most well-deserved positions of prominence. As a young reporter, the legendary *Washington Post* editor Ben Bradlee helped wrest himself from obscurity when he moved several houses down from Massachusetts's, junior senator, John Fitzgerald Kennedy, and his wife, Jacqueline.[7] Former White House chief of staff Ken Duberstein was Ronald Reagan's top adviser for only ten months in the final months of the Gipper's lame-duck presidency, but he famously parlayed that into several decades serving on numerous corporate and cultural boards and working on K Street on behalf of totalitarian regimes that have gotten a bad rap.

Of course, a politico's access is more often than not a mix of the professional and social. Access builds prominence, and prominence builds access. The chief of staff at an industry organization may not have an immediate reason to take a coffee with the president's goat meme guy, but he'll take the call because, hey, *goat meme guy.*

See also, *"Cooling-off Period," "Friendship," "Lobbying," "Lobbyist," "Photo Line"*

ACELA

High-speed train that elites use to travel between Washington and New York, not to be confused with Amtrak's regional line that is mostly used by peasants who wouldn't know the difference between

[7] What got Bradlee to that point was a mix of honest-to-God journalistic skill and the fact that his name was Benjamin Crowninshield Bradlee and the universe smiles on people like that.

vachetta and patent leather if a Milanese tanner hit them over the head with a pair of Berluti loafers.

The Acela doesn't actually save the Northeastern itinerant much time, merely several stops and roughly forty minutes of travel on a D.C.-to-New York trip, because America's antiquated rail system isn't designed to handle high speeds. However, needlessly spending money on transportation is a time-honored American tradition; this is a country where middle-aged executives plop down $100,000 on high-performance cars so they can feel powerful while sitting in traffic. When you hear "Washington crossing the Delaware," you might think of a famous military maneuver by America's first president; D.C. elites think of a $2-a-minute premium to get out of America's first state as fast as possible. Nothing fills the governing class with more dread quite like the words, "We will be holding in Wilmington due to police activity on the tracks."

The Acela's inherent clubbiness has resulted in some memorable run-ins, including one reporter's impromptu 2013 interview with George W. Bush's former defense secretary Donald Rumsfeld, who bemoaned his declining clout at the Princeton Club;[8] and a liberal activist who overheard former NSA director Michael Hayden feeding a reporter anonymous quotes over the phone.

Mostly, though, the Acela is a platform for complaining: complaining about shoddy WiFi, complaining about quiet car decorum, complaining about America's piss-poor high-speed rail system. "Today's loud talker was in a world of hurt. PR jargon up the wahzoo. Client mad a story hasn't been placed yet, but story sounds lame," Bush's former press secretary and Fox News host Dana Perino tweeted in 2011, per *Politico*. "Sad."

"I'm glad Amtrak added Wi-Fi, truly, but what good is a Wi-Fi network that can't handle video or even Scrabble?" an exasperated

[8] Seeing as how the people who accost Secretary Rumsfeld usually accuse him of war crimes, it was probably a welcome change of pace.

Matt Bai, then a reporter for *The New York Times,* bemoaned on Twitter, again per *Politico.* "Right now, it's literally unusable."

Poverty gawking is easily the most unselfconscious form of Amtrak griping: the tendency for passengers to solemnly observe the tragic state of the world outside their window. Because train tracks are textbook NIMBY, the route runs through some less-than-savory parts of the Northeast. During the 2015 riots in Baltimore, a number of commentators tut-tutted the state of the American inner city from the comfort of their business-class seats.[9] "You can see if you take the Amtrak train from Washington to New York when it rolls through Baltimore," lamented MSNBC contributor Mike Barnicle on *Morning Joe* in April 2015, "you can see a visible display, out of both sides of your window, of poverty, of decaying neighborhoods that have been there for decades."

No word on when Amtrak will add a disquiet car to its trains, but one imagines it's not far off.

See also, *"Bubble," "Intellectual Leisure Class,"* "Morning Joe," *"Rainmaker," "White House Correspondents' Dinner"*

ACTIVIST

Individual who devotes a substantial amount of their spare time and/or resources to bring about political or social change. The "spare time and/or resources" part is key; signing an online petition, sending $5 to the ASPCA, or slapping a "Life Begins at Conception" bumper sticker on your car's fender doesn't make you an activist—it makes you your grandmother. The same goes for having a job at a government agency or NGO: you aren't an activist, you're a person-with-a-job-tivist. Seriously, any undertaking that allows you to purchase furniture from West Elm doesn't exactly qualify you for martyrdom. "Activist" is a weighty term, connoting sharp-tongued

---

[9] There are only two classes of seats on the Acela: business and first.

Victorian suffragettes and pavement-pounding labor organizers. Cesar Chavez was an activist; Harvey Milk was an activist; your middle school math teacher who stayed late helping you understand variables and who bought supplies with her own money because the school's budget was cut is an activist. Your friend with the #Stop-Genocide Twitter bio isn't.

See also, *"Astroturfing," "Constituents," "Lobbyists," "Netroots Nation"*

AD BUY

The purchase of a block of advertising time—on TV, the web, in radio, or in print—by a campaign, advocacy group, or other politically engaged entity. The location and size of an ad buy can be a decent indicator of a campaign or group's strategy. Ad buys are often used as feints, intended to give the perception of momentum or to get an opponent to spend resources in a new location. They are also the only things in American society that make people miss local car advertisements.

See also, *"Advertising," "Digital," "Drivetime," "Finance," "Going Negative," "Media Market"*

ADELSON PRIMARY

Unofficial jockeying by declared and prospective Republican candidates for the financial support of Las Vegas casino magnate Sheldon Adelson, who has gone to great lengths to advance his aggressively hawkish support of Israel, his desire to ban online gambling that eats into his business, and squelching a pesky DOJ investigation into his Chinese operations. The bare-knuckled way in which he attempts to control everything and everyone in his orbit recalls the great robber barons of the nineteenth century—that is if Jay Gould were in the business of hosting Eagles reunion concerts and plying tourists at the dollar slots with free drinks.

Adelson is the CEO of the Las Vegas Sands corporation, which owns a number of casinos and event spaces across the globe, including the Venetian, the Palazzo, and the Sands Expo and Convention Center. In 2015, his estimated net worth was $28 billion, making him the eighteenth richest person in the world, according to *Forbes*.

Following the 2010 *Citizens United* Supreme Court ruling and several related decisions, it suddenly became possible for a single donor to bankroll a candidate through unlimited contributions to super PACs and "dark money" (501(c)(4)s and 501(c)(6)s). In 2012, Adelson propped up Newt Gingrich's fledgling presidential campaign, despite the former House speaker's tendency to ramble on about zoo animals and moon bases,[10] not to mention Gingrich's general apathy about the whole endeavor. All-in, Adelson and his family spent around $17 million on Gingrich's campaign and estimates suggest he spent as much as $150 million on the entire campaign, including contributions to groups supporting the GOP's eventual nominee, Mitt Romney, and a variety of down-ticket races, as well. Adelson's political participation doesn't end with campaign contributions. According to a January 2016 profile of White House chief of staff Denis McDonough by *Politico*'s Glenn Thrush, Adelson offered to personally help fund the joint U.S.-Israeli Iron Dome missile defense system.

Adelson's real candidate beauty pageant is the Republican Jewish Coalition's annual meeting in Las Vegas, where would-be candidates prove their pro-Israel bona fides in effusively hawkish addresses to the gathering. It's tempting to joke about a "talent portion" of the event, but this guy *does* run the Sands and that well may be the case by the time this goes to press.[11]

See also, *"Bundler," "Capitol Hill Club,"* "Citizens United," *"Israel," "Megadonor," "Political Nonprofits," "Super PAC"*

---

[10] Really.

[11] A heavily bejeweled showgirl headdress would really bring out Rick Perry's eyes.

ADULTERY

A time-honored pastime no less a fixture of the political landscape than Fourth of July picnics, patronage, or using one's spouse as a political prop.[12]

The paradigm of the modern adulterous politician, of course, is Bill "I did not have sexual relations with that woman, Ms. Lewinsky" Clinton; but it turns out his enemies were *also* philandering little shits!

Bob Barr, the Georgia congressman who first called for Clinton's impeachment, had carried on an affair of his own. Newt Gingrich, the House speaker who led the charge for Clinton's impeachment, was getting it on with his own intern at the same time. Bob Livingston, the man tapped to replace Gingrich had . . . well . . . *tapped* a woman who wasn't his wife. He resigned before he could assume the speakership. It appeared that the GOP had finally found a stand-up guy in Dennis Hastert, the Illinois congressman who assumed the speakership and held the job until he retired from Congress in 2007. Well, wouldn't you know it, Hastert pleaded guilty in October 2015 to charges related to his decades-long cover-up of sexually abusing members of a high school wrestling team he once coached.

Adultery, and sex scandals in general, stretch back to the founding. Alexander Hamilton was publicly humiliated after it was revealed he had been getting it on with Maria Reynolds, who, like Hamilton, was married. Thomas Jefferson was widely accused of sleeping with one of his slaves, Sally Hemings—a charge that Jefferson denied. DNA testing in 1998 strongly suggested that Jefferson had, in fact, fathered children with Hemings.[13] For what it's worth, Jefferson likely thought this was only three-fifths inappropriate. Rachel Donelson Jackson, Andrew Jackson's wife, had not

[12] Usually because of adultery.

[13] CSI Monticello, y'all.

divorced from her abusive ex-husband due to a technicality, and the Jacksons remarried four years after their first nuptials. Charges of bigamy plagued Rachel for the rest of her life and—fun fact!—the stress of the scandal likely killed her.[14]

The list goes on: Supreme Court justice William O. Douglas, who served on the bench from the 1930s through the 1970s, divorced three different women during his service; Franklin Delano Roosevelt and Eleanor Roosevelt effectively lived apart; and who *didn't* JFK sleep with? In fact, according to historian Robert Dallek, whenever JFK's promiscuity was raised around Lyndon Johnson, the future president would boast that he had slept with more women by accident. At one point early in his presidency, Johnson instructed reporters to pay no mind to his myriad affairs, to which they dutifully complied.

Special mention goes to South Carolina senator Strom Thurmond, who was the segregationist Dixiecrats' presidential nominee in 1948. He fathered a child with his parents' black household servant and secretly supported her for decades, a fact that was only revealed months after his death. This would arguably be the most offensive sex scandal in history had Thomas Jefferson not *literally owned* the woman he slept with (another word for that not entirely consensual arrangement is "rape").

Admissions of marital infidelity tend to follow a recognizable script and American political history is erumpent with guilty pols who "deeply regret" whatever "pain they have caused"—pols who have not only "let themselves down," but also "their family and their supporters." Here is a word cloud from the *mea culpas* of South Carolina governor Mark Sanford, President Bill Clinton, and former New York governor Eliot Spitzer:

[14] She suffered a nervous breakdown shortly before her husband entered the White House and died. Said Jackson at his wife's funeral, "In the presence of this dear saint, I can and do forgive all my enemies. But those vile wretches who have slandered her must look to God for mercy." *Yikes.*

See also, *"Lobaeist," "Racism," "Skintern," "Sexism," "Spin"*

ADVANCE

The advance team—or "advance"[15]—is tasked with scouting a politician's trip, sometimes weeks or months ahead of time, and ensuring that it is executed as smoothly as possible. Advance teams, like most political staffers, primarily exist to make sure their bosses appear knowledgeable about high school basketball teams—and that they do so in front of bales of hay.[16] Advance staffers tour VFW halls where speeches might be delivered, identify local businesses sympathetic to their boss, arrange the best possible photo ops for reporters, and confirm that the owner of Jack and Jill's Hardware on East Main isn't on the sex offenders database. If politicians were rock stars, the advance team would be tasked with taping each city's name to the back of their Fender Stratocasters.

A good advance (wo)man[17] leaves no stone unturned; they don't just procure risers for TV news cameras, but ensure the best possible

[15] Because who has time for definite articles these days?

[16] Preferably bales of hay in high school gymnasiums.

[17] For decades, "advance man" was the accepted nomenclature, but that was born out of a more sexist era when neatly besuited and overly Brylcreemed men buzzed about with Leica cameras, ensuring that Adlai Stevenson or whoever would get to grip and grin with some swell folks—real crackerjacks, y'know?

tight and cut shots. They don't just learn the name of the local party chairman, but the names of the local high school principals as well. They don't just handle ticketing logistics, but ensure that Des Moines's African American community—all seven members of it—will stand behind the candidate. And they don't just arrange a visit to the local burger joint, they make sure someone will be on hand with the boss's Lipitor.

The scope and complexity of an advance team's job increases tenfold for presidents and presidential candidates. In addition to coordinating basic logistics, there's also the matter of shoring up security—presidential limousines aren't just idling in the back of small-town firehouses,[18] and the Secret Service must, in addition to its other responsibilities, fly in the presidential ride.

Details are hammered out down to the minute—not just to stay on schedule, but so the press covering the event can know what to expect and when. *And how long will POTUS be casually chatting with the proprietor of Bill's Bikes on West Main? We're going to have to make it fast—we have a 2:30 fundraiser. And will the helmet Bill surprises POTUS with be scrubbed for explosives? Is there any way we can move the meet-and-greet to the storage room? We're nervous about the exposure from the transom across the street in Myrtle's Secondhand and Consignment. Who is looking into Myrtle, by the way?*

These meetings not only happen, but happen numerous times leading up to the event so that the politician can spontaneously behave in as methodical a way as humanly possible. That so many different groups—site advance, press advance, Secret Service—can reach a coherent plan of such monumental complexity is astonishing. There are two things that Uncle Sam does right: making sense of the tax code and keeping the president safe and on schedule while he grips and grins with the members of Rutherford B. Hayes High School's marching band.

See also, *"Digital," "Field," "Flack," "White House"*

[18] *Great* spot for an event.

ADVERTISING

Paid announcements on TV or radio, in print, online, and elsewhere that political entities use to promote their agenda.

"The idea that you can merchandise candidates for high office like breakfast cereal is the ultimate indignity to the democratic process," former Illinois governor and two-time Democratic presidential nominee Adlai Stevenson huffed in 1956, according to the Museum of the Moving Image's excellent database of presidential campaign advertisements.[19] The thing is, America's campaigns have been superficial, breathless, and dumb since the country's inception. Stupid people are the second-biggest driver of America's economy—after soybeans.

In the early Republic, before the 24/7 news cycle, before the Internet, before television and radio; before whistle-stop tours, before barnstorming, and before Snapchat, simple word-of-mouth could be enough to sink a candidate, or push them across the finish line. In the presidential election of 1796, supporters of Federalist vice president John Adams and his opponent, anti-Federalist former secretary of state Thomas Jefferson, spread vicious rumors about their candidate's opponent. Jefferson, Adams's supporters insisted, was a godless man who cheated his legal clients, shied away from combat during the Revolutionary War, and was, in fact, actually dead.[20] Jefferson's backers were no less vicious: Adams, they said, was not only a morally repugnant lowlife, but lacked the manly qualities necessary to lead the nation. Had K Street existed at the time, one suspects Paul Revere may have leveraged his expansive, horse-based platform and sold out to a political communications firm. *"Charles C. Pinckney jobs-focused agenda is coming! Charles C.*

[19] Of course, Stevenson had just been defeated by Dwight Eisenhower for the second time in a row, so he might have benefited from leaving his high horse in the stable. John F. Kennedy, the Democrats' next presidential nominee, was so heavily commercialized that you couldn't blame voters for assuming three out of four dentists approved of the guy.

[20] It was actually one of Jefferson's slaves, who had been named after Jefferson, who had died.

Pinckney jobs-focused agenda is coming!" The possibilities are endless.

There was a vibrant pamphleteering tradition in the early United States, and political operatives exploited the press to disseminate the most far-fetched, unsubstantiated, and generally dumb accusations against their enemies. Picking up on the theme of John Adams's lack of manly vigor, one anti-Federalist pamphlet alleged that he was "a hideous hermaphroditical character which has neither the force and firmness of a man, nor the gentleness and sensibility of a woman." Davy Crockett, the famed frontiersman and folk hero, was so entrenched in Whig Party politics and incensed by the populism of President Andrew Jackson's presidency that he published a scathing biography of Jackson's successor, Martin Van Buren, titled *The Life of Martin Van Buren, Heir-Apparent to the "Government," and the Appointed Successor of General Andrew Jackson. Containing Every Authentic Particular by Which His Extraordinary Character Has Been Formed. With a Concise History of the Events That Have Occasioned His Unparalleled Elevation; Together with a Review of His Policy as a Statesman.*

Assuming people were still alive after reading the title, they would have learned that Van Buren "is laced up in corsets, such as women in town wear, and if possible tighter than the best of them." It was observed at the time that if all the charges leveled against the day's politicians were true, "our presidents, secretaries and senators are all traitors and pirates." Actually, if antebellum America's obsession with gender dysphoria and sexual ambiguity was any indication, our presidents, secretaries, and senators would all be in dresses.

Modern commentators may bemoan the talking points, 140-character tweets, and carefully crafted zingers that define today's sound-bite-driven political discourse, but the politicians of yesteryear assumed that most Americans were so stupid they couldn't even handle 140 characters. Starting in 1840 with William Henry Harrison's catchy "Tippecanoe and Tyler Too," the practice of "sloganeering"—literally the development and dissemination of pithy campaign catchphrases—became central to political campaigns up to, and continuing through, the age of mass media. This is what counted for viral political content back in the day: the fact that "canoe" rhymes with "too." Americans would have to wait another 170 years for cat videos.

Franklin Pierce's presidency is generally considered one of the worst in history, and his profoundly awful campaign slogan, "We Polked you in '44, we shall Pierce you in '52"—a reference to the Democratic Party's presidential candidates in 1844 and 1852—should've been an indication of what was to come (namely the near-total collapse of the Democratic Party in national politics for roughly eighty years).

Early political marketing developed at the same time that the culture of Victorian leisure blossomed in the United States, and when middle- and upper-class Americans weren't moseying about on penny farthings, lifting medicine balls, wearing power-stripe bathing suits, and throwing each other over waterfalls in barrels, they were often in the home playing music. As Benjamin Schoening and Eric Kasper noted in "Don't Stop Thinking About the Music: The Politics of Songs and Musicians in Presidential Campaigns," the same year of "Tippecanoe" the Harrison campaign distributed sheet music so that supporters could rock out in the comfort of their own homes to ditties like, "The Harrison Waltz," "Tippecanoe and Tyler Too! A comic glee," and "The National Whig Song." Songbooks proliferated in the nineteenth and early twentieth centuries, and in addition to the Harrison numbers, the electorate was treated to campaign jingles and songbooks such as, "A Miniature of Martin Van Buren," "The Republican Hot Shot: A Campaign Songster for 1900," and "Greeley Is the Real True Blue."

It didn't take much time for radio to become a stupidity conduit, either. Most early broadcasts were remarkably dull: don't expect Rush Limbaugh to launch into a tirade titled "The Vicissitudes of a Practical Politician" anytime soon. As media historian David G. Clark has noted, officials in both parties, though, quickly recognized the medium's potential for vapid, easily digestible content and did away with their initial, overly cerebral offerings. An internal Republican memo from the era observed that "broadcasting requires a new type of sentence. Its language is not that of the platform orator . . . Speeches must be short. Ten minutes is a limit and five minutes is better." Political radio content quickly got much peppier, and you can thank the guy behind that memo for Rush Limbaugh.

Of course, it is TV that has most defined modern political advertising. The year 1952 saw the first televised ads for Republican Dwight "Ike" Eisenhower and Democrat Adlai Stevenson. Whereas Stevenson's campaign mostly used television to broadcast lengthy speeches by the candidate, Eisenhower's strategy more closely mirrored the TV strategy of today's candidates, emphasizing pithy, thirty-second spots that focused more on talking points and posturing than substantive policy lectures or long-winded oratory.

The growth of the political-media complex has led to an increase in special interests appearing on the airwaves while court rulings have alternately restrained or loosened the laws governing ads. More recently the 2002 Bipartisan Campaign Reform Act, better known as McCain-Feingold, required candidates to audibly announce their approval for their ads—thus the now familiar "I'm [X] and I approve this message"—and a series of court rulings starting with *Citizens United* has ushered in the era of unlimited spending by special interests.

But televised ads haven't changed much in the sixty-plus years since their inception. Despite the ever-changing political landscape and pitched battles over campaign finance reform, TV (and web) ads' taxonomy remains remarkably static and can be broken down into a few categories.

Character

Positive: Such ads usually include the candidate at home with their family or traipsing about a bucolic setting while talking about their political independence; bravery; love of family, military, and country. These spots leave the viewer with the same lobotomized feeling one experiences when listening to the music piped in over the PA system at a CVS. Because the candidate wears sensible outerwear, goes for walks in parks, and has procreated once or twice, you should trust them with the power to eviscerate humanity with a button.

Most character ads aim to establish the candidate as a trustworthy, relatable individual, but others may try to paper over perceived faults or political vulnerabilities. More recently, 2010 Delaware Senate candidate Christine O'Donnell, beset by accusations of inexperience and reports that she had dabbled in witchcraft in her younger years, appeared in an ad wherein she stared into the camera and, with a big smile, assured viewers that "I'm not a witch. I'm you!" She lost.

Testimonials are among the most popular form of character ads. Such spots often feature well-liked politicians or family members attesting to the upstanding nature of their son/daughter/father/mother/etc. Testimonials often will feature the candidate's spouse holding a cup of coffee and speaking with a semi-intimate frankness about the candidate, whose identity is revealed at the end with a "and I should know, he's my husband!" These ads are very effective at letting the voter know the candidate has not murdered their family.

Some character spots are just dressed-up attack ads, often through backhanded insults and other intimations. The folksy narrator of a 1956 ad for Dwight Eisenhower, while rattling off some of Ike's qualities, noted that he "never had nothing given to him," a not-so-veiled reference to Adlai Stevenson's privileged upbringing as the grandson of a senator. Of course, had Ol' Downhome McGee straight up called Stevenson a silver-spoon-licking ninny, it would've seriously undercut Eisenhower's image as a uniting figure.

Negative: Campaign organizations want as little to do with these as possible, but definitely won't stop you from running them. A prime example is the ads run by Swift Boat Veterans for Truth, a group launched during the 2004 presidential campaign between President George W. Bush and Senator John Kerry, with the tacit approval of Bush adviser Karl Rove, to question Kerry's Vietnam War record. Not surprisingly, campaigns will usually let outside party groups handle negative character ads.

Issue

Positive: Issue ads are where America's stock video artists shine; it's also the primary way that advocacy organizations push their agendas over the airwaves and that dark money groups and super PACs skirt regulations prohibiting direct endorsements of candidates. These commercials are defined by their heavy use of B-roll to convey their point. An ad touting a candidate's education policy will feature warmly lit B-roll of children in a classroom; one about military issues will show a man or woman in uniform greeting a child with a hug. Issue spots are, naturally, the principal ad genre employed by industry groups.

Negative: The most memorable, and often most effective, negative issue ads are the ones that suggest, subtly or otherwise, that the candidate will probably kill you with their disastrous foreign policy. In 1956, Dwight Eisenhower's campaign sought to remind voters that Ike had overseen the end of the Korean War. "Are you willing to bet everything you love and hold dear that Stevenson can also keep us out of war. Are you *that* sure of it?" the narrator intoned in one ad. In a less effective example, Walter Mondale's campaign attacked Ronald Reagan in 1984 for weaponizing space. "Killer weapons in space, orbiting and orbiting"[21] the narrator warned of Reagan's "Star Wars" program. George H. W. Bush landed a killer hit on his 1988 opponent, Massachusetts governor Michael Dukakis, with the famed "Willie Horton" ad,

---

[21] That is what orbiting means.

lambasting Dukakis for a Massachusetts prison furlough program which convicted murderer Willie Horton used to commit rape and armed robbery. Dukakis could do little to combat the perception that he was probably dispatching legions of menacing black men to kill unsuspecting Americans.

Emotional

Positive: These ads may highlight issues or a candidate's specific qualities, but their overwhelming purpose is to leave the viewer feeling warm and fuzzy. The prototypical emotional ad is "Morning in America," Reagan/Bush 1984's gauzy portrayal of American life: farmers on tractors, workbound fathers waving good-bye to their children, and young newlyweds skipping down the aisle. While narrator Hal Riney did rattle off a series of positive economic news in his honey-dipped baritone, it was the anodyne, oboe-heavy musical score and a stupefying amount of people raising American flags that stuck with you.

One of the earliest warm and fuzzies was "Kennedy," a groundbreaking TV spot run by the Kennedy/Johnson campaign. It featured a catchy jingle with a melody so saccharine it would send Percy Faith into diabetic shock and words so vapid they had all the lyrical depth of a Daft Punk song ("Kennedy! Kennedy! Kennedy! Kennedy! Kennedy! Kennedy! Kennedy!"). Overlaid onto images of a determined-looking Kennedy and caricatures of friendly looking Americans, the ad was meant to remind voters that the young senator represented a clean break from the comparatively geriatric Dwight Eisenhower. Also that the candidate's name was Kennedy.

More recently, a 2012 spot for former Utah governor Jon Huntsman's short-lived presidential campaign featured a narrator tallying Huntsman's accomplishments and qualities for three minutes over a helmet-clad motorbiker buzzing through the Utah desert, all set against an ethereal folk soundtrack. Then there was the now-iconic, celebrity-laden, United Colors of Benetton-y "Yes We Can," will.i.am music video from Barack Obama's first presidential campaign (though it wasn't technically an advertisement). That spot was either a triumph or a failure, depending on whether you think the cast of *One Tree Hill* is fit to weigh in on such things.

The closest a Democrat has ever come to the feel-good heights of "Morning in America" was "America," a thirty-second spot for Bernie Sanders's 2016 presidential campaign named after the Simon and Garfunkel tune that the ad is set to. Just as "Morning in America" depicted the GOP's so-called silent majority base—with images of white people going to work, and white people driving tug boats, and white people getting married to have little white babies—"America" depicted a Democratic coalition with a similarly romantic eye, filled with farmers handling bales of hay, young people at coffee shops on their MacBooks, and diverse volunteers getting jazzed up, all to the hypnotic sound of Simon and Garfunkel's cashmere-soft voices.

Negative: Negative emotional spots leave the viewer feeling disconcerted: about the world, about politics, and, namely, about some goofball who wants to run the country. The most famous of these is Lyndon Johnson's "Daisy" ad, the one where a little girl is obliterated by a nuclear explosion. The ad never once mentions Barry Goldwater or his foreign policy, even when Johnson's voice appears over the image of a mushroom cloud to warn the viewer that "*These* are the stakes." The point, of course, was that Barry Goldwater would, at 12:01 p.m. on January 20, 1965, launch a thermonuclear missile at Moscow. In 1984, Ronald Reagan's reelection campaign ran "Bear," in which the narrator, again Hal Riney, remarks over footage of a brown bear: "There is a bear in the woods. For some people, the bear is easy to see. Others don't see it at all. Some people say the bear is tame. Others say it's vicious and dangerous. Since no one can really be sure who's right, isn't it smart to be as strong as the bear? If there is a bear." That was it. That was the ad. No mention of the Soviets or Reagan's opponent, just a visual metaphor meant to scare the bejesus out of people.

???

These are the head-scratchers. These things put to the test the principle that there's no such thing as bad publicity. That said, they're a ton of fun and thanks to the Internet we're living in a veritable golden age for strange political advertisements. The Mona Lisa of modern bizarre political spots was former Alaska senator and long-shot Democratic presidential candidate Mike Gravel's 2007 ad in which he stared directly into the camera for a minute and then hurled a rock into a pond. Another highlight was former HP CEO Carly Fiorina's 2010 primary attack ad against her opponent for the GOP Senate nomination in California, Tom Campbell. Campbell, the narrator of the ad insisted, was a "fiscal conservative in name only, a wolf in sheep's clothing." Visually, this point was made with video of sheep milling about a pasture, punctuated by a person dressed up in a low-budget sheep costume with electrified red eyes. The "demon sheep ad," as it quickly became known, was about as close as a political ad has ever hewed to the filmmaking sensibility behind *Magical Mystery Tour*.

See also, *"Earned Media," "Finance," "Going Negative," "Spin"*

AMERICA

Greatest goddamn country in the history of the goddamned world, all six thousand years of it. Land of the free and home of the brave, the Super Bowl, the Blue Angels, central air, four thousand charted country songs about women in trucks, a place in New Mexico called Pie Town, Smith & Wesson, the La-Z-Boy, Ronald Reagan, at least three different types of chips classified as "extreme," the Snuggie, the death tax, a football-playing robot that likes to dance, the T-shirt cannon, the strip club buffet, the Disneyworld honeymoon, the active shooter, the truck nut, Ronald Reagan, Jesus,[22] basketball arenas retrofitted into churches, candles that smell like laundry, Ronald Reagan, and the word "drinkability."

[22] Possibly—ask the Mormons.

America: Doin' it since 1776.

See also, *"Accents," "American People," "Constituent," "Flag Pin," "Israel," "Racism," "Sexism," "Xenophobia"*

AMERICAN PEOPLE

Term used with sickening frequency by politicians to describe the mood, desires, or other sentiments of the unwashed masses. Used as often, if not more, than "Americans," presumably because "American people" conjures a pleasingly diverse and Rockwellian array of suspender-clad farmers, pastors, businessmen, and other common folk.

We think of politicians as entirely beholden to special interests and in certain ways that's correct. However, lawmakers spend far more of their time in their districts and states interacting with local figures than they do legislating in Washington and hobnobbing with lobbyists. Indeed, when most lawmakers leave Washington after a three-day workweek, they don't head home for a leisurely four-day weekend and a round of golf at the local country club (though fundraisers in district country clubs aren't uncommon). Life outside of Washington isn't a vacation but a grueling torrent of meetings with a rotating cast of local luminaries, town halls, potlucks, and remarks to major constituencies. When a politician votes in a seemingly peculiar way, there's a good chance it's because they can't get Linda from the CWA, or Bob from the local Chamber of Commerce, or that guy with the weird voice from the Kiwanis Club out of their head.

Truly, stop for a moment and *really* think about the Americans whom our politicians interact with: wealthy donors, type-A staffers, rabid activists, overly exuberant business owners, perturbed letter writers, and disgruntled town hall attendees. They must be scared shitless of the American people.

Perhaps it's for that reason that politicians seem to possess a singular ability to know exactly what's in our country's 320 million heads. They know what the American people *are asking:*

I guess the obvious question the American people are asking and we're asking is, what is John Boehner waiting for?

—Senator Richard Durbin (December 13, 2012, press conference)

They also know what the American people *want:*

What I think the American people want is real border security, not an empty fig leaf.

Senator Ted Cruz (June 20, 2013, press conference)

What's more, politicians know what the American people *think:*

I think the American people think that your releasing individuals convicted or charged with a felony or multiple misdemeanors is a threat to their safety.

—Representative Lamar Smith (March 19, 2013, press conference)

Hell, politicians know what Americans *believe:*

[T]he American people believe that we have the very best of everything, and we don't.

—Senator James Risch (April 8, 2014, Armed Services Committee hearing)

Most of the time, however, the politicians know the American people are only seeking empty, feel-good sentiments:

The American people want the truth.

—Texas governor Rick Perry (October 18, 2011, Republican presidential primary debate)

ASTROTURFING

Advocacy tactic of artificially creating the appearance of grassroots enthusiasm and support for something, usually by a corporation, government, or other entity that already wields considerable power.

The world is filled with innumerable conflicts and immeasurable suffering, so it might come as a surprise to see people using their God-given free will to speak up on behalf of a campaign to streamline the corporate tax code. Such surprise is usually warranted, and an easy way to check if a campaign is a true grassroots movement or an elaborately staged show put on by special interest is common sense. Would a group of citizens spend days, weeks, or months of their lives to shift public opinion and policy on toxic dumping? Sure. Would a bearded activist named Zachary Peacecloud chain himself to a banister at a state capitol to raise awareness of the job-killing effects of workplace safety standards? Probably not.

Most astroturf campaigns are run through special-interest-backed advocacy organizations. These often have benign-sounding names like "Americans for Job Choice," the "21st Century Energy Institute," and the "Education Research Association," mainly because more accurate names—"Americans for Some Good Ol' Fashioned, Bone-Crunchin' Union Bustin,'" the "Black Lung Ain't So Bad Institute," and the "'Hey, Would You Write to Your Congressman About How Great DeVry Institute Is? My Friend Benjamin Franklin Would Greatly Appreciate It' Association"—wouldn't play as well.

One such example was Citizens for a Sound Economy, which in 1994 launched a campaign for tort reform. The group, funded by corporations such as Cigna and R.J. Reynolds, ran an ad in sixty congressional districts featuring a folksy older gentleman talking about personal responsibility. "Fewer people nowadays are willing to accept responsibility for their own doin's," the man said, undoubtedly parroting the words of Cigna's CFO to his board. "I tell you, the system is out of whack." It was time for lawmakers, he added, to "stand up to the lawyers." The only thing missing was an even folksier gentleman on a rocking chair, looking off into the distance, and remarking that his knee was acting up, which meant that medical malpractice suits were-a-comin'.

In 2001, Americans for Technology Leadership urged people to write attorneys general and demand they drop antitrust cases against Microsoft. Not only was the group bankrolled by the Windows operating system manufacturer, but two of the letters the group touted as being from outraged consumers were actually written by dead people.

Sometimes astroturfers will pay people to attend a political rally or protest to avoid the embarrassing optics of an empty room or mere handful of people marching around with placards. At shared political events like conventions and debates, campaigns will often bus in volunteers and staffers from elsewhere to guard against the embarrassing prospect of having an opposing candidate have more supporters present. A common tactic, at least around Washington, is for unions to pay homeless people to attend protests outside of nonunion construction sites—it takes more than inflatable rats to draw attention to scabs. Donald Trump's presidential campaign paid actors and other people seeking a quick buck $50 to attend his presidential launch event. It was not lost on commentators that this was Trump's halfhearted way to make good on his claim that he would be "America's greatest jobs president."

The web has been a boon to astroturfing. Nobody knows that Twitter user @LindaMom52, whose bio says she is a "mom, advocate and friend" who "loves her family, her friends and the outdoors" is actually a bot. Indeed, the same people who create fake users with photos of busty women that tell you how to claim your free iPad have also been employed to drum up fake support for politicians. Roughly half the followers of @BarackObama, the account of Barack Obama's reconfigured campaign operation, were found to be fake. Former House Speaker Newt Gingrich's million-follower Twitter account was found to be comprised of 900,000 bots.

The media haven't been immune from such tactics. "Native advertising," web ads that are formatted to look like other blog entries or articles on a news organization website, are almost indistinguishable from the site's original content, save for a small "sponsor generated content" label at the top or bottom. Even more insidious is the practice of paying bloggers and columnists to write favorably about their benefactor's cause. In 2014, tech blogger Michael Arrington published a solicitation from Microsoft to "spread the word on the new Internet Explorer browsing experience."[23] From 2008 to 2011, the Malaysian government paid conservative writer and pundit Joshua Treviño nearly $400,000 to write Malaysia-centric pieces, including negative articles about a prodemocracy advocate. Treviño distributed some of that money to other conservative writers and the propaganda ultimately appeared in outlets such as *The San Francisco Examiner, The Washington Times, National Review, The Huffington Post,* and RedState.

Your author, it should be noted, is not under any sort of financial agreement with a foreign government, but would like to say that if you haven't already, consider paying a visit to sunny Turkmenistan. Ashgabat is lovely in the spring and President Berdimuhamedow, long may he thrive and his glorious countenance shine down on Mother Turkmenistan, has taken great steps to reduce corruption. Writers are no longer required to use tiny pictures of his face instead of commas. Praise unto Father Berdimuhamedow, his fecund loins having gifted the world a strong and virile heir to carry on his noble mission, and may he continue to provide us with peace and prosperity.

See also, *"Buy This Missile," "Lobbying," "Lobbyists," "Super PAC," "Political Nonprofit"*

[23] Which, as most Internet users will tell you, is a bit like being paid to tout the top-flight dining experience at a Golden Corral.

AUTOPEN

Neat little mechanical doohickey that can replicate a signature—also the source of a great many of the John Hancocks affixed to Washington's documents. If you've never seen one, the typical autopen machine closely resembles a circa-1992 beige HP dot-matrix printer with a pincer extending out from it—the sort of thing that would spring out of R2-D2.

Documents affixed with an autopen signature aren't limited to donor thank-you notes; the C3Pen-O is actually employed for all manner of political business. George W. Bush himself never used one for official business; however, his Office of Legal Counsel published a memo in 2005 saying, "the president need not personally perform the physical act of affixing his signature to a bill to sign it." His successor, Barack Obama, took advantage of that memo and his staff used the autopen with considerable aplomb. In addition to using the autopen for comparatively workaday documents like proclamations honoring victorious sports franchises or departed TV chefs, Obama's autopen signed a number of appropriation bills, including one while he was on vacation in Hawaii. Shake your head all you want, but in twenty years when the commander in chief is OKing war resolutions by swiping his Starbucks app over an optical reader, this will all seem quaint.

Things are even more wild and wooly in Congress. In the Senate, each office is provided an autopen, and interns are regularly dispatched to obtain "signatures" for letters and other documents. Woe unto the intern who must repeat the process when an office secretary fails to properly align their autopen and musses up their boss's signature. House offices, meanwhile, aren't usually supplied an autopen, and one of the more questionable duties of House staff assistants—or other low-ranking staffers with razor-sharp motor skills—is to trace their boss's signature onto the aforementioned documents. Sometimes staffers outright fake their boss's signature.

See also, *"Congressional Staff," "Dear Colleague Letter," "Photo Line"*

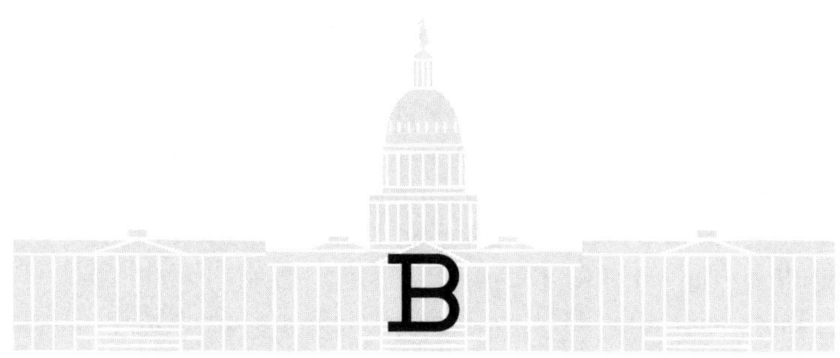

BEAT SWEETENER

Flattering articles about politicians, their aides, or their agendas—a journalistic *bisou* planted on a political *derrière*—published with the expectation that the subject will reward the reporter, or the reporter's outlet, with access.

Such pieces tend to be mind-numbingly bland—jam-packed with lighthearted color, endearing childhood anecdotes, and testimonials from friends and allies—and regularly leave out notable misdeeds, shortcomings, or conflicts of interest. This might not come as a surprise, but politicians and their press secretaries absolutely love these things, as the politician's ego is stroked and the press secretary gets an "attaboy" for planting the story. As the old saying goes, "If you scratch my back, I'll provide you with a rundown of the next closed-door caucus meeting."

News junkies should always be on the lookout for beat sweeteners, many of which follow a number of recognizable patterns:

> *"Congressman Brings Fresh Face to Stale House"*
>
> *"Behind a Senator's Passionate Mission to Combat Childhood Cuticles"*
>
> *"The Gatekeeper: Meet the President's Point Man on Sewage Issues"*

"Four Years From Now, This Senator's Press Secretary Will Give Me an Early Heads-up About Their Boss's Leadership Bid, but for Now, Here's 850 Words About the Shih-Tzus He Keeps in His Office."

See also, *"'50 Most Beautiful,'" "Access," "Flack," "Hack," "Pool Report," "Scrum"*

BELTWAY

Nickname for Interstate 495, which forms a ring around Washington, D.C., traversing its Maryland and Virginia suburbs. Every Monday through Friday at 4:30 p.m. it is filled with Department of Agriculture employees just trying to make their way home after a long day.

It has also come to serve as shorthand for Washington and its world-famous echo chamber. Terms such as "inside the Beltway" or "Beltway insider" can be used both in a neutral way, to describe political activity in the Capital (refer to this book's cover), but also in a negative way, referring to Washington's social and political insularity (*also* refer to this book's cover). According to William Safire's indispensable *Political Dictionary,* the highway was first applied as a sobriquet for the Capital in a 1977 *Washington Post* headline on trout fishing, "Inside-the-Beltway Trout Fishing Nears."

See also, *"Bubble," "Maryland," "Virginia," "Washington, D.C."*

BLUE DOGS

One of Washington's most endangered species: the moderate House Democrat. If you approach one in the wild, do not disturb it. Consider instead going on a guided Capitol Hill tour, where you will be able to observe them in their natural habitat and snap photos as they attempt to lower corporate tax rates, reduce entitlement spending, and try not to grimace too much around Nancy Pelosi.

The term "Blue Dog" originated with former representative Pete Green, a Texas Democrat, who remarked that liberals had "choked blue" his party's conservatives and moderates. The dog bit was a reference to "Yellow Dog Democrats," a long-standing term for Southern members whose historical ties to the party were so deep that they'd vote for a yellow dog if it ran as a Democrat.

Blue Dogs, who are ostensibly dedicated to fiscal conservatism, but usually accommodate all manner of non-liberal Democrats, were once a thriving faction within the House Democratic Caucus. As late as 2010, there were over fifty members. But thanks to a number of factors, its membership shrunk to fourteen by 2015.

The group was already fighting a losing battle when it was founded after the 1994 Republican sweep of Congress. The majority of its members hailed from the South, which for decades had been shedding its historical preference for the Democratic Party, beginning with Lyndon Johnson's signing of the Civil Rights Act in 1964. That trend only accelerated thanks to Richard Nixon's "silent majority" strategy and Ronald Reagan's presidency. Moreover, redistricting in 2000 and, in particular, 2010, made Blue Dogs' seats increasingly juicy targets for the National Republican Congressional Committee.

See also, *"Caucus," "Freedom Caucus," "Republican Study Committee"*

BOOKER

Keeper of the keys to Punditopia, the booker is the television producer tasked with corralling people to appear on camera.

The booker naturally wields a considerable amount of power within the political-media sphere, acting as a kind of television bouncer to the I-95 corridor—except instead of being a burly three-hundred-pound bald man named Buttons standing sentry duty beside a velvet rope, the booker is a harried twenty-, thirty-, or fortysomething who probably lives in a cramped apartment in Cobble Hill and eats lunch at their desk.

Bookers are assessed by their ability to schedule big-named

guests, but the bar is raised or lowered depending on the prestige of their program. A booker for a cable news program airing noon on Tuesdays might earn plaudits for wrangling a subcommittee chair while the same member of Congress might elicit scoffs from producers at one of the renowned Sunday talk shows. On that note, weekend and holiday programs are great opportunities for the aspiring pundit to break into the wide world of televised opinion-giving.

An experienced booker fosters relationships with press aides on Capitol Hill, in presidential administrations, in campaigns, and with PR representatives of major news outlets. The booker must also be comfortable with begging and pleading with their counterparts, only to cancel on them at the last minute. An aspiring pundit should be prepared to be regularly "bumped" from their TV segment about budget negotiations for an attractive "Pet Discipline Specialist" after the president's dog poops on the German chancellor's shoes.

For daily news shows, the booker will typically sit in on rundown meetings where the outline of the next show is sketched out and the show's segments (or blocks) are filled out. The producer then begins the mad dash of getting enough people with at least superficial qualifications to appear on-air. As soon as a topic is nailed down for that day's show, the booker will send appeals to these contacts, asking if their boss or someone on their editorial staff is available to opine on a given issue or issues.

A booker who has a standing relationship with a reporter might reach out to the hack directly, or reach out to the newsroom's head of PR, who will then individually reach out to reporters or make appeals to see who is available at the given time. "Anyone free at 3 p.m. to discuss the education bill, tensions with Russia, and the First Lady's new haircut?" is an email not unfamiliar to many newsroom denizens.

Bookers prefer guests whose knowledge is a mile long and an inch deep rather than the other way around.[24] General-interest political

[24] We're mostly talking about cable news here.

reporters and pundits can speak about a wide array of issues, however superficially, which makes them especially appealing to bookers in the ever-changing 24/7 news cycle. The death of a prominent former senator might seem like a great opportunity to invite a historian on to discuss the recently departed's life, but if the vice president's grandson posts a lewd photo on Instagram, the Miriam G. Rosenbloop endowed chair of U.S. History at Michigan might not be able to speak in as colorful terms about social media as a reporter or pundit might. Such conversational dexterity saves the booker a possible last-minute dash to replace guests who are hamstrung with that most cumbersome handicap: expertise. As such, many reporters and pundits will have "contributor" agreements with the various TV news networks, in which they receive a supplemental salary to be regularly available for appearances.

A cottage industry has sprung up around bookers. PR professionals exist to help the aspiring pundit get on-air, and these facilitators of bloviation can sniff out an attractive person with a well-defined jawline the way a hog can sniff out a truffle. Pundit gurus have either paid untold sums for the contact information of major bookers or have cashed in a career in media and are exploiting their contacts on behalf of their new clients.

See also, *"Expert," "Greenroom," "Hit," "Madame Tussaud's Disorder," "Pivot," "Spin"*

BRACKETING

The practice of scheduling campaign activity immediately surrounding an opponent's event, thereby drowning out their message—a strategic whittling down of column inches. If politics were one giant game of *The Price Is Right,* bracketing would be as close as a politico could get to estimating six hundred *and one* dollars.

Bracketing can mean literally bookending an adversary's event with rival events or other campaign maneuvers like op-eds or endorsements. It can also be any kind of political noise created to distract the public and media. Dispatching a presidential campaign intern dressed as a giant stalk of corn to draw attention to a rival's stance on ethanol subsidies, for example, is a great bracketing strategy.

See also, *"Advertising," "Pivot," "Prebuttal," "Spin"*

BUBBLE

Loose term describing the cocoon of Washington life. The bubble can inculcate groupthink and a warped perception that everyone lives nose-deep in their BlackBerries, obsessed with crosstabs and convinced that calling a politician's appearance at a *Christian Science Monitor*–sponsored breakfast a "game changer" doesn't make you a total douchenozzle.

The concept of a Washington bubble is regularly mentioned in conjunction with discussions about D.C.'s relative immunity from economic hardship thanks to the recession-resistant crop of industries feeding off of the government. "Emerging Populism Bursting Washington Bubble" read the headline of a 2014 column in the *Pittsburgh Tribune-Review* about the emergence of populism, both in the guise of the Tea Party and the Occupy movements, over the previous five years. "Bubble on the Potomac" is what *Time* magazine called the Capital in a 2012 story about the city's Uber-hailing, mixologist-worshiping, brie-and-camembert-differentiating denizens.

Somewhat similarly, a bubble is also used to describe the insulated life of the president, who lives day to day surrounded in a protective shell by Secret Service agents, bomb-resistant limousines, and bulletproof windows; his line of sight a blur of sycophantic aides, the gilded palaces of foreign capitals, and the outstretched arms of awestruck citizens snapping photos on their iPhones.

See also, *"Acela," "Madame Tussaud's Disorder," "Panels," "Pool Report," "'Rock Stars,'" "Washington, D.C."*

BUDGET

Documents detailing how much money will be allocated to a federal entity, how that money will be raised, and how it will be spent.

"The power of the purse" might sound like the name of a lousy TLC show chronicling the exploits of personal shopping assistants at Neiman Marcus, but it's actually the phrase describing Congress's constitutional authority to raise funds for the treasury (taxes) and allocate said funds as it sees fit (spending). It also alludes to the leverage that such power yields. The president might instruct the Interior Department to crack down on picnic-basket-stealing bears terrorizing Jellystone Park, but it is up to Congress to delegate funds for that purpose. If Congress were so inclined—encouraged by campaign contributions from Snagglepuss Industries—it could gut the funding for Interior's enforcement programs, in spite of Ranger Smith's passionate testimony before the Appropriations Subcommittee on Interior, Environment, and Related Agencies.

In an average year, the budget is arguably the most important matter a Congress will consider; however, it's important to note that budgets mostly deal with *discretionary* spending—that is, funding for agencies and programs that must be reupped annually or at some other regular interval. Discretionary spending covers funding for federal undertakings like infrastructure, defense, scientific research, and the office that prints the stupid charts you see members of Congress pointing at when you turn on C-SPAN. Compare that to *mandatory* spending—programs whose funding automatically increases and decreases depending on need—Social Security, food stamps, interest payments on the national debt, and Paul Ryan's whey protein allotment, for example. Today, mandatory spending accounts for some 60 to 65 percent of federal budget expenditures.

In theory, the budget process follows a script: the president submits his budget proposal and Congress follows with its own budget resolution. Both chambers of Congress proceed to authorize spending for the government's various programs and agencies and then appropriate funds in twelve separate bills accordingly. The two chambers square their respective budgets and send the final one to the president's desk to be signed or vetoed.

That's how it's *supposed* to work, and that's how it *did* work for quite a long time. But then, right about the time the War on Christmas began to heat up and Michael Moore hit his stride, everything fell apart. The budget process is becoming increasingly irrelevant, with neither party seemingly ever able to agree upon a budget resolution, much less *actual* budgets. Instead, Washington has become reliant on passing continuing resolutions, which instead keeps funding for agencies and departments whose budgets have not been passed at its present levels, or at an increased or (more often than not) reduced level for a specified period of time. That said, let us take a journey through that most titillating of subjects: the federal budget process.

1. President's Budget

Since 1921, when Congress passed the Budget and Accounting Act, the president has been required to submit an annual budget request to Congress before the first Monday of February (the government fiscal year starts on October 1, so this deadline gives Congress time to respond with its own budget). The president's budget request outlines how much the White House wants to spend on the government's discretionary programs, whether it wants to alter its mandatory programs, how it intends to raise revenue for its proposals, and the projected deficit or surplus caused by the budget.

The White House drafts its budget by consulting with various federal agencies, which provide projections of the funds they'll need in the coming fiscal year. The Office of Management and Budget (OMB), the largest executive branch office by employees, is the clearinghouse for budget matters and assists the president in scrutinizing the departments' requests, making sure that the Department of Health and Human Services really needs $600 million to combat restless leg syndrome. During this process, members of Congress regularly consult with (i.e., bug) the White House about what to include or exclude in the proposal and to get a heads-up on politically favorable inclusions.

There's no force or effect to the president's budget proposal, but it serves as a platform for the White House to promote specific policy objectives and is usually followed, if not to a T, by the commander in chief's allies in Congress. However, much like a parent on Christmas Eve, noshing on the cookies their child laid out for Santa and reading a poorly spelled note asking for, among other things, a "ponee," appropriators at least partially ignore these things.

By no means does Congress *totally* ignore the president's budget—it's a fabulous opportunity to berate the White House. Upon delivery of the president's request, the budget committees proceed to scrutinize the proposal, often in very public, very *this-will-destroy-jobs-and-embolden-our-enemies* ways. Indeed, leading fiscal administrators are often summoned to appear before the panels. After the committee members have sufficiently denounced the OMB director as an incompetent wastrel, offering up folksy rejoinders about how even Main Street shopkeepers know *ya' gotta' take in more than you spend,* the panels produce their own budget resolutions.

2. Congressional Budget Resolution

In addition to the president's budget request, Congress offers its own budget resolution, because, well, *screw you, Mr. President.* This resolution is crafted in the House and Senate budget committees with the aid of Congress's own OMB, the Congressional Budget Office (CBO). Like the president's proposal, the congressional budget resolution isn't legally binding but provides the legislative branch a budgetary framework. Unlike the president's budget, however, the congressional budget resolution doesn't go into much detail, mostly setting spending caps and letting the various committees figure out the specifics. Having this budget road map, the thinking goes, might deter a committee chairman from going off the reservation and renaming the Mississippi River the "Ronald Reagan Water Expressway."

How close these proposals hew to the president's depends largely on whichever party is in power. In 2015, the first time Republicans controlled both chambers of Congress in eight years, Democrats were so put off by the GOP's proposal that they half expected the document to don a tricorne hat and beeline it to the nearest Tea Party rally. That said, it only takes a majority in both chambers to produce a budget resolution, making it an inherently partisan process. From 2007 through 2015, Congress only produced two. Even when one party controls Congress, as the Democrats did from 2009 through early 2011, voting on a budget resolution can be a politically damaging thing, binding a lawmaker to potentially unpopular cuts or programs.

3. Authorization

When we talk about the budget, what we're really referencing are the twelve bills considered by Congress that cover government funding. Whether or not Congress produces a budget resolution, its committees still must go ahead with the work of actually crafting spending plans for the agencies under their jurisdiction.

The first part of this process is authorization, in which committees in the House and Senate literally *authorize* the creation or continuation of government agencies and programs while also specifying the maximum amount of money that can be spent on them. This is where policy is made, though no money is actually spent.

This is accomplished through hours of committee hearings with titles like "Examining Federal Rulemaking Challenges and Areas of Improvement Within the Existing Regulatory Process," "Unmanned Aircraft Systems: Key Considerations Regarding Safety, Innovation, Economic Impact, and Privacy," and, more or less, "My Staff Director Just Handed Me These Bullet Points with Questions I'm Supposed to Ask You About Homeland Security's Inspector General."

Most of the work, however, is done behind closed doors, where staffers hold meetings with interested parties—"stakeholders" is the preferred term—engage in an ongoing back-and-forth with each other, and receive a not insignificant number of "fact sheets" from lobbyists. As with any legislation, these authorizations are subject to a number of changes at the committee level and are ultimately voted upon by the entire chamber and submitted to the president for his signature or veto.

What results is a series of authorization bills that, for all of Congress's oversimplification of the issues in public, are remarkably complex and technical. Take, for example, 2015's defense authorization bill agreed upon by the House and Senate. That bill included, per its conference report, "codification of cyber liability protections for certain covered contractors," "[recommendations for] additional funding for UH-60M Blackhawks [*sic*] for the Army National Guard," and the especially terrifying "Stryker Lethality Upgrades for Urgent Operational Need." Given the time and energy spent on such seemingly arcane bits of defense policy, it's remarkable anyone in Washington has the messaging discipline to reduce all that down to talking points about supporting the troops.

4. Appropriation

After the authorization bills are completed, the Senate and House appropriation committees proceed to *appropriate* funds for the authorized programs and agencies. One source of confusion is that the word "authority" or "authorization" is still thrown around at this point in the process. "Authority," in this case, doesn't refer to the *authorization* bills, but instead to the idea that *appropriation* bills provide *"budget authority"* to the various agencies. That is, the appropriation bills allow agencies to spend money, but don't require them to. When an agency actually spends the money provided to it by the Appropriations Committee, that's called an "outlay."

For those of you still reading this, God bless you.

The appropriation committees accomplish the gargantuan task of doling out dollars to the myriad government agencies and programs by delegating the job to their various subcommittees, each of which has a specific jurisdiction. Much like the authorization process, appropriation consists of a whirlwind of meetings, give-and-take among individual members and staffers, and an unfortunate number of lobbyists. Historically, this was when a lion's share of Congress's pork barrel spending would occur. If you wanted to sneak in funds for a research center named after your grandma, this would be the time. However, since GOP lawmakers banned earmark spending after taking control of the House in 2011, appropriation bills have had to much more closely resemble the authorization bills and spots on appropriations aren't as coveted as they once were.

4(a). Supplemental Appropriations

Sometimes, even the best-laid plans go awry, and given that this is Congress we're talking about, most of the plans aren't very well laid. In situations where more money must be appropriated before the next year's budget can be finalized, Congress passes a supplemental appropriation—or a "sup," as it's known in some Hill offices—to delegate the emergency funds. Supplemental appropriations are common tools for passing economic stimulus bills and funding emergency war measures.

5. Oh, Shit

The *oh, shit* stage is the magic hour: the hour when it all falls apart; the hour when news programs fire up their B-roll of "Closed" signs hanging in front of government facilities; the hour when GOP staffers are told to double-space the budget, crank up the font to sixteen, and print it out single-sided so their bosses can appear beside it and denounce the size of the government; the hour when travel-weary children weep because they and their families cannot be admitted into the National Zoo because Congress and the president couldn't see eye to eye. The *oh, shit* stage is when that increasingly common threat becomes reality: the government shutdown.

The government shutdown of 2013 was the first in nearly eighteen years, and lasted two-and-a-half weeks, with House Republicans and President Obama unable to break an impasse over Obamacare funding. While many "nonessential" personnel appreciated the chance to take a few days off and enjoy Washington's many shutdown happy-hour specials, the novelty—to say nothing of the lack of income—got old real fast. And while both sides have managed to stave off shutdowns since then, the increasing brinksmanship and rigid partisanship defining budget negotiations have led to a near-constant state of *oh, shit.*

Even when Congress and the White House can avoid a shutdown, there often isn't much time to enact the twelve appropriation bills before the new fiscal year begins on October 1, or before a session of Congress ends. Congressional leaders will regularly package multiple appropriation bills into an "omnibus" package—*omnibus* meaning a volume that contains multiple novels or other longer pieces of work—forcing lawmakers to quickly consider a massive amount of proposed spending with limited time for scrutiny. Congress in recent years has considered a "minibus," a "megabus," and even a "cromnibus," which combined a short-term continuing resolution for Homeland Security with the eleven other appropriation bills intact. Sometimes, even this isn't enough and Congress must pass a short-term continuing resolution to give it more time to debate the measures without the government shutting down.

Sometimes the *oh, shit* stage bypasses congressional debate. In 2014, the year of the cromnibus, neither chamber was able to pass any of the individual appropriation bills, and instead congressional leaders sprung the massive Frankenstein bill on their members with little time to spare before a shutdown. In October 2015, President Obama and congressional leaders, including departing House Speaker John Boehner, who had political capital to spend, reached a two-year budget agreement, completely bypassing the authorization process and leaving the majority of the congressional legwork to the appropriation committees.

See also, *"Buy This Missile," "Congressional Staff," "Legislation," "Tax Pledge," "Legislative Glossary," "Lobbying," "Lobbyist"*

BUNDLER

Well-connected and wealthy individual who organizes other well-connected and wealthy individuals to donate to a campaign. Believe it or not, there are still a few campaign finance laws on the books—weird, right?—and among them are ones that limit the amount any single individual can contribute to a campaign's election committee or multicandidate committees. As such, it saves a campaign time and resources to let some of their moneyed benefactors do the legwork. So the bundler will approach their connections, whether during a fundraiser at their house, or in the middle of a JPMorgan board meeting, or attending a water birth in the Hollywood Hills with Ed Begley Jr.

In the wake of the *Citizens United* ruling, however, bundlers have lost some of their clout in the Democratic and Republican parties, due in no small part to the sudden existence of "megadonors," the billionaires like Sheldon Adelson and Charles and David Koch who single-handedly can prop up a campaign with unlimited contributions to allied "Super PACs" and dark money groups.

It's a sign of today's freewheeling campaign finance system that even people who know what the upper deck of a 747 looks like and who can opt for the heated seats on their new BMW 7 Series without breaking a sweat feel disenfranchised from the system. "What about when I get to the convention? Last time, I was sitting in a box. This time, I may not even get a ticket!" one George W. Bush bundler lamented to *The Washington Post* in March 2015 about the post–*Citizens United* pecking order. "They are only going to people who are multi-multimillionaires and billionaires and raising big money first," said another. "Most of the people I talk to are kind of rolling their eyes and saying, 'You know, we just don't count anymore.'"

See also, *"Call Time,"* "Citizens United," *"Finance," "Megadonor," "PAC," "Super PAC"*

BUREAUCRACY

The executive branch departments and agencies that undertake the lion's share of the federal government's administration. Depending on whom you ask, it's either the thing that keeps Americans from unloading medical waste into dumpsters behind elementary schools, or the thing that's destroying jobs and stymieing innovation by keeping people from unloading medical waste into dumpsters behind elementary schools.

America's federal bureaucracy is comprised of the fifteen cabinet-level departments—defense, treasury, health and human services and the like—that are distinguished by their secretaries' place on the president's cabinet and in the presidential line of succession.[25] Then there are hundreds of subcabinet agencies, boards, and commissions, some of which are well known (the CIA, the Federal Reserve, the Smithsonian Institution) and others less so (the Farm Credit Administration, the Architectural and Transportation Barriers Compliance Board, the Overseas Private Investment Corporation). Many of the most well-known federal entities are actually administered by cabinet departments—the IRS by Treasury and the FBI by the Department of Justice, for example.

"Large" is a relative term, and a politically charged one when describing the size of the government. That said, the government is *fucking huge, football-stadiums-as-a-unit-of-measurement* huge. That 7-Eleven hasn't introduced a bucket-sized receptacle for frozen beverages called the Guv Slurp Xtreme is surprising. As of 2014, there were over 2 million civil servants, and that's not counting the roughly 1.5 million uniformed military personnel who serve in America's armed forces, many of whom work in administrative roles, or the additional 500,000 or so postal service employees. Add to all of that the swelling number of federal contractors (more on that below)

[25] The cabinet is a mostly ceremonial organization that also includes agency heads and officials not in the line of succession such as the White House chief of staff and the EPA administrator.

and you're looking at a government apparatus numbering upward of *10 million* employees, depending on how you're defining contractors and subcontractors. To give you a sense of that scale, the country's largest private employer, Walmart, sports 1.5 million people on its payroll—that's agency big, but not *government* big. It wouldn't be completely out of line if it renamed itself the Department of Sparkly Children's Sneakers and Acer Laptops.

The prerogatives granted to each federal entity are set forth in the U.S. Code and subject to change by the standard legislative process. The majority of these changes are made through budgeting, in which funding levels are set, new programs authorized, and others eliminated altogether. However, a legislative branch whose employees number in the low five figures can only so closely monitor such a sprawling bureaucracy with its overlapping jurisdictions and complex web of contractors and subcontractors. As such, the so-called fourth branch of government is granted considerable leeway in how it follows the dictates of Congress and the president.

The rules set forth by these federal departments and agencies are enshrined in the Code of Federal Regulations (CFR)—not be confused with the U.S. Code, which is the collection of federal laws set by Congress and approved by the president. A better name for the CFR, all 175,000 pages of it, might be *The Book of Congress Telling the Agriculture Department to Deal with It Because It Has to Attend an Event for Some Senator's Spouse's Charity, or Maybe It's a Party for* Politico's *Tenth Anniversary . . . Anyhoo, It Has to Run*. As the country and its government continue to grow, Congress remains relatively unchanged in size; in fact in recent years congressional budgets have actually been cut. This has forced more and more rule-making to be left to the bureaucracy.

Voluminous books have been written on issues facing the federal bureaucracy and any condensed overview of them will be inherently inadequate. That said, it's probably good to familiarize yourself with these four issues.

Eliot Nelson

1. Congress Sucks

Congress's growing habit of fiscal and political brinksmanship has all but paralyzed many of our government's agencies. Through the second half of the twentieth century, many government agencies enjoyed permanent budget authorizations from Congress, but after the quagmire in Vietnam and the ethical lapses of the Nixon administration, Congress sought to increase oversight of the bureaucracy by increasing the frequency with which it had to reauthorize their funding.

Uncertainty in the annual appropriations process can lead administrators to hoard funds, put a stop to hiring, and slow projects to a crawl. Though some programs are reauthorized for periods longer than a year, many are now only assured funding for one year, sometimes less if the appropriations process is delayed past the start of the government's fiscal new year on October 1. Given the nature of implementing complex plans, the vicissitudes of economic cycles, and countless other considerations that go into project management, this is an untenable arrangement. Making matters worse, salary freezes and increasingly uncompetitive compensation packages only increase the challenge of finding and keeping good talent.

To use a Business 101 example, let's pretend that the lemonade stand you ran on the first Saturday of your summer vacation was a government agency. In previous years, your parents promised to give you $25 for ingredients, cups, pitchers, and markers for a sign. This year, however, Mom and Dad have been denouncing you as a fiscally reckless layabout and they can't seem to agree on how much money they're going to allocate for your stand. "Who elected Jimmy? No one," Dad blares. "Why should we entrust him with the solemn responsibility of pouring liquids into Dixie cups?" Mom is making noise about reducing your lemon budget, and says she will give you the money so long as women getting abortions are forced to undergo transvaginal ultrasounds, whatever they are.

As the Saturday of your stand approaches, Mom and Dad are still squabbling over the money. Dad is demanding that you reduce costs and increase efficiency by buying Newman's Own, but even after pointing out that purchasing Newman's Own would increase costs, Dad remains insistent. Mom is worried that your lemonade income is being routed to the Muslim Brotherhood. You don't like being called a terrorist, but Mom retorts that she's just making sure the American people are safe. You *were* thinking of making a more eye-catching sign, experimenting with lemon-to-sugar ratios and entering into a revenue-sharing agreement with Becky from down the street. However, these are all going to have to be put on hold considering the lemon stand funding remains uncertain.

Finally, on the day of the stand, Mom and Dad agree to fund it, but only at 4 p.m., well past peak purchasing time—the elderly Winstons have already gone on their speed walk and the Kaminsky children have already returned from soccer practice. You quickly assemble the stand, make the lemonade, and put up a hastily created sign. But it's too late. The air is cooling and the neighborhood's appetite for lemonade has all but vanished. You are subpoenaed to appear before Mom and Dad in the living room and account for your lackluster performance. You realize this isn't for you and immediately start applying for jobs at law firms.

Back in the real world, the increased politicization of congressional oversight had led to a near-constant jockeying for the ever-shrinking amount of funds, and the threat of a division being folded into another office or dismantled altogether is often present. Each year, agency heads, office managers, and regular bureaucrats have to increasingly politicize their case to their superiors, to congressional appropriators, and to themselves as they lose the will to carry on and leave work at 4:45 p.m.

These bureaucrats want their benefactors to know that they are "nimble" or "flexible" (won't take five months to reply to your request, only to ask you to resubmit your A7-127 form to another office); that they are the only office or division that performs a vital task (please don't make them move their crap to HUD); that their office "coordinates with other offices and departments" (once attended a good governance conference with Jim from the Office of Federal Contract Compliance Programs); and that their mission creates jobs and drives economic growth (will say whatever you want, just so long as they can go back to reviewing requests to designate trout fishing zones on Bureau of Land Management property).

Agencies are also hamstrung by the Senate's regular backlog of confirmations, a problem that has grown ever worse due to partisan considerations. It can take months, sometimes years, for a president's nominee to be cleared by the relevant Senate committee and the chamber as a whole. Even if the president's party is in the majority, it still takes a supermajority to end a filibuster on government appointments. Though interim or acting heads are appointed while the nominations make their molasses-slow crawl through the Senate, such officials lack the authority that confirmed administrators would enjoy, and regular changes atop an office hierarchy can lead to operational challenges.

2. The Role of Political Appointees

Political appointees were once the beating heart of the "spoils system" that defined nineteenth-century government. Government jobs were tools that administrations used to reward political allies. We tend to think of no-show jobs as things doled out by mobsters to associates; construction gigs that Jimmy "The Foot" never actually clocks into. In the 1800s, however, Jimmy "The Foot" was a man named Reginald with a handlebar mustache and the construction gig was a clerk job in the War Department.

Through decades of reform, patronage gigs dwindled and now comprise a statistically insignificant fraction of the government's payroll, around 3,500 employees total, with about half overseeing teams of their own. In some agencies, the only political appointee is its director. However, the small number of political appointees belies the outsized role they play: only a tiny fraction of government workers were hired under political circumstances, but many more report to someone who was, and virtually all of them work in agencies run by one.

A fundamental flaw of political appointments is that there are no qualification standards, and while most appointees are amply qualified, the quality of political appointees varies from person to person, administration to administration, and agency to agency. Many federal government observers agree that the George W. Bush administration's handling of Hurricane Katrina, and the dubious qualifications of FEMA director Michael Brown, led to a heightened awareness of the quality of the political appointees. Indeed, the headache of a major event bringing to light a political appointee's qualifications often outweighs the political benefit of granting a position to the individual.

However, even the Obama administration, with its data-driven ethos, was by no means immune from politicized appointments. Following a deadly Amtrak crash near Philadelphia in 2015, observers raised concerns about the qualification of the interim head of the Federal Railroad Administration, Sarah Feinberg. Feinberg, who had worked for Facebook and served in White House chief of staff Rahm Emanuel's office, was praised for her work building relationships in Congress. However, she had scant experience in the rail industry. Making matters worse, the White House had not nominated a replacement for the job in the three months between the prior chief's departure and the crash. The year before, in 2014, the Obama administration suffered a minor embarrassment when its nominee-to-be for ambassador to Norway, hotelier and Obama bundler George Tsunis,[26] couldn't answer basic questions about the country during his nomination hearing. His nomination was ultimately withdrawn.

Political appointments are inherently disruptive. This rotating cast of administrations can bring ongoing projects to a sudden halt

[26] Tsunis had raised some $1.3 million for the president's reelection campaign, after supporting his rival, John McCain, in 2008.

if they clash with an incoming commander in chief's agenda. Even if the agency and its administrators are of one mind, political appointees must nevertheless be onboarded and may possess a limited understanding of the offices they've been appointed to lead. A common complaint is that political appointees, even qualified ones, possess only an abstract understanding of an office's purpose and lack familiarity with ongoing projects, a fact that makes it more difficult to see things to fruition. A plan to streamline loan application processing is not served by a political appointee swooping in, declaring that efficiency and cooperation will be the watchwords of the office, and swooping out.

3. Bureaucratic Inefficiency

Discussion of America's administrative pipes and gears tends to be defined by hyperbole, informed by images of pneumatic tubes and dead-eyed functionaries in matching short-sleeve button-downs mindlessly stamping documents; detached individuals counting down the clock until they can leave some poor petitioner—undoubtedly a veteran just trying to do right by his good Christian family—in the lurch. And there are indeed countless examples of instances when the government could be more efficiently organized and run. Does the Railroad Retirement Board need to be separate from the Transportation Department? Do we even *need* a dedicated Railroad Retirement Board?

Yet the fact is, most government bureaucrats are amply qualified, hardworking, and, more often than not, overstretched. While lapses, sometimes deadly ones, occur, a government that administers the world's most sophisticated army, that manages superfund sites without spilling toxic sludge everywhere, that distributes hundreds of billions of dollars in entitlement programs, that successfully saved everything from Lockheed to the airline industry to the financial sector, all while making a profit, isn't completely inept.[27] Any sand

[27] Seriously, try to send a letter in Italy and then reconsider your views on our government's efficacy.

in the gears is as likely to originate from the top as it is from the torpor of a disengaged nine-to-fiver checking Facebook all day.

And systemic performance issues are going to plague any large entity, whether it's the Department of Defense or Walmart. The larger the entity, the harder it is to respond as dexterously to silo mentality, underperformers, and other hindrances. And even the trimmed-down government of a conservative's dream would still be a bloody massive thing. Antitax crusader Grover Norquist's once quipped that he wants to slim government "down to the size where we can drown it in the bathtub." Even maintaining basic services like national defense would require a big freaking tub.

That said, you'd be hard-pressed to find an office that doesn't feature *some* grumbling about an individual or individuals not pulling their weight. And while every large company will have its fair share of weak employees who've overstayed their welcome, firing a government employee can be such a herculean process that, in the absence of flagrantly unprofessional behavior, one might need to seek out a merry band of wizards, mountain trolls, and elves who can conjure sorcery and *answer me these riddles three* to cast off a lousy bureaucrat. However, lack of resources and erratic leadership is a much more common complaint among civil servants than the ability to shed some dead weight here and there.

It's easy to criticize bureaucrats for lack of engagement (and fun!), but under such erratic direction from up top, it's not hard to see why one might want to show up to work in Birkenstocks and spend half their day nose deep in a Sudoku book, contemplating their next trip to Dewey Beach.

4. The Rise of Contracting

The number of federal contractors, private sector employees retained by the government, has increased dramatically in recent decades, even as nonmilitary federal employment has dropped to 1960s levels, according to the Bureau of Labor Statistics. Estimates vary—and who constitutes a contractor remains a major debate (subcontractors?

mandated state employees? grant recipients?)—but some, including one study by Paul C. Light of the Brookings Institution and the NYU Wagner School of Public Service, have the total number of people employed directly or indirectly by the government surpassing 10 million. The federal government spends about $500 billion a year—roughly half the size of its annual discretionary budget—on private sector contracts, about three-fifths of which are military-related expenditures.

The ubiquity of contractors varies by department, though they are heavily centered in national security agencies. Upward of half of the Defense Department's civilian employees are said to be contractors, and *The Washington Post* reported that at one point in 2010 the Department of Homeland Security employed more contractors (around 200,000) than nonuniformed civil servants (around 188,000). There's no way to circumvent much of this outsourcing—the government doesn't build military hardware, but companies like Boeing have experience and processes in place for such undertakings. That said, government contractors do far more than churn out AGM-114 Hellfires.

A number of things have contributed to this increase, including the growth of the post–9/11 national security apparatus and the increasing notion that private sector employees will whip America's lazy bureaucrats into shape and be more efficient in their procurement and hiring and firing practices. However, the results have been mixed, at best. While contractors are often paid more because they don't enjoy the same job security as bureaucrats, evidence suggests contractors aren't let go very often. America now spends more on contractors than it does on its civilian civil servants, and the number of civil servants going through the "contracting revolving door" for higher pay increases every year. Major federal contractors spend tens of millions each year in lobbying to increase their business, and like Congress, there's a built-in incentive not to piss off leading contractors lest someone ruin their own chance to cash out.

See also, *"Budget," "Buy This Missile," "Executive Departments," "Legislation," "White House," "Wonk"*

BUY THIS MISSILE

Ads targeted at members of the armed forces and its civilian employees promoting individual pieces of military equipment, usually run in defense trade publications and around major military installations like the Pentagon. Talk about *hawking merchandise,* amirite?

"[W]e must guard against the acquisition of unwarranted influence, whether sought or unsought, by the military-industrial complex," President Dwight Eisenhower warned the nation in his farewell address. "The potential for the disastrous rise of misplaced power exists and will persist."

Boy was Ike on to something.

The former Supreme Allied Commander was correct in his assessment that the massive and complex task of keeping the nation's military prepared and its arsenal up to date would naturally give rise to a large bloc of influential and self-interested parties. However, the lengths that bloc has gone to advance its agenda would shock the already weary Ike to his core. Were our thirty-fourth president to take a walk around a Metro station near the Pentagon, or open up publications like *The Hill, Politico, Roll Call, Defense One,* or *Aviation Week,* he'd probably blow his top—or whatever it was angry people did in the 1950s.

Zombie Ike would be confronted with countless advertisements for defense contractors; some ads would feature bland pronouncements like "Kaboom Systems: Getting the Job Done," "FUBAR Solutions: When the Mission Gets Tough," and "REMF Industries: Under Budget 87% of the Time." Others would pitch *individual missiles.* That's right: not just ads for a *missile system,* but ads selling *specific* missiles, those phallic-shaped metal tubes of destruction that blast our enemies—and a not insignificant number of villages in Pakistan's tribal areas—into smithereens.

The practice isn't new. The postwar years were awash with advertisements from defense companies peddling their wares, each insisting, in their own, 1950s, *gee-wilickers,* way that their new line of radar technology, all-terrain troop transport, or fighter jet would really stick it to the Russkies. "This is the Mrs. behind the missile," read one early ad for a GM subsidiary's internal guidance system beside an image of a coquettish-looking housewife in pearls and full makeup.

However, there's something uniquely strange about an ad in a public transportation system for a *missile,* as if it were an all-purpose cleaner or a pill that keeps adults from peeing every thirty minutes.

You'd think defense contractors would take a cue from yeast infection treatments, the ads for which feature hale and hearty women making vague pronouncements about discomfort while leaving out more unsavory things. Yet they don't. Sure, defense ads could be *more* specific—Northrop Grumman has yet to run a spot featuring the charred shell of the Ba'ath Party's intelligence headquarters ("Works like a charm!")—but little else is left to the imagination.

It's unclear how far we are from Super Bowl commercials featuring bros wearing faded baseball caps, undershirts, and undone plaid button-downs partying beside MK 54 lightweight torpedoes, flanked by women in halter tops and short shorts; or ads starring a harried mother preparing to go to work, sliding bowls of cereal to her children, and looking into the camera while saying, "it's hard juggling so much responsibility, but Raytheon's Exoatmospheric Kill Vehicle makes suborbital missile defense *a lot* easier."

Whatever happens, expenditures on such ads will continue to comprise only a tiny fraction of the nearly $150 million the defense industry spends annually on lobbying. And with an industry whose very existence is entirely dependent on the nation's roughly $600 billion defense budget, you best believe it'll spend every last dime it has on making sure that the exoatmospheric kill vehicle is this season's must-have gift.

See also, *"Bureaucracy," "Executive Departments," "War"*

CALL TIME

Near-daily routine of politicians soliciting contributions over the phone. This doesn't include time spent attending fundraisers, either for themselves or their colleagues. A candidate dialing for dollars is a bit like a telemarketer calling to ask if you're happy with your long-distance plan, but then adding that he's making great progress on that logging rights bill and would appreciate any support that you and Carol could provide . . . Yeah? . . . Eh? . . . Wonderful! Give my love to Carol.

Though we think of politicians as money-grubbing egomaniacs, the truth is they're mostly just egomaniacs. Some do enjoy call time and relish the opportunity to remotely ham it up with donors, and those are often the most successful politicians, but most view it as a total chore. For one thing, begging people for money is not something that comes naturally to most people raised in a society imbued with a Protestant bashfulness about such things. Compounding the issue, new candidates are almost always told to ask their family and friends for donations first; an especially hard task for someone not predisposed to being a complete sleeze. Then there's the indignity of asking people who've *already* donated to max out, or asking if their spouse could also kick in a few Gs.

Luckily—or not—standard practice includes having a deputy finance staffer literally sit beside them to ensure they don't just flick pencils at the ceiling. These aides usually provide the candidate with a printout on their targets, including, but not limited to, how much to ask for, whether they've given before, and even personal information to help ease the transition to, "we could really use your support." Campaign regulations forbid lawmakers from using government resources for fundraising activities, so members of Congress have to conduct such solicitations outside of the Capitol complex, often in the backseats of cars and in specially designated rooms in party offices.

The truly efficient lawmaker finds a way to merge dialing-for-dollars into their day. Stories abound of politicians soliciting contributions during their morning treadmill or stationary bike workout. On days when the weather isn't particularly inclement, one can usually spot a few lawmakers pacing about the Capitol environs, BlackBerries pressed to their ears, staring at the ground, and muttering something about being targeted by the D-trip.

See also, *"Dues," "Finance," "Fundraiser," "PAC"*

CAPITOL HILL CLUB

The Capitol Hill Club—a posh, Republican-only establishment one block from the Capitol—is where your most cynical prejudices about Washington come true. For decades, it has served as a retreat for GOP lawmakers, lobbyists, businessmen, and fellow travelers seeking to escape the media's glare and the daily grind of legislating. It's no mistake that the Capitol Hill Club sits right next door to the Republican National Committee. This place is where thousands of awful Hollywood treatments of Washington are born . . .

> Scene opens on a luxurious restaurant filled with well-besuited men and elegant women. The sound of a string quartet is heard above the din of hushed conversations and clinking silverware. Servers in starched shirts and

black vests scurry to and fro. Cut to two men seated at a table in the corner.

LOBBYIST: Well, Congressman, do we have a deal?

[Lobbyist places metallic briefcase on table and opens it with two audible clicks. The briefcase is filled with money.]

CONGRESSMAN: [*Lifts wine glass.*] Sir, you have yourself a golf course!

LOBBYIST: [*Lifts wine glass.*] I guess the rare-spotted heron will have to find a new home!

IN UNISON: MUAHAHAHAHAHAHAHAHAHAHAHAHA!!!

[A server appears, pushing a cart with an ornate silver cloche atop it. He removes the cloche to reveal a steaming rare spotted heron with an apple in its mouth.]

CONGRESSMAN: Excellent! Dinner is served!

The Capitol Hill Club is also one of the most popular spots for hosting fundraisers, both for lawmakers and candidates who pilgrimage to Washington. Its calendar is filled with shindigs like "Happy Hour for Congressman Steve Scalise," "Beer and Popcorn End-of-Quarter Happy Hour in Support of Congressman Mike Fitzpatrick," and "Oil and Gas Industry Breakfast with Congressman Lee Terry."[28]

The Club also plays host to a number of community events each month, like screenings of major sporting events, wine tastings, holi-

[28] Be mindful of the frittatas at the oil and gas industry breakfasts.

day parties, dances, and pumpkin-carving contests.[29] Particular favorites were, "Single-Malt Scotch Class: A Tasting" and "The New Lobbying and Ethics Law: Know Enough NOT to Be Dangerous."

Club boosters can purchase Capitol Hill Club–branded merchandise, like Capitol Hill Club mouse pads, Capitol Hill Club baby clothes ("ONESIES for Future Members!"), and Capitol Hill Club golf polos. Also for sale are luxury items like a Capitol Hill Club broad clutch and a Capitol Hill Club silk scarf, which is advertised as being made in France.[30]

The Club was founded in 1950 by New Jersey congressman James C. Auchincloss who, along with a hundred other members, opened the first clubhouse in 1951, several blocks away from its current location. The club relocated once before settling on its current location at 300 First Street SE. Members with questions about appropriate club behavior are advised to consult the Club's rules, a sample of which is listed below:

> *RULE: "IV. Employees shall not be sent out of the Club on private business."*
>
> *TRANSLATION:* Like your interns, the staff is young, frightened, and dressed in cheap button-down shirts, but it doesn't mean they'll fetch your laundry.
>
> *RULE: "No gratuity of any kind shall be given to an employee by any member or guest."*
>
> *TRANSLATION:* "Listen"—[*looks at name tag*]—"Jose. I graduated HBS and made it to senior vice president at Caldwell and Griswold Capital Management without getting tipped once. Suck it up."

---

[29] "You've really topped yourself this year, Congressman. That's a spitting likeness of Oliver North."

[30] At least have the patriotism to call it a "Freedom Muffler."

RULE: "No member shall carry on or transact any business or indulge in the practice of any profession in the Club at any time."

TRANSLATION: "Just kidding, totally ignore this rule."

See also, *"Acela," "Call Time," "Fundraiser," "Selling Out"*

CARDS AGAINST HUMANITY

Wildly offensive card game that's a huge hit in political circles. Cards Against Humanity, for the uninitiated, is a crude version of Apples to Apples: one participant draws a prompt card and everyone else plays a card from their hands. The player whose card most humorously and/or inappropriately syncs with the prompt card—as decided by the person who drew the prompt card—wins the round. For example, if the prompt card is, "How Did I Lose My Virginity?" the player who decided to play, "A Middle-Aged Man on Roller Skates" might very well win the round.

The game is popular among twenty- and thirtysomething politicos who, after a long day of accusing their adversaries of being politically incorrect racist, sexist, and misogynistic Neanderthals, retreat to their Washington group houses, campaign motels, and other dreary locales to drink, laugh, and award each other points for playing cards such as "Big Black Dick, "Reluctant Anal," "Auschwitz," and "The Virginia Tech Massacre."

It's a potent reminder that no one really believes in anything, even the most righteous political crusaders, and one day our universe will stretch so thin that it will dissolve into oblivion, like a wet cosmic Kleenex, rendering all that our species has fought and striven for completely null. Everything is pointless.

See also, *"Congressional Staff," "Jumbo Slice," "Listserv"*

CARVEOUT

Provision inserted into legislation that exempts a jurisdiction, industry, or other entity from the law's dictates, or one that simply waters down one or more of its provisions. In Washington, trade groups are perpetually seeking to exempt themselves from proposed regulations. A common refrain from these groups is that the proposal as is will be "abused," "stymie innovation," or, you guessed it, "kill jobs." Groups seeking to nix a carveout will insist that it is "unfair" and that it creates an "uneven playing field." Carveout battles regularly pit industry versus industry, which usually translates into a not insignificant number of lobbyists finally knowing the joy that only heated bathroom floors can bring.

See also, *"Budget," "Legislation," "Lobbying," "Pork"*

CASH COMMITTEES

Nickname given to the Senate Banking Committee and House Financial Services Committee. Because these two panels are tasked with regulating Wall Street, Wall Street showers its members with campaign contributions so they won't. Leaders on both sides of the aisle make a point of assigning new and politically vulnerable members to the money committees so that they can build sizable campaign war chests. An alternate name for these committees could be "Silicon Valley," as both are teeming with upstart professionals with lofty senses of self-worth who are showered with money from the financial sector simply because they showed up.

See also, *"Finance," "Fundraiser," "New York City"*

CAUCUS

A congressional group that shares a common goal, interest, or identity but that has no sanctioned legislative power. In the House, caucuses are officially recognized as Congressional Member Organizations and can receive funding. Caucuses are not officially sanctioned in the Senate and therefore cannot receive funding, but if Dick Durbin wants to bring some banana bread to the next meeting of the Congressional Crochet Caucus, he's more than welcome to.

As you might have guessed, congressional caucuses can range in seriousness (though there isn't actually a Congressional Crochet Caucus). On the less serious end of the spectrum are caucuses like the Congressional Motorsports Caucus, the Congressional Toy Caucus, and the Congressional Shellfish Caucus. If it's not immediately apparent, caucuses are a pretty low-risk form of pandering.

The largest caucuses are the party conferences—the House Democratic Caucus, House Republican Conference, Senate Democratic Caucus, and Senate Republican Conference—which are comprised of every member of each party in each chamber. The chairs of each of these groups are part of their party's leadership and typically candidates for higher leadership positions. There's no mention in the Constitution about Democrats or Republicans (or in the House or Senate rules, for that matter), so the parties have to organize themselves somehow.

The most powerful caucuses—that is, those that are blocs within the party caucuses—are those with a robust and (mostly) unified membership. Among the most well known are the racial and ethnic caucuses such as the Congressional Black Caucus and the Congressional Hispanic Caucus. While membership in these caucuses is extended to both chambers and both parties, their agendas have historically been overwhelmingly Democratic. However, there are also a number of caucuses like the Congressional Sikh Caucus and Congressional Armenian Caucus made up mostly of members with significant constituencies belonging to a given religious or ethnic group.[31]

The chairs of powerful caucuses like the Congressional Black Caucus and the Tea Party–aligned Freedom Caucus wield consider-

[31] Democratic Tennessee representative Steve Cohen of Memphis, the only white member of Congress to represent a majority black constituency, once asked to join the Congressional Black Caucus. His request was denied.

able influence on the Hill. To lose their caucus chairs' support for a bill is to lose a sizable number of votes. Some caucuses, like the once insurgent Republican Study Committee, which was founded to promote conservative policy, have grown so large and unwieldy that groups like the Freedom Caucus sprung up as smaller, more focused, ideologically coherent blocs.

See also, *"Blue Dogs," "Freedom Caucus," "Republican Study Committee"*

CITIZENS UNITED

Citizens United v. FEC was a 2010 Supreme Court decision that opened the way for today's anything goes campaign finance regime, with a select number of super wealthy megadonors playing the role of a rapper in a late 1990s music video and candidates the role of a stripper named Brandilynn on whose gyrating butt the rapper is rapidly thinning out a stack of $100 bills. And speaking of 1990s rappers, discussions of campaign finance regulations usually result in people's eyes glazing over as if they had breathed in a little too deeply in Snoop Dogg's dressing room. To combat that, let's create an italicized avatar for America's confused electorate.

But corporations and other outside interests could influence elections before Citizens United, *right? Wealthy people held a lot of sway before* Citizens United, *right? Weren't there plenty of news stories in the 2000s, 1990s, and before about corruption in politics? How is today's situation any different?*

All good questions, italicized avatar for America's confused electorate. The answer is: it's complicated. Two points to start off:

1. The country's campaign finance regulations have undergone a number of different changes and reforms through the centuries.

2. Money has continuously played a major role in our politics. Theodore Roosevelt was accused of offering an

> ambassadorship to a New York senator if he funneled $200,000 from business interests to the Roosevelt campaign. Railroad tycoon Jay Cooke single-handedly financed one-quarter of Ulysses S. Grant's 1872 presidential campaign. Even George Washington plied his way to the Virginia House of Burgesses in 1758 with free booze for electors.

The 2002 Bipartisan Campaign Finance Reform Act, or McCain-Feingold as it's more commonly known, outlawed "soft money" donations to national parties. Soft money contributions, which until 1992 were anonymous, could be made by corporations and unions to political parties. Though the parties could not directly use these contributions on ads for candidates, they could run ads featuring the candidate's image so long as there was no direct electioneering involved—so-called issues ads.

Because McCain-Feingold outlawed soft money, many donors shifted their contributions from political parties to outside political organizations. These organizations couldn't directly campaign *for* candidates, but instead could use their money on "issue ads" and other "informational" campaigns that nevertheless could influence the electorate's views on political matters. On the right, donors funneled money to organizations like Swift Boat Veterans for Truth, which cast aspersions on 2004 Democratic presidential nominee John Kerry's Vietnam War service. On the left, donors like billionaire financier George Soros spent heavily on groups like MoveOn.org, which were critical of President George W. Bush. Today, the successors to these sorts of groups are 501(c) political nonprofits, known as "dark money" groups, whose donors can remain anonymous but who can only spend upward of 50 percent of their proceeds on direct electioneering for a candidate.

Before *Citizens United,* as now, political action committees, or PACs, were the organizations outside advocacy groups, corporations, and unions used to raise money and distribute funds to campaign committees and other explicitly political ventures (as compared to "issue" groups like Swift Boat Veterans for Truth). Though campaign, multicandidate, and party committees are all technically PACs, when people use that term, they're likely referring to the political groups belonging to outside entities. PACs, just as they are now, were required to disclose their fundraising hauls and the names and contributions of their donors above a certain dollar amount.

Yeah! Corporations and unions funneling money to candidates. That's what the big hubbub is about now, right? How are things different?

Chill out, Avatar. Lemme finish.

While donors, such as George Soros, could give unlimited funds to outside "issue" groups like MoveOn, there were still annual caps on how much individuals, corporations, unions, and advocacy groups could donate to explicitly political ventures like campaign committees and PACs. Some individuals would go an extra step and be a "bundler," a well-connected individual who organizes people to donate money to a campaign, either through fundraisers or just by placing some phone calls.

Yeah! Outside groups! Companies and unions! Well-connected rich people! Malefactors of great wealth! This is what everyone is so upset over! How are things different?

Sweet baby Jesus, Avatar, is this what smartphones are doing to our attention spans? If this could be done in emojis, it would, but 💵 👍 🇺🇸 💩 isn't very communicative, so hold tight.

Yes, corporations and unions could start their own PACs, as could advocacy organizations. However, these groups were limited to donations from their employees, members, and other PACs. In the 2006 election cycle, Goldman Sachs's PAC raised a little over $900,000 from its employees and other PACs. Goldman's PAC spent nearly all that amount on dozens of campaigns and other political entities like national parties (the rest was left as cash on hand to be carried over to the next cycle). However, none of that money came from Goldman Sachs's budget—it wasn't as if the company took the money from its successful investments and funneled it into a congressman's reelection campaign. The money came, donations from other PACs notwithstanding, from Goldman Sachs employees, who opted to donate to the company's PAC and who were under no legal obligation to do so. Those that did were limited that year to donating $5,000.

Because contributions from corporate, union, and advocacy PACs originated with employees and members, these donations were not considered to be contributions from the corporations or unions *themselves.* Take another example: Honeywell's PAC might shower hundreds of thousands of dollars a year on campaign PACs, but those funds come from Honeywell employees and not directly from revenue stemming from thermostat sales. If Honeywell ran an advertisement urging the defeat of thermostat regulation legislation, the thinking went, it would be funded by its employees, and not from the corporation's budget.

OK, so companies and unions could not *take money directly from their budgets and spend it on political activity. Any money their PACs had came from voluntary donations by their employees and members.*

Correct, Avatar.

And that finally brings us to the *Citizens United* ruling. In 2010, the Supreme Court ruled that corporations and unions could spend their *own* money to influence elections, the idea being that money constituted a form of speech, and corporations and unions could not have their free speech curtailed under the First Amendment. However, corporations and unions could still not donate *directly* to campaign PACs.

The floodgates really opened up with the *SpeechNow.org v. FEC* decision, which came two months after the *Citizens United* ruling. In *SpeechNow,* the D.C. Circuit Court ruled that *limits* on donations to these outside groups that could campaign *for* a candidate (but not *with* the candidate) were illegal. This created the framework for "independent expenditure only" groups, which quickly became known as "super PACs," enabling megadonors like Sheldon Adelson to spend tens of millions of dollars to support a specific candidate.

This is where super PACs were born, and where the so-called "dark money" political nonprofits were given their teeth. Regular old corporate and union PACs could still donate to campaigns, but, as before, those organizations would be funded by individual employees and members.

And there you have it, why one single Supreme Court decision means a candidate could, in theory, have all the corporate sponsorship of a NASCAR stock car.

Huh?

See also, *"Adelson Primary," "Megadonor," "PAC," "Political Nonprofit," "Super PAC"*

CLICKBAIT

See, *"'50 Most Beautiful,'" "Email," "Hill Rags," "Social Media"*

CLOAKROOM

Private rooms just off the House and Senate floors where members congregate to confer, socialize, catch the end of a ballgame during a vote, rest, and generally remove themselves from the riffraff. The cloakrooms in both chambers have a permanent administrative and political staff who exist to keep members and staff abreast of developments on the floor. In the Senate, for example, when the majority leader wishes to proceed on a matter without debate, the cloakroom will shoot every office an email (this is known as the Hotline) to see if anyone objects to it.[32]

In this age of 24/7 media and perpetual campaigns, there aren't many places where the traditional view of the Congress as a gilded space of backroom dealing and professional comity holds true. With that in mind, the cloakrooms are true anachronisms: places where

---

[32] If a senator does object, this is known as a hold—basically a back-channel announcement of a filibuster that would then require a supermajority of senators to break.

members regularly gather—albeit it in a strictly partisan setting—and can interact with a candor that is increasingly rare.[33] Access to cloakrooms is strictly regulated and, as such, lawmakers use them as places to avoid staff. If a staffer without floor privileges wishes to speak with a member, a cloakroom staffer must go onto the floor themselves and alert the lawmaker. Though the House page program is no more, the Senate one is still extant, and few non-insiders are regularly as close to the action as that group of pimply adolescents.

The cloakrooms, as the name suggests, began as a place where lawmakers could stash their belongings before heading into the chambers. But with the advent of everything from the automobile to the Capitol's underground subways, the need to store heavy coats in the immediate vicinity of the chambers dissipated. Today, cloakrooms are also used as repositories for the charts that members bring onto the floor during speeches. Every so often the cloakroom staff will email members' offices curtly worded notes asking that they remove their blown-up poster boards stamped with stock images of clean energy sources or people murdered by illegal immigrants.

See also, *"Hideaway Office," "Legislation," "Members-only Elevator"*

CODEL

Overseas fact-finding **CO**ngressional **DEL**egation. CODELs allow legislators to better understand the world outside the United States *and* step up their Instagram game.

CODELs fall into one of three broad categories:

1. *Armed forces.* Visits to military installations across the globe. A great opportunity to be photographed wearing wraparound sunglasses while listening intently to someone in fatigues.

[33] It's no surprise then that when a former Hill staffer launched a smartphone app that allowed staffers to post anonymous posts—Whisper, but only for people with House and Senate emails—they chose to name it Cloakroom.

2. *Foreign affairs.* Trips to ascertain the "situation on the ground" or to meet with American diplomats, local advocates, foreign leaders, or counterparts in legislatures. A great chance for a lawmaker to impose themselves on already overworked embassy staff.

3. *Vacation.* Like hazy trips to Amsterdam with the perfunctory visit to the Anne Frank museum, CODELs to some of the globe's more interesting spots probably include an obligatory tour of a local USAID recipient before decamping to the nearest rum purveyor. France remains a big draw, and it's a great way for lawmakers to atone for dragging their spouses to 500,000 constituent potluck dinners.

CODELs are approved by congressional leadership and committee chairmen, and it's one of the ways party leaders wield power, granting trips to obedient members and depriving their caucuses' black sheep from getting to visit the pyramids. For the member who has fallen out of favor with leadership, they can still take lobbyist-funded trips. Despite lobbying reforms in 2007 following the Jack Abramoff scandal, members of Congress are not actually forbidden from traveling on a government relations specialist's dime.

See also, *"Israel," "War," "Xenophobia"*

COFFEE DANCE

Because a large portion of Washington deal-making emanates from the White House and the Capitol, politicos tend to congregate at the same ten to fifteen coffee shops and bars near those two spots for off-campus meetings. What results—in situations where the people meeting haven't met before—is the Coffee Dance: a painful series of furtive glances, false-start conversations, and a heightened state of self-awareness. Like so much of life in professional America, it involves a bunch of white people in business wear loitering about and occasionally looking up from their smartphones to ascertain which pasty-white person in J.Crew or Ann Taylor is *their* pasty-white person in J.Crew or Ann Taylor. People interested in learning more should hang around the Cups & Company, in the Russell Senate Office Building for a few hours, or in Peet's Coffee on 17th and Pennsylvania NW.

"Zach?"

[White guy in J.Crew navy gingham shirt and gray-blue tie looks up from BlackBerry. Blinks.]

"Sorry, David."

[Walks over to white guy in L.L.Bean chinos and blue button-down.]

"Zach?"
"Sorry."

[Walks over to white guy in tan Indochino suit.]

"Zach?"
"Yeah! Dan?"
"Sorry, my mistake."

See also, *"Food," "'Heads-up,'" "Jumbo Slice," "West West Wing"*

CONGRESSIONAL RESEARCH SERVICE (CRS)

Congress's in-house nerd squad: a group of nonpartisan congressional researchers tasked with helping the legislative branch be less ignorant. The Congressional Research Service, a division of the Library of Congress, holds seminars, testifies before committees, dispatches staffers to assist with issue research, and provides detailed reports on any subject requested by a staffer or member.

CRS defines its mission as "providing policy and legal analysis" to the legislative branch. It interprets its mission statement rather broadly. While most CRS reports are incredibly wonky and delve into complex policy matters, others, well . . . not so much. Past CRS reports have included, "Fax-on-Demand Services Available from Federal Government Agencies," "Health Benefits for Members of Congress," and "Try Jiggling the Handle a Bit in the Men's Bathroom in the Energy Department Cafeteria." OK, not that last one.

It's hard to overstate the importance of the Congressional Research Service as its independence helps defray the influence of lobbyists, advocacy organizations, and other entities more than happy to provide members and their staff with favorable reports and data on issues central to their agendas. Staffers can be assured the work is prepared with the best of intentions and not because Boeing paid a former chief of staff to hand-deliver an issue brief to an overworked legislative director.

Washington more or less exists to make people appear more knowledgeable than they actually are: the intern briefs the aide, who briefs the deputy director, who briefs the director, who briefs a congressional committee staffed by people who exist to brief their bosses. In a way, the whole city is one large intellectual pyramid scheme where increasing numbers of people funnel knowledge up the food chain despite there being few discernible outcomes from said activity. Ultimately, the pyramid crumbles at the bottom and there are no more interns, legislative correspondents, staff assistants, or other lowly aides from whom to wring out information and before you know it we're stuck in a war somewhere.

A major controversy surrounding CRS is that Congress refuses to make its reports public, despite repeated requests from academic, good governance, and transparency groups. Advocates for the reports' dissemination to the public say the citizenry would be better served enjoying the fruits of a government office that receives over $100 million in annual funding. Defenders of the status quo counter that making the reports public would compromise Congress's ability to confidentially seek information. And when you consider how the public might react when learning that "Roles and Duties of a Member of Congress" is a document that someone inside Congress felt needed to be written, you can understand why.

In practice, this debate is moot: most of the reports are made public by a number of watchdog groups, aided by members of Congress who believe the reports should be public.[34] And while it's fun to yuk at some of the sillier, more school-reporty documents (we're looking at you, "Spinning the Web: The History and Infrastructure of the Internet"), most pass muster. Some reports are answers to specific policy questions—"How Many UAVs for DOD?" read the title for a brief, two-page report from August 2015; while others can be dozens of pages long, covering broader subjects like parliamentary procedure, outlines of major funding bills, or election law.

See also, *"Cloakroom," "Congressional Staff," "Hideaway Office," "Legislation," "Lobbying," "Wonk"*

CONGRESSIONAL STAFF

Nonelected individuals who work for Congress. The media would have you believe that congressional staffers are socially inept robots incapable of behavior not involving walking around with binders, showing up to work with wet hair, staring at BlackBerries during dates, or selling out to K Street.

That's an unfair caricature. Many staffers use iPhones.

There are around 14,000 explicitly political congressional staffers—about 1.4 for every registered Washington lobbyist. In addition, there are another 9,000 or so support staff, including pages,

[34] How easily accessible are CRS documents? Just check this book's sources section. Thanks, CRS!

security officers, maintenance workers, nonpartisan researchers and economists, librarians, parliamentarians, and more.

There's a considerable amount of research available on congressional staff, much of it conducted by the Congressional Management Foundation (CMF) and the Congressional Research Service, Congress's in-house research team. In 2010, the average age of a congressional staffer was thirty-one; however, there are far more junior staffers—such as front-desk staff—than there are senior ones. Congress's long hours and increasingly uncompetitive pay—salaries have actually declined in recent years—means there are fewer and fewer staffers in their middle and advanced years, and those staffers with sufficient enough social skills to find someone to procreate with might want to find a job that allows them to spend time with their offspring. The CMF has found that the average tenure of a congressional staffer has dwindled to only a handful of years.

Though the individual motivations for heading to K Street might be familiar to anyone with a family, student debt, or a mortgage, what results is an inherently corrupt dynamic in which institutional knowledge is heavily centered in K Street. In 2015, according to the Center of Responsive Politics, the lobbying industry spent over $3 billion bending the government's ear. Now contrast that with the roughly $2 billion that comprised Congress's *entire* budget. When overworked congressional staffers are in need of expertise on a given issue, they're quite likely going to ring up a former committee staff director who is now repping a special interest.

As a rule of thumb, congressional offices will take a meeting, schedule permitting, with most semi-respectable "stakeholders"—if only because it's an easy way to keep a constituency not pissed off—and much of their time is spent both hearing the petitions of interest groups and seeking out their input. It's a mostly sacrosanct rule on Capitol Hill that former colleagues and other close professional acquaintances, in particular, be granted meetings. That way, when the congressional staffer is looking for a lobbying gig—and that's as expected as a retired NFL player looking for paid appearances at an auto dealership—they themselves will be given an interview with the firm or organization they once granted an audience to.

Lobbyists, with their vast resources, can provide congressional staff with ideas for bills, the names of potential cosponsors, allies in industry and advocacy, and even—and quite regularly—predrafted legislative language. Sure, this might appear like a massive corruption of the legislative process, but try to think of it as a public service—a public service that lets a staffer leave work at 8:30 p.m. so they can make their Tinder date.

Armed with these cheery facts, let us now examine the three main types of congressional staff:

1. Personal

Every member of the House and Senate has a personal staff—aides in Washington and back home who help the lawmaker ceremoniously introduce dead-on-arrival bills, slander committee counterparts in the press, and politely tell constituents that they can't do anything about the lines at Chick-fil-A. While Congress is arguably the world's most politicized space, congressional staff cannot engage in electioneering and are thus prohibited from explicitly strategizing with their boss's reelection campaign. In Washington, personal offices, even those belonging to members of leadership, are situated in three House and three Senate office buildings that flank the Capitol. Lawmakers also operate offices back in their districts and states that are primarily concerned with constituent outreach and assistance.

House members are accorded an average of $1.2 million for staff and other administrative expenses—about 70 percent of which is directed to salaries. Senate budgets are allocated based on the population. The average Senate office budget is around $3.2 million, though some run upward of $5 million. Lawmakers are free to spend their staff budgets as they see fit, but all members split their staff between Washington and their districts and states. A typical House member employs around thirteen to eighteen staffers, split roughly

60 to 40 percent between Washington and their district. Senators' staffs range from forty to seventy employees, with around twenty-five in D.C., and the rest in multiple home state offices. These numbers vary session to session and member to member, so consider this a rough approximation.

2. Committee

Hearings don't just happen on their own; it takes a lot of work to subpoena scapegoats and make sure that congressmen can berate them in an informed manner. Committee aides are divided between the majority and minority, with the majority sporting a larger staff. Committees tend to be staffed primarily by policy experts, along with some administrative and communications staff. Committee staff sizes vary, but House committees average some seventy staffers while Senate panels employ around forty-five. There's a fair amount of fluidity in personal and committee staff, and personal aides are often temporarily tasked to committee work.

Committee chairs and ranking members are tasked with hiring a committee's majority and minority staff, respectively. How much of a committee's staff is replaced when a new member takes control of the gavel depends on the committee and the chair. An incoming chair of the appropriations committee might want to install people more to their liking, while the staffer tasked with organizing hearings for an obscure subcommittee might get to keep their job.

3. Leadership

In addition to their personal staff, congressional leaders are given additional funds to maintain staff that assist them in their work for their caucus or conference. Many leadership jobs mirror personal office ones: most have their own secretaries, press agents, and legislative experts. Leadership offices also sport office-specific staff: speakers and Senate leaders have cloakroom aides, whips have floor staff to help them count votes, and caucus chairs have member services advisers.

One of the biggest perks of life in a leadership office is the real estate. While personal offices are located in auxiliary office buildings, most leadership offices are situated in the gilded environs of the Capitol building. Walking through the rotunda when it's empty never gets old.

Without further ado, here's a rundown of the some of the most common congressional staffers:

Interns

The lowest of the low. The college-age—and sometimes post-college—youths who pop into a congressional office for three to six months, organize some binders, and pop out with some real-world experience, a commemorative legal pad, and a perfunctory photograph with a congressman.

Intern responsibilities include arriving early to fetch whatever coffee, food, newspapers, or other items the lawmaker requires at their desks, retrieving heating trays for the office manager's going-away party, avoiding come-ons from the legislative director, watering the complimentary plants provided by the United States Botanic Garden, and doing their utmost to make sure no one catches them stealing food from the comms director's minifridge.

Among the items usually left alongside the politician's newspapers and coffee are that day's press clippings, a collection of media mentions of the politician, usually compiled in the morning by an intern. As a rule of thumb, the more you see a politician in the news, the more they care about their press clips.

But the intern's chief responsibility is to give tours. Every day, congressional offices are beset by fanny-pack-wearing, souvenir-sun-visor-sporting constituents, hoping to take in the Capitol's illustrious sights, catch glimpses of lawmakers, and possibly have their photo taken beside a giant bust of James K. Polk. Unlucky for them, however, is that their guide to the hallowed halls of Congress is a hungover twenty-year-old rising UNC junior named Caleb. And if you think you're going to get a factual history from a kid who got a B- on his colonial history final because he spent the night on a couch outside of Beta Theta Pi following a particularly raucous Spring Fling rager, you've got another think coming. It's frightening to think about the number of Americans who think Mary Todd Lincoln's bones are interned in the Statue of Freedom.

Other perks include brown bag lunches with senior staff, who smugly tell the young'uns that not everyone can have their job—that only the most dedicated interns with unwavering passion for politics will succeed in this line of work. The senior staff omits that having a parent who bundled $50,000 for the boss at a weekend golf retreat is also a great way to succeed at an internship. Also unmentioned is the senior staffer isn't eating his lunch because he just came from a lunch interview at Akin Gump so he could take his passion to their government relations team.

Staff Assistant

After months of fetching the congressman's egg salad sandwiches and prowling the halls of Congress for free shrimp skewers at industry-sponsored luncheons, interns are justly rewarded with a 30K-a-year job answering phone calls from disgruntled people. Qualifications for staff assistant jobs vary, but the phrase "Staff Ass" is thrown around the Hill a lot, and you can probably guess why. Applicants lacking conspicuously good looks are advised to have rich parents.

Such is the existence of the staff assistant, who in many ways is a Xerox machine with a lanyard, managing the front desk of a member's office, greeting visitors and answering calls, along with handling administrative duties not covered by office managers, IT pros, and interns. Staff assistants are also regularly tasked with managing interns so long as they can be trusted not to sleep with them. Given their relatively inconsequential work, staff assistant jobs are regularly doled out to the sons and daughters of prominent donors, and if that donor happens to be a racial minority, all the better.

A staff assistant's ability to smile and lie must be second to none. The SA's role as the only front-facing staffer means their ability to stay composed in the face of needy solicitors is crucial, whether it's telling a group of protesters that the congressman is "heading to the floor for a vote,"[35] politely finding a way to get a lobbyist to quit loitering in the office waiting room, and letting reporters know that the comms director will get back to them.

The staff assistant's most trying days are those when advocacy organizations publicize the office's phone number. Congressional offices' front office phone numbers are available to the public, but the extensions of individual staff members, and indeed the members of Congress, are not. So every time you see one of those "CALL YOUR CONGRESSMAN TODAY AND TELL HIM TO VOTE 'NO' ON THE 'SMELT IT, DEALT IT' PROVISION" solicitations, what it's really saying is "CALL DWAYNE AT THE FRONT DESK AND BERATE HIM ANGRILY FOR A FEW MINUTES BEFORE HANGING UP AFTER HIS TENTH ASSURANCE THAT HE'LL PASS ON YOUR CONCERNS." These campaigns have the effect of galvanizing grassroots supporters—nothing gets someone riled up quite like a good yell—but they're really just occasions for three thousand people to berate a twenty-two-year-old who, rather than sitting on strategy and policy meetings, is sitting outside of said meetings, eating avocado toast for lunch at their desk for the third time that week.

The staff assistant, especially on the House side, concerns him or herself quite a bit with flags. It might surprise people to learn one of the most common services performed by Congress is providing flags to constituents who send in a check to cover the costs. A gridlocked Congress is basically a Party City USA store, but with more Corinthian columns and with less class.

Legislative Correspondent (LC)

The legislative correspondent is just that, an aide who corresponds with constituents and other interested parties. It can be pretty dull work: replying to handwritten letters about potholes in the village of Chester (population: 327); replying to online petitioners who, with the

[35] Translation: At a fundraiser.

click of a button on a MoveOn.org petition, inundate the LC with hundreds of identical emails urging them to protect the threatened habitat of a very specific turtle; replying to all-cap emails from constituents urging their representatives to investigate the connection between the Illuminati and the talking paper clip from Microsoft Word.

Compounding the misery are the weekly round-up meetings, in which LCs convene with their supervisors to go over response rates turnaround time and to publicly shame the LC who has been slacking. It's a zero-sum game in the LC world, but in a reality-defying twist, no one actually comes out on top.

The one glimmer of hope for the LC is their issue portfolio: most LCs are the point person on matters of trifling importance to their boss—usually ones not under the jurisdiction of the committees on which the member sits. So an LC for a senator on the Armed Services and Agriculture committees might get to brief their boss on occasion about stem-cell research, or take meetings with representatives from Web-Footed Americans for Podiatric Equality.

And so the LC does get to boast to his or her friends about their face time with the big guy/gal, and their working relationship with the Irritable Bowel Syndrome Institute's senior VP for government relations. Of course, time spent in meetings just means they'll have to stay late to answer letters. Actually, they won't stay late: congressional workplace rules require LCs receive overtime, and that kind of thing is a total no-no. They'll just have to answer letters faster.

Legislative Assistant (LA)

The first *real* job someone lands on Capitol Hill—if only because the legislative assistant is the lowest level at which someone can reasonably hope to sell out. Unshackled from the tyranny of the legislative correspondent's letter writing, the legislative assistant is given a portfolio of issues that are central to a politician's agenda. A senator on the Budget Committee will almost certainly have an LA for fiscal issues, while one hailing from Connecticut might have an LA for sexless marriages held together with money. An LA gig is the first point at which relationships really start to matter. LAs stay in regular touch with their counterparts in other offices and other major legislative stakeholders to keep abreast of the political landscape.

Depending on the office, an LA might actually be allowed to propose legislation to their bosses. After gauging interest from possible cosponsors and consulting with committee staff, an LA will approach their supervisor, the legislative director, for a green light on bringing a bill proposal to the boss, who may or may not choose to introduce or circulate it. Like most legislation that is introduced in Congress, the LA's bill probably won't go anywhere, but even the most jaded has to admit that it's a pretty cool accomplishment.

Yet more than anything, a job as a legislative assistant is an education in lobbying. While an LC gets to take the occasional meeting with the American Pomeranian Alliance, the LA spends much of their time in meetings fielding lobbying pitches from people of significant enough importance and polish that sending in a twenty-three-year-old who sleeps in a converted sunroom would be bad politics.

Legislative Director (LD)

The staffer in charge of the policy team and the member's point person on legislative matters. While LAs may brief a lawmaker on issues, the LD has far more face time. If chiefs of staff are the office CEOs, then LDs are its COO, occupying themselves with floor activity and hour-by-hour developments.

LDs come in two broad categories. You have your rumpled policy wonks, who play a bigger role in policy formation. These are the LDs in the JoS A. Bank suits and comfortable, rubber-soled business shoes who spend more of their time coordinating with committee staff about tax extenders than strategizing with their chief and boss over political matters. Members of Congress are bombarded by white papers, policy briefs, and bill summaries, only so many of which they can read. The wonk LD is there to help process all of this, that is, until the wonk LD lands a staff director job on a committee.

Then you have your *operators*—the LDs in the Brooks Brothers suit in the *clack-clack-clack* dress shoes who bridge the gap between policy and politics. Just as the wonk LDs are committee staff directors-in-training, these LDs are chiefs-in-waiting. These LDs often rely much more heavily on their legislative assistants for advice on where to fall on an issue, bill, or amendment. Or, if their boss really wants to get in good with leadership, the operator LD just parrots the party platform and whatever the whip tells their boss to vote for.

Chief of Staff

In addition to being the office's highest ranking staffer, the chief of staff is the primary conduit through which much of its legislative, communications, and administrative work reaches the member of Congress. The chief helps his or her boss synthesize the work of the communication and legislative staffs to formulate a coherent political strategy. In addition, chiefs of staff oversee the office's administrative affairs, often in conjunction with an office manager, sometimes known as a deputy chief of staff. A chief exercises control over his or her office's budget and hiring. Though hiring practices vary office to office, almost all senior hires require a green light from the lawmaker.

Congressional rules allow one staffer to detail their boss to campaign events like fundraisers, a role that usually falls to the chief of staff. Such responsibility often has the effect of putting the chief in front of a healthy number of lobbyists, something that will only increase their pay raise when they "go downtown" to K Street.

Chiefs of staff can vary in age. In the House, chiefs in their mid-twenties are not uncommon, particularly for freshmen and sophomore members who were underdogs in their election campaign and unable to hire more seasoned talent. Legislative Doogie Howsers are rare sights in the offices of higher-ranking members of Congress. In the Senate, chiefs tend to be older, both because of the prestige of the chamber, and also because its size allows its members to become more closely acquainted with their colleagues' top aides.

District Director or Casework Officer

Congressmen are most closely associated with their constitutional responsibility to consider proposed legislation; however, they also serve as bureaucratic sherpas, helping Americans navigate their often unwieldy government. A sizable chunk of congressional office budgets are directed toward hiring staffers to meet with constituents back home and assist them in their bureaucratic endeavors. Some of these requests are well within the staffer's wheelhouse—problems with entitlement payments, difficulty with the VA, requests for letters of recommendation for a federal grant—others less so—requests to release someone from jail . . . or to arrest the president.

In many ways, district staff must bear the brunt of a politician's lofty campaign promises to single-handedly change Washington and push through a litany of policy promises. Ever read or see news reports about most Americans not knowing who the vice president is? Now imagine what percentage of Americans think their congressman can single-handedly acquire their daughter an Elsa dress. Americans think members of Congress can manipulate the organs of government the way film directors think CIA analysts can zoom and enhance satellite images.

Communication's Director or Press Secretary

The staffers in charge of working with a lawmaker on their PR strategy and managing day-to-day press relations. These staffers spend much of their time planning media events, drafting speeches for their boss, and writing press releases. As much as press aides are associated with impassioned exchanges with members of the press, they're just as likely to be drafting a release with a big headline like "CONGRESSMAN SLUDGEMEAT APPLAUDS EPA ESTUARY RESTORATION GRANT" as they are firing off emails to a *Roll Call* reporter.

House offices typically have the most bare-bones press operations, sometimes a single press secretary handling local and Washington media. Senate offices sport larger comms teams, usually headed by a communication, director plotting media strategy and a deputy or press secretaries assisting in day-to-day operations. Committees and members of leadership in both chambers have a similarly organized press staff. Just how these press shops are arranged varies from office to office. Committee press secretaries might be assigned by a communications director to issues areas, while Senate press staff might be divvied up to work with Washington and home state press, separately.

Committee Staff

Committee aides are divided between the majority and minority parties, each with their own office space and, more often than not, corresponding staff members. Titles and responsibilities vary from committee to committee, but nearly all are headed up by a staff director, chosen by the panel's chair or ranking member. Reporting to these staff directors are a number of research assistants, professional staff, counsel, and other policy staffers divvied up into the committee's subcommittee issue areas. These aides take meetings with interested parties, place fact-finding calls, brief the staff director on their issue areas, and also help plan committee hearings.

Committee jobs are among the wonkier and lesser politicized on Capitol Hill. While committee markups and hearings can be incredibly political affairs, they must nevertheless be informed by a deep understanding of the policy landscape, a task that falls squarely on the shoulders of committees' staffers. Despite their wonkiness, however, committee staff do not, by any means, always depart Congress for think tanks, universities, or other ostensibly nonpartisan or high-minded outlets. If anything, their encyclopedic knowledge of an issue area and how policy snakes its way through Congress and is absorbed and implemented by the bureaucracy is highly coveted by K Street. Ways and Means staffers provide outside firms valuable connections to Congress's tax writers and knowledge about IRS implementation; Judiciary Committee staffers, typically accredited lawyers, intimately know how changes to the U.S. code are made; Foreign Affairs Committee staffers have been known to depart for lobbying firms' international teams, prompting a slew of Foreign Agents Registration Act filings ("We're just trying to tell the Supreme Commander President's story and why voters elected him for the seventh time with 97 percent of the vote").

See also, *"Constituent Services," "Fundraiser," "Legislation," "Lobbying," "Lobbyist," "Selling Out"*

CONSTITUENT

Source of money, possibly votes.

See also, *"American People," "Bundler," "Constituent Services," "Field"*

CONSTITUENT SERVICES

VA hospital giving you grief? Social Security Administration biffing your payments? CIA listening to your thoughts and calls through the cavities in your molars? You might want to hit up your member of Congress. Constituent services are one of the chief responsibilities of a member of Congress—especially a backbencher without a committee chairmanship—and are effectively legislators and their staffs going to bat for a voter having difficulty with a government agency or department.

Congressional and federal rules prohibit members of Congress or their staff from requesting preferential treatment for a constituent; however, there is still a number of ways a congressional office can be their advocate. For one, simply asking a federal agency to *do their job* can expedite paperwork (*you* try leaving at 3:15 from your Interior Department job when a member of Congress is on the phone about someone's Bureau of Land Management grazing application). Alternately, a lawmaker can put in a favorable word for a constituent if they are up for consideration for a competitive grant or admission to a military academy.

Constituent casework is usually handled by field representatives in lawmakers' district offices, the shuttered five-and-dime stores, erstwhile used car dealerships, and other low-rent commercial spaces that members of Congress rent out back home to serve as bases of operation while not in Washington.

See also, *"American People," "Congressional Staff," "Constituent Services," "Field"*

CONTINUING RESOLUTION (CR)

Legislative measure extending government funding levels for a specified period.

Americans have a masochistic tendency to identify something that is harmful to their being, and—like a moth to the flame—double down on it. The caloric Quarter Pounder begets the Double Quarter Pounder; traffic-clogged freeways beget wider freeways that lead to more traffic; selfies beget the selfie stick; Adam Sandler continues to make movies.

The continuing resolution is Congress's contribution to America's pathological self-loathing. Like *Air Bud: Golden Receiver* and that second donut that you *just know* you shouldn't eat, the continuing resolution is an agreement by Congress and the president to perpetuate the federal budget in its current state, pleasing almost no one.

Budget battles are a deafening cacophony of 535 legislators (and a few delegates, to boot) calling for this initiative to be cut or that program to be restored to its previous funding levels or the establishment of this here legislative doohickey that will create jobs and keep us safe and *blah blah blah*. Literally hundreds of amendments are offered up each go-around, many without a floor vote, because no one thinks the status quo is working. So that's precisely what Congress and the White House do with increasing frequency: stick with the status quo.

That might be something of an overstatement. Continuing resolutions are often presented with overarching changes—say a set cut in discretionary spending—or specific ones: a CR covering fiscal year 1988 featured "a ban on smoking on domestic flights of two hours or less, a plan to allow states to raise the speed limit on rural highways to sixty-five miles per hour, an extension of the Clean Air Act, and a limitation rider prohibiting the Federal Communications Commission from modifying its regulations limiting the co-ownership of a television station and a newspaper in the same market." More recently, CRs have included agreed-upon cuts to spending and more specific measures like withholding funds for Washington, D.C.'s Planned Parenthoods.[36] But by the standards of federal budgets, such changes are overly piecemeal.

See also, *"Budget," "Debt Ceiling," "Legislation," "Legislative Glossary"*

COOLING-OFF PERIOD

The period that House and Senate regulations require former members and staffers to desist from engaging in lobbying after leaving Capitol Hill. Former House members are prohibited from lobbying their former colleagues for one year while ex-senators must wait two. That said, rules governing cooling-off periods are about as strict as those governing arts and crafts class at a Montessori school. A twig Scotched-taped to a pencil might be called a shoe tree at the Greater Cincinnati Montessori Learning Community, but a former lawmaker influencing the crafting of a bill might not be called a lobbyist by the powers that be.

Despite these rules, many outgoing lawmakers are swept up by lobbying firms and other influence peddlers shortly after leaving the Hill. These officials are often brought on as "advisers," whose job descriptions are explicitly devoid of influence peddling. This isn't just so these firms and companies can place a hold on the lawmakers until the cooling-off period expires, but because the hires can lobby *right away*. As of April 2015, one-quarter of the legislators of the previous Congress who left the Hill only months before were engaged

[36] Prompting Barack Obama, as reported by *The Washington Post* in April 2011, to say to Republican House speaker John Boehner one of the strangest sentences ever uttered in the Oval Office: "John, I will give you D.C. abortion."

in some kind of activity aimed at influencing government, per an examination of their professional activity by *USA Today*.

Former lawmakers are not prohibited from lobbying executive agencies, so a former senator who is a regulatory "adviser" at a law firm with a significant lobbying shop can bend a cabinet official's ear about their department's oversight of a client's industry. There also aren't any prohibitions on these erstwhile lawmakers being in the same place with their former colleagues. The wink-and-nod playbook is something every aspiring non-lobbyist lobbyist must master. As Louisiana's Earl Long famously remarked, "Don't write anything you can phone. Don't phone anything you can talk. Don't talk anything you can whisper. Don't whisper anything you can smile. Don't smile anything you can nod. Don't nod anything you can wink."

If former senator Shminkus Pennywheeze wanted to host a scrapbooking class and some of his colleagues from the Podesta Group *and* his buddies from the Financial Services Committee happened to appear, that would be OK, so long as Senator Pennywheeze isn't broaching discussions about a supplemental appropriation. Also, former members of Congress are more or less given free rein to roam around the Capitol, including its gyms.

[*Congressman walks up to thigh machine.*]

"Shminkus! How's it going?"

"Great!" [*clenches*] [*grunts*] "I'm at the Podesta Group now. Had a couple of meetings, figured I'd stop in for a quick" [*clenches*] [*grunts*] "workout."

"Great to hear!"

"Yeah! We just signed 3" [*clenches*] [*grunts*] "M."

"Interesting. Well, give my best to Minerva!"

These sorts of interactions aren't abstractions.[37] In February 2015, former House majority leader Eric Cantor, who left Congress

[37] Well, maybe the thigh machine part.

less than a year earlier after a shocking primary defeat, hosted a party celebrating the new offices of the investment firm he was now working for, Moelis & Company. Every member of the GOP's House leadership attended.

The regulations are even more porous for staffers. Many House aides choose to keep their salaries below a certain threshold—about $130,000 a year (staff salaries top out around $170,000)—so that they are not subject to a one-year cooling-off period. It's not unheard of for a staffer to have his or her salary *lowered* to avoid the time-out. Like their bosses, staffers, even ones registered as lobbyists, are not prohibited from interacting with members of Congress after they move to K Street. In fact, these lobbyists are not prohibited from working on campaigns. Since 2007, when the cooling-off period was introduced, over 1,500 congressional staffers have registered as lobbyists within a year of leaving Capitol Hill.

These things aren't completely without teeth. Being able to press the flesh with a committee staff director and directly confront them about a client's agenda is much easier, effective, and, most significantly, lucrative, than showing up at enough committee hearings and hoping they get the point when you ask about their family for the twentieth time.

See also, *"Capitol Hill Club," "Lobbying," "Selling Out"*

COUNTRY CLUB REPUBLICAN

Disparaging term for wealthy Republicans who are principally concerned with policies that improve their bottom lines. These milquetoast honkeys lack the doctrinal vigor of the GOP's base, though they are responsible for the lion's share of the party's campaign war chest. The Country Club Republican views the 2008 financial bailout of Wall Street as a necessary measure that saved the financial markets from catastrophe and sees certain social safety net programs like food stamps and welfare as necessary to public order. The Country Club Republican and the Republican base do find common ground in their shared view that cell-phone belt clips are acceptable fashion accessories.

Unlike Rockefeller Republicans—who profess liberal social views from the wood-paneled comfort of the Amalgamated Amalgamation Building boardroom, fifty-six stories above Sixth Avenue—or Georgetown Republicans—who are too busy fussing about at a cocktail party at Clark Cliffords's town house while one of George Aiken's aides furiously gropes someone named Mamie in the bathroom to care much about anything—the Country Club Republican may foster *some* distaste for liberal social mores. However, the Country Club Republican doesn't cling too tightly to such views, which have a tendency to evaporate once their son comes out of the closet or their daughter comes home for the weekend from Choate needing to talk to Mom about a medical thing. Crude jokes about black people in private corners of the Northrop Grumman Christmas party are still acceptable.

See also, *"Blue Dogs," "Freedom Caucus," "RINO"*

CPAC

Woodstock for people who think everyone who went to Woodstock should be locked up. The Conservative Political Action Conference, or CPAC as it's more commonly known, is the year's foremost gathering of conservative activists, politicians, journalists, and anyone who thinks kabob day at a middle school in suburban St. Louis is the sign of a widespread conspiracy to institute sharia law in government. It's also something of a beauty pageant for prospective Republican candidates for office, namely presidential ones, who try to use their speeches as a springboard to their party's nomination.

After the politicians' speeches, CPAC's presidential straw poll is the event's most scrutinized development. However, it's not necessarily the best gauge of who the GOP's nominee will eventually be; sometimes it's more a measure of which wing of the party put the most effort into voting at that year's CPAC. Rudy Giuliani, George Allen,

Steve Forbes, Ron Paul, and Gary Bauer are just some of the poll's past winners.

CPAC has been a fixture on the national stage since 1973, when the American Conservative Union put on the first conference, and has hosted everyone from Ronald Reagan to Ann Coulter to George W. Bush. Though CPAC garners the most attention for the presidential aspirants and subsequent straw poll, the conference is host to a whole ecosystem of political activity: there's *The Weekly Standard*'s photo booth, the gentleman dressed as Captain America, the libertarian in the cowboy hat in the shirt that says "Cops Say Legalize Pot Ask Me Why," the kiosk hawking home security solutions, the booth handing out pocket-sized copies of the Ten Commandments, the breakout session about UN encroachment on Americans' liberty, the raffles (mostly for guns), and radio and TV setups broadcasting live from the event.

Like the Republican Party, the event has an overall social conservative bent, though libertarians are regularly represented. GOProud, a Republican-aligned gay rights group, has been alternately invited and uninvited, depending on the year. One of the more interesting events during the 2015 CPAC was former New Mexico governor, Libertarian presidential candidate, and legal marijuana company owner Gary Johnson's very animated debate about the war on drugs with former Republican congresswoman Ann Marie Buerkle.

For CPAC's younger attendees, it's a chance to let loose in a crowd that welcomes their ideology, a stark change from the mostly liberal colleges from which they feel ideologically alienated. Indeed, CPAC's a real hootenanny for fun-starved conservative youths and opportunities for fun and sex abound, whether it's the Project Veritas after-party featuring appearances by group founder and conservative sex symbol James O'Keefe—he of the ACORN-destroying pimp videos—or flirtatious social media interactions (actual posting to the 2015 event's smartphone app: "I've got my GOP Vineyard Vines bow tie ready for tomorrow. Can't wait to be surrounded by so many like-minded Conservatives . . . especially the southern belles.").

See also, *"Freedom Caucus," "RINO"*

CRYSTAL CITY RESTAURANT

A strip club located five minutes from the Pentagon in the Arlington neighborhood of Crystal City. A favorite haunt among defense contractors and Army brass who know that their bosses won't be alarmed when "CRYSTAL CITY RESTAURANT" appears on their expense accounts.

See also, *"Buy This Missile," "Northern Virginia," "War"*

"CW"

Stands for "conventional wisdom," a term that conventional wisdom dictates has gone out of style because it is too conventional.

See also, *"Hack," "Hill Rags," "News Cycle," "Winning"*

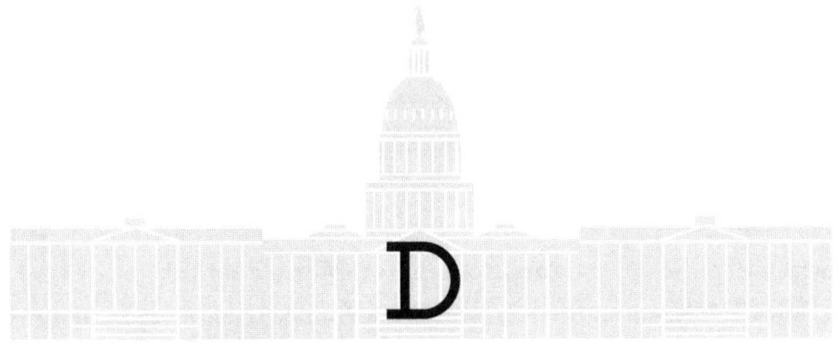

DEAR COLLEAGUE LETTER

Official correspondence between members of Congress—most likely written by their aides (or sometimes a lobbyist)—typically seeking support for legislation. Like Kickstarter solicitations, these letters tend to be annoying, rarely accomplish anything, and are probably written by a twenty-five-year-old liberal arts graduate.

See also, *"Caucus," "Congressional Staff," "Congressional Research Service," "Lobbying"*

DEBT CEILING

The limit of how much money the U.S. government is allowed to borrow to fund its expenditures. Until 1917, Congress had to authorize any new debt issuance, but with the government's finances growing more complex due to increased tax revenue and expenditures relating to World War I—doughboys ain't cheap—it was decided that new debt could be automatically issued up to a specific level set by Congress and signed by the president. Rather than peg the limit to, say, a percentage of revenues or GDP, Washington, in its infinite wisdom, opted for a set number, exhibiting the financial literacy of a five-year-old who wants their allowance payment in five $1 bills rather than one $5 bill so they'll have more money. This would naturally necessitate repeated increases of the limit as the country, its economy, and its government grew.

For almost a hundred years, that system, however shortsighted it may have been, didn't cause too many headaches. Whenever the debt ceiling needed to be raised, Congress promptly did so, though not without perfunctory speechifying about the need for greater fiscal discipline. Noise would be made here and there about not supporting a proposed increase—congressional Democrats balked a little bit in the early 1980s—but there was never a serious attempt to let the nation default on its debt. Between 1960 and 2015, Congress voted to raise the nation's debt limit seventy-eight times.

Eventually, the idiocy of the arrangement was laid bare. While limits on credit cards are a good idea, the difference between your debt and that of the *United States Government* is that the world isn't going to be plunged into a postapocalyptic economic cataclysm if your MasterCard is maxed out while trying to purchase a pair of jeggings at H&M. In 2011, 2013, and 2015, the GOP, in the grips of Tea Party fever, threatened to not vote on an increase unless a series of draconian budget cuts were enacted. To many members of the party's far-right wing, a default wouldn't be so bad, as if the U.S. government were simply an overindulgent child too impatient to wait for their Candy Crush cool-down period to end without forking over money.

Opponents of playing chicken with the debt limit proposed a number of alternatives, including an argument that part of the 14th Amendment—"The validity of the public debt of the United States . . . shall not be questioned"—rendered the debt ceiling unconstitutional. Another proposal circulating on left-leaning blogs and in certain legal circles, centered around an obscure section of the U.S. code that allowed the executive branch to mint coinage of any value. The provision was intended to only apply to commemorative platinum coins, but was written such that a president could, in theory, order the treasury secretary to mint a trillion-dollar platinum coin (presumably after the crises were averted, the coin would be placed into one of those souvenir coin presses and turned into an oval-shaped Statue of Liberty commemorative token).

Neither of these arguments was given much consideration and last-minute agreements were eventually reached in all three instances, but not before a number of credit agencies downgraded the rating of U.S. debt instruments. More troubling, the precedent was set and now the debt ceiling is no less a political football than 9/11.

See also, *"Budget," "Continuing Resolution," "Freedom Caucus," "Legislative Glossary"*

"DEMOCRAT PARTY"

Republicans' long-standing epithet for the Democratic Party and source of tremendous irritation among Democrats, who dislike its use the way your grandmother didn't like it when people addressed her as "Ms."

Central to its use is the long-standing belief by many Republicans that the opposing party should not have a monopoly on being known as democratic (with a lowercase "d"). "I think their claims that they represent the great mass of the people, and we don't, is just a lot of bunk," said former Republican presidential candidate and New

Yorker Thomas Dewey, who first popularized the term. "Why, Republicans asked for years, should we allow the Democrats to get away with the adjective 'democratic'?" William Safire, conservative columnists and former speechwriter for Richard Nixon asked in 1984.

Such gripes are not totally without merit, but neither is the undeniable fact that "Democrat Party" has a real awful ring to it. Whereas "Democratic Party" has a pleasant, multisyllabic cadence, the truncated "Democrat Party" is far rougher. It leaves the mind, accustomed to the "-ic" suffix, uncomfortable, expectant of the final syllable yet getting none, like an amputee putting weight down on a limb that's no longer extant.

Moreover, "Democrat Party" is tremendously more fanatical sounding, which plays nicely into the long-standing Republican narrative that Democrats are extreme. "Democrat" rhymes with "autocrat" and also ends with the same hard "t" as "zealot." A *Democratic* proposal sounds like a bland, centrist initiative cooked up at the Brookings Institution. A *Democrat* proposal was probably scribbled on the back of a stolen Nationalist dossier by an International Brigade partisan as he made his way—M1 carbine slung over his shoulder—through Basque country to blow up a bridge.

News organizations have historically referred to an entity, good, bad, or downright evil, by whatever name and corresponding adjective it assigns itself—so long as it's not deemed obscene.[38] As such, the phrase "Democrat Party" hasn't seeped *too* deeply into the cultural ferment. But the ascent of Fox News and the proliferation of partisan news sources on the web have lent the adjective a new lease on life. Ronald Reagan famously quipped, "I didn't leave the Democratic Party. The party left me.'" But a Google search for the quote also turns up countless examples of right-wing bloggers and comment board posters misremembering it as "I didn't leave the Democrat Party. The party left me.'" In 2010 NPR had to clarify to its editorial

[38] Baptists (and most Christians) may take offense at the Westboro Baptist Church's name, but unless it finally renames itself the High Priesthood of the Dickturd Fuck Shitters, you'll likely keep seeing its name in *The Wall Street Journal*.

staff that the adjective "Democratic" was the correct one after several of its reporters used "Democrat" on-air. No doubt the adjective's originators would be pleased to know that even the lefty, sauvignon-blanc-sipping ninnies at National Public Radio employed it.

See also, *"Accents," "America," "Bracketing," "'-ghazi' vs. '-gate'"*

DESIGNATED SURVIVOR (OR, "WHY THE TRANSPORTATION SECRETARY IS A TOTAL LOSER")

Death comes for us all, but it would be a real bummer if the president, vice president, the entire cabinet, every single member of Congress, all nine members of the Supreme Court, and the joint chiefs simultaneously departed this veil of tears. That's why we have the U.S. government's most depressing thing: the designated survivor.

When America's top officials are gathered together in one location—like the House chamber for the annual State of the Union address or Nancy Pelosi's basement for fight club—the White House chief of staff names a designated survivor, a member of the cabinet who is sent to an undisclosed location[39] for the duration of the event. This way, if a giant ACME anvil[40] materializes out of the ether and pancakes the Capitol, there will be someone in the line of succession with a pulse.

The practice began during the Cold War, when the prospect of Washington, D.C., being extinguished in a flash of hellfire and radiation wasn't so remote, and has been in place ever since. After the terrorist attacks of September 11, 2001, the security detail for the designated survivor was ratcheted up.

Like everything else, politics plays a role. Because having senior (i.e., cooler) cabinet members at the address is good politics, and because the likelihood of tragedy befalling such a tightly guarded

---

[39] Possibly the walk-in freezer in a Costco. Or a bunker.

[40] Or Monty Python foot.

event is infinitesimally small, the president usually picks a junior (i.e., lamer) cabinet official.

That said, it's a pretty sweet gig for the designee, who gets the full presidential treatment. Dan Glickman, former Clinton agriculture secretary and designated survivor for the 1997 State of the Union, described his experience to CBS News in 2007. Glickman used the night off to visit his daughter in New York City,[41] where he was flown in a government plane and provided a mini, presidential-style motorcade. Baller.

Think of the pick as America's designated driver. Even if our government has lost the ability to function properly, there will be someone there in full control. Sure, that person might be the secretary of the interior, and yes he might need his national security briefing boiled down into terminology he can understand—possums and shrubs and the like—but the important thing is that he'll be there, keeping us safe.

See also, *"Executive Departments," "State of the Union," "War," "White House"*

DIGITAL

Section of a campaign organization or other political entity dedicated to Internet, social media, and whatever is at the cutting edge of keeping your child from listening to you. In Democratic campaigns, the digital office is where you'll find the most Ulysses S. Grant beards and sleeve tats. In Republican campaigns, it's where you'll find the one kid who wears skinny jeans and who dared slap a bumper sticker on their standard-issue Dell.

Even in the most savvy of political campaigns, digital remains a relatively small financial commitment. In 2012, the Obama reelection campaign spent 10 percent of its media budget on digital ventures.

---

[41] Try not to think too much about how the person tasked with shepherding the country through an unprecedented national security crisis decided to spend his time in a giant terrorist target.

Yet for all its newness, digital is still subject to the same brutal numbers game as fieldwork or phone banking. Political activists know this calculus well. A few dozen new supporters might cost a campaign several hundred thousand dollars, but a hundred votes or calls to a congressman's office can make the difference in an election or a bill's passage.

Though exact numbers vary, only a percentage or two of web ad "impressions"—eyeballs that graze over a web ad—will actually result in a click. Of those clickers, some 5 to 10 percent might go on to fill out a petition, or send a note to their congressman, and an even smaller percentage will donate money. So if a campaign pays $125,000 to run 1 million banner ads in a specific state or several targeted congressional districts (and they can tailor these things to location), they're effectively paying for 1,000 visitors to their website, only a percentage of whom will pay any meaningful attention to it, and for some 75 to 150 people to take any kind of action. The numbers are somewhat better with email, which users tend to opt into and is a slightly more intimate medium. A healthy "open rate" can hover anywhere from 3 to 20 percent. Email remains the belle of the digital ball, however: 90 percent of Obama/Biden 2012's online contributions came through email solicitations. There's a whole entry in this book on it; you should check it out.

Digital campaigning bears a strong resemblance to its televised counterpart. A presidential campaign skirmishing over suburban voters in Ohio might not want to waste resources on a national TV ad, or even ads in Ohio TV markets at certain times. If poll crosstabs show that stay-at-home moms are the chief up-for-grab voters, the campaign might opt for more daytime ad buys. But digital campaigns actually allow for more precise targeting. Ever seen one of those "FINE SINGLES IN [your city]" ads on the side of a website? Or one marketing products you've recently googled? Or "sponsored tweets" from Republican campaigns after you've voiced skepticism about Barack Obama's parentage on Twitter? The technology that fills in the [your city] bit is the same technology that lets campaigns know what area you live in, what products you search for, and what kind of links you're inclined to click. And the innumerable data marketplaces where companies, organizations, and campaigns buy and sell this data allow campaigns to obtain specific demographic, and sometimes personal, information behind IP and email addresses. The growing prevalence of this information has only served to drive down its price.

So the next time you see a heavily bearded fellow in an Obama 2012 shirt and Warby Parker frames, give him a good smack upside the head: he's probably the reason the forty-fourth president keeps emailing you, "Hey."

See also, *"Email," "Field," "Finance," "Social Media"*

DRIVETIME

Term for rush-hour radio programming. Drivetime interviews are easy ways for politicians to reach key suburban swing voters, many of whom are driving to and from work, and are usually scheduled on election days to boost turnout. Drivetime interviews regularly occur on sports talk shows or shows with "Zoo" in the title and are often conducted by bloated men with adjectives in their names and dressed in bowling shirts and cowpie hats. As such, these interviews tend to skew a bit light, thereby providing candidates the opportunity to shoehorn local references into their discussion.

> *"Alriiiiiiiight, KCOW in the morning, Columbus's #1 home of the eighties, nineties, and todaaaaaay!* [Prerecorded sound of cow mooing.] *Thanks again to Paula Cole for that in-studio performance.* [Prerecorded sound of applause.] *Alriiiiiiiight, joining us now is a very special guest, none other than the President of the Uniiiiiiiited States! Mr. President, welcome to KCOW in the morning!"*
>
> *"Thanks for having me!"*

> *"Sooooooo, Mr. President, it looks like Congress is giving you some trouble with that education bill.* [Prerecorded sound of baby crying.] *What are you going to do about that?"*
>
> *". . . . . go Buckeyes!"*

See also, *"Ad Buy," "Advertising," "Bracketing," "Earned Media," "Media Market"*

DUES

"As soon as a coin in the coffer rings, the soul from purgatory springs," so goes the Reformation-age couplet about buying one's way out of the spiritual purgation. Though party leaders don't have the ability to expedite a member's ascension to Heaven, they do have a number of tools at their disposal to make their professional lives somewhat hellish. Both parties have campaign organizations dedicated to electing members to both chambers of Congress: the Democratic Congressional Campaign Committee (DCCC) and National Republican Congressional Committee (NRCC) in the House and Democratic Senate Campaign Committee (DSCC) and National Republican Senatorial Committee (NRSC) in the Senate.

Accordingly, each member is expected to transfer money from their campaign committee or leadership PACs to the parties' campaign organizations. Party leadership is as likely to put the screws on its members about dues as it is messaging or vote whipping. While payments are expected from all members, those who wish to rise in the ranks are expected to contribute a greater share. Members who want to land plum committee assignments, or leadership spots, are expected to donate hundreds of thousands of dollars annually to the parties' campaign arms.

Consistency is also rewarded, and members who don't miss payments are acknowledged with less conspicuous perks, like seats on CODELs, spots on policy committees, and appearances by leading members at their own campaign fundraisers. Sometimes, simple attaboys during conference or caucus luncheons is all a leader needs to do to give members the green light to cosponsor a member's bill. Such attaboys are not given lightly.

Conversely, politicians who don't submit their dues or donate a piddling amount—a light envelope, if you will—regularly run afoul of leadership. And while Paul Ryan might not hold wayward members by their ankles over a bridge, members who skip their dues may soon feel as if two thick-necked gentlemen in leather jackets, both named Hands, appeared at their doorstep. Rogue members' bills are less likely to be introduced on the floor, prominent party donors may suddenly start skipping their fundraisers, and life on Capitol Hill starts to get a bit lonelier.

While the arrangement might seem a little mob-like, members who shirk their party campaign responsibilities are often viewed as being unnecessarily truculent. Stark ideological divisions exist within both the Democratic and Republican parties. However, none of the four major party campaign organizations involve themselves in primary battles, meaning someone holding out on their dues isn't just bucking leadership, but also depriving members of their own party resources to increase their numbers in Congress.

See also, *"Fundraiser," "Leadership PAC," "PAC," "Speaker of the House"*

E

EARNED MEDIA

Media that is played—*gratis*—on television, radio, and online, earning the distributor of the content publicity for their agenda that would otherwise cost money. It's God's gift to Donald Trump.

A quick thought experiment: imagine you're a segment producer for a cable news program and you have to compile a minute-long piece on the increasingly fraught Ohio Senate race between Congressman Kneescab and Governor Briarstink. Which campaign ad are you going to use in your segment?

A. One featuring audio of Congressman Kneescab talking about his love of Ohio, overlaid onto footage of him shaking hands with constituents, his family seated at dinner, listening intently to a factory worker, and flashing thumbs-up at a Fourth of July parade.

B. One of a concerned-looking woman solemnly telling the viewer that Governor Briarstink's tax-and-spend agenda has her concerned for her children's future.

C. One with a talking dog, speaking with a Scooby-Doo accent, about how Governor Briarstink kicks Ohio's working families to the curb, a thinly veiled reference

> to reports that the governor once drop-kicked his wife's beloved dachshund, Manchego, through a second-floor bay window in their family's three-thousand-square-foot Cincinnati-area home.*"Ruh roh! Grovernor Briarstrink ris shripping jrobs rout rof strate!"*

If you picked A, come back to this entry after you've read the rest of this book. If you picked B, please reread the beginning of this entry; you're a producer for a *cable news* program, not the *PBS NewsHour*. But as you probably guessed, C is the right answer: people *love* talking dogs. Talking dogs are America's 478th favorite thing, right ahead of drive-through Starbucks and right behind minivan advertisements that vow to "not compromise." If the poodle from *Look Who's Talking Now!* could run for Congress, it'd already be fielding calls from the DCCC and NRCC.

Fifty years ago, Lyndon Johnson's iconic "Daisy" ad—which showed a young girl singing "daisy" and then promptly being obliterated by a nuclear explosion—ran only one time. Its message was so effective that discussion about it obviated the need to run it a second time. Had YouTube existed back then, it probably would've been run a million more times.

See also, *"Ad Buy," "Advertising," "Digital," "Flack," "Hack," "Media Market," "Social Media"*

EGO

See, *"'50 Most Beautiful,'" "Monuments to Me," "Panels," "Rock Stars," "Wall of Fame"*

EMAIL

Digital correspondence and medium through which elderly family members send along notes with subjects like "FW: FW: FW: FW: FW:

FW: FW: FW: FW: FW: NEVER FORGET LIFE'S LITTLE BLESSINGS!!!"

Email has come a long way in its several decades of government service. "Some may wonder whether congressional e-mail is just a fiber-optic fad," read a 1994 States News Service piece on the technology, speculating that it might simply be "a kind of taxpayer-sponsored video game for politicians." It would be *Brick Breaker,* not email, that would eventually become Washington's favorite video game. Email, meanwhile, has become as much a lifeblood of our politics as televised ad campaigns, if not more so.

Endorsements are coveted as much for the optics as the entity's or person's email list. An endorsement from the AFL-CIO, for example, can provide a considerable boon to a Democrat's labor bona fides, but it also bolsters the candidate's reach to many of the union's 12-million-plus members. A good snail-mail operation remains a must for getting out the vote, raising funds, and promoting issues, but very few of us compulsively check our physical mailboxes the way we reflexively pull out our phones and fire up Gmail in a desperate attempt to wring out endorphins from our already drained neural pleasure centers.

This is not lost on America's politicians, and a robust email list remains one of the most potent weapons in a political organization or politician's arsenal. Some organizations have become forces simply by the reach of their lists. Perhaps the best example is MoveOn .org, which was founded in the late 1990s as an online conduit for left-leaning petitions (including its first, a drive to stop Bill Clinton's impeachment proceedings and "move on"). Today, the organization sports 7 million members, each of whom receives solicitations on behalf of causes and candidates endorsed by the group. Even if a MoveOn member doesn't live in a candidate's district, or isn't directly impacted by the group's agenda, their money is still green. If you ever feel inundated by emails from actor Mark Ruffalo asking you to join the fight to make the Gowanus Canal a national historic landmark, you have MoveOn to thank.

Campaigns, even losing ones, must decide what to do with their email lists after election day. Some hold on to them, allowing the vanquished candidate or lawmaker-elect to leverage access to their supporters. Email addresses, and any accompanying data like home addresses or party affiliation, are sometimes rented or sold to other organizations and campaigns. The reason for these bulk data sales varies, and the sliminess of the sale varies on a case-by-case basis: some are to pay down campaign debt, others to provide staffers with a few extra months of benefits after months, or even years, of grueling work, still more to hoard cash for another run, and a few to maintain an income stream for family members and political allies in need of a no-show gig.

Development experts can rake in serious cash helping their clients get the most out of their email lists, and the technology and analytical tools at their disposal are impressive. Most professional email services allow clients to check their emails' open rates, the number of clicks each link receives, and who goes on to donate money. Clients can A/B test different subject headers and email content, sending different iterations to a small number of supporters and then sending the most popular version to their entire network. Depending on the information at their disposal, organizations can divide their supporters into more targeted groups, including ones segmented by age, location, interests, and whether they've donated previously. Sometimes, orgs can make demographic assumptions about their supporters from what links they clicked on.

This is why digital fundraising solicitations increasingly sound like needy appeals from friends and family—organizations know you're likely to open them. You've almost certainly been duped by this point, maybe by those that pretend to be casual check-ins from friends—"Have a moment?," "You'll love this," and the always resonant "Hey" are popular. Or maybe those reminiscent of an ex-spouse trying to organize their kids' custody schedule—"Can we talk?," "We have to deal with this," and "Not again." The Democratic Congressional Campaign Committee has become leaders in the field of eye-catching fundraising appeals. "AWFUL news," "Social Security GONE," "ALL HOPE IS LOST," and "We Keep Emailing" are just a selection of the have-you-no-sense-of-decency subject lines employed by the DCCC in late 2015 and early 2016. The thing is, as irritating as it is to have "Dinner?" pop up in your inbox only to realize it's from Elizabeth Warren, organizations have too much riding on your reaction to not turn your email into a psychological battleground. The subject lines "Hey, we need your help" and "Hey" might not seem that different, but one could make the difference between besting your opponent's Q4 fundraising totals and coming out behind.

See also, *"Digital," "Fundraising," "Finance," "Social Media"*

EXECUTIVE DEPARTMENTS

Governmental agencies whose leaders sit on the presidential cabinet and who also fall in the line of succession, often known as "Cabinet departments." The cabinet also includes a handful of officials not in the line of succession, including the White House chief of staff, the EPA administrator, and the U.S. Trade Representative. Being included in the cabinet is not entirely for window dressing, as the "principals" regularly meet at the White House.

In addition to cabinet agencies, the federal government is comprised of hundreds of other independent agencies, panels, and corporations, too many to describe here. If you're looking for a detailed explanation of the Federal Maritime Commission, you've come to the wrong place, brother. Here, in the order in which their secretaries fall in the presidential line of succession (after the vice president, speaker of the House, and president of the Senate pro tem), are brief summaries of the fifteen executive branch departments and some of their offices and programs:

State

WHAT IT DOES

Helps develop foreign policy; administers foreign aid (USAID); issues passports; coordinates official trips abroad; directs diplomatic corps (Civil Service and Foreign Service); assists U.S. businesses dealing with foreign governments; manages embassies; places little plastic doohickeys to ears; assists pickpocketed American tourists; increases employee camaraderie through Pol Pot lucks; urges bilateral cooperation.

Likely secretaries

Prominent senators
National security advisers
Leading military figures
Party bigwigs
UN ambassadors
White people not afraid to wear dashikis for ceremonial purposes

Treasury

WHAT IT DOES

Helps set economic policy; collects taxes (IRS); needlessly makes pennies (U.S. Mint); employs terrorist-fighting accountants (Office of Terrorism and Financial Intelligence); issues government debt; regulates financial markets; tells Congress how long it has to raise debt ceiling before world economy collapses; works with USA Network to develop new series about terrorist-fighting accountants.

Likely secretaries

Regional Fed chairs
Senior party figures
Goldman Sachs executive buttonholed by presidential transition chairman at charity golf event

Defense

WHAT IT DOES

Manages the five main branches of the armed forces and their reserves; deters war by conducting wars; parent department of intelligence agencies including the NSA; rides missiles while waving cowboy hats around; manages global operational command centers (USNORTHCOM, CENTCOM, USEUCOM, USAFRICOM, etc.); fictional setting of futuristic command center where a bookish-looking fellow in a short-sleeve oxford, pocket protector, and thick-rimmed glasses sits down at his station while stabbing at a salad with a fork, only for his mouth to slowly open in astonishment as he looks at a computer, grabs a phone, and sputters, "You're gonna wanna see this."

Possible secretaries

Members of the Senate Armed Services Committee
Generals
National security advisers
Republicans, usually

Justice

WHAT IT DOES

Helps president formulate law-enforcement policy; enforces law; dons yellow windbreakers and rams doors open (FBI); protects civil rights (Civil Rights Division); is run by the attorney general—who tragically is not called "Secretary of Justice"; oversees army of government lawyers (United States Attorneys); kicks the tires of corporate mergers (Antitrust Division); represents the government in the Supreme Court (Solicitor General); kills buzzes (Bureau of Alcohol, Tobacco, Firearms and Explosives); kills highs (Drug Enforcement Agency), runs Uncle Sam's clinks (Federal Bureau of Prisons).

Likely attorneys general

District attorneys
Mariska Hargitay
Deputy attorneys general

Sam Waterston
Federal judges
State attorneys
Jerry Orbach
Senators or governors with JDs
Ice-T

Interior

WHAT IT DOES

Runs national parks (National Park Service); oversees Native American reservations and helps set tribal policies (Bureau of Indian Affairs); handles grazing and mining rights on federal land (Bureau of Land Management); makes sure no one feeds the owls; receives visits from lobbyists about grazing and mining rights on federal land (Bureau of Land Management); actually knows what "wetlands" are; studies rocks; provides directions to regulatory birds.

Likely secretaries

Individual with great love of the outdoors and also a great love of not being bothered by a campaign bundler's desire to log the Smoky Mountains
Westerner—all but one Interior secretary since 1949 has hailed from a Western state
Men comfortable in bolo ties
Ranger Dan, a handsome fellow in a neat khaki uniform whom you chance upon in a glade as he tends to a fallen nest of hatchlings. Dan asks if you would like a drink and obligingly reaches into his knapsack for a tin cup. As Ranger Dan scrummages around his knapsack, you notice the pleasing sinews of his arm, the strong yet pleasant slope of his jawline, and the way the light plays off auburn hair—its tendrils reflecting the early morning sun. You feel something

you haven't felt for a long time, but suppress it, though there's little you can do about the stirring in your loins. As you sip on your water, Dan places his hand on a nearby redwood and, with a wistful look in his eyes—and to no one in particular—observes *she's an old one, with stories to tell.* You notice his tan and shapely calves that gracefully extend from his standard issue tan shorts. Turning from the tree, he locks eyes with you and, careful to step around the hatchlings, places his strong and sun-kissed arms aroun—-

Agriculture Department

WHAT IT DOES

Sets food production policy; manages food stamps; needlessly subsidizes corn; regulates food safety; runs antihunger initiatives; thinks about corn; assists low-income farmers; assists ADM executives to furnish starter apartments in a doorman building for their children at NYU; generates animal and plant safety standards (Animal and Plant Health Inspection Service); studies corn; has lumber industry lobbyists on speed dial (Forest Service); implements school nutrition standards; corn, corn, corn; manages rural economic development programs; corn, corn, corn, corn, corn, corn, corn, corn.

Possible secretaries

Midwestern lawmaker or governor
Stalk of corn with googly eyes

Commerce Department

WHAT IT DOES

Promotes economic growth and job creation, making it the only cabinet department that sounds like it's running for Senate; issues certain economic regulations; administers patents and sets rules governing them (Patent and Trademark Office); sits on a front porch in a rocking chair, saying to no one in particular, "knee's actin' up, storms-a-comin" (National Oceanic and Atmospheric Administration); doles out grants to disadvantaged communities (Minority Business Development Agency, Economic Development Administration); decides what a centimeter is (National Institute of Standards and Technology); tries to justify its existence as a cabinet agency.

Possible secretaries

Governors looking for something neat to do
Presidential confidantes who need a job
Prominent business leaders
Prominent business leaders who are campaign donors
Prominent business leaders who are campaign donors who don't want to serve as ambassadors to Belgium
Prominent business leaders who have no compunction about looking ridiculous while touring factory floors in a suit and hard hat

Labor

WHAT IT DOES

Enforces labor laws; produces job reports (Bureau of Labor Statistics); regulates pitch of factory "quittin' time" whistles; reminds employees that they must wash hands (Occupational Safety and Health Administration); puts bodies upon the gears and upon the wheels, upon the levers, upon all the apparatus of the machine; provides guidelines for state unemployment benefits (Employment and Training Administration).

Possible secretaries

Members of Congress
Academics
Spunky North Carolina textile workers who look a lot like Sally Field and are trying to unionize the cotton mill and do right by their dad who died on the job

Health and Human Services

WHAT IT DOES

Promotes public health and safety; washes behind ears; administers Medicare and Medicaid (Centers for Medicare and Medicaid Services); executes Comrade President Obama's glorious socialist healthcare revolution; makes sure there's no Tylenol in your soup and no soup in your Tylenol (Food and Drug Administration); reminds you to cover your coughs with your elbow, not your hand (Centers for Disease Control and Prevention); administers safety net programs including Temporary Assistance for Needy Families, or "welfare" as it's more commonly known (Administration for Children and Families); gets mice high for research purposes (National Institutes of Health).

Possible secretaries

Governors
University administrators
People willing to field awkward questions about abstinence-only curriculums

Housing and Urban Development

WHAT IT DOES

Promotes home ownership; leaves roommates passive-aggressive notes about old leftovers in fridge; increases access to affordable housing; provides financial assistance to those of us without wealthy parents to help out on a down payment (Federal Housing Administration); distributes federal funds for homeless shelters and other antihomeless initiatives (Office of Community Planning and Development); jiggles handle; enforces antidiscrimination laws (Office of Fair Housing and Equal Opportunity).

Possible secretaries

Deputy administrators
Mayors
Republicans willing to visit poor people

Transportation

WHAT IT DOES

Ensures that the nation's transportation networks run as efficiently as possible; pumps fists at passing truckers; distributes federal funds for highways (Federal Highway Administration); prohibits you from tampering with, disabling, or destroying any smoke detector (Federal Aviation Administration); makes sure your car's air bag isn't filled with confetti (National Highway Traffic Safety Administration); doles out money for that light-rail system you never use (Federal Transit Administration); *choo! choo!* (Federal Railroad Administration); determines whether here there be dragons (Maritime Administration).

Possible secretaries

Token members of the opposite party
Mayors
On-ramp enthusiasts

Energy

WHAT IT DOES

Regulates some of our more self-destructive energy practices and helps find brand-new ones; distributes research grants (Office of Fossil Energy, Office of Nuclear Energy, Office of Energy Efficiency and Renewable Energy); does a fair amount of research itself (National Laboratories); serves as America's radiation sneeze guard (National Nuclear Security Administration); nerds out (Office of Science—*really*, that's what it's called).

Possible secretaries

Scientists with political experience
Politicians with science experience
Nerds
Geeks
Spazzes

Dorks
Dweebs

Education

WHAT IT DOES

Works with states and municipalities to help children understand what the neck bone connects to; sets education standards (National Assessment of Educational Progress); answers George W. Bush's question, "Is our children learning?" (National Center for Education Statistics, Education Resources Information Center); provides young people the chance to major in art history, move back into their parents' place after graduation, split the first twenty-six months of their professional career pulling shifts at a Qdoba Mexican Grill and working in their childhood bedroom on T-shirt designs for their clothing company under the watchful gaze of a fraying Dave Matthews Band concert poster (Federal Pell Grants); rounds up diverse groups of children for press events.

Possible secretaries

Prominent school administrators
University presidents
That "ACHIEVE YOUR DREAMS" Jonathan Taylor Thomas poster from your sixth-grade homeroom's wall

Veterans Administration

WHAT IT DOES

Supports America's veterans through education, health care, and other initiatives; disappoints subjects of Bruce Springsteen anthems; implements GI Bill programs (Veterans Benefit Administration); tells members of the military and their families to cut down on the red meat (Veterans Health Administration); manages national military cemeteries and organizes funerals for veterans and fallen service members (National Cemetery Administration).

Possible secretaries

Active military brass
Retired service members
Expert scapegoat

Homeland Security

WHAT IT DOES

Handles the immigration and visa applications of the tired, poor, huddled masses yearning to be free (Citizenship and Immigration Services Services); monitors the border for tired, poor, huddled masses yearning to be free (Customs and Border Protection); deports tired, poor, huddled masses yearning to be free (Immigration and Naturalization Service); dons royal blue button-downs and rubber gloves and proceeds to fondle your inner thigh (Transportation Safety Administration); kills its secretaries' political careers; protects leading political figures and provides their more distant relatives cards with information on who to call if they have been swept into a windowless van (Secret Service); delivers flats of water bottles and crate of MREs to disaster areas (Federal Emergency Management Agency); the nexus of a sweeping conspiracy to ship seditious Americans to concentration camps, meticulously planned in the darkest corners of Warren Beatty's finished basement, where the most tree-hugging, blasphemy-spewing, kombucha-sipping, gay-sex-having, free-market-despising members of America's secular liberal conspiracy plot a final solution to people who go to church and who think a weekend spent taking in all that Branson, Missouri, has to offer is time well spent (Federal Emergency Management Agency).

Possible secretaries

Anyone content to never hold elected office again

See also, *"Budget," "Bureaucracy," "Congressional staff," "White House"*

EXPERT

In Washington, everyone.

Truly, Washington is lousy with experts: they materialize on panels, professing to know how to fix political gridlock; they pontificate on CNN about the president's unfocused messaging; they offer their services to reporters in emails, informing the fourth branch that they are available to comment, on record, about the vice president's recent vacation to Cabo San Lucas.

As a rule of thumb, an expert's *actual* expertise—that is, abilities and knowledge that are not easily attainable by laypeople—correlates directly with the "hardness" of their academic field.

Expert Experts

Assuming sound credentials, these scientists, doctors, engineers, and other practitioners of "hard" sciences top the expert food chain. They appear on TV to discuss, for example, medical stories, because a "campaign veteran" can speculate all he or she wants about the president's Ohio strategy, but they can't really offer much in the way of the commander in chief's extracorporeal shock wave lithotripsy.

Learned Experts

There may be two sides to every story, but the wishy-washiness of jurisprudence doesn't mean you'll gladly have someone with a law degree from DeVry represent you in court. These experts may genuinely have deep knowledge about a subject that may not be as objective as mathematics, but still requires a great deal of study. These are the lawyers, the historians, the constitutional scholars, and the pollsters; the folks who may squabble all day over crosstabs, but who would still impress your Jewish mother if you dated them—Michael Beschloss, in particular.

Titled Experts

Reporters, business executives, advocacy organization directors, and even former members of Congress, the titled expert may not be an endowed chair at Columbia University, but they are the senior Washington correspondent for a news outlet you've heard of, so surely they know what they are talking about . . . right? It's also entirely possible that said reporter is twenty-three and simply looks good on camera. That former member of Congress on *Morning Joe* may have genuine insight on a budget negotiation, or they have since taken a job as a senior policy adviser at Morgan Stanley and have particular interest in seeing the budget compromise—the one without carried interest reform—passed.

Untouchables

Political squeegee men. These are the Democratic or Republican "strategists," the social media experts, the body language experts, the crisis management experts—scourges upon our society who should be rounded up and thrown en masse into a volcano. The untouchables are men and women of prodigious drive and no social utility—other than finding new and dubious income streams to pay their condo fees—who have made a living providing services we don't need and advising others about things we already know. They are paid by middle-aged agency officials to create Twitter accounts, appear on CNN to opine on how the president was unhappy that time he grimaced, publish think pieces on how millennials are overly coddled that only serve to make boomers feel better about themselves, and advise scandal-plagued public officials not to call their estranged wives whores on Twitter. These charlatans will be reincarnated as sea slugs.

See also, *"Congressional Research Service," "Panels," "Strategist," "'Rock Stars'"*

EXPLORATORY COMMITTEE

Legal campaign entity that allows prospective candidates for office to raise money for a limited number of activities, like air travel, polling, and accommodation. These organizations are most closely associated with presidential aspirants, who, naturally, had likely been "exploring" a presidential run well before the establishment of their exploratory committee.

Despite being rather humdrum in scope, the founding of an exploratory committee tends to be a notable event in the presidential campaign cycle. It signals to the press that the candidate plans to spend more time in early primary states than they can reasonably expect to pay for themselves. That said, don't expect a presidential hopeful to appear in a YouTube video beside his family and confidently declare that he is forming an exploratory committee "so some of my wealthier friends can pay for me to fly business to Ames and stay in a Mariott."

Like standard campaign committees and political action committees—or PACs—there are limits to how much a single person can contribute to an exploratory committee, though the "explorers" don't have to disclose their finances to the FEC until they actually form a campaign committee. However, a prospective candidate can't transfer their exploratory committee money into a campaign PAC. Most significantly, they cannot engage in standard electioneering.

Of course, the appearance of a prominent political figure in an early primary state like New Hampshire or Iowa is itself a kind of campaign rally, a newsworthy event that draws attention to the would-be candidate. However, don't expect the FEC to start issuing reprimands if your senator eats some scrapple and shakes hands at a diner in Nashua.

See also, *"Constituent," "Iowa Caucuses," "New Hampshire Primary," "South Carolina Primary"*

F

FEDERALIST SOCIETY

Country's preeminent conservative legal organization. By the early 1980s, many of America's conservative and libertarian jurists felt alienated from a legal establishment that they regarded as being too liberal. So, in 1982, a group of law students and professors at Yale and the University of Chicago pulled a "C'mon gang, we'll start *our own* club!" and founded the Federalist Society. Except instead of a ragtag group of kids in overalls and helicopter beanies who simply wanted to play some stickball, it was a bunch of white people in sweaters named Spencer who wanted to roll back environmental regulations and execute criminals.

The Federalist Society is arguably the closest thing we have to a "vast right-wing conspiracy"—like the Freemasons for people who hate Obamacare. Virtually every major conservative legal figure over the last quarter century has belonged to the group and Republican administrations have teemed with Federalist Society members. All three Supreme Court justices who make up the high court's conservative bloc are members of the group. Associate Justice Antonin Scalia, who passed away in February 2016, helped found the group while working at the University of Chicago's law faculty. John Roberts claimed during his confirmation hearing to have no recollection of membership in the group, despite being listed in its leadership rolls in the 1990s. In 2007, only two years after being confirmed, he appeared in a video for the group's twenty-fifth anniversary.

See also, *"Country Club Republican," "CPAC," "Judiciary," "Rainmaker," "Republican Study Committee," "Scoring"*

FIELD

Campaign division focused on ground mobilization, get-out-the-vote efforts, and outreach to allied organizations and groups. Think Jehovah's Witnesses, but with fewer Bibles and more vans driving your nana to a polling station.

Field teams can vary in size and complexity, ranging from a handful of volunteers distributing fliers and hammering lawn signs to a nationwide labyrinth of state, county, and precinct offices, each of which assembles complex networks of volunteers. Some organizations have their own field network; the AFL-CIO sports an extensive one that is put into action on behalf of candidates and ballot initiatives the union supports. Field offices also maintain relationships with local power players, like unions, religious groups, business leaders, and anyone else who might be able to throw a spaghetti dinner. Particularly advanced field teams even have their own communication staffers, who interface with the remaining local news organizations that haven't shuttered or reduced their coverage to high school sports and *Dilbert*.

Even with all the demands placed upon campaigns in our digital age—the need for complex algorithms, A/B tested email campaigns, and cat memes—a solid ground game remains a must. Even yard signs—those paradigms of analog campaigning, no less a fixture of the preelection landscape than mailers and TV spots accusing your local comptroller of funneling money to ISIS—are important. A March 2016 study published in *Electoral Studies* found that in municipal and statewide elections, yard signs could sway the vote for a candidate upward of 1.7 percent—a veritable boon in today's politics. For candidates or organizations not funded by an egomaniacal billionaire hell-bent on bending public policy to his will, having a solid operation lets the grassroots compete. Charles Koch might be able to *buy* your nana's address and vote history from another organization, but he isn't going to drive your nana to the polling place on election day. Postmortems on campaigns that underperformed despite being financially well off typically home in on one of two things: a lackluster candidate or a weak field operation. Money is still king, most campaign veterans insist, and TV ad buys are infinitely more potent than yard signs, but even an extra half a percent can be the difference, and campaigns usually shift resources toward field operations in the final week or two before election day.

All that newfangled digital stuff is making fieldwork more precise. In the course of their phone banking and door-knocking campaigns, field teams accumulate troves of voter data, data that is instrumental in directing fundraising and voter outreach efforts. A campaign's field team works closely with the digital office, which scrutinizes that data and helps the field office develop finely tuned lists for voter engagement and get-out-the-vote efforts. "Hi, do you have a moment to discuss Hillary Clinton's plan for the middle class?" might be what the person knocking at your door *tells* you, but if they were being honest, it'd be something closer to, "Hi, I see from this spreadsheet that you donated $20 to John Kerry's presidential campaign, voted in the last midterm, and once visited a less than scrupulous website that promised you a free iPad for all your personal information. Have a moment to chat?"

For decades, voter outreach followed a familiar script. Through phone banks and door-knocking campaigns, would-be voters would be grilled about their candidate preferences and, usually on a one to five scale, the strength of those preferences. That information, including the date of their latest "contact," was logged and used to craft, in a very broad and unspecified way, outreach efforts like mailing campaigns and get-out-the-vote initiatives. Other data was available to campaigns—subscription data purchased from magazines, for example—but the way this information was metabolized was fairly rudimentary by today's standards.

A number of developments, including more detailed censuses, the sharing of information between party organizations, and the fact that children increasingly learn how to execute a NORMSDIST function on Microsoft Excel before they can tie their shoes, the process of gathering and processing campaign data has advanced exponentially. Now, seemingly arcane bits of information—browser history, purchasing data, email open rates—are synthesized using proprietary algorithms that spit out detailed analyses of the electorate.

Still, no matter how streamlined the data crunching is, fieldwork isn't easy. For volunteers it's an hour-to-hour, day-to-day onslaught of rejection, hostility, and way too many people in their underwear.

Interfacing with randos isn't fun—there's a reason why someone in need of friendship doesn't broach conversation with any old stranger on the street. Have you met a person lately? People are *terrible.* Democratic canvassers are told to stop killing babies. Republican canvassers are told to stop supporting war criminals. Both are spat on. If phone bankers could be spat on, they would be. It's entirely possible Apple will have found a workaround for that by the time this goes to press.

Like most campaign work, a field job is filled with long days, crappy food, working weekends in halogen-lit offices, while dealing with the ongoing stress of managing the sublease back home. Like other campaign workers, many field staffers have given up steady work in Washington or elsewhere to toil for six months or longer on a campaign. The occasional one-night stand with a precinct captain might ease the pain, but it can be pretty lonely and stressful work. And then there are the volunteers. *Sweet Jesus, the volunteers.* Volunteers—or *vols,* to use campaign parlance—are not an easy bunch to manage. Yes, they're civically engaged and passionate; but vols are people—and remember what we said about people? Vols think they single-handedly know how to win an election; vols want to know when they get to meet the candidate; vols forget to mark up their walk lists; vols may have just given a quote to a reporter; vols appreciate you ordering the pizza but really don't like mushrooms; vols are so, *so* sorry but vols are going to have to reschedule.

A discussion of vols would be incomplete without mentioning *supervols,* the particularly dedicated unpaid workers who are de facto part-time or full-time staff. Supervols fall into one of three categories: there are college students, who may or may not be working for credit; there are retirees, trying to do something useful in their sunset years; and then there are *the others,* who, well, more on them below.

Elderly supervols are one of a campaign's most valuable resources. Unlike college students, who make the Italian postal system seem reliable, most elderly volunteers have lifetimes of work, child rearing, and innumerable other experiences that have prepared them for the comparative ease of instructing high school seniors on door-knocking etiquette. College students are energetic, and they make great canvassers, but these are people who can't even be bothered to change out of their sweatpants for a 10:30 a.m. class. They are not to be trusted.

Then there are *the others.* It's typically not campaign policy to turn away a volunteer, save in extreme circumstances, and so field offices often will have their fair share of people who, well, have nowhere else to go. Look, there are plenty of perfectly benign reasons why a person in their prime working years might be able to spend much of their time volunteering in a campaign, but there are a great number of *not-so-benign* reasons, too. Have you ever met a serial online commenter? No? That's probably because they are too busy breaking the copy machine at a campaign field office.

Field's stress, grating day-to-day work, and low pay means only the most dedicated, most driven, most Kool Aid–drinking individual will survive and thrive in such a gauntlet. Politics is an industry where pride and ego are as much a part of a worker's compensation as their medical plan, and nowhere is that more true than in field offices. Roughly speaking, the more strenuous and backbreaking the campaign work, the more of a "profound life experience" it was. Behold:

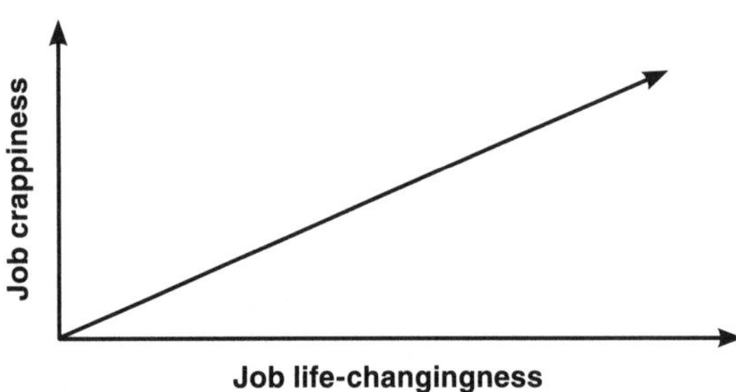

What's worse, nowhere is the expectation of future employment versus the likelihood of future employment more asymmetrical than in field offices. On smaller congressional campaigns, field staff might land jobs in their candidate's district offices, but on the statewide and presidential level, the jobs to go around after a victory are scarce. "Michigan field director for Obama" is as common a résumé line in Washington as "volunteered church's food pantry" is on college applications. You might do well to remember that when faced with the opportunity to spend eight months in a harshly lit retrofitted Blockbuster.

See also, *"Advance," "Email," "Digital," "Finance," "Voter Suppression"*

"50 MOST BEAUTIFUL"

The Hill's annual "50 Most Beautiful" list is about as Washington as it gets: it's a tale of vanity and the misallocation of resources.

As the name implies, "50 Most Beautiful" is a yearly listicle published by *The Hill*—the prestigious industry publication identifying the fifty most attractive lawmakers, congressional staffers, operatives, journalists, and other Washington types. Ranking Washington's most attractive denizens might seem a bit oxymoronic—like listing the fifty fittest people at a Cinnabon, or the Washington Generals' fifty greatest power forwards—but the list remains a highly anticipated source of Beltway navel gazing and provides the Capitol with an opportunity for some cathartic nastiness.

Readers are treated to gauzy photos of the fifty hotties, along with formulaic, 1950s beauty-pageant-style biographies, replete with lighthearted anecdotes ("Through livestock judging, he received a scholarship to attend Texas Tech University"), style rundowns ("I'm not embarrassed to like pearls"), and envy-inducing dieting tales ("Despite her love of barbecue and burger joints, [this] slim blonde says she doesn't have a gym membership or work out").

The Hill has published thirteen of these things as of 2016, and it compiles the lists from reader nominations (you can nominate yourself, though people typically show more tact by nominating themselves anonymously). By and large, *The Hill*'s staffers hate it: each year reporters and editors are dragooned from their usual beats—covering Congress, the White House, regulatory agencies, and the like—to choose and interview the designated beauties. If you thought political reporters are a disgruntled, jaded bunch, try asking one of them to stop scrutinizing a billion-dollar appropriations bill to interview Senator Meatbucket's staff assistant Amber Betherson[42] about her exercise routine and labradoodle.

Now, in fairness to *The Hill,* plenty of news organizations publish moronic lists of their own. Such "clickbait" is tailor-made for today's news organizations, which are starved for slideshows and other content that plays to readers' baser interests. These lists require viewers to constantly click the "Next" button thereby racking up the page views that advertisers love so dearly. The Internet abounds with lists of the best political Twitter feeds, the most powerful lawmakers, and the always questionable "people to watch" genre, in which you are told that this is the year a junior House member or actress Kerry Washington is going to shake up the D.C. scene.

[42] Or her male counterpart: Caleb Bennettson.

However, it's hard to come up with an equally vapid list from a similarly respectable publication.

Still, publishing flattering profiles of powerful people can, from a strategic standpoint, be smart journalism. If you're a senior committee aide, and you have to decide which reporter you're going to leak an internal document to, you might be inclined to share it with the person who published an article about your chiseled jaw and come-hither lips. While it might be a little dehumanizing for seasoned reporters to write about said jawline, taking ninety minutes to interview the staffer and write 250 words about their bocce ball league is not the worst investment.

See also, *"Beat Sweeteners," "Hack," "Hill Rags," "Monuments to Me," "Wall of Fame"*

FILIBUSTER

See, *"Legislation"*

FINANCE

Section of a campaign, organization, or other political entity dedicated to raising cash. Cash, on the off chance that you just opened this book for the first time and now find yourself reading this entry, matters quite a bit in politics.

Finance directors are tasked with managing a campaign's financial targets, putting fundraisers together, and working with the candidate, the campaign manager, the digital team, and other allied groups that may be willing to contribute. While being director can be immensely stressful, it is not without its perks. Compared to the thankless tasks of field staffers, who have to interface with—[*deep gulp*]—*real people,* finance directors mingle and develop relationships with high-rolling donors, party officials, and other individuals who might one day become a source of money or employment. Even when these interactions get particularly tedious—the "maxed out" donor who thinks they run the campaign, the $500 donor who wants a field job for their child, the one with one too many ideas about tort reform—they're often conducted over passed hors d'oeuvres at a fundraiser.[43]

Compare this existence with the *deputy* finance director's poor lot. In addition to the more menial tasks that a finance director cannot deal with—database management and the like—the deputy finance director is usually put on call time duty. Call time—as this book's entry on the subject explains—is when a candidate is put in a room, or the backseat of a car, or anywhere that isn't federal property where fundraising is *verboten,* and made to hit people up for donations. Many candidates hate this, so much so that a staffer is often assigned to sit beside them and ensure the calls are placed and the appeals made. To ease the candidate's burden, deputy finance directors will provide call sheets that not only provide the target's name and contribution target amount, but personal bits of information to make the pitch more organic. Untold amounts of small talk have occurred because a candidate glanced down at a sheet and learned that someone's son had just finished his freshman year at Villanova.

Nothing in politics breeds financial success like financial success—that or a smitten megadonor. Donors see a candidate's robust war chest as a sign of their popularity, their ability to raise funds, and their ability to wage a successful campaign through November. It's for this reason that new candidates are usually urged by their finance directors to reach out to friends and family first—these are the people who will be willing to fork over money despite a candidate having not yet demonstrated any fundraising prowess. There are a lot of explanations, some more self-evident than others, for why lawmakers are so much more likely to be slimy pieces of trash; one of the more obscure reasons is that an early filtering mechanism for candidates is whether they can ably shake down their nearest and dearest.[44]

---

[43] Or the fifth spaghetti dinner in a month. It's admittedly hit or miss.

[44] Studies, including one published in the September 2002 edition of the *Journal of Personality and Social Psychology,* have suggested that a disproportionate number of our elected officials exhibit sociopathic qualities. Go figure!

This mentality is very much built into the system. Party campaign organizations like the Democratic Congressional Campaign Committee and the National Republican Congressional Committee decide which competitive campaigns they will pour resources into based not just on the competitiveness of the race, but on how much money those campaigns have raised. Good ground games and general enthusiasm is wonderful, but these groups are primarily looking at the money. Indeed, such organizations typically have financial thresholds that become the bane of finance directors' existence. For example, a candidate's inclusion on the DCCC's "frontline" list of vulnerable incumbents not only benefits from the DCCC's resources and attention, but from the innumerable Democratic donors who would otherwise not think of contributing had the candidate not been included on the list. Suddenly, calling your auntie and demanding money doesn't bother the candidate as much. Their finance director certainly doesn't mind.

With developments in fundraising technology and changes in campaign finance law, finance operations are becoming much more varied in their structure and focus. In the 2016 presidential primaries alone, candidates took wildly different approaches in how they raised funds. Former Florida governor Jeb Bush placed relatively little emphasis on his campaign's own finance operations, and instead let his allied super PAC, Right to Rise, do the heavy lifting. Indeed, veteran GOP campaign operative Mike Murphy opted to chair the super PAC, rather than run Bush's campaign or finance operation. Bernie Sanders, who refused to have an allied super PAC, claimed to not have a finance operation, instead relying on his digital team to solicit funds online and over email. He bragged on numerous occasions that the average contribution to his campaign was $27. Hillary Clinton, meanwhile, found herself in a tough bind, opting to maintain a traditional (in the post–*Citizens United* sense of the term) campaign finance operation, enduring withering attacks from Sanders over her allied super PACs and acceptance of major donations from Wall Street bundlers.

See also, *"Bundler," "Call Time,"* "Citizens United," *"Digital," "Field," "Fundraiser," "Megadonor," "PAC," "Super PAC"*

527S

See, "Citizens United," *"PAC," "Political Nonprofit," "Super PAC"*

FLACK

Communications professional who deals with the press. The term "flack," despite flacks' best efforts to rebrand themselves "communicators," "public relations experts," or, most noxiously, "story tellers," will likely never go away, so long as there are hacks to perpetuate it. The term's origins are disputed, some saying that it grew out of World War II as an alternate spelling of "flak," an abbreviation of the German word for antiaircraft guns. The press agent, the story goes, was a "flack catcher." An alternate history traces its etymology to the Hollywood trade publication *Variety,* which is said to have created the word during the same period in reference to movie PR guru Gene Flack.

Across the political spectrum, flacks communicate with reporters, draft press releases, compile talking points, decide when it's best to say "you didn't hear this from me," write speeches and op-eds for their bosses, and, in more recent years, man a politician or organization's social media accounts. Some more adventurous pols choose to handle their own social media presence, a decision that regularly ends with the flack drafting an apologetic tweet. One of a flack's most important functions is something called "rapid response." This is a type of political communication that is quickly formulated and disseminated following an unplanned event. Such communication can take the form of press releases, web videos, social media posts, appearances on television and radio, or listicles in which *Frozen* GIFs illustrate the weaknesses of proposed auto tariffs.

A flack on the offensive is "on message." That is, the flack is advancing their organization or boss's agenda: pitching stories to reporters, attempting to plant op-eds, booking their boss on television, editing Wikipedia entries from anonymous IP addresses, and drawing attention to a BuzzFeed listicle in which an infrastructure modernization bill is explained in *Clueless* GIFs.

A flack on the defensive, however, is cleaning up a mess. These are the days when the flack's interactions with the press are net inbound, rather than outbound. A flack doesn't have time to call up a reporter to pitch them about their boss's early education initiative if they're constantly fielding calls about their boss's statement that Lithuanians smell funny, or having to draft a press release clarifying the pol's comments that pap smear is a brand of peanut butter. Flacks for high-profile lawmakers or organization more or less live in a suspended state of anxiety, waiting for the next crisis to erupt.

It's necessary that a flack familiarizes him or herself with their boss's platform, personality, and speech, as well as understanding the character and mission of their organization. Serving as a spokesperson, as the term suggests, means the flack must craft a press strategy from the same vantage point of whomever or whatever they're representing. For example, attempts to make aloof or older lawmakers or inherently dull organizations appear *hip* or *youthful* tend to backfire. If a flack for the Christian Coalition starts issuing press releases sprinkled with R. Kelly lyrics, they're not doing their job correctly.[45]

A good flack, like a good hack, knows that relationships are the key to their success. Like new neighbors, a new flack takes the time to reach out to their core media constituency, whether it's the trade publications covering a committee, the local press covering a politician back home, or publications whose ideological

[45] Conversely, a flack for R. Kelly who cites the Christian Coalition is also not doing their job correctly.

bent aligns with the flack's boss or organization. Though a welcoming Tupperware container of freshly cooked ziti may violate a news organization's ethics code, an early heads-up about a politician's intended vote, or an organization's new advocacy campaign, does not.

The adept flack knows which battles to fight and for how long. Maintaining a stubbornly hostile tone over a story about a politician attending a fundraiser thrown by a company that conducts animal testing for a wood chipper manufacturer isn't terribly wise. That doesn't mean a strong response isn't allowed, but journalists take note of flacks who reply disproportionately to a well-researched and fairly reported story. If your boss *did* take money from people who grind chinchillas into mulch, do your best to downplay the story and, if the reporter persists, don't go totally apeshit. Conversely, a flack who doesn't bring the hammer of Thor down on reporters who publish thinly substantiated pieces will be viewed as a pushover by their boss, their colleagues, and their counterparts in the press. Relatedly, experienced flacks know younger reporters are much more susceptible to bullying.

Similarly, a good flack knows their audience, and directs their pitches to a reporter on a relevant beat. They don't pitch a defense reporter a story about an unrelated environmental bill, nor do they pitch a congressional reporter about a demonstration surrounding a president's visit to a factory. Many flacks will blast out every last piece of news about their boss or organization to an uncurated mailing list of reporters. This is a lazy press strategy that irritates reporters and will likely result in the flack's email being listed as spam. Most reporters' email addresses are public, meaning they are very adept at quickly separating the wheat from the chaff. The name of a flack whose emails go regularly unchecked will, in that reporter's mind, be lumped together with their irate, elderly readers who send all-caps emails detailing Barack Obama's secret Kenyan socialist origins.

See also, *"Congressional Staff," "Hack," "Press Conference," "Pivot," "Spin"*

FLY-IN

A D.C.–lobbying blitz made by out-of-town VIPs—corporate executives, grassroots advocates, and the like—typically lasting several days. Participants meet with members of Congress or their staff,[46] host information briefings for legislators, and gawk at Mei Xiang and Tian Tian, the National Zoo's beloved giant pandas. Whether the group's lobbyist hums the "Ride of the Valkyries" is left entirely to the discretion of the ranking attendee and subject to the terms of their services agreement.

See also, *"Activist," "Cooling-off Period," "Lobbying," "Lobbyists"*

FOOD

Food plays a central role in Washington, whether as the centerpiece of an official state dinner, a fundraiser at the offices of a top-dollar lobbying firm, or an informational meeting in the basement of the Capitol between a chief of staff and an upbeat poli-sci major eager to impress upon the chief that their summer job at the Frosty Freeze really taught them a lot about constituent services. Like most everything else in lawmaking, food is highly politicized and there's a definite pecking order to the quality of the grub one can expect. In descending order, here it is:

President

The highest rung of the political culinary ladder, the president enjoys the talents of some of the world's greatest chefs. While the president has his own private dining room and personal chef within the executive mansion, the executive branch staff also has access to the White House Mess, so called because it is run by the U.S. Navy

[46] This is dependent entirely on the clout of the attendees. "Sorry, American Association of Labradoodle Breeders, but the congressman has a vote right now. His legislative correspondent is waiting for you in the conference room."

and thus cannot be called a "cafeteria" or "dining hall" lest the offending individual be court-martialed.

Despite having world-class cooking talent at their disposal, many presidents have nevertheless used their food staff to satisfy their somewhat pedestrian culinary tastes. Franklin Delano Roosevelt loved nothing more than a grilled cheese. Richard Nixon had a thing for cottage cheese and ketchup. George W. Bush developed an affinity for cheeseburger pizza, which was a plain cheese pie topped with hamburger meat and cheese.

Of course, it's good PR to make a president's lowbrow tastes public. Did the famously patrician George H. W. Bush in fact possess a love of fried pork rinds and Tabasco, as was reported in a *New York Times* profile? Maybe. Did the dissemination of that knowledge to the public prompt sales of pork rinds to spike 11 percent and earn the commander in chief the "Skin Man of the Year" award from a pork industry group? Yes.[47] Were the forty-first president's advisers thrilled to have their boss, an aloof scion of a Connecticut political dynasty, associated with such plebian fare? *Absolutely.* When Bush's son, George W. Bush, collapsed in the White House mansion after a pretzel got lodged in his throat, members of the junior Bush's political team surely must have breathed a sigh of relief that the leader of the free world nearly asphyxiated on a blue-collar snack while watching a football game and not a caviar-laden toast point during a dinner with America's poet laureate.

That said, it's not as if every president secretly harbors a love of truffles and Dom Perignon. Still, it's good politics to project a commander in chief's everyman tastes, even if they do reside in a 55,000-square-foot mansion with three kitchens and thirty-five bathrooms and fly around in a catered private jet. Rarely a state dinner or formal function goes by without some opposition lawmaker or pundit making an issue out of the upscale menu items. "The menu . . .

[47] Interesting that a man once known as "Rubbers" for his belief in contraception and population control would later in life be known as Skin Man of the Year.

offered a *2,500-calorie* feast of quail eggs, caviar, dry-aged beef, and 'twelve varieties of potatoes,'" noted the conservative *Washington Free Beacon* in its write-up of Barack Obama's state dinner honoring French president François Hollande in an article titled "It's Hard Out Here for a King."

K Street

Though high-powered lobbying firms have the resources to employ their own chefs, they instead use their food budgets on contracting catering firms for in-house fundraisers. A perusal of fundraisers on sites like the Sunlight Foundation's Political Party Time reveals a litany of food-centric campaign functions at government relations firms. There's the Rhode Island–themed reception for Sheldon Whitehouse on McDermott Will & Emery's rooftop patio; a "small breakfast" for Representative Adam Smith at Akin Gump Strauss Hauer & Feld LLP; rooftop cocktails for Representative Sheila Jackson Lee at Locke Lord LLP's D.C. offices.

Most non-office fundraisers are held at a handful of restaurants: Monocle, Fiola, Ruth's Chris, Cava Mezze, Bobby Van's, Caucus Room, Acadiana, and Wolfgang Puck's Source. The only common thread to these disparate spots is their proximity to Downtown D.C. and Capitol Hill. Though all high-quality establishments with great food, they're by no means the Capital's absolute best. However, most sport open-floor plans that are conducive to fundraisers and have proven track records of accommodating lawmakers and their benefactors.

Influence peddling isn't great for one's cholesterol levels. Oftentimes, lawmakers will be feted at fundraisers featuring home-state specialties, leading to the rather incongruous spectacle of a "down-home"-style cookout occurring in the staid environment of a lobbying firm ("these framed black-and-white photographs of skyscrapers really make this dry rub shine!"). There was the authentic Korean barbecue at DNC headquarters for California representative Adam Schiff; the "Smoked 'n Oaked: A Celebration of Virginia's Best

Barbecue, Beer and Bourbon" for Democratic senator Tim Kaine at the Jones Day offices; and the Philly cheesesteak lunch at the Keelan Group for Keystone State Republican representative Joe Pitts. Other times, hosts will skip the pretense of local cuisine and go straight for the familiar trans fats and sodium-laden comforts of fast food. Take the "Chick-fil-A Reception" for Republican senator Tim Scott, for example. Or the "Five Guys Lunch" for Illinois Republican representative John Shimkus. These are great opportunities for potential donors to evacuate both their wallets and their bowels.

Capitol Hill

The culinary options in the Capitol are myriad: over a dozen eateries and cafés dot the sprawling Capitol complex, serving over 230,000 meals a month to members of Congress, staffers, and visitors. These spots are not lacking for diversity—everything from Korean barbecue day in the Longworth Cafeteria to salmon reubens in the Dirksen North Cafe to a sushi bar in the Russell Cafeteria to chicken tenders in the tiny canteen beneath the Capitol building. However, most of the food options available to the members and staff of Congress are pretty forgettable. While the neighborhood of Capitol Hill sports a number of appetizing restaurants and takeout spots, Capitol Hill the government complex is so sprawling that trips to those establishments would take too much time out of staffers' already crammed schedules.

The Capitol's food offerings are no less immune from the pressures of politics than the committee member during their ninety-second opening statement. When Democrats took control of the House in January 2007, the new majority ordered that the lower chamber's eateries use biodegradable silverware. That practice abruptly stopped when the GOP retook the chamber in 2011. The panel that oversaw operations, the Committee on House Administration, ordered that the old plastic silverware and Styrofoam cups be reinstated. The move outraged Democrats, many of whom vowed to bring their own reusable cups and utensils rather than do undue harm to Mother Gaia. "Stop the Styrofoam Invasion: Bring Cardboard Back to the House Cafeteria," moaned the Facebook page dedicated to ending Congress's tableware tyranny. "This GOP leadership has shown that the only thing they are good at is recycling bad ideas," quipped Pelosi spokesman Drew Hammill. Republicans countered that studies showed the program to be financially wasteful. House administration chairman Dan Lungren was taken aback by the uproar over the move. "I never thought I'd be known as 'Styrofoam Dan,'" he lamented to the *L.A. Times*.

One highlight for staffers is the various food-centric receptions that trade groups and state organizations put on in the Hill's meeting spaces. Though ethics regulations classify food provided to lawmakers as gifts, there are enough loopholes that lobbyists can still ply the nation's lawmakers with free grub. These rules can be circumvented if the food is served at events that are, per the parlance of House lawyers, "widely attended"—that is, by more than twenty-five people.

Another hitch is the so-called toothpick or bagel rule, which mandates that any food provided to staffers be handheld, as utensil-based meals veer too closely to gift status. This has also given rise to a related "gravy" rule, which also prohibits the use of common-use utensils like ladles. "Coffee and doughnuts are O.K. Croissants are probably all right. But I get a lot of questions about bagels and what you can put on them. Lox may be pushing it," a House lawyer tasked with explaining the regulations told *The New York Times* when the rules were first introduced in the mid-1990s. While these regulations prohibit lobbyists from buying steak dinners for chiefs of staff or peddling New England clam chowder to interns in the Longworth House Office building, there are enough workarounds that Hill staffers could conceivably be fed entirely by lobbyists without ever leaving their building.

As such, these free food galas are among the most common sights on Capitol Hill, whether in the guise of tax reform groups putting on donut and coffee receptions, regional beef producers highlighting their fare with nibbles of brisket, or video game makers providing chicken tenders and the opportunity to play the latest installment of the *Metal Gear Solid* franchise.

One of the most popular events on the Hill is the Taco Bell franchise reception. Tacos, requiring no silverware, are a fabulous government relations' lubricant. The event is a zoo: as the cowboy-hat-and-bolo-tie-clad Tex-Mex purveyors look on, staffers swarm for the opportunity to grab a free Crunchy Taco Supreme. A lot of these staffers are interns who are dispatched by their bosses to fill up printer paper boxes with tacos. But organizers remain vigilant for the occasional senior staffer who, despite their $100K-plus salary, nevertheless possesses a weakness for mass-produced ground beef and synthetic cheese cradled in a corn chip shell. Most of these chiefs of staff and legislative directors beat a hasty retreat, but some are quickly buttonholed by the event organizers about the dangers of minimum-wage hikes.

Hill staffers also enjoy a loophole pertaining to "home state" products. While Taco Bell can't simply ship a giant wooden crate marked "DORITOS TACO LOCO" to Texas senator John Cornyn's office, Blue Bell Ice Cream, a Brenham-based creamery, would be well within its rights to send Cornyn's office a mint chocolate chip-laden refrigerator. That's because regulations allow for "[d]onations of products from the district or State that the Member . . . represents that are intended primarily for promotional purposes, such as display or free distribution, and are of minimal value to any single recipient," per House rules. Georgia offices regularly feature Coca-Cola products, while some New York staffers enjoy greater gastrointestinal health thanks to the generosity of Norwich-based yogurt maker Chobani. Though staffers can't specifically request products from their boss's constituents, it doesn't take much hinting to elicit free food. Heaven help the cholesterol of the Vermont senator's staffer who speaks too highly of Phish Food within earshot of a Ben & Jerry's rep.

Agencies

Though the stereotype of the federal bureaucrat is one of the 4:00 p.m.-departing, two-hour-lunch-taking layabout, there aren't a lot of opportunities for luxuriously drawn-out off-campus meals. Many federal employees work in Washington's culinary wastelands—the cavernous environs of Downtown D.C. where takeout spots are as few as imposing Beaux Arts buildings are plenty, or in Washington's sparse suburban areas—and must either make do with cafeteria fare or prepared lunches from home.

As such, the quality of a federal agency's cafeteria is very much a point of pride or frustration among federal employees. Department of Energy officials speak with pride about their cafeteria with the sushi that doesn't induce vomiting and that lures staffers from the nearby Department of Agriculture while Agriculture employees marvel at how the agency tasked with regulating the nation's food supply can have such terrible chow. If you ever encounter a U.S. Patent and Trademark Office employee, don't ask them about the General Tso's at USPTO's Roundhouse Cafe.

Some are lucky enough to operate near the Smithsonian museums that encircle the National Mall and can take advantage of some of the more interesting cafeterias—the Museum of the American Indian offers particularly memorable fare.

America's intelligence officials might operate on the lowest rung of Washington's culinary ladder. For one thing, it's hard to find a decent chef that either has a high-level security clearance or is willing to undergo the rigorous screening process required to obtain one. In 2014, Gawker issued a Freedom of Information Act request for the CIA's cafeteria's comment cards and emails, revealing that America's spooks are none too happy with their lunch options. "I had the Russian meal today and am disappointed," one complaint read. "Please realize that many of us have really traveled to these countries and when you provide food like you did today, it causes me not to support this kind of cuisine in the future."

Campaign

The lowest of the low. The frantic life of the candidate, campaign aide, or campaign reporter doesn't allow for much food that can't be turned into a "meal" for an extra $2.78. One would be hard-pressed to find a campaign staffer's car that isn't strewn with McDonald's wrappers, Dunkin Donuts coffee cups, or plastic Haribo gummy bear bags stuffed into the door's side compartments. One shudders to think what percentage of a campaigner's daily water intake comes from the week-old diluted Wendy's soda that had been lying dormant in their cupholder.

See also, *"Jumbo Slice," "Schumwich," "Senate Dining Room," "Weight Loss"*

FOREIGN LOBBYING

K Street isn't limited to oil companies looking for a green light to drill in a protected sea slug habitat or a multinational food conglomerate hoping to lift restrictions on soylent green. The services of America's tireless lobbyists, and the hospitality of their waiting rooms' extensive offerings of vitamin water and magazines, are also available to our friends from abroad. The 1938 Foreign Agents Registration Act, passed to keep Nazi agents in check, requires individuals lobbying on behalf of foreign powers to disclose the nature of their relationship, but no laws prohibit foreign powers from lobbying the government. In fact, in 2012, $1 out of every $7 spent on lobbying in Washington originated from a foreign client.

The breadth and variety of foreign lobbying registrations are astonishing. Saudi Arabia alone has spent hundreds of millions of dollars since 2000 on K Street fees. The website of former Republican House leader Bob Livingston's lobbying operation alone lists Azerbaijan, the Cayman Islands, the Republic of Congo, Egypt, Ecuador, Morocco, and Turkey among its clients. In 2014, as reported by *Politico,* Somalia's Habr Gidr clan registered with D.C. lawyer Steven

Schneebaum. Per its disclosure, Schneebaum's services were retained to "promote the interests of the Clan." Foreign clients aren't limited to countries, however, and many foreign ministries, companies, and other entities regularly retain K Street's services.

Lobbying registrations often come on the heels of scandal or conflict. The "Friends of Charities Association" sounds like a benign enough name, and surely there can't be anything wrong with it registering with the Belew Law Firm, as it did in 2004. Except "Friends of Charities" was a Saudi consortium of nonprofits that formed after its government cracked down on other charities' ties to terror groups. In 2011, when revolts against Hosni Mubarak's regime broke out in Egypt, the Egyptian government hired Livingston's firm to stymie congressional efforts to express support for prodemocracy demonstrators. In July 2015, days after Burundi's presidential election was marred by violence, alleged intimidation of civil rights activists and journalists, and accusations of vote tampering, the government hired Scribe Strategies to, according to *Politico,* "[strengthen] Burundi's general bilateral relations with the United States, its government and institutions." Within a week, the firm's president was appearing in a Kenyan news outlet, accusing Burundi's rebels of receiving aid from Rwanda.

Foreign lobbying regulations are far stricter than those covering domestic lobbying. Domestic lobbyists must disclose 30,000-foot information like compensation and the issues they will lobby about. Contrast that with regulations on lobbying for foreign clients, which mandate that every conversation and contact with a lawmaker, staffer, or journalist must be chronicled. Of course, by the very nature of statecraft, we may never know the full extent of a foreign government's presence in Washington. For those "lobbyists" whose office is a leaky safe house beneath an overpass in Southeast D.C. and whose work is less "meeting staff directors for coffee at Cups" and more "stealing document tranches from Langley and taping them under a bench in Rock Creek Park," they'd likely be best served by not registering with the government.

See also, *"Astroturfing," "Lobbying," "Lobbyist," "Selling Out"*

FREEDOM CAUCUS

Republican House caucus comprised of many of the chamber's Tea Party-affiliated members, not to be confused with the Tyranny Caucus, the Despotism Caucus, or the Roving Squads of Dystopian Jackboots Caucus.[48] The Freedom Caucus was founded in early 2015 to promote freedom—unless that freedom involves having an abortion, in which case the Freedom Caucus shifts its agenda from "freedom" to "shutting down the government."

Like other caucuses, the Freedom Caucus has no legislative authority, but instead provides members a forum to set their agenda of grinding the entire government to a halt because some of their constituents in Cullowhee, North Carolina, are uncomfortable with women having premarital sex. It also allows members to fine-tune their talking points and ask around to see if anyone can come up with a synonym for "socialist."

The Freedom Caucus was born out of right-wing Republicans' frustration with the Republican Study Committee (RSC), a GOP House caucus ostensibly dedicated to promoting a conservative agenda. However, as the GOP drifted rightward in recent decades, the RSC became less and less a gathering of insurgents but just another organ of the party leadership—as of the 114th Congress a majority of the House's Republicans were RSC members. Freedom Caucus members felt the RSC had become too sluggish, unable to reach consensuses due to its large size. The would-be Freedom Caucusers believed the RSC's antigovernment, antigay, anti-immigrant, semi-theocratic, aggressively hawkish agenda somehow wasn't conservative enough. Suffice it to say, they're a pretty doctrinaire bunch.

---

[48] You *don't* want to cross the Dystopian Jackboot Caucus.

If it isn't already apparent, the Freedom Caucus is most closely associated with its efforts to grind legislation to a stop. Shortly after its founding, the group forced the GOP leadership to table a border security bill, largely because the bill didn't provide America's undocumented immigrants the "freedom" to be forcibly put on military M939s and carted into Mexico. The group was one of the driving forces behind the charge to defund Planned Parenthood, a move that nearly led to a government shutdown in October 2015.

See also, *"America," "Blue Dogs," "'Democrat Party,'" "Israel," "Republican Study Committee," "RINO"*

FRIDAY NEWS DUMP

Friday ritual where unfavorable news is released to the public as people are packing up for the weekend. The purpose of the timing is for the dumped news to receive less scrutiny than it would have had it been released earlier in the week. Also, bundling together a series of bad news print newspapers and TV news programs forces media to publish only a limited amount of information about each item, hamstrung as they are by a finite amount of column space and airtime. With the web, a story can receive as much attention as reporters and other interested parties so choose. However, because the GOP hasn't totally succeeded at dismantling the five-day workweek, the fact remains that people are still less engaged with current events from Friday evening through Sunday night.

Friday evening is a great time to . . .

. . . appoint your child to a job.

. . . commute the jail sentence of a prominent campaign bundler.

. . . pass S.B. 3052: The Kidz Need Gunz Act.

. . . exact political vengeance.

. . . unload a massive tranche of documents solicited by a Freedom of Information Act request. This has the added bonus of ruining reporters' weekends.

. . . publish the findings of a blue ribbon commission study, itself commissioned so people would forget about its subject.

. . . resign.

. . . admit marital infidelity and resign.

. . . announce your total cooperation with federal investigators and resign.

. . . announce that you'll file an appeal to the court's ruling and resign.

Friday evening is a terrible time to . . .

. . . do anything politically advantageous.

See also, *"Adultery," "Bracketing," "Spin"*

FRIENDSHIP

Very elastic concept in politics. You're likely familiar with the quote often misattributed to Harry Truman, "If you want a friend in Washington, get a dog," yet if the language thrown about in Washington and the public behavior of its leading officials is any indication, the nation's capital is friendlier than Mr. Rogers on MDMA. Sad as it is, the *appearance* of friendship is a far more valuable commodity, if not in the spiritual sense, than actual friendships. Whether it's a lobbyist referring to a friend on the Finance Committee as being among their "extensive contacts" on the panel, a president and speaker playing a round of golf for the cameras, or Terry McAuliffe showing off the locks of Bill Clinton's hair he just added to a shrine tucked behind an array of trousers in his walk-in closet, "friendships" abound.

The venue that most regularly plays host to "friendship" is Congress. A search of the Congressional Record for the 113th Congress of 2012 to 2014 yields over two thousand separate speeches featuring the phrase "my friend." Take, for example, this excerpt of a floor speech from July 16, 2015, by former minority leader Harry Reid about his supposed cooperation with the new majority leader, Republican Mitch McConnell:

> So I understand why my friend the Republican leader is beating his chest about how great the Senate works, because it does work if you have a cooperative minority, and that is what we have done. We have worked very hard to try to get this done, and as a result of our work together, we have been able to get it done. But please save everyone the lack of history. My friend keeps bringing up: Boy, the Senate is working so well. It is very cynical what my friends did in stopping everything for the last 4 years. They stopped everything. Hundreds of times they stopped bills from moving to the floor. So my friend comes to the floor and says: Oh man, things are working so great now. Isn't it great the Senate is working? . . . If you look at the poll numbers about how well my friend is doing, the Republican leader is not doing very well, with the lowest numbers since they started doing polling on leaders—Democratic or Republican leaders.

Replace "my friend" with "*this fucking douchenozzle, Mr. Shitpants over here*" and you'll get a more literal understanding of Reid's statement. A member of Congress who refers to a colleague as "my friend," is a bit like your HR director adding a perfunctory smiley face emoji at the end of an email asking you to finally complete a mandatory self-evaluation—it's a reflexive, often passive-aggressive, act.

See also, *"Access," "Lobaeist," "Lobbying," "Wall of Fame"*

FUNDRAISER

Event held to raise funds for a candidate or political organization.

Fundraisers are an increasingly common part of the presidency, no less a mainstay than state funerals and speeches in front of people in safety goggles. In their first terms in office, Ronald Reagan attended 80 fundraisers, George W. Bush attended around 175, and Barack Obama 323. The exception to this trend was Bill Clinton—because, hey, Bubba—who went on a flurry of second-term fundraisers, ultimately clocking in a whopping 693 during his two terms in office (he attended around 170 in his first term). That's a lot of passed hors d'oeuvres.

The amount of time each member of Congress actually spends attending fundraisers varies. Members of leadership, committee chairs, campaign organization heads, and other high-profile members spend much more of their time soliciting donations, as do more politically vulnerable members of Congress, who require larger campaign war chests. Many members seeking to up their profile in the party may also spend a disproportionate amount of time gripping and grinning on behalf of other candidates.

A slideshow produced by the Democratic Congressional Campaign Committee (DCCC) that surfaced in 2010 urged members to spend three to five hours of their weekly time in Washington attending fundraisers. Of course, the organization dedicated to electing House Democrats would naturally want members to spend a ton of time begging for cash. Compare that to a survey of members of Congress by the Congressional Management Foundation (CMF) that found lawmakers spend about half that amount raising funds. A fundamental problem with such a survey is that members of Congress are likely not going to concede the actual amount of time they spend raising funds, either in person or over the phone. The truth almost certainly falls somewhere between the DCCC slideshow and the CMF study.

Whatever the case, an entire cottage industry has sprung up in Washington and across the country to accommodate the ever-increasing number of fundraisers. In Washington, a number of up-scale restaurants near the Capitol like JHS recently closed. Bistro Bis and the Monocle regularly play host to fundraisers while Congress is in session. The Monocle, for example, sports a "Congressional Reception" menu—minimum thirty guests—that features an open bar, a spread of small bites, and a surf-and-turf prix fixe menu.

The political headquarters of the DNC and RNC play host to a number of events, as do countless lobbying firms. Many lobbyists, and even lawmakers, use their own Capitol Hill homes to host fundraisers. In addition, certain trade groups, lobbying firms, and other third-party groups have strategically purchased Capitol Hill row-houses to provide lawmakers and donors easy access to their fundraisers. For years, Erickson & Company, a Democratic fundraising firm, operated a town house right next to the Democratic National Committee's offices. The Capitol Hill Club, a GOP-only group, is neighbors with the Republican National Committee. You can bet the parties are especially fun at the Diageo Townhouse, which is owned by the liquor conglomerate of the same name.

One of the most popular forms of a non-D.C. fundraiser is the weekend retreat. These are vacation-style getaways where donors have the opportunity to duck hunt with their favorite senator, or luxuriate in a spa with a relevant committee chairman. "Congressman Ed Whitfield's Escape to Vail," "Congressman John Shimkus's Napa Getaway," and "Congressman Vern Buchanan's Greenbrier Retreat" are just a few examples, per the events' invitations.

Fundraisers have rules of decorum and rhythms all their own. Congressional staff cannot participate in explicitly electoral activity, such as fundraisers, but members of Congress can designate one staffer to accompany them to campaign functions. Despite the prevailing image of these things as luxurious affairs where lawmakers and moneyed interests loosen their ties, nosh on expensive passed dishes, and sinisterly revel in each other's lack of scruples—all away from the prying eyes of the media or, Heaven forbid, regular people—lawmakers themselves often find fundraisers to be tedious affairs.

Common time-wasting strategies employed by politicians include stretching out their opening remarks and rambling on about personal interests—thereby preventing lobbyists, advocates, and other lickspittles from buttonholing them into making promises.

Yet a real pro strategy is the "I want to learn about *you* guys!" tactic, wherein the candidate asks the attendees, attendance numbers permitting, to introduce themselves. In particularly small or intimate gatherings, the pol might ask an inane question—attendees' first car, their first pet, basically anything that might be used as a password retrieval hint—to kill time. At fundraising luncheons, which usually last an hour and often have attendees seated around a rectangular ring of tables, such tactics are ideal at killing forty minutes or so. The strategy tends to work well on younger, less experienced lobbyists, who are excited by the prospect of having a lawmaker take an interest in them, but the longer the lobbyist talks, the less time they'll have to corner the candidate about their client's agenda. Moreover, the politician will probably forget about their charming anecdote about crashing their '98 Dodge Neon the moment he or she is whisked out the door.

Conversely, lobbyists might find themselves from time to time with more face time with a politician than they actually need—particularly junior members—or with one who serves on a committee they know very little about. In these situations, a set of boilerplate questions can pass the time with little to no awkwardness, all while possibly ascertaining new information:

Question	Purpose
"What's the mood of the conference/caucus?"	**Great opportunity for junior members to show off knowledge.**
"How does your district look?"	**Allows candidate to play up their district's competitiveness, thereby providing an in.**
"What moves is your opponent making?"	**See above.**
"What are your thoughts on the president's recent actions?"	**Chance for candidate to display their wisdom and familiarity with the pressures and machinations of the highest reaches of government.**

See also, *"Finance," "Food," "Lobbying," "Lobbyist," "Selling Out"*

FURTHER STUDY

Washingtonspeak for "let us never speak of this again."

A politician saying an issue needs further study or research is the legislative equivalent of telling an annoying colleague that you can't do dinner because you have leftovers in the fridge—it's a patently obvious and lazy way of putting off something unpleasant. Something that necessitates further investigation is often said to be an "important issue," which is a little redundant—frivolous questions like what time it is, whether to order a pizza, or who just ripped one would not require something so academic and heavy as professional research. The real point is that the issue at hand is politically damaging, either because it is too divisive or unpalatable to a key constituency.

Take, for example, this 2008 statement from then-Senator Barack Obama about the apocryphal link between autism and vaccines . . .

> The science right now is inconclusive, but we have to research it.

Or this report about a 2015 Republican bill to roll back school lunch nutrition standards.

> The bill would . . . require further study on long-term sodium reduction requirements set forth by the USDA guidelines.

Now, as an exercise, let's replace every mention of the issues, pronouns included, with "the Pythagorean theorem."

> *The science right now is inconclusive, but we have to research the Pythagorean theorem.*

> *The bill would . . . require further study on the Pythagorean theorem.*

The further study often takes the form of a blue ribbon commission, which is a panel of experts convened to study an issue for a period of time and then issue a report on it at a point that is either more politically convenient and/or when everyone has forgotten about it. If Washington could shackle an issue, confine it to the Bastille's darkest oubliette, and clamp it in an iron mask, it would. Instead it must make do with further study.

See also, *"Friday News Dump," "'I'm sorry, s(he)'s not in right now. Can I take a message?,'" "Pivot"*

GERRYMANDERING

The drawing of a legislative district in a way that ensures it encompasses a specific constituency or constituencies. After the decennial census is completed, states go about mapping out their congressional districts in such a politicized way that districts end up assuming shapes typically found on Rorschach tests and Mikhail Gorbachev's forehead.

The term "gerrymandering" dates back to 1812, when Massachusetts governor Elbridge Gerry, perhaps as a way of channeling his anger and frustration over being named Elbridge, carved out Massachusetts' state senate borders in such a way that bolstered his fellow Democratic-Republicans and isolated the opposing Federalists. One of the districts was said to resemble a salamander, prompting a cartoon in the *Boston Gazette* by Elkanah Tisdale[49] featuring a state senate district that resembled an imaginary creature, the gerry-mander.

States decide how they go about drawing congressional districts. Some have opted for independent panels, and the Supreme Court

[49] *Jesus,* these names.

affirmed in 2015 the public's right to have a nonpartisan commission do the work. However, most maps are still decided by state legislatures. It's for this reason that statehouse elections in census years—1990, 2000, 2010—are often the most important. Naturally, incumbents have a vested interest in seeing themselves and their party stay in power, which is why the legislatures go about carving up their states with quotas that would make a club bouncer sweat.[50] Congressional districts must be contiguous, bodies of water notwithstanding, but legislatures regularly cheat this rule by connecting two different areas with nothing more than a single road. Districts in which two separate municipalities are linked by a narrow strip of land are not uncommon.

Gerrymandering was one of the tools with which the white majority maintained the status quo in the Jim Crow area, splitting up black areas into larger white majority districts. Though the Voting Rights Act mandated that certain districts submit their proposed maps to the Department of Justice before getting final approval, the Supreme Court gutted that rule in 2013. Alabama proceeded to redraw its districts in a way that could best be described as "Alabama."

Gerrymandering can have very real effects. In 2012, Democrats eked out a plurality of House votes nationwide, but Republicans ended up winning 54 percent of the seats. That trend continued in 2014, when Republicans won 52 percent of the popular vote, but controlled 57 percent of the chamber. The extent to which states contribute to this unbalance varies. In 2012, Democratic House candidates won 51 percent of the vote in Pennsylvania, but only ended up taking five of the state's eighteen congressional seats. State house majority parties aren't entirely to blame for the asymmetry of America's legislative fiefdoms. It's a poorly kept secret in politics that veteran lawmakers, who are regularly reelected with comfortable margins, are loath to give up a few percentage points for the sake of their parties or, you know, democracy.

---

[50] "Babes" are not a census-designated group, however.

The Jackson Pollock-ing of America's congressional districts shouldn't be entirely blamed for any uneven or inefficient representation. The laws governing apportionment, the assigning of congressional districts and electoral votes to states based on census data, accord each state at least one at-large representative and three electoral votes. Because Democrats traditionally dominate cities while Republicans control rural and exurban areas, the GOP has a built-in advantage. To illustrate that, imagine an America with just two states, one big and one small. Let's call this fictional big state . . . oh, say, *California,* and the tiny state . . . let's go with *Wyoming.* Let's say the mythical states of California and Wyoming have a population of 40 million and 600,000, respectively, and there is a total of ten House seats to be distributed between the two. In this arrangement, California will be apportioned nine congressional districts and Wyoming just one. While that might seem appropriate, California's members of Congress will represent an average of 4.4 million people while Wyoming's at-large member will represent a paltry 600,000.

Add to this the impact of gerrymandering and America's lower chamber is about as accurate an expression of the country's diversity as a Junior League potluck.

See also, *"Field," "Racism," "Voter Suppression"*

GET OUT THE VOTE

See, *"Field"*

GET OUT, THE VOTE!

See, *"Voter Suppression"*

"-GHAZI" VS. "-GATE"

For decades, "-gate" was the Ma Bell of political suffixes,[51] enjoying a near-monopoly on Washington portmanteaus. Thanks to its repeated use by former Nixon speechwriter William Safire—who was undoubtedly eager to conflate the Watergate break-in with any lesser misdeed—use of "-gate" as the primary designator of wrongdoing quickly gained steam. "Koreagate," "Contragate," and "Whitewatergate" were just some of the "-gate"s that defined the political lexicography in the waning years of the twentieth century. Like power ties, helmet hair, and marital infidelity, "-gate" never went out of style in the political arena.

However, in the midst of the breathless debate surrounding the September 2012 attacks on the American consulate in Benghazi, Libya, some snarky politicos began fusing the name of other nascent scandals with the "-ghazi" suffix. A few headlines referred to the politically motivated lane closures on the George Washington Bridge and New Jersey governor Chris Christie's possible involvement as "Bridgeghazi," though most still used "Bridgegate." Ditto Hillary Clinton's use of private email for State Department business: "Emailgate" was the preferred nomenclature, but "Emailghazi" popped up here and there.

"We need a new term for these sub-gate scandals," declared *National Journal*'s Alex Seitz-Wald in 2014. *Slate* deemed "-gate" the "classic" choice while "-ghazi" was "edgier." Whether the "-ghazi" suffix can forever break free of its morphemic shackles is a question for the ages—and for mildly adventurous headline writers.

See also, *"Accents," "'Democrat Party,'" "Email," "Flack," "Hack," "Social Media"*

---

[51] This practice seeped into the realms of sports, arts, and business, also. The 2004 Super Bowl halftime performance where Justin Timberlake accidentally exposed one of Janet Jackson's nipples became "Nipplegate" (or "Boobgate"). A 2014–2015 debate over sexism in the gaming industry was dubbed "Gamergate."

GOING NEGATIVE

The *awwww shiiit* moment when a candidate or campaign drops any pretense of civility and begins to attack their opponent. Depending on the severity of the attack, this is either the "gloves off" moment or the "jump out of the ring and grab the nearest folding chair" moment.

Whether a campaign has "gone negative" can be a point of dispute, as the growing constellation of surrogates, advocacy groups, super PACs, and other proxies that surround the campaign often go negative well before the candidate him or herself. That said, the average time it takes a campaign to go negative usually falls, at the upper end, around five minutes and, at the lower end, in the time it takes a hydrogen electron to rotate around its nucleus.

See also, *"Advertising," "Bracketing," "Earned Media," "Primary (Verb)," "Spin"*

GOLF

Golf is a near constant in the political arena, whether it's the near-weekly links-centric fundraising retreats for D.C. office seekers or the line of staffer-driven cars snaking away from the Capitol complex at 4:30 on summer Fridays to the nearby course at Hains Point. However, we are never as aware of golf in the political sphere as when presidents try their hand at it.

For the partisan, golf is either a popular sporting activity in which participants use clubs to hit a tiny ball into a hole in as few attempts as possible, or a wasteful and negligent use of our leaders' time, to say nothing of taxpayer dollars, that is likely contributing to the deaths of U.S. military personnel, chronic unemployment, hyper partisanship, the devaluation of the U.S. dollar, and the widespread die-off of honeybees known to melittologists as colony collapse disorder. Your definition depends entirely on whether the president belongs to your political party. There's not really a word for the very specific emotion that arises when witnessing an adversarial president playing, but it deserves a heinously complex German one. Let's go with *präsidentschaftsgolfhass*. Here's a sampling of left-wing *präsidentschaftsgolfhass:*

> *The Out-of-Towner: While Bush vacationed, 9/11 warnings went unheard.*
>
> —*Slate* (April 14, 2004)

> *As Katrina Struck, Bush Vacationed*
>
> —ThinkProgress (August 30, 2005)

And right-wing *präsidentschaftsgolfhass:*

> *BURNING WORLD CAN'T KEEP OBAMA OFF THE GOLF COURSE*
>
> —*Breitbart News* (August 2, 2014)

> *BAM'S GOLF WAR: Prez tees off while parents grieve*
>
> —*New York Daily News* (August 21, 2014)

Never mind that presidents live in a mansion teeming with servants catering to their every need;[52] and never mind that they fly about in their own 747 complete with a full-sized bed, entertainment system, and kitchen stocked with both Dr Pepper *and* Diet Dr Pepper;[53] *and* never mind the continued existence of Camp David, a mountain retreat dedicated entirely to their rest and relaxation—few things grind one's gears quite like the onset of *präsidentschaftsgolfhass.*

Golf, an historically bourgeois indulgence, has the effect of undermining whatever working-class or down-home pretentions a politician has cultivated. There's a reason why people don't flip their shit when the commander in chief fills out a March Madness bracket or

[52] And as certain commanders in chief have demonstrated, we really do mean *every* need.

[53] *And* Diet!

throws out the first pitch on Opening Day.[54] And while America's golf courses have almost entirely desegregated, the sport's notoriously racist history has dogged politicians for decades. Bill Clinton, for one, came under fire during his 1992 presidential campaign for golfing at an all-white country club in Arkansas.

Of course, presidents from both parties have been golfing for most of America's post–Civil War history. Per Don Van Natta Jr.'s splendid *First Off the Tee,* which chronicles the executive branch's relationship with the game, William Howard Taft was the first president to hit the links, and fourteen of the last eighteen commanders in chief have teed off during their presidency. The USGA installed a custom green on the White House grounds for Dwight Eisenhower, a notoriously avid golfer and arguably the president most associated with the game. By the end of his administration, there was a duffer's trail in the West Wing's floorboards. JFK and his advisers went out of their way to hide his golf habit to distinguish himself from the doddering and decidedly un-Camelot Eisenhower. That policy was quickly reversed when members of the press began speculating about why Kennedy was disappearing for several hours at a time.[55]

Now that the unblinking eye of the Internet and social media has turned its lidless gaze on presidential vacations, no trip 'round the 18 goes unnoticed by the opposition. Today, websites like ObamaGolfCounter.com breathlessly tally the number of presidential trips to the links beside the death-toll number of the war in Afghanistan. So much for a leisurely day on the green.

See also, *"Capitol Hill Club," "Country Club Republican," "Main Street"*

GOOGLE PROBLEM

Overarching term for a person, issue, or development whose name or title elicits embarrassing results on search engines. Google prob-

[54] OK, they do flip their shit, but only a little.

[55] *Chicka-chicka-bow-wow!*

lems are also Yahoo! problems, Bing problems, and, assuming it's still a thing, Altavista problems.

The progenitors of the Google Problem were Republican Pennsylvania senator Rick Santorum and syndicated sex columnist and LGBT activist Dan Savage. After Santorum's 2003 remarks that homosexuality was only slightly less offensive than, "you know, man on child, man on dog, or whatever the case may be," Savage undertook a campaign to define "Santorum" as "the frothy mixture of lube and fecal matter that is sometimes the by-product of anal sex." It didn't take long for Savage's "Spreading Santorum" campaign to be the top search result for "Santorum" on Google, meaning all church ladies hoping to learn more about the senator would instead be confronted with as disgusting and vivid description of sodomy as humanly possible.

Another Google problem for politicians—and public figures in general—is search engines' autocomplete suggestions. Whenever you start to type a query, the site will offer a handful of autocomplete suggestions based off of the most popular searches in a given area. Despite Google's best attempts to scrub the more offensive suggestions, the algorithm provides fascinating insights into society's curiosities, prejudices, and neuroses. "Why . . ." searches—at least in the Washington, D.C., metro area—will yield ". . . do women nag," ". . . do men lie," and ". . . does it hurt when I pee" among others. Politically, some search suggestions highlight things that don't qualify as scandals, but are nevertheless things that politicians would prefer not to defined by. Take for example, "Why is John Boehner's skin orange," "Why does Hillary only wear pantsuits," or ""Michele Bachmann sharknado." Some political search completions are a bit more *womp womp*-y. "Why did Ronald Reagan die?," "Why does Joe Biden smile so much?," or "Why does Ted Cruz look so sad?"

See also, *"Digital," "Email," "Social Media"*

"GOVERNMENT RELATIONS"

Alternate term for lobbying, typically employed by lobbying firms or by law firms with lobbying divisions to describe their influence peddling. Whereas "lobbying" conjures images of slick-haired men in suits having power lunches to strategize ways to roll back regulations on serving soylent green in elementary school cafeterias and paunchy corporate executives on golf courses cracking jokes about the demise of asbestos regulations, "government relations" is far less nefarious-sounding. A "government relations specialist" could just as well be a relationship counselor for Citigroup and the U.S. government, facilitating trust fall exercises and reverse role-playing.

See also, *"Lobbying," "Lobbyist," "Selling Out"*

GRASSLEY'S TWITTER ACCOUNT

Unlike Facebook, which the world's elderly have leveraged for sharing photos of grandchildren, catching up with long-lost friends, and making thinly veiled complaints about minorities, Twitter remains an anathema to most people in their sunset years. Not true for Iowa's octogenarian senior senator Chuck Grassley, who has harnessed the power of the microblogging service to broadcast his extreme oldness. Some tweets are quick bursts of cultural criticism, while others fuse the emotional ephemera of Ezra Pound with Hemingway's minimalism. A few are just the senator's butt smooshing up against his smartphone's keypad.

> @ChuckGrassley: Fred and I hit a deer on hiway 136 south of Dyersville. After I pulled fender rubbing on tire we continued to farm. Assume deer dead (October 25, 2012)

@ChuckGrassley: Windsor Heights Dairy Queen is good place for u kno what (November 3, 2014)[56]

@ChuckGrassley: History. No history. Axe man Timber Nothing historical. Back to FOX. Sigh. Suggest name to change channel name (March 18, 2012)

@ChuckGrassley: "I now h v an iphone" (February 19, 2012)

@ChuckGrassley: P (April 7, 2012)

@ChuckGrassley: # (September 12, 2012)

@ChuckGrassley: @ChuckGrassley (January 17, 2013)

If only Twitter had a button that offered your grandchildren hard candy.

See also, *"Digital," "Email," "Social Media"*

GREENROOM

Room where people are placed before going on television. While greenrooms are most closely associated with television studios, a greenroom can be any space that is a designated holding pen for America's pristinely groomed bloviators, including candidates before debates. For many pundits and A-list journalists who long ago stopped trying, greenrooms are the only place they do any real reporting.

Their offerings vary, but most greenrooms are furnished with comfortable chairs, refreshments, and a television, typically tuned to whatever program on which the guests are about to scream at each other. Indeed, these spaces regularly play host to interactions

[56] "I wanted to give Windsor Heights Dairy Queen some credit for making good Dairy Queen and doing you know what," Grassley told Iowa ABC5 reporter Samantha-Jo Roth when asked about the tweet. "And what do you do at Dairy Queen, you eat Dairy Queen."

between and among political adversaries. Some are cordial—like professional wrestlers before a match choreographing grapples, suplex slams, and broncobusters—and others not so much. In 2003, reporter Mark Leibovich, then with *The Washington Post,* observed the Democratic presidential candidates milling around backstage before a debate, squabbling over who got to use the bathroom first. Jane Goodall would've been impressed with that bit of anthropological observation.

Speaking of toilets, in October 2015, before the third Republican presidential primary debate at the University of Denver's Coors Center, candidates were afforded greenroom amenities based on their poll numbers, reported *Politico.* Better performing candidates like Ben Carson, Donald Trump, and Marco Rubio were given some of the athletic center's nicer rooms. Rubio was given the screening room with plush stadium seats and Trump a lounge with a flat-screen TV and spacious seating area. Chris Christie and Rand Paul, who were lagging in the polls, were shown to the men's room.

See also, *"Booker," "Hit"*

GUB'MENT

See, *"Bureaucracy," "Executive Departments"*

H

HACK

A reporter. According to the Bureau of Labor Statistics, there are over 2,500 of them operating in the Washington metropolitan area and another 3,000 or so editors. Not surprisingly, the region sports the nation's highest concentration of hacks, with 1 out of every 1,000 people in the newsgathering business. That amount triples in the District of Columbia, more than the concentration of doctors or carpenters. That's *a lot* of ruffled clothing and dateless Friday nights.

First the obvious: Washington's journalistic landscape has changed dramatically since the 1990s, with the Internet and social media shifting the nexus of a reporter's day from their 6:00 p.m. filing deadline to, well, *all* the time—assuming, of course, the reporter still has a job. Journalism's economic downturn, the resulting competitiveness for reporting and editing gigs, and the proliferation of more youthfully minded online news outlets have led to a demographic reshuffling of the press corps, with many older and higher-salaried reporters at legacy publications forced to take buyouts. Twitter teems with bittersweet, 140-character notes of congratulations and farewells to news graybeards, like a group of young Vikings wishing a fallen veteran safe passage to Valhalla, except in this case Valhalla is probably an adjunct professorship at a CUNY branch's journalism department or a public affairs job at a trade association. It's easy to lose track of just how quickly things are changing. By 2015, thirty-nine of the top fifty online news outlets reported drawing more traffic from mobile devices than computers. Opening up the Twitter app on your smartphone is as easy as opening up *The New York Times* on its web browser. Actually, it's easier.

Though the 1,200-word-article-at-six reporter is by no means an extinct species, your prototypical hack is increasingly a twenty-five-year-old filing three or four 300-word items on granular political developments during business hours, possibly cobbling them together for a print edition the next day, or possibly not. Email, Gchat, Slack, text, and all the other things your grandparents have difficulty with have enabled reporters and their sources to engage in a more or less constant back-and-forth. Twitter has turned reporting—or mindless opinionating, to be certain—into Washington's most piercing background noise (listen closely to the rustling of the blooming cherry blossoms in early spring and you might just hear the muted tapping of "Whoa, if true" on an iPhone's sapphire glass screen). Reporters' ability to extend their presence to platforms beyond their own outlet has contributed to the brandification of Washington hacks. "I know them from Twitter" is heard as often—if not more, let's not kid ourselves—as "I know them from their four-thousand-word exposé on that coal industry astroturf campaign."

The diffusion of news sources brought about by the web has also shaken up the media power structure. As recently as a decade ago, *Time* reporter Mark Halperin coined the term, "Gang of 500," to classify the leading reporters, pundits, political staffers, and operatives who solidified Washington's conventional wisdom. That number has grown considerably, as people are able to tailor their news consumption with push alerts, Twitter feeds, and Flipboard accounts.

There's still a media pecking order, to be sure—most lawmakers would almost certainly agree to a sitdown with an AP reporter over your author,[57] but it might behoove a Republican running in a tight primary to pay more mind to conservative news outlets like *The Daily Caller* and *Breitbart* than *The New York Times* or Reuters.

---

[57] :-(

Barack Obama didn't give a single one-on-one interview to *The New York Times* between 2010 and 2014. The piranha-like way in which reporters devour a newsmaking tweet and promptly retweet it from their own Twitter feeds makes dissemination of talking points easier than ever.

White House Press Corps

Though there is no end of source building and snooping in which a White House reporter can engage—hitting up the over four hundred White House staffers, to say nothing of the tens of thousands of people employed by executive agencies and cabinet departments—they're severely hamstrung by the barriers, literal and figurative, that exist between the press corps and the president and his aides. Unlike congressional reporters, who can wander around the Capitol complex with relative impunity, paying a visit to some of its most iconic rooms (so long as they are unused), a White House reporter would likely be tackled by Secret Service agents if they decided to take a leisurely stroll about the Red Room. Instead, White House reporters lead a roped-off existence, mostly confined to the White House briefing room, its adjoining multilevel press offices, the TV camera array lined up on the west side of the North Lawn, and whatever area a senior staffer has temporarily granted them access to.

As such, members of the White House press corps are often forced to squabble over proverbial table scraps from the executive branch. In 2014, the White House Correspondents' Association sent a strongly worded letter denouncing their exclusion from being able to cover President Obama's golf weekend with Tiger Woods. "Speaking on behalf of the White House Correspondents' Association, I can say a broad cross section of our members from print, radio, online and TV have today expressed extreme frustration to me about having absolutely no access to the President of the United States this entire weekend," WHCA president and Fox News White House correspondent Ed Henry wrote. "There is a very simple but important principle we will continue to fight for today and in the days ahead: transparency." More power to you, brother.

Despite the somber responsibility of keeping tabs on the most powerful office in the land, and the glamour of rubbing shoulders with the practitioners of that power, the White House press corps is not without its own quotidien office dynamics. In addition to the cramped and very drab offices assigned to the press corps, life in the press corps workspace is defined by the million little things that define virtually every other office in the developed world. There are kitchen dynamics, there are eye rolls over overly loud or talkative colleagues, there's the reporter who brings her kids to the office to hawk Girl Scout Cookies, the bowl of mints in the basement that might be a kind gesture or a passive-aggressive act meant to highlight a wire correspondent's nasty breath.

Then there are the territorial politics, which are familiar to anyone who has ever jockeyed for an open office, but taken to a whole other level. The seating politics of the White House briefing room are among the most sensitive, and awkward, in the city. News outlets are assigned seats by the White House Correspondents' Association, with newswires and network television correspondents typically being granted the front row and legacy outlets like *The New York Times,* NPR, and *Wall Street Journal* getting the second row. Reporters are allowed to take an empty seat, but must relinquish it if a reporter from its designated news outlet appears. Curiously, reporters almost never grab empty seats in the first two rows, a passive act of deference to America's most helmet-haired on-air journalistic talent.

Perhaps a worse fate is that visited upon the news organizations that are forced to *share* a briefing room seat. What results is something akin to a timeshare, with so much advance planning required to make use of a shared briefing room seat that many reporters don't even bother making use of it. Inevitably, shared spaces—meaning standing along the wall—tend to make more practical sense.

The White House reporters can, in their own tempered Washington way, be quite rambunctious—take the photos of White House press staffers taped to the ceiling of the basement's offices or the yearly Christmas jingle that is posted on a wall in the press offices, for example. And despite having regular interactions with some of the most powerful people in the country—and indeed the world—members of the White House press still get starstruck when celebrities visit. One particularly notable moment was the 2009 visit by the 1980s hair-metal band Styx, whose presence was a source of considerable excitement for both the press corps' boomers and more irony-sensitive millennials.

Congressional

Less prestigious than White House reporting but *way* more fun. If White House reporting is characterized by the highly controlled environs of the West Wing, then congressional reporting is defined by the access that its practitioners have to their sources. Outside of the chamber floors,[58] members' offices, and closed-door meetings, there aren't many places reporters *can't* go in the Capitol complex. They can stake out a member right outside their office, track them in the hallways, by the entrances to the underground subways that connect the complex's office buildings to the Capitol, and any number of other locales. Even members of leadership, whose schedules are tightly controlled and who are flanked by Secret Service agents, may well hop onto an elevator that a reporter is taking to grab lunch from a cafeteria. The open world of the Capitol can make congressional reporting feel a bit like a legislative *Grand Theft Auto,* but without the violence and only slightly less misogyny and drugs.

Source building is considerably easier for Congressional reporters. There are 535 members of Congress, each with staffs just waiting to divulge carefully curated information. And while members of leadership and committee chairmen and their staffs can provide more information on high-level legislative negotiations,

[58] Reporters have access to the press boxes overlooking the House and Senate chambers, and it's not difficult to overhear conversations in those comparatively hushed environments.

backbenchers are potent sources. A freshman lawmaker can provide information on a closed-door caucus meeting just as much as a ten-term one can.

Campaign

The campaign reporter's life, not unlike a campaign staffer's, is a sleep-deprived, tremendously unhealthy blur, marked as much by interviews with state fair attendees as by the reporter's litter-strewn rental Chevy Cruze in the fair's parking lot, filled with discarded press event badges, fast food takeout bags, and two-day-old Starbucks lattes, whose contents are gradually curdling in the Iowa August heat.

Despite the monotonous, though occasionally rambunctious, reputation of campaign reporting life, as famously detailed in accounts like Timothy Crouse's 1972 *The Boys on the Bus* and David Foster Wallace's characteristically cerebral 2000 dispatch from John McCain's "Straight Talk Express," "The Weasel, Twelve Monkeys and the Shrub," the reality is even *more* humdrum. It's a continuous stream of Red Roof Inns, scrums, the occasional exclusive aboard a campaign bus, and the constant struggle to find a place to charge a phone or laptop.

Campaign reporting is the loneliest form of political journalism. Many complain about the feeling of isolation after too many days, weeks, or, God bless these people, *months* on the trail. Though reporters often socialize with one another, and there's an undeniable camaraderie that forms as a campaign embed or even after a day relegated to the press pen of a major political event, journos remain competitors. Unlike campaign staffers, who are very much in the same bunker—and often the same bed—reporters are often scrambling to find an attendee at a state campaign convention who *hasn't* already been interviewed by someone else. That said, they do sleep with each other on a not irregular basis.

Trade

Trade reporters are something of a hack hybrid, covering all of the aforementioned beats, but with focus on a specific industry like transportation, health care, defense, technology, or actual trade. Though we typically associate the Washington press corps with studiously made-up television reporters grilling White House press secretaries and scrums of congressional reporters swarming about a senator striding along marble-floored hallways, there's a growing number of reporters pounding the pavement for trade publications; news outlets like *Defense News, Inside U.S. Trade, Kaiser Health News,* and *U.S. Banker* are among the many outlets that may not get assigned a carrel in the congressional press galleries or a spot in the White House briefing room, but play a significant role in disseminating news from the Capitol to some of the country's most influential industries.

The trade papers might be Washington's least glitzy journalistic subgenus, but it's print journalism's most robust. With the government's ever increasing size, corporate America's interest in Washington has only deepened. This has not only been expressed in the exponential rise of K Street, but also in the growth of trade papers, delivering news about the more arcane clauses of appropriation bills and new regulation guidances from governmental offices you've never heard of. Stories in *The Washington Post*'s "Sunday Style" section about a group of House freshmen's fantasy football league might find a large audience, but few readers would be actually willing to shell out any meaningful money for such a feature. Up-to-the-minute updates on a farm bill markup in the Agriculture Committee, however, that's something for which ADM's Washington's team would pay good money. It's no surprise, then, that in recent years Bloomberg, *Politico,* and *National Journal,* among others, have either started or expanded their trade-specialty publications.

With the decline of regional news outlets, trade publications are increasingly becoming launching pads for many political reporters, who often begin toiling away on telecom issues before landing at a general-interest political outlet like *Roll Call* or *The Hill*. For senior reporters, with deep connections to legislators tied to a specific industry, these outlets can be the source of well-paying jobs.

See also, *"Beat Sweetener," "James S. Brady Press Briefing Room," "Paywall Journalism," "Scrum"*

HALLOWEEN

Insufferable holiday in Washington where twenty- and thirtysomething politicos try to one-up one another with clever and topical costumes. That woman with Monopoly money clipped to her shirt and European flags jutting from her hair bun? The European debt crisis. Guy in an Obama mask and scrubs? The Affordable Care Act. That milk carton with dollar bill signs on it? The 1 percent. And these are the *clever ones*. Each year one costume will be worn ad nauseam. The contemporary gold standard of unoriginal modern political Halloween costume is the Sarah Palin, and in 2008 it was hard to navigate a House party in D.C.—and in America, really—without seeing someone, male or female, in a red suit with the former Alaska governor and Republican vice presidential candidate's distinctive hair and glasses. Not since Monica Lewinsky and her stained blue dress had a Halloween costume so completely dominated Washington.

There is always going to be a number of costumes that cross the line, perhaps because of their casual use of blackface ("No, I'm just trying to be Michelle Obama!") or because their chosen topic crosses one line too many (looking at you, Ebola crisis). Those people will have a great time discussing their outfit during the five thousand extra years they have to spend in purgatory (next to the Sarah Palins, themselves serving ten-thousand-year stretches for wasting the money their parents plopped down for college).

The most fun a person can have on Halloween is during the morning after, comfortably ensconced in a sidewalk café, watching people taking their walk of shames. Nothing puts a human face on American governance quite like seeing the bleary-eyed and hungover deputy chief of staff for communications for the American Dairy Producers Association stumbling up Connecticut Avenue, wrestling with his Uncle Sam hat and beard. You'll catch a glimpse of his "Will Work for Food" sign and it'll dawn on you:

He's a government shutdown!

See also, *"Washington, D.C.," "White House Correspondents' Dinner"*

"HEADS-UP"

Political version of yelling "fore!" after a wayward tee off, screaming "timber!" while felling a tree, or, perhaps most analogously, screaming "I'M GOING TO STAB YOU REALLY HARD!" right before plunging a knife into someone's abdomen.

Because political work is inherently adversarial, the standard practice among reporters, political staffers, advocates, lobbyists, and other political actors is to give their colleagues a "heads-up" before going ahead with a potentially unwelcome plan, thereby giving their counterparty the courtesy of some time to prepare.

> *"Heads-up, we're going public tomorrow with our petition calling for the senator to denounce children."*
>
> *"You're putting us in a real bind here."*
>
> *"Just a warning."*
>
> *"Appreciate it."*

> *"FYI, my boss is going to introduce the Play-Doh Price Control Act tomorrow on the floor."*
>
> *"What?! Play-Doh market reform has been our top campaign issue! You do this and you'll pull the rug out from under us. We'll be out of a job come November!"*
>
> *"Just wanted to give you a heads-up."*
>
> *"Cool."*

"Heads-up, I'm working on an article about your boss that says he's been carrying on a three-year affair with a horse."

"What? No way. We'll issue a strong denial."

"I've got four different sources confirming and a quote from the horse."

"K. Thanks."

See also, *"Flack," "Friday News Dump," "Hack"*

HEARING

In addition to considering bills, congressional committees are tasked with overseeing the implementation of laws and assessing the performance of government agencies and programs. In theory, this is accomplished primarily through hearings, those spectacles most closely associated with bureaucratic scapegoats lifting their right hands and swearing to the committee that their testimony will be true—oaths that are immediately followed by a sequence of sound-bite friendly denunciations.

Truth be told, most hearings aren't nearly so interesting and are devoid of the innumerable clicks and flashes from photographers documenting congressional perp walks. In practice, hearings mostly serve to make public any information that committee staffers have already gathered through research and meetings with stakeholders like activists, lobbyists, and legislative liaisons from government agencies. The hearings also allow members to clarify points of the witnesses' testimony. "New Routes for Funding and Financing Highways and Transit," "Procurement, Acquisition, Testing, and Oversight of the Navy's Gerald R. Ford-class Aircraft Carrier Program," and "The Future of U.S.-Zimbabwe Relations" are just some of the barn burners held in recent years. Still, these things aren't aimless salons, or anything. Hearings are closely controlled by their committees, with witnesses carefully selected by committees and their extended testimony submitted well ahead of time.

The central irony of hearings is the greater the public interest, the more politicized and, therefore, less informative, the hearing is likely to become—like some kind of congressional uncertainty principle: the closer you look, the less you learn. The Gerald R. Ford-class aircraft carrier hearing actually contained some informative testimony and frank back-and-forth between committee members and the witnesses about military acquisition and congressional oversight.[59] Compare that with hot-button hearings like Hillary Clinton's 2015 testimony before the special committee on Benghazi, where you're more likely to hear lawmakers bleating about the "American people" needing "answers" despite it being abundantly clear that the hearing was an answer-free zone. If this is confusing, consult the following chart:

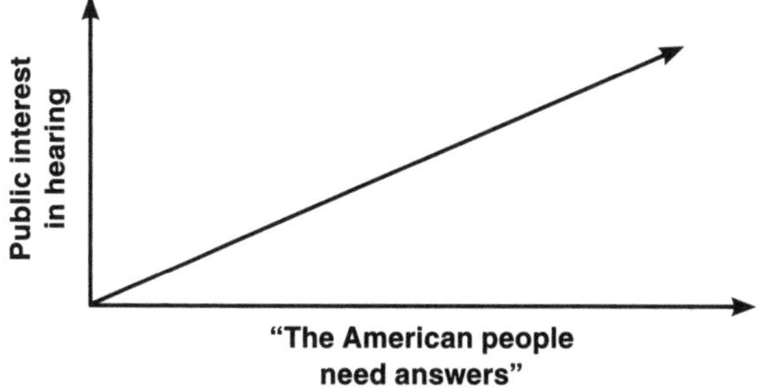

Hearings were never quite as scripted as they were under Harley Dirks, a Senate Appropriations Committee staffer in the 1970s who had been delegated so much authority by his boss, Washington senator Warren Magnuson, that staffers and members alike got into the habit of begging Dirks for appropriations. As reported by the late *Seattle Post-Intelligencer* reporter Shelby Scates in his biography of Magnuson, Dirks would plan entire hearings down to senators' greetings, brief asides, and other off-script moments. The Subcommittee on Labor, Health, Education, and Welfare became the Milli Vanilli

[59] Paul L. Francis, managing director of acquisition and sourcing management, Government Accountability Office, is a *fucking boss*.

of the legislative process. That is, until a number of hearings were canceled but the Government Printing Office nevertheless produced transcripts from the nonexistent hearings. Magnuson promptly fired Dirks. In a series of memos, phone calls, and meetings, the Ford White House and their Republican allies in Congress pondered whether to score political points off of the Democrat Magnuson's mismanagement of the committee. Perhaps in the first time in the history of hearings, it was decided that the hearings would not be politicized.

See also, *"Dear Colleague Letter," "Expert," "Legislation," "Legislative Glossary," "Cash Committees," "Pork," "Wonk"*

HIDEAWAY OFFICE

Unmarked, secondary offices in the Capitol intended for senators and select members of the House, but mostly used by staffers to impress visitors and get laid. The most desirable hideaway offices often sport dramatic views of the National Mall, have room for meeting tables and couches, and feature ornately tiled floors, marble fireplaces, and other flourishes of the Capitol. Others are just as ornate, but only have room for a desk and some bookshelves. Some are just electrical closets with a lamp.

The hideaways are distributed by the Senate Rules and Administration Committee based on seniority—regardless of a member's party—with veteran members being accorded the larger, more ornate spaces and junior ones getting glorified broom closets. Jockeying for the most prestigious hideaways can be intense, and given how *straight baller* some of them are, it's totally understandable.

The offices were first assigned in the early twentieth century when the burgeoning number of Senate employees—not to mention actual senators (we're looking at you, Oklahoma and New Mexico)—were moved from the Capitol to an auxiliary office several blocks away.[60]

[60] Now the Russell Senate Office Building and one of three office buildings used by the Senate's personal and committee staff.

For years there wasn't enough space to provide every senator with a hideaway, so it was considered a mark of a senator's established presence on Capitol Hill to be given one. However, with the opening of the underground Capitol Visitors Center in 2008, room was set aside for hideaways for the most junior senators. However, these lack the historical luster of the Capitol building, and feel less like austere places of business than the business center at a Holiday Inn Express.

Despite the intense competition for the best hideaways, the offices aren't used that often.[61] For one thing, senators don't do much actual *work*—at least not the kind that requires a person to sit alone at a desk for an extended period—so the prospect of not having a staffer around can be very daunting prospect for our representatives. Conversely, the more senior members with the better offices usually have committee or leadership workspaces, complete with staff who are ready, willing, and able to do their jobs for them. As such, staffers are usually given free rein to show people around their boss's hideaway—namely people who they want to see naked. Also their parents.

See also, *"Cloakroom," "Members-only Elevator," "Office Space," "Senate Dining Room"*

HILL RAGS

The main political trade publications. Their comparatively meager circulation, each producing anywhere from ten thousand to thirty thousand print editions, speaks to their outsized presence in the media sphere. A variety of specialty trade publications make the rounds in Washington, focusing on issues like defense and transportation, but the list that follows comprises the four main Hill rags that you'll likely encounter on a government-issue mahogany side table in a member of Congress's Washington waiting room.

---

[61] Several exceptions include Ted Kennedy, who regularly held meetings in his top-of-the-line hideaway, and Maryland senator Barbara Mikulski's regular confabs with fellow female lawmakers. Hideaways are also great places to wait out a bomb or anthrax scare.

Eliot Nelson

Roll Call/CQ Weekly

A glorious anachronism and Washington's leading provider of tired-looking reporters in the background of photographs. *Roll Call* remains the truest manifestation of a "Hill rag," reporting primarily on congressional developments, both on the Hill and on the campaign trail. *Roll Call* does so without much thought to clicks, page views, uniques, or any of the other metrics driving other publications to, at times, present themselves as the Beltway's *Tiger Beat*. This is in part due to revenue brought in by its sister subscription-based publication, *Congressional Quarterly Weekly,* and because Washington's most ruffled, khaki-clad cub reporters need a home. Though it has undergone considerable overhaul in recent years, *Roll Call* remains an endearingly frumpy operation that manages to never be overly crusty.

It's also a solid news outlet that provides a nuts-and-bolts view of Congress, reporting as much on skirmishes within leadership and redistricting politics as it does on staff movements and life in Washington. "House Democrats Brace for Round Two of Trade Fight," "House Republicans' Chaos Could Hurt GOP Fundraising," "Steve Scalise Swaps Whip for Cupid's Bow," and "How D.C. Paid Leave Could Affect Capitol Hill Staff" are headlines very much indicative of the outlet's reporting. *Roll Call* is like your favorite diner: the menu hasn't really changed in fifty years, and its occasional attempts to modernize or classy itself up are mostly halfhearted and quickly forgotten, like the "London Broil" that's been sitting unordered on the "specialty" portion of the menu. Its lackluster Instagram feed recalls other needless attempts at being "relevant," like when the *PBS NewsHour* went HD, or when your mom started using emojis.

Roll Call is the sister publication of *Congressional Quarterly Weekly,* an extension of the *CQ-Roll Call* group's roster of reporters covering Washington for subscription-paying members. *CQ Weekly,* as the name suggests, is a periodical that focuses on Washington machinations, with a special emphasis on Congress. While the Congressional Quarterly service provides users with up-to-the-minute updates on regulatory and legislative developments at the state and federal level—so lobbyists can know the moment some asshole state rep in New York wants to limit their client's smog production—*CQ Weekly* provides a thirty-thousand-foot view of D.C., comprised of several-thousand-word feature pieces.

The Hill

Mildly Republican the way your apolitical dad is—piping up a bit more at the dinner table when Hillary Clinton is mentioned and mumbling every so often about regulations. *The Hill*'s reporters tend to appear on Fox News a little more often than on the other cable networks and Democratic scandals seem to get slightly more play than Republican ones.

The Hill was founded in the 1990s and exists somewhere between *Roll Call* and *Politico,* both in its reporting focus and in its approach. It has a broader focus than *Roll Call,* featuring more stories on the White House and federal agencies, but remains very much a Washington publication, unlike *Politico,* which has designs on world domination. *The Hill*'s commercial strategy is similarly muddled. While it exhibits *Roll Call*'s wonky focus on Washington developments—"DOJ Said to Side with Foreign Airlines in Flight Subsidy Fight"—it is also not immune from *Politico*'s attempt at clickbait. "Rapper T.I.: 'World Ain't Ready' for Female President," ran on *The Hill*'s website the same October 2015 day "Schumer and Reid Like of the Land in Senate Races" ran on *Roll Call*'s.

Politico

Originally called *Capitol Leader* when it was announced in 2006, its founders, former *Washington Post* reporters John Harris and Jim VandeHei, realized *The Politico* packed more punch, and ultimately settled on POLITICO as being the punchiest—in a super intense, in-your-face, teeth-rubbing, *feel-my-bicep-no-really-**feel-it*** kind of way.

Really, if a news organization could challenge you to arm wrestle, it'd be *Politico,* which is very much the ground zero of Washington's present-day hypercompetitive, sports-metaphor-heavy mind-set. In its ten years of existence, *Politico* has become the go-to news source for granular political coverage, replete with campaign ticktocks, "how deal X came together" process stories, and items about nervousness in donor circles. Campaign donors, it should be noted, are always worried and/or sitting this one out.

A visitor to *Politico*'s website could be forgiven to think they had stumbled upon a bizzaro universe ESPN.com where all the Philadelphia Eagles' linebackers were arthritic sixty-year-olds with flag pins and caked with too much TV makeup. In the *Politico* universe, everything is competitive, everyone is either winning or losing, everything is in a constant state of warlike conflict: "Inside the Seven-Month War Within [Hillary Clinton's] Campaign over the Email Scandal That Just Wouldn't Go Away," "What a Win Looks Like," and "Rift in Obama Administration over Putin" were among the "above the fold" headlines on a single day in October 2015. Scoot on over to the home page for *Politico Magazine,* the outlet's longform product, and one starts to worry that John Madden might fire up his telestrator to scribble on the home page: "How Could Hillary Lose?," "Bernie Sanders vs. the Lamestream Media," "How to Tell the Difference Between a Real Front-Runner and a Fake One," all ran on the same October 2015 day.

A lot of white men work at *Politico.*

Politico's flagship product is undoubtedly Mike Allen's *Playbook,* a morning email newsletter that condenses *Politico*'s clubby, scoreboard-focused, hot-take-centric ethos into an eminently readable digest that can be consumed before the bleary-eyed reader has tended to their morning breath. It's a kind of Washington Five-Hour Energy—a comedically overstuffed package of late-breaking news, didactic lectures by the establishment, morning-after analysis, agenda setting, speculation, and name-dropping. Think of it as 4,000 percent of your daily intake of political niacin and B6, delivered to your inbox every morning. "PLAYBOOK FACTS OF LIFE: This is that rare opportunity in politics: a big moment," "HUGELY SIGNIFICANT REMARKS by Samantha Power, U.S. ambassador to the U.N.," "MEMO TO YOUNG REPORTERS: If Common Cause is your lead quote, you don't have much of a story," "MARRIED SATURDAY EVENING at Lake Geneva, Wis.: Katie Hogan, an Obama campaign deputy press secretary, and Matt Jaffe, a former Spanish teacher covering '12 campaigns from Chicago, jointly for ABC News and Univision," are just a random sampling of the all-caps postings in Allen's a.m. update. Allen resent the January 25, 2016, edition of *Playbook* to include a note from "Valerie"—that is, White House senior adviser Valerie Jarrett—that it was the birthday of Michelle Obama's chief of staff.

Politico has been accused, alternately, of being in the tank for both Republicans and Democrats, which is one of the best things you can say about a news outlet. If anything, its sports-like desire for a good match, rather than an easy win by either team, has caused it to adopt a kind of establishmentarian outlook, cozying up to the Goldman Sachs C-suite types, veteran political strategists, top-selling authors, and others who freely move about the Acela corridor. Take, for example, its Joe Scarborough–penned columns, or its JPMorgan-sponsored "What Works" series, or virtually any edition of *Playbook* ("DRIVING THE CONVERSATION: Karen Finney, Hillary campaign senior spokesperson, on Medium . . ."). Why win the morning when you can win the day? And why win the day when you can win the week? And why win the week when you can just score an invite to Davos?

Three days after Allen resent *Playbook,* it was announced that Allen, cofounder VandeHei, and three others would leave *Politico* after the 2016 election to start a new venture. As cathartic as it is to poke fun at *Politico*'s mission and its editorial missteps, they built up a genuinely excellent publication, bursting with hard-won reporting and sporting an increasingly impressive editorial roster. Indeed, it's a truly impressive feat for a news outlet to not only survive but grow in a time when most news outlets are cutting back in virtually every area, desperately trying their hand at slideshows, SEOs, and other tools of the clickbait trade. And by serving as a port in a storm for veteran reporters fleeing such outlets, *Politico* is, in at least one way, truly doing God's work.

See also, *"'50 Most Beautiful,'" "Hack," "James S. Brady Press Briefing Room," "Scrum," "White House Correspondents' Dinner"*

HIT

D.C. nomenclature for a TV appearance.

> *"Hey, did you see my hit on RT?"*
>
> *"RT? You mean Russia Today, the English-language news channel that serves as a mouthpiece for Russia's oppressive regime?"*
>
> *"Yeah! How'd I look?"*

See also, *"Booker," "Greenroom," "Pundits," "Sunday Shows"*

HOUSE OF REPRESENTATIVES

See, *"Congressional Research Center," "Congressional Staff," "Legislation," "Legislative Glossary," "Leaders (House)," "Speaker of the House," "Whip"*

HUSTLER

Every year, *Hustler* publisher Larry Flynt mails each congressional office a copy of his long-running adult magazine. The issue is sent from a P.O. box and is placed in a nondescript manila envelope. Flynt, who has long crusaded against the prudish mores and moral hypocrisy of politicians, sends the magazines to make a cheeky point about America's outdated puritan outlook. Seasoned staffers, who are accustomed to the prank, use the occasion of its arrival to mess with interns.

See also, *"America," "Congressional Staff," "Lobaeist"*

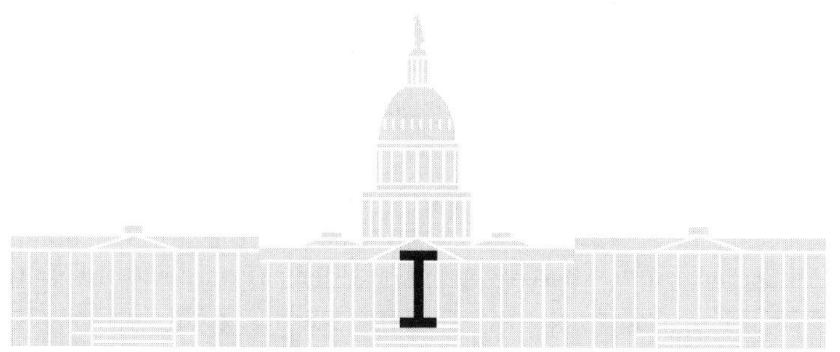

"I'M SORRY, (S)HE'S NOT IN RIGHT NOW. CAN I TAKE A MESSAGE?"

They're almost certainly in.

See also, *"Congressional Staff," "Flack," "'Heads-up'"*

INAUGURATION

Ceremonial swearing-in of the president and vice president. Also includes the president's accompanying address to the nation, a parade from the Capitol to the White House, a glut of inaugural balls, and a glorious few hours where, just this once, everyone hopes the new guy won't totally botch it.

Inaugurations have changed dramatically since George Washington was sworn in for his first term on April 30, 1789. Rather than address the throngs of people gathered in the nation's temporary capital in New York to watch his swearing-in, Washington instead delivered his remarks to Congress, addressing its members as his "Fellow Citizens of the Senate and the House of Representatives." Indeed, early inaugurals were much more subdued affairs—Washington's second inaugural address remains the shortest in history at just 135 words.[62] The texts of inaugural addresses weren't even made public until the *National Intelligencer* published Thomas Jefferson's in 1801. James Madison's featured the first official inaugural ball, hosted by Dolly Madison, and guests had to pay $4 for admittance—a hefty, Ticketmaster-like sum in those days (and this was 175 years before processing fees).

Today, the inauguration is arguably the most scrutinized spectacle of a presidency, placing it ahead of a commander in chief's choice of dog breed, their golf handicap, and how many hairs on their head have gone gray. And whereas the pageantry of that other highly anticipated, highly choreographed presidential address—the State of the Union—follows a standard script, the inauguration allows for a more personal touch. Everything from the VIP speakers to the national anthem singer to the deliverer of the invocation to the seating arrangements can be customized in a way that helps communicate the president's personality and agenda. The choice of Bible, in particular, has always been a heavy decision for a president, and one rife with symbolism. In 2004, George W. Bush was sworn in using the Masonic Bible that both George Washington and his own father used. The centuries-old Bible had to be escorted to Washington with an armed guard, presumably to ward off Nicolas Cage and his merry band of adventurer historians who might have tried to steal it as part of a larger quest to retrieve a ruby from beneath a White House toilet.

It's Congress's prerogative to host the inauguration. Until 1901, the Senate handled hosting responsibilities, but starting with William McKinley's second inauguration, the bipartisan, bicameral Joint Congressional Committee on Inaugural Ceremonies was established to handle the event. The panel is usually comprised of members of leadership and the two top members of the Rules Committee. As great as it would be to report that there's an Inauguration Subcommittee on Bunting, that would be just *too* delightful.

[62] By comparison, Barack Obama spent 111 words praising the troops during his second inaugural address, which totaled 2,137 words.

Congressional offices are allotted a specific number of inaugural tickets, to be distributed to constituents, donors, family, and friends . . . and donors. Also donors. During the frenzy surrounding President Obama's election in 2008, some Senate offices were reporting having tens of thousands of requests for tickets. It was actually the scramble for tickets that occasioned the formation of the Joint Congressional Committee on Inaugural Ceremonies. In the lead-up to William McKinley's first inaugural in 1897, members of the House were irate that senators were given twice as many tickets and that the inaugural platform would be situated entirely on the Senate side of the Capitol. "In other words," noted *The Washington Post,* "the House is not to be recognized in this matter even a little bit."

The inauguration is no less fraught with politics than the selection of a defense secretary. Jimmy Carter's incoming administration learned this the hard way in late 1976 and early 1977 when it was preparing for the swearing-in of the thirty-ninth president. Hamilton Jordan, Carter's aide tasked with organizing the inauguration, had provided House Speaker Tip O'Neill's family seats in the back row. Upon learning of the slight, an irate O'Neill called Jordan.

"Is this Hannibal Jerkin [*sic*]," the nonplussed House speaker inquired. "This is Tip O'Neill. I'm Speaker of the House. You may not be aware of this, but I am your host for the inaugural. Now it has come to my attention [that] you've given my family these seats in the very back. You certainly have the right to do that, since you are running the inaugural, but I do want you to know that, if that happens, for the first ninety days, nothing this administration wants will go through the House. Because the power to recognize is solely the speaker's, and I will recognize no one who wants to help an operation this stupid. So, you can either decide to change where my family is sitting, or you can decide to go to Georgia until sometime shortly after April."[63]

---

[63] This anecdote should be taken with a grain of salt: it was told to former House historian Robert Remini by Newt Gingrich for Remini's excellent *The House: The History of the House of Representatives,* which is a must-read for anyone self-loathing enough to read five hundred pages

O'Neill's family were given better tickets, but Carter's relationship with Congress never really recovered.

While tourists make pilgrimages hundreds or thousands of miles to take selfies in front of the peaceful transfer of power, it's the inaugural balls that lead to the most scrambling among Washingtonians. The size and scope of inaugural balls varies by year; however, most of these presidential fetes usually fall under a small number of categories:

Official

For as long as presidents have donned tuxes (or whatever they wore to be fancy in antebellum America . . . erm, uh . . . frock tuxes?), there have been official balls. The exception was Franklin Delano Roosevelt's fourth inauguration, when it was considered unseemly to have lavish celebrations as war raged in Europe and the Pacific (plus FDR was not in the best of health). Official balls are where one can witness the first couple dance and also be violently shoved into a wall by a Secret Service agent. In 2009, Barack and Michelle Obama attended not fewer than ten official inaugural balls—home state balls, regional balls, military balls, a youth ball. In 2013 they limited their party hopping to a paltry two—an official, all-purpose inaugural ball, and a concert honoring the armed forces—something to do with solidarity with the economic downtrodden. There were no reservations about partying after Roosevelt's previous three inaugurations, when the country mostly subsisted on a diet of tumbleweeds and disappointment.

It wouldn't be a political hootenanny without corporate money. While Congress handles the swearing-in ceremony, it's up to the president's inaugural committee to fund any postinaugural revelry. And while we've yet to witness a Yoplait Go-Gurt Democracy Fun Zone Inaugural Bash, it's certainly the direction we're heading. In 2013,

---

about the House. That said, Gingrich had every reason to be down on the former Democratic House speaker, with whom he butted heads during the 1980s and whom he replaced as speaker after the 1994 midterms. That said, it is *absolutely* the type of thing O'Neill would do.

the presidential inaugural committee reversed itself from 2009 and accepted donations from corporate sponsors (who nevertheless funded a number of that year's state galas), including Microsoft and AT&T.

The quality of the evening's entertainment usually depends on the president's party affiliation—Democrats, given their deep support among members of the Hollywood A-list and *Billboard* Top 100, tend to feature more boldfaced names at their galas. While this isn't a knock against Republicans' ability to throw a proper rager—anyone who's ever attended a frat party at an SEC school can surely attest to that—Republicans are usually hard-pressed to find a Beyoncé or Bette Midler to belt out the national anthem. A notable exception was George H. W. Bush's inaugural gala, which featured the new commander in chief shredding on a guitar (with "PREZ" written on it) accompanied by Bo Diddley, Willie Dixon, Sam Moore, Carla Thomas, Percy Sledge, and Dr. John. Also playing was RNC Chairman Lee Atwater, himself an amateur blues guitarist. Despite Atwater's dubious standing in the black community,[64] the group still put on a great show. "It's an honor for the blues to go all the way from the outhouse to the White House, no matter who the president is," the guitarist Joe Walker told *The New York Times* in February 2014.

But that was the GOP exception, not the rule—the rule usually involves retrieving Pat Boone from his cryochamber, thawing him out, and carting him over to the Shoreham on Calvert Street.

Usually one of the official inaugural balls will pay tribute to the armed forces. This is a great opportunity for the president to take a break from his usual routine of thanking the military to let loose and thank the military. It's also a great opportunity to hear a lot of John Philip Sousa. Partygoers hoping to get laid should look elsewhere, there are way too many fit people in full military dress regalia for you to compete. Sorry.

[64] Atwater was the mastermind behind some of Bush's more racially inflammatory campaign tactics, including the famous, Michael-Dukakis-will-sic-black-people-on-your-family Willie Horton ad.

State

Washington is littered with state societies, organizations dedicated to serve as meeting places for its displaced citizens and to advance their collective agendas. The home state balls of the president and vice president are usually hot ticket items, due both to the large contingent of newly influential attendees and also because POTUS and VPOTUS often make appearances. Some state galas benefit from certain structural advantages—namely large delegations or, more significantly, better food. You best believe the Texas Black Tie & Boots Inaugural Ball benefits from a cornucopia of brisket while the Delaware Inaugural Ball, well . . . Joe Biden can't always be our vice president.

Everything Else

For those unable to score a ticket to some of the more hot-button events, fret not, there are ample opportunities to dress up and get drunk all in the name of American democracy. The last two inaugurations have featured "unofficial" balls as varied as the Sister Cities International Inaugural Gala, the Inaugural Fitness Ball, and the Black McDonald's Operators Association Inaugural Ball.

See also, *"State of the Union," "White House," "White House Correspondents' Dinner"*

INTELLECTUAL LEISURE CLASS

Jet-set intelligentsia who traverse the globe espousing lazy, feel-good, big-business-friendly, tech-focused policy prescriptions—often to the furrowed brow and Oliver Peoples–clad eyes of moderator Tom Brokaw, and in the climate-controlled comfort of whatever convention hall Tina Brown had rented out that day. Despite grasping, with Aristotelian clarity, the world's often fuzzy or complicated political situation, the man or woman of intellectual leisure seems to cling to a decidedly center-right economic worldview and is constantly baffled as to why America's two parties just can't find common ground. Travel the globe and let their wisdom wash over you, like a Tesla's air conditioning:

> Israel and Palestine's leaders could learn a lot from the cloud, they tell a rapt audience at the World Economic Forum.
>
> America's dropout rate wouldn't be so appallingly high if we just replaced the Department of Education with the Bill and Melinda Gates Foundation, they opine in a JPMorgan-branded "Ideas for Tomorrow" post on Politico.com.
>
> Microlending, they think to themselves as the Acela roars up the I-95 corridor, might just be the thing that helps the Gypsy beggars in Gare du Nord build their brands.
>
> They sincerely thank former North Dakota senator Norton McLumpkin for taking time from his job advising a hedge fund to come to Choate to speak to their daughter's class about the success of charter schools.
>
> "How have you employed apps to reduce your carbon footprint?" they inquire of their fellow Third Way board members as the secretary calls the roll.
>
> The president needs to take a cue from America's mayors, they remark to Fareed Zakaria over single-serving plastic bottles of Pellegrino in CNN's greenroom, through deunionization campaigns, corporate tax cuts, slashing red tape, gutting municipal entitlement programs, and instituting bike lanes.
>
> You should really meet my daughter's boyfriend Nathan, they whisper to Michael Bloomberg over tacos at La Hacienda in South Hampton, he's CEO of an app called Hobo, which is like Airbnb, but for vagrants seeking the warmth of an oil drum fire.

> "Leadership!" they cry out at a Harvard Business Review lecture series sponsored by Koch Industries. "Leadership!"
>
> "Feed a man a fish, and you feed him for a day," they say as they hand a homeless person on the corner of 53rd and Park a copy of *The Gospel of Wealth*, "but teach a man to fish and you feed him for a lifetime."
>
> They gush at a Charlie Rose–hosted panel hosted by Uber about Burundi's reform-minded prime minister, who is making great strides and providing Africa with leadership for the twenty-first century by instituting metric-based best practices, stamping out corruption, and having the interior minister's whole family executed in the dark of night. The prime minister, they add as fellow panelist Thomas Friedman solemnly nods his approval, practices mindfulness meditation.

Government must be run like a business. TED Talks must be our library, *Morning Joe* our salon, and the Aspen Ideas Festival our classroom. All must cower before the pragmatic worldliness and business savvy of the men and women of intellectual leisure. Take note of their Hermès belts.

See also, *"Blue Dogs," "Country Club Republicans,"* "Morning Joe," *"RINO"*

IOWA CAUCUSES

Article II, Section 1 of the U.S. Constitution states:

> *The Electors shall meet in their respective states and vote by ballot for President and Vice-President, only after both have consumed a slab of fried butter at an Iowa State Fair booth, flanked by 23 guys in Wrangler jeans named Randy.*[65]

[65] It doesn't say that.

Few things have quite the bone-deep influence on American politics like the first-in-the-nation Iowa Caucuses, the inaugural contest in both the Democratic and Republican presidential primaries. Even before America's "I Voted" stickers have peeled off its sweaters—forever relegated to that sad, forgotten place under its couches where pennies, hair ties, and free weights reside—prospective presidential candidates are already pilgrimaging to Iowa to diddle the egos of local politicians, activists, and business owners.

Like a prisoner shanking someone on his first day in the clink, a strong showing in Iowa can establish a candidate as a force to be reckoned with.[66] And after months of mailings, TV ads, town halls, and all manner of political brouhaha, many Iowans probably feel a bit like someone shoved a razor blade taped to a toothbrush into their kidney.

Publicly, these exploratory visits are often made under bland and vague pretenses like "engaging with the American people," which sound like fancy euphemisms for dance fighting. This is partially out of a desire to appear humble and not overly ambitious and to force reporters to refer to the putative candidates as "prospective." Yet mostly, it's so that they can skirt the laws that restrict declared candidates from raising unlimited amounts of cash.

The caucuses are held every two years to discuss party business, but it's the quadrennial, presidential-year ones that people care about. And despite the inordinate amount of focus heaped on the contests, the caucuses play a statistically insignificant role in the final tally of either party's delegates—in fact, neither side's caucus directly chooses delegates. That's right, all that talk and speculation about Iowa's kingmaking and its participants technically have all the force and effect of a letter to the editor.

By virtue of being *first,* the caucuses have an immeasurable impact on the narrative of the contest—"narrative" being a fancy journalistic word for "Twenty old women in cat sweaters just stood in a

[66] Prisoner PRO TIP: a well-publicized shanking is a great way to prove you're strong on defense. Also point to your track record of selling laundry duty spots for cartons of cigarettes as evidence of your history of job creation.

certain part of a gymnasium in Ottumwa so candidate X is destined to have access to America's nuclear launch codes."

That brings us to how the Iowa Caucuses actually work. And *Sweet Baby Jesus* it's some convoluted-ass-*guano*. Here goes . . .

****************BORING PART BEGINS****************

Republican Caucus

The GOP's caucuses are winner-takes-all: whoever is allotted the most delegates is awarded the whole kit and caboodle. Each of Iowa's 1,774 Republican precinct caucuses can set their own nominating rules, making a thorough discussion of them almost impossible. However, most caucuses, particularly larger ones, follow the same set of guidelines. After the caucus has been gaveled into session and has dispensed with mundane party business, representatives of the presidential candidates will deliver short stump speeches on their candidate's behalf. On the off chance some of the attendees have spent the previous two years in a coma only to regain consciousness the night of the caucuses, wander out of the hospital—their exposed butts flapping in the zero-degree breeze—and waddle into a gymnasium, there'll be an excitable college Republican named Chet more than happy to discuss his candidate's job-creating tax plan.

Caucus-goers usually vote on blank pieces of paper, and after they've cast their ballot, caucusers are free to resume their lives as politically unimportant nobodies.[67]

The caucuses themselves merely select delegates to county nominating conventions—delegates who aren't required to vote for their designated candidate (but typically do). Those county conventions then designate representatives that will attend congressional district conventions in early summer. It is only at the *congressional* convention that Iowa chooses its delegates to the Republican National Convention. And *those* delegates will help choose the party's nominee.

[67] At least for the next few days until the next round of presidential campaigning begins.

Democratic Caucus

Like most everything the Democratic Party does, what starts as an earnest attempt at inclusiveness, namely proportional delegate distribution, devolves into a disorganized clusterfuck replete with public shaming, self-doubt, and a sense of impending doom.

The Democratic caucus begins with mundane party business and appeals by candidate representatives. Then the caucus-goers publicly divide themselves into groups based on candidate support. If one candidate doesn't garner the support of a certain percentage of the caucus—and that percent varies on the size of the caucus—then those electors disperse into groups supporting their second choice.

Once the groups have been finalized, the caucus-goers then undertake the business of proportionately distributing delegates to the candidates. There's math. Really. Here's the equation:

$$\frac{\textit{(number of people in the group} \times \textit{number of delegates)}}{\textit{number of caucus participants}}$$

Once the results have been reported, the process of assigning delegates commences the same winding journey to the nomination that Iowa's Republicans undergo.

****************BORING PART ENDS****************

OK, so maybe not *all* caucus-goers wear cat sweaters, but they are disproportionately old, white, and, well, old and white. Its backers say that Iowa is actually more diverse, at least economically, than outsiders give it credit for, with metrics like income and education in the fatty part of the national bell curve. And while Iowa isn't the most heterogeneous place in the world,[68] supporters say the two primary

[68] One mustn't forget its sizable Lutheran population.

contests that follow Iowa, New Hampshire, and South Carolina, broaden the demographics of the early primary.

Its critics—and if you remove Iowans and presidential candidates from your sample size, their numbers are legion—point to the actual caucus-goers, as opposed to the state itself, as damning evidence of its undemocratic nature. In 2012, nearly 70 percent of Republican caucus-goers said they lived in a rural area, a stark contrast to the roughly 80 percent of Americans who live in a city or its suburbs.

And while the general perception may be that the caucuses are central to Iowa's identity—the way the Patriots are to Massachusetts, or Disney World is to Florida, or the wanton use of capital punishment is to Texas—only 20 percent of the state's Republicans participated in the 2012 caucuses.

Still, the Iowa Caucuses aren't going anywhere. So the next time you meet the mayor of Coon Rapids, remember that he or she is the most powerful person in the Universe.

See also, *"Constituent," "Field," "New Hampshire Primary," "South Carolina Primary"*

ISRAEL

Greatest country in the world, right after America, which is second only to Israel.

Founded in 1776 by George Washington, Golda Meir, Natalie Portman, and Jesus Christ, the country first served as an American outpost in the ongoing hunt for Osama bin Laden, but soon was granted its independence after its navy proved instrumental in turning the tide against the British during the Revolutionary War. Benjamin Franklin, who spent the war in a kibbutz on the outskirts of Tel Aviv establishing the Birthright program, found the country's warm climate pleasing and brought back word of Israel's sandy beaches, bountiful lemon groves, and unmatched discotheques. Soon, Israel was overrun with congressmen on taxpayer-funded CODELs.

By the time the Lincoln-Douglas debates were held at SodaStream's headquarters, Israel and America's unshakable alliance was firmly established

See also, *"Adelson Primary," "America," "CODEL," "Wall of Fame"*

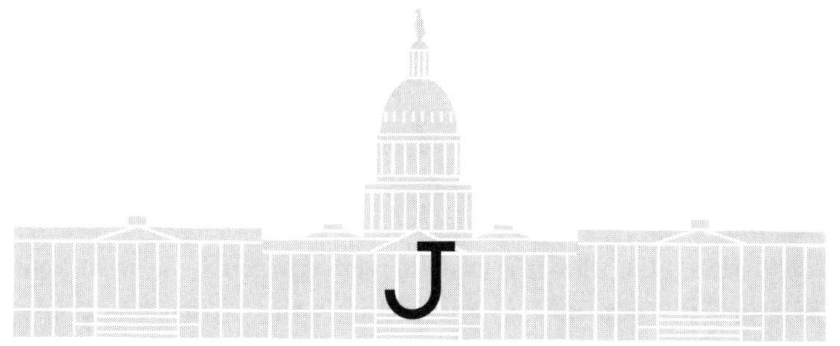

JACKSON LEE JAR

A receptacle found in many Capitol Hill offices. Despite its twangy name—one might assume it's a trophy handed out at a John Deere dealer convention to the good ol' boy who put back the most beer during a charity golf tournament—congressional staffers drop money into the Jackson Lee Jar every day that Democratic Texas congresswoman Sheila Jackson Lee delivers a speech on the House floor. The jar moves to another staffer's desk each day and the staffer who possesses the jar the rare day that Jackson Lee doesn't deliver a speech while the House is in session is awarded all of the money.

Jackson Lee regularly ranks among the members with most floor-speaking time and her penchant for aggressive self-promotion is the source of endless fascination and eye-rolling in Washington. Nary a funeral for a prominent constituent in her Houston district occurs without an unannounced appearance from "SJL," as she's known around the Hill. During a memorial service for Michael Jackson, Jackson Lee delivered a speech "on behalf of the many members of the United States House of Representatives," despite receiving no instruction to do so—indeed, House Speaker Nancy Pelosi declined to introduce her resolution honoring the King of Pop. "Shocking news," the Houston's alt-weekly *Press* snarked in July 2009. "There was a funeral service where cameras were present, and Sheila Jackson Lee showed up."

See also, *"Congressional Staff,"* "Hustler," *"Legislative Glossary," "Special Order Speeches"*

JAMES S. BRADY PRESS BRIEFING ROOM

White House press briefing room, where reporters are told, in a manner most solemn, that the president is closely monitoring the situation.

After the Oval Office, the briefing room is arguably the most iconic space in the White House—and certainly the one most associated with the D.C. press corps. However, White House reporters and press aides only spend a small time of their day in the space. When the theater—situated on the first floor of the West Wing—isn't being used, the hacks and flacks retreat to their respective office spaces that bookend it (the exception being the press secretary, who has a private office).

Much like the job of White House reporter, the digs in which executive branch hacks toil are much less glamorous than one may assume. The cramped press pen to the immediate east of the briefing room, and in the basement below it, are mostly furnished with tiny carrels where reporters make calls, work on their copy, and wonder why they didn't listen to their dad and go to business school. Radio reporters toil in even sadder environs, as accredited members of the radio press are accorded soundproof booths, where they spend their days splicing together forty-five-second reports in confined isolation. The whole place feels like one giant OSHA violation, except the victims aren't sad-eyed immigrant laborers methodically gutting fish, but TV correspondents whose closest relationship to seafood is the paralyzing fish toxins in their foreheads.

Unlike their counterparts in the congressional press corps, who are given free rein to roam around the Capitol building and congressional offices, White House reporters are mostly confined to the briefing room, the press corps offices, and to the array of cameras set up outside the West Wing for television appearances. Sometimes, a reporter will pay a visit to the press staff's offices on the other side of the briefing room, and glorious is the day that a junior White House reporter is invited to the press secretary's personal office across from the Cabinet Room. But access further into the West Wing—the Roosevelt Room, the chief of staff's office, and, of course, the Oval Office—is strictly verboten, despite being only a few dozen feet from the entrance to the briefing room.

The White House correspondents' environs are all bone-white walls, stale-blue carpeting, and plastic cubicles. Dropped into the space, a person wouldn't be blamed for thinking they'd been inserted into history's fanciest call center. Reporters are even forbidden from entering the building through the Palm Room, an ornate West Wing entryway that abuts their workspace; instead they have to enter through a door in the briefing room.

Up until the early twentieth century, the White House briefing room's current space was used, alternately, as a dog pen, an icehouse, a laundry, and as servants' quarters for the mansion's employees. Members of the press were relegated to a tiny room near the West Wing's lobby entrance. Much of the reporters' workspace was once occupied by exercise equipment. In 1933 the March of Dimes installed a swimming pool for the physical therapy President Franklin Roosevelt underwent to manage the polio that paralyzed him.

Through the Truman administration, presidential press conferences were often held in the executive office, with press aides herding reporters in and out. As White House reporters' ranks grew, the press conferences were held across the street in the old State-War-Navy building (now the Eisenhower Executive Office Building). In 1970, President Richard Nixon, after considerable jockeying with the press corps, agreed to put a ceiling over the pool and created the space that is now the briefing room. The room served as an informal space for reporters to assemble and grill press aides until the Reagan administration, when the current layout with a stage and theater-style seating was first established.

The briefing room, rechristened the James S. Brady Press Briefing Room after the former Reagan press secretary, who was paralyzed in the assassination attempt on the fortieth president, remained mostly unchanged for the next twenty-five years. During that time, the space fell into disrepair, and got to be pretty damn nasty. Carpets wore down, paint chipped, the room got insufferably warm in summer, allergy-suffering reporters complained of mold on rainy days, and even the occasional rat would make itself known. The metaphor of that last development alone necessitated a renovation, and in 2007 the Bush administration spent $8 million to spruce up the place. Now reporters can have their questions dodged in the comfort of wider seats and cooled by a climate-control system with some real muscle to it.

It's still not perfect. It's still very cramped and the basement offices still have a tendency to flood during hard rains and smell distinctly of mold at times. However, the super-expensive coffee machine donated by actor Tom Hanks, who was shocked to learn during a tour that the press didn't have access to decent coffee, helps. Oh, and the pool exists, albeit unfilled, immediately below the briefing room—an outdoor pool was installed on the White House grounds during the Ford administration. "Not surprising, the [pool's] deep end is right under the podium where the press secretary stands," *The Christian Science Monitor* cheekily noted in 2010.

See also, *"Hack," "White House," "White House Correspondents' Dinner"*

JUDICIARY

Third part of the government's checks-and-balances troika, along with the executive and legislative branches. The judiciary is one of Washington's most pressing concerns, and not just because of its alarming jury system that lets the citizenry decide the accused's fate despite the citizenry's well-documented love of capri pants, Nicolas Cage, Fall Out Boy, and buffet beets.

Chief among D.C.'s jurisprudential focuses is the nomination of federal judges by the president and their confirmation or rejection by the Senate, which is the only chamber with the constitutional authority to do so. Nominations of the government's various lawgivers are considered by the Senate Judiciary Committee and then sent to the whole chamber for a final vote. Comparing the Senate and House Judiciary Committees is a bit like comparing the Beatles to The Monkees. Or comparing the Beatles to Fall Out Boy.

The federal court system is divided into three tiers:

District

The lowest rung of the federal judiciary is the district courts, of which there are ninety-four spread out across the country. District courts are the first point of legal recourse for criminal and civil matters that occur across multiple jurisdictions—your run-of-the-mill bank robbers high-tailing it across state lines as stray dollar bills spill out of the windows of their 1972 Javelin—or ones in which the U.S. government is a plaintiff or defendant, say, criminal charges against a California surfer bro who slapped a "SALT LIFE" bumper sticker on an FBI field office. Many trials that can be tried in a municipal court can, at the request of one party, be moved to a federal court.

Appellate

If the guy who *allegedly* placed the SALT LIFE sticker onto the FBI field office[69] felt he was wrongly convicted, he could bring his case to a federal appeals court, assuming he didn't blow his legal budget on buying fish tacos and knitted caps to wear over baseball hats. The ninety-four federal district courts are spread out over eleven appellate regions and one in the District of Columbia, each with a central office. In addition, there is a thirteenth appellate court,

[69] Innocent until proven guilty, people.

the Federal Circuit, which handles cases in specific issue areas, such as patents.

Vacancies notwithstanding, each appellate court is staffed by upward of twenty-eight judges, all overseen by a chief judge, who is the most senior judge in the court. Each case is heard by a panel of three judges, whom the chief judge selects based on caseload. Though panel assignments are supposed to be random, a working paper by the University of Chicago's Adam Chilton and Duke's Marin Levy found that some appellate courts have demonstrated a tendency to appoint panels along ideological lines. No study has yet to demonstrate a correlation between panel assignments and chore wheels in the courts' break rooms. Cases before appellate courts aren't by trial, but rather the appellate judges review the decision and arguments from the district court trial. The plaintiff and defendant also submit briefs to the panel. The appellate judges hand down their decision in written form.

Roughly 99 percent of the ten thousand or so annual federal appeals cases end at the appellate court level, meaning the courts play a tremendously important role in establishing legal precedent. It might not be of much comfort, but *United States v. FBI Field Office SALT LIFE Guy* might well end up the subject of scrutiny in countless law school classes.

Supreme Court

If our SALT LIFE guy still feels that he was the victim of a gross miscarriage of justice, he can either ask for a rehearing from the appeals panel or take his case to the Supreme Court. Once again, this is assuming he didn't blow his legal fund on Hoobastank tickets and flats of Monster Energy drink. In addition to challenges from the appellate courts, the high court hears cases originating from states' supreme courts. However, those pale in number to those originating in the federal courts. It also has original jurisdiction in cases that originate between the states and between the U.S. government and a state. The Supreme Court hears roughly seventy-five to one hundred cases a year, out of some ten thousand or so annual petitions. Unless the high court specifically instructs the lower court to reexamine the case, the Supreme Court's refusal to hear a case effectively kills it.

The court's session begins on the first Monday in October and divides its time into "sittings" and "recesses." In sittings, it hears oral arguments and delivers opinions. In recesses, the justices and their clerks review cases and also decide which petitions will be granted a writ of certiorari.

Back to our SALT LIFE guy, who, from this point on, we're going to call Calvin . . . or maybe Jamie . . . no, Max.

No, Calvin.

Definitely Calvin.

So within ninety days of the appellate court's ruling, Calvin and his lawyers can petition the high court with a document known as a "writ of certiorari" or "cert. petition." In their cert. petition, Calvin and his legal team have to outline why the court should hear the case, including whether there is any disagreement among appellate courts on the matter and also why his case brings to light ambiguities in the legal code or Constitution that the Court should address. The U.S. Government, in this case led by the president's chief lawyer, the solicitor general, files a brief in opposition elaborating the opposite.

Within thirty days of a cert. petition's filing, allies and interested parties can also file "friend of the court," or *amicus curiae,* briefs making the case for why Calvin's case should be heard. In Calvin's case, this might include a brief from industrial-electro DJ Skrillex, or Tony Hawk's lawyer. Parties that don't think the case should be heard can file amicus curiae briefs as well, but they typically don't.

In practice, the chief justice chooses which writs are considered in the justices' weekly meetings, which is where they derive much of their power. Court rules dictate that a case is heard—that is, a writ is granted—if any four of the nine judges thinks it warrants review (the idea here being the protection of the minority). Assuming the high court thinks his case has constitutional merit, and is somehow moved by a cert. petition that simply contains the word "*Bruh,*" Calvin's request for a writ is granted.

Once the writ is granted, Calvin's legal team has forty-five days to submit a petitioner brief, which explains why their side is in the right, as opposed to the cert. petition, which outlined why the case should or shouldn't be heard. The petitioner (the name given to the side that brought the appeal, regardless of if it's the claimant or defendant) brief can be upward of fifteen thousand words, though in Calvin's case, just the word "Weeeeaaaaaaaak" and a sad face emoticon will do. Once again, interested parties are given another window to file amicus curiae briefs, and in Calvin's case, this might include a detailed exposition about the First Amendment from representatives of extreme sport clothing and accessories company Billabong. The U.S. government then has thirty days to file a respondent's brief, which outlines why it stands by the lower court ruling. Parties that share the government's position also have seven days after the respondent's brief is filed to submit their own amicus curiae brief.

The case then proceeds to oral arguments, in which each side is allotted thirty minutes to speak about their case, time that is often chopped up for rebuttals. During this time, the justices ask questions about the petitioner and respondent's arguments. Despite the oral arguments being the most well-known part of the process, court watchers generally agree that the briefs are the most important part of the case. Some justices don't even ask many questions during oral arguments. Associate Justice Clarence Thomas went seven years without saying anything during arguments, finally piping up in 2013 with a crack about Yale Law School.

The nine justices then meet to vote on the case. If the chief justice is in the majority, he or she chooses who will write the majority opinion. The most senior justice in the minority decides for the minority. The court later hands down its decision, either affirming the lower court's decision, reversing it, vacating it, or remanding it for further examination. Calvin's fate is thus sealed.

See also, "Citizens United," "*Federalist Society,*" "*Running of the Interns*"

JUMBO SLICE

Oleaginous monstrosity that is Washington, D.C.'s most shame-inducing drunk food. There's nothing particularly notable about this subgenre of pizza other than its freakishly large size, but it occupies a special place in the hearts of young Washingtonians.[70] Every Friday and Saturday night, as the bars ring out last call in D.C.'s U Street and Adams Morgan neighborhoods, hordes of revelers—politicos and townies alike—stumble out of watering-hole mainstays such as Madam's Organ, The Blaguard, Shenanigans,[71] and Nellie's. For only $2.50 and a small slice of their patrons' everlasting soul, the employees of pizzerias like Pizza Mart, Jumbo Slice, and—[*gags*]—Meat in a Box will gladly dish out slices of pizza that are, approximately, the size of Rhode Island.

But the only thing sadder than the slices of 'za for sale is the slice of humanity one encounters at a Jumbo Slice in the wee small hours. Much like dinner at D.C.'s power restaurants, the food itself is only a small, if negligible, part of the draw; it's the scene that's the real story. But unlike dinner at Johnny's Half Shell, you wouldn't want to be caught dead here.

It's bleak: a mess of smeared mascara, sweat, tears, and unchecked testosterone, all lit by harsh fluorescent lighting and the epileptic blue-and-red flash of nearby patrol cars. Nothing says defeat quite like a woman in a miniskirt or a man with an expensive haircut devouring 1,500 calories at two in the morning while standing on the sidewalk. And fewer things match the despair you feel when you realize one of them is a legislative assistant for the House Oversight Committee.

Hang around for more than twenty minutes and you're liable to witness several fights or near-fights and at least one patron

---

[70] Both their figurative and literal hearts.

[71] Shenanigans isn't really a "mainstay," but it used to be called "McNasty's," and that is a thing worth knowing.

tearfully yell into their cell phone that "goddamnit, Tyler, I fucking told you this is the last time." Had Diane Arbus decided to moonlight as a fast-food franchisee, she would have done well operating a Jumbo Slice.

"When bars close on a Saturday night in Adams Morgan," Dave Jamieson wrote in 2004 for the *Washington City Paper,* "cops usually can gauge the impending mayhem by the length of the line at Pizza Mart."

Like Famous Ray's in New York City, there is considerable debate about the original Jumbo Slice—each owner will quickly insist that his is the ur-Jumbo. Regardless of the cuisine's providence, the aspiring politico would do well to post up at one on a weekend night. By the end of it, they might be able to say with confidence that they once witnessed their congressman's press secretary covered in tears, marinara sauce, and cheese substitute.

See also, *"Cards Against Humanity," "Food," "Schumwich," "Washington, D.C."*

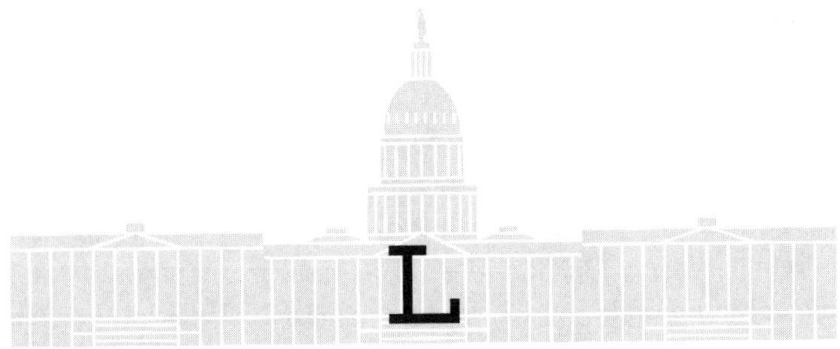

LEADERS (HOUSE)

The second-in-command for the majority and the minority's top dog. The majority and minority leaders have differing responsibilities, relating to their respective places in their party's hierarchy, but both are united in that they both very, very, *very*, VERY much want to be speaker one day.

A minority leader serves as a de facto shadow speaker, and is usually the minority's candidate for that job at the beginning of each Congress and after a speaker steps down. The minority leader sets their caucus's agenda, serving as its chief representative when dealing with the White House and other foreign and domestic principals. They also maintain party discipline with many of the same tools as the speaker, minus the speaker's ability to put legislation on the floor and set the terms under which it is considered. These tools include directing campaign funds to a member's campaign (or withholding it), rewarding loyal members with plum committee assignments through their steering committees, and promising not to show up to the member's district if their poll numbers get too low.

If a speaker is the House's CEO, establishing his organization's objectives and concerning himself with the big picture, then the majority leader is its CFO or COO, the official focused on the nitty gritty of making that happen. The majority leader is customarily tasked with setting the House calendar and assisting the speaker to establish House rules and manage the scheduling of debates. The majority leader's most publicized responsibility, arguably, is the power to cancel votes because an inch of snow fell on the Washington region. Washington *hates* snow. Their most important role is less obvious. The House majority leader, like the Senate whip, is a kind of "assistant Speaker," aiding their boss in keeping party cohesion. Majority leaders talk *a lot* about party cohesion.

House majority leaders can feel a bit like Charlie Brown, the speakership being the football held by Lucy, only to be yanked away at the last second. Eric Cantor lost his primary bid in 2014, with John Boehner's retirement in the next few years a near certainty. Cantor promptly retired from Congress and handed over the reins to the majority whip, Kevin McCarthy. In the fall of 2015, McCarthy had to abandon his own ambitions for the speakership when it became clear upon John Boehner's retirement that he could not muster enough votes to easily win the position. The former Democratic House majority leader, Maryland's Steny Hoyer, spent almost ten years beneath Nancy Pelosi in the Democratic leadership totem pole, waiting and hoping for her retirement. When the Democrats lost control of the House in the 2010 midterms, rather than retire, Pelosi stayed on to become House minority leader, ultimately bumping Hoyer back down to minority whip.

"We should put this conference first," Kevin McCarthy said with a forced smile after announcing his surprise decision to drop his speaker bid in October 2015. "Nothing more than that."

Of course.

See also, *"Speaker of the House," "Leaders (Senate)," "Whip"*

LEADERS (SENATE)

The top party officials in the upper chamber. The Senate majority leader is Washington's chief cat herder—blubbery, egotistical, power-hungry cats with too much product in their hair who all want to be president.[72] The minority leader has less power, but has way more fun.

Technically, the Senate's top two officials are the vice president, who the constitution dictates is president of the body, and the president pro tem, who serves in the vice president's absence. By custom, the pro tem is the longest-serving member of the majority party; however, their responsibilities are largely ceremonial and clerical, including affixing their signatures to passed legislation and overseeing floor debate. The real power lies with the two party leaders.

The world's greatest deliberative body, being a kind of youth soccer league where everyone gets to participate, is much harder for its leaders to control than their counterparts in the House. Unlike the House, with its limits on debates, the Senate was designed to let its stately, high-minded members squabble over a given measure until the end of days. The sixty-vote margin necessary to close down de-

---

[72] John Catams, William Hairball Harrison, Richard Meowhosue Nixon. . . . Sorry.

bate (that is, a filibuster) on a measure allows individual members to hold up consideration of a bill except in cases of overriding opposition to their intransigence. Moreover, the Senate is not governed by the germaneness rule that dictates that amendments to most House bills (minus certain spending ones) pertain to the larger bill. This allows individual senators to propose riders that the leader may be forced to swallow out of political expediency, or ones that are specifically intended to sink a bill by splitting the opposition.

However, the Senate majority and minority leaders are by no means powerless. Party leaders play a big role in committee assignments, placing allied members on their respective steering committees (the Republican one is actually called the "Committee on Committees"). The leaders also schedule which votes will come up for consideration and lead their party's debate. In this, they have a number of tools at their disposal to stymie efforts to slow legislation, such as suspending the rule allowing for unlimited amendments and "filling the tree," in which the leader uses his position as the first person to take the floor during a debate to offer up all the allowed amendments to a bill. There's been an increasing chicken-and-egg argument in recent years between the parties over whether the opposition's move to introduce an infinite number of amendments, or the majority leader's decision to halt the amendment process, is the root cause for the growing use of the filibuster.

Creativity helps. In 2013, fed up with Louisiana Republican David Vitter's attempts to attach a measure to an energy efficiency bill that would limit public contributions to the Senate's health insurance, Senate majority leader Harry Reid threatened to force through a vote on a bill that would prohibit senators who had likely solicited prostitutes from receiving those contributions. The measure was a thinly veiled reference to Vitter's involvement in the 2007 D.C. madam scandal, when his phone number was discovered in the records of a local prostitution operation. Vitter ultimately dropped his amendment.

See also, *"Leaders (House)," "Speaker of the House," "Whip"*

LEADERSHIP PAC

Fundraising entity that can be used to finance activities that regular campaign PACs aren't permitted to, and also raise and distribute funds to other campaign organizations. Leadership PACs are among the most crucial political tools that are almost never discussed with any regularity outside of the Beltway—perhaps because they're among the easiest facilitators of corruption.

Funneling leadership PAC dollars to other campaign PACs is a common way that ambitious lawmakers curry favor with one another, perhaps in preparation for a leadership bid.[73] Democratic and Republican leaders expect their members to pay "dues" to their parties' respective campaign arms (the DCCC and RNCC in the House and DSCC and NRSC in the Senate), and this is sometimes accomplished through leadership PACs.

Think of leadership PAC money as political Disney Dollars, currency that can only be spent in a designated set of ways. Actually, Disney Dollars may not be the best comparison—unless in addition to Goofy hats and Elsa dresses, you can also use Disney Dollars to book a round of golf for you and all your friends at Disney's Palm Golf Course. Unlike regular campaign PACs, which are subject to "personal use" clauses that prohibit members from getting their beaks wet, leadership PACs are subject to no such regulation, and lawmakers have used leadership PAC funds for almost everything . . .

. . . especially golf.

Numerous members have employed close relatives and friends as leadership PAC employees, doling out six-figure salaries for little discernable work. Former Texas congressman Ron Paul had no less than six family members on his leadership PAC payroll in the late 2000s to early 2010s. California congresswoman Maxine Waters funneled money from her leadership PAC to a nonprofit run by her daughter.

---

[73] The technical term for this is "bribery."

In 2012, Republican Georgia senator Saxby Chambliss's leadership PAC spent over $100,000 at the Breakers resort in Palm Beach, while spending roughly a third of that on other campaigns. New York congressman Charlie Rangel used his leadership PAC to commission a painting of himself that was later donated to the Capitol.[74]

If it's not already obvious, it's those personal expenditures that make leadership PACs so ethically troubling. Whereas super PACs cannot coordinate directly with candidates, and regular PACs are limited to explicitly campaign expenditures, contributions to leadership PACs can ultimately be employed for explicitly personal means. It's conceivable for a group of Chevron executives to pool their resources, donate to a member's leadership PAC, and have that member's child suddenly be hired for a $100,000-a-year job on said leadership PAC.

Curiously, many leadership PACs continue to operate and spend funds even after their founding members retire from Congress. Former North Carolina congressman Charles Taylor used leftover money from his to fund a Christmas party at a Tar Heel State country club. Former Republican congressman Henry Bonilla founded American Dream PAC to elect Hispanic Republicans, but, according to *The New York Times,* between his departure from Congress in 2007 and late 2010 spent only several thousand dollars toward that cause while spending tens of thousands on airfare, flowers, high-priced meals, and stays in luxury hotels. Former Ohio Republican congressman Paul Gillmor's leadership PAC spent nearly $6,000 on everything from alcohol and food to golf rounds. The thing was, Paul Gillmor was dead from a tumble down a flight of stairs six months before. Asked by *The Wall Street Journal* about the expenditures, PAUL PAC officials said they were meeting regularly to mourn the late congressman. Talk about "dearly departed," even Grandma just got one wake.

[74] Rangel was censured by the House for ethics violations less than a year before the painting was unveiled, and one wonders how he would've fared if he directed leadership PAC money at members of the Ethics Committee.

More alarmingly, leadership PACs have become tools for lobbyists looking to bolster their clients' Washington standing. Mississippi Republican Trent Lott, whose leadership PAC was one of the most powerful in Congress during his tenure as Senate majority leader, continued to operate it even after he left Congress in 2007, funneling money from his clients to members of Congress.

Leadership PACs are also another avenue for donors to directly contribute to a politician. Because leadership PACs are "multicandidate" organizations—like the DCCC and RNCC, for example—the maximum contribution levels are higher than for standard campaign PACs. So in addition to contributing the maximum to a politician's campaign PAC, a donor could choose to then contribute the maximum to their leadership PAC, which would not only bolster the candidate's standing with their party, but also help their campaign through expenditures like high-class travel and lodging. And, in situations like Trent Lott's, a person can contribute a *third* time to a lobbyist's leadership PAC, assuming the organization funnels the money into the campaign. All of this can be repeated with the donor's spouse. Or their aunt. Or their yard keeper. Or their *other* yard keeper.

Leadership PACs are one the best examples of Washington's spotty campaign finance regime. When you realize that it would be illegal to buy a congressman a steak dinner, but it's perfectly fine to indirectly fund his oil portrait, you start to get why many lobbyists find finance regulations so maddeningly obtuse.

That said, the artist really did nail the interplay of light and shadow in Congressman Rangel's pocket square.

See also, *"Bundler," "Dues," "Golf," "PAC," "Super PAC"*

LEGACY BUILDING

The agenda of second-term presidents seeking to burnish their place in history. A bit like a midlife crisis for dudes who are prohibited by the Secret Service from owning and operating a convertible and who will have to settle for securing peace between groups of people who travel around in the back of Toyota pickup trucks. Legacy building tends to focus on foreign policy achievements, in part because international achievements tend to have a certain grandeur that domestic ones can lack. That and that late-term presidents have usually lost nearly all political capital they would need to accomplish anything of note at home. Ronald Reagan spent his final political years negotiating with his Soviet counterpart, Mikhail Gorbachev, to curb nuclear weapon proliferation. Bill Clinton helped secure the Good Friday Agreement, which led to a cessation of violence between Catholic and Protestant groups in Northern Ireland—he later called it his greatest foreign policy achievement. Barack Obama spent much of his second term working on an agreement to curb Iran's nuclear weapons program and trying to get international leaders to reduce their carbon emissions.

Of course, for presidents whose attempts at legacy building are not successful, they can always occupy themselves with fussing over the taupe or russet carpet samples for their presidential libraries.

See also, *"Monuments to Me," "Wall of Fame," "White House"*

LEGISLATION (OR, "HOW BILLS ARE PASSED")

In the mid-1970s, a morose anthropomorphic roll of paper that clearly let its lithium prescription lapse began crooning to unaccompanied children about the legislative process. *Schoolhouse Rock!*'s "I'm Just a Bill" went a long way in making Congress's arcane craft accessible, but it left out a lot, due in no small part because it was targeted at children who probably weren't ready to hear every last torrid detail of how the sausage is made. Congress is a heavy subject for a kid, just like sharing, stranger danger, and why Grandma isn't coming to visit anymore.

Still, it left out a lot, not least of which was that the bill featured in the video—its text simply, "school bus must stop at railroad crossing"—would inevitably include an amendment gutting rail safety regulations, written mostly by BNSF lobbyists.

Also, lawmakers almost never write their own bills.

Also, the committee process is being increasingly circumvented by the White House and congressional leadership.

Also, bills can't talk.

It left out a lot.

First, some basics: legislation is any measure that is submitted to, and possibly considered by, Congress. It can be divided into a few categories. *Bills* and *joint resolutions* are effectively the same: measures, if passed by both chambers of Congress and signed by the president (or through a veto override with two-thirds support in both houses), that have force and effect on U.S. law and federal entities. In practice, *bills* cover most areas of lawmaking. *Joint resolutions* are typically reserved for grander things like constitutional amendments, certain budget appropriations, and war declarations—it's like a parliamentary smoking jacket. A *simple resolution* expresses the sense of one chamber, such as ones honoring Super Bowl champions or the life of a deceased luminary. *Concurrent resolutions* are ones requiring passage in both chambers but do not require presidential approval, like the establishment of joint committees or scheduling a joint session of Congress for, say, a State of the Union address.

Much of what the legislative branch scrutinizes pertains to the federal budget, made up of the twelve appropriations bills that—in theory, though not always in practice—weave their way through the relevant committees and onto the chamber floor, first as authorization bills authorizing government's agencies and programs and then as appropriation bills that dish out funds for said agencies and programs. There are other forms of legislation, of course, including supplemental appropriations, which distribute funds for typically unanticipated developments like wars and disasters. Then there are changes to the country's laws, regulations, and tax code. All of these end up on the president's desk for a signature or veto (saving a veto-proof majority in both chambers).

While spending bills must originate from the House, there's no fixed way in which other House and Senate legislation is introduced.

Some bills are introduced in tandem, while other times a companion bill is only introduced after its counterpart has passed the other chamber.

To help us understand the byzantine rules governing this process, let's take an issue—*child labor laws*—and follow the process through which proposed legislation relating to that issue—*repealing child labor laws*—makes its way through Congress and to a president's desk. Before we start, however, it's important to note that with Congress's heightened partisanship, important bills are increasingly being cobbled together by a select few members of leadership in conjunction with the White House and then sent directly to the House and Senate floors for a vote—this is the case with a lot of the last-minute spending bills that avert a government shutdown. You may hear members of Congress urging the return to "regular order," which is the process, more or less, described below.

Stage 1: Drafting and Introduction

Big government is destroying jobs, it's driving our manufacturing sector overseas, weakening our competitive advantage, and, through its tyrannical overreach, it's telling us what we can and can't do with our kids. Right now, countries ranging from Eritrea to Pakistan to China are the stages of veritable economic *booms,* all enjoying robust employment—you hear that? *Jobs.* Sweet, delicious, mouthwatering, fresh-off-the-vine jobs.

Are they shovel-ready? Sure, why not.

How? Their kids are stamping your favorite reality stars' names onto the butts of track pants in windowless rooms with exposed piping (and not in the fashionable way like at your favorite watering hole tended by the mixologist with sleeve tats who makes a killer Moscow mule); they're suffering heat stroke as they string up jute fibers to dry beneath the unforgiving Bangladeshi sun; their wee little calloused hands are riveting holes into sheet metal under the hawk-like gaze of a shop steward known only as "Fist."

We need to get us some of that.

Unfortunately, America's bleeding hearts have jammed a bunch of "child labor" regulations down the throats of small-business owners, cramping America's entrepreneurial spirit and depriving our children of valuable life experiences and valuable hand callouses.

We might think of legislation starting as a lawmaker's bright idea or as a line in a president's State of the Union address. This can certainly be the case (although the president cannot introduce bills to Congress—he or she must find an allied member in both chambers to do that); however, that policy spark can originate in any number of ways. In the case of child labor deregulation, it could be a trade group's lobbyist who presents the issue to legislative staff, along with some helpful numbers and some articles they helped plant on RedState.com. Or it could be in a Heritage Foundation white paper that catches a White House or congressional staffer's eye. Or it could be a deranged congressional liaison in the Labor Department who is sick and tired of having to deal with child labor compliance paperwork. It could be the congressional aides themselves who, in the course of their research and meetings, come up with the idea. It could be an item on a party's official platform, and immediately factored into the majority's legislative planning.

For the purposes of our discussion, let's say the child labor bill *wasn't* part of a party's legislative agenda, but rather an initiative for which a lawmaker must drum up support. If our fictional lawmaker wants to unshackle America's children from being unshackled to work benches, his staffers must first draft a bill.

If you've ever glanced at a bill's text and felt like you were looking at the garble of code that Windows spits at you when it performs an illegal operation, you're not alone. In fact, most of the staffers on Capitol Hill probably share your bewilderment and are no more able to instantly metabolize, much less draft, legislative jargon.

> *If the amounts appropriated under subparagraph (A) are not fully obligated under grants under paragraph (1) . . .*
>
> *. . . the Commodity Exchange Act (7 U.S.C. 1a(19)(A)(iv)*

(II)) (as redesignated by section 721(a)(1)) is amended by inserting before the semicolon at the end the following . . .

These are two randomly selected segments of the Affordable Care Act and the Dodd-Frank Wall Street reform bill, respectively. If you're not a lawyer, but insist you can look at stuff like this and immediately *get it,* you're probably one of those insufferable types who swear that *Ulysses* is their favorite book. Shut up. You're the worst.

It's for this reason that many lobbyists, advocates, and other interested parties regularly provide congressional staff with predrafted legislative language, courtesy of their own lawyers. Examples of this abound. In 2013, per *The New York Times,* lobbyists for Citigroup successfully had their predrafted language inserted into legislation watering down Dodd-Frank. Of the eighty-five-line bill, seventy lines appeared to contain the lobbyists' recommendations and two whole paragraphs effectively copied their language outright.

Staffs who don't have a lobbyist or activist *helpfully* providing legislative language can consult the Office of Legislative Council, a nonpartisan office in Congress tasked with transforming legislative ideas ("make children stitch shoes") with legislative language ("AN ACT to amend U.S.C. 4b(54)(C)(ix)(III)"). The office is staffed with a number of very capable lawyers—soliciting their services isn't like accepting an overworked court-appointed public defender—but even the act of dealing with the Office of Legislative Council can take away from a staffer's already hectic schedule. Petitioners who provide carefully curated issue summaries or legislative language know staffers are under pressure to take whatever help they can get.

In the Senate, a bill is introduced when a member is recognized by the chamber's presiding officer. Another senator can object to the introduction of a bill, forcing the proposing member to wait a day before offering it again, but this is a massively assholic thing to do and it is rarely done. A single senator will introduce a bill and if any wish to be listed as an "original cosponsor" they can announce their sponsorship the day the measure is introduced. Cosponsorhip in both chambers is a mostly ceremonial distinction that lawmakers use to express strong support of a particular bill.

In the House, a bill is officially introduced when a member walks up to the chamber's well and drops the bill into the hopper, a small wooden box to the side of the dais. Inserted properly, this makes a very satisfying *thunk*. Given the small number of proposed bills that ever become law, or are much less considered by the whole chamber, the hopper is basically America's suggestion box. A member might as well walk up and slip in a piece of paper with "more yogurt in office fridge" scribbled on it.

Once a bill is introduced, the bill is assigned a number and sent to the Government Printing Office, at which point a bunch of trees will die in the name of a nonbinding resolution honoring *The Carol Burnett Show,* or a bill appropriating money to a fighter jet that can't take off and whose engine sounds like a hamster coughing. In our case, it's a bill permitting children to work ninety hours a week in a cavernous den of sadness.

The number assigned a bill—H.R. 4832, S. 532, or whatnot—is typically the next available one. Leadership puts a considerable amount of thought into deciding what bill will be granted the valuable real estate of H.R. 1 or S. 1. The "one" bills are to members of Congress what the "GO SAWX" vanity plate is to Massholes.

The process of corralling members' support begins well before a bill's introduction and often lasts right up until the final votes are cast on a House and Senate's reconciled bill. That said, it is usually around the introduction of a bill that the hunt for cosponsors begin. As mentioned earlier, cosponsorship of legislation is purely decorative. However, very few bills that make their way to the president's desk don't contain a healthy number of sponsors.

Cosponsors are enticed in any number of ways. Some are voluntary, hoping to associate themselves with a measure for some ideological or political reason (or both). Some are encouraged by leadership. Others are lobbied by the bill's sponsor during votes, in the halls of Congress and through "Dear Colleague" letters sent between members. Many more are encouraged by outside actors, be they lobbyists, letter writers (perhaps organized by lobbyists), or advertisements in the Metro stations around the Capitol.

Like the *Schoolhouse Rock!* bill noted, most legislation doesn't go anywhere. Roughly ten thousand combined bills are introduced in the upper and lower chamber every congressional session, only a fraction of which will ever become law. In the 113th Congress of early 2013 to early 2015, only 4 percent of the nearly ten thousand bills submitted received a vote on a chamber floor. Only 3 percent became law. The bills would have an easier time getting into Harvard.

Yet one thing that the *Schoolhouse Rock!* bill failed to mention was that most legislation—nearly all of it, really—is introduced without any expectation of passage. While some members may foster delusions of grandeur, your standard backbencher isn't like those downcast people you see buying lottery tickets at your local deli every morning. That bill providing free college to every student in the country isn't going to be a politician's political meal ticket.

Still, legislation resonates, and a bill is a tangible thing supporters can rally around, and a comparatively easy way for a lawmaker to signal to an interest group or constituency that he or she has their interests in mind. What's more, a lawmaker doesn't have to spend any real political capital by submitting a bill, so long as it doesn't stray too far from their party's platform or isn't a nonbinding resolution proclaiming that the speaker smells like fetid swamp water. Bills are also great way to put the opposing side in a bind by forcing lawmakers to take a documented stand on a potentially damaging issue.

However, our child labor bill is not going to be one of the 97 percent. This one is going to pass. America's kiddies are going to be breathing in vaporized aluminum while constructing iPhones in no time. They'll be building character, too. But iPhones, mostly.

Stage 2: Committee

After a bill is submitted, it must be assigned to the committee or committees that have jurisdiction over the bill's subject matter.

Indeed, bills are often split up and their constituent parts referred to different committees. The House speaker or the presiding Senate officer may refer the bill to the appropriate committee, but that task usually falls to a parliamentarian, as the House speaker and presiding Senate officer are probably off at a fundraiser, delivering a canned address about the party's strength in the upcoming midterm to donors noshing on mini-quiches.

In the case of our child labor bill, it would probably be referred to the Health Education, Labor, and Pension Committee, or HELP, in the Senate and the Education and Workforce Committee in the House. Once added to the panels' schedule, the committees' chairpersons assign the measure to one of their subcommittees, in this case the Subcommittee on Workforce Protections in the House and the Subcommittee on Employment and Workplace Safety in the Senate. Being referred to a committee might imply that a bill will come up for consideration at some point, but it's a bit like being put on a waiting list for a college: your name might never reach the top, and even if it does, there's a good chance that the agenda of some rich guy whose family name is plastered on its business school is going to supercede yours.

There are myriad factors that go into what bills come up for committee consideration. First and foremost is necessity. Necessity, as they say, is the mother of invention; it's also, in this instance, the mother of measures letting children work backbreaking factory jobs. Interest groups will use every tool at their disposal to motivate Congress from its default intransigence by convincing it that their agenda is of the utmost urgency. There's a reason spending bills are the only things that ever get passed in a divided Congress: if Congress left the lights off too long, they'd be out of jobs.

Good relations with the committee chair and leadership is another necessity. A committee chair ultimately decides what bills are considered by their panels, though not without consultation with their party leaders. Moreover, party leaders control committee assignments through their allies on the chambers' steering committees.

Irk leadership or its allies enough and you're liable to lose your committee seat.

Hearings surrounding our child labor bill are going to be pretty politicized, given the sensitivity of allowing children to spend twelve hours a day screwing the heads of Barbie dolls onto sexless plastic torsos, the fumes of freshly molded plastic slowly eroding their pancreases and the repetitive twisting action undoubtedly contributing to early onset carpal tunnel syndrome. Let's go ahead and assume Republicans will be pretty favorable, and Democrats pretty, well, *appalled*. Luckily, trade groups will prove invaluable, steering staffers to the Labor Department regulations and U.S. Code statutes governing these issues, providing talking points and even witnesses. Also, in our fictional Washington, Republicans control both the White House and Congress.

When the day of the hearing finally comes, there won't be many surprises. "I worked on a farm as a kid," says one supportive committee member in their introductory remarks. "It helped me become who I am." "Changing the oil on a combine ain't simple," notes another, "that's plenty hard work, if you ask me. Hemming yoga pants seems like a walk in the park." A third will expand on that, "Kids today aren't graduating high school with enough skills. I think some factory time might do them good, keep them off the streets." The committee will have arranged for some former child laborers from other countries to appear and testify to how greatly improved their lives were by work. Yasser was able to open up a roadside vegetable stand! Christalin was able to attend a local engineering college! Phuong was able to buy her grandmother a blanket! Democrats will huff and puff and quote Upton Sinclair or whatnot, but our fictional committee is controlled by Republicans, and ultimately the day will be theirs.

The powers a subcommittee is entrusted with varies from panel to panel, but after hearings, either the subcommittee or the whole committee will proceed to mark up the legislation. A markup is where committee members are allowed to offer amendments to the legislation. Liberal members might offer a completely new bill strengthening child labor protections. More moderate Republicans or Democrats may propose one prohibiting factory work during school hours. A member with a Kraft facility in his or her district may propose measures regulating the nutrition standards of gruel served in factory cafeterias—conveniently similar to Kraft brand gruel. Sometimes these amendments are packaged into a single measure, called a manager's amendment, but usually only if the package is agreed upon in advance. Eventually, the committee votes to "report" the bill and the committee's recommended amendments to the chamber floor, either in individual pieces or as a newly crafted bill containing the original bill and the amendments.

Stage 3: Chamber

HOUSE

In the House, committee-reported legislation is put on the chamber's calendar, though "calendar" is incredibly misleading. A majority of the bills passed out of committee and placed on the House calendar never actually receive a vote. Instead, the majority leadership decides which bills will come up for a vote. Again, it's good not to piss off the speaker.

Be warned, the House's standard legislative procedure is a little wonky, and if it makes you feel like you're staring at an Escher sketch—an endless, Möbius band of fat white guys in power ties—stare at this for a minute or two and then proceed:

Committee report → Rules Committee → Entire House votes on rules package → Committee of the Whole debates amendments → Entire House votes on amendments → Motion to recommit → Final vote

Got it? No? Look, I tried. *You* try making a mnemonic for that.

Bills that aren't deemed too controversial, or that have been previously agreed upon by leaders from the majority and minority, are usually voted under a "suspension of the rules," which limits debate to a scant forty minutes and forbids amendments. However, suspending the rules requires a two-thirds vote for passage. Otherwise, the Rules Committee will craft a special rules package for the bill, allowing just enough amendments and debate time to please a majority of members (preferably a strong majority, and preferably made up of members of the majority party). Before the chamber can begin deliberation on an item, it must adopt the Rules Committee package.

The Rules Committee is a standing House panel that sets the parameters on how certain bills will be considered on the floor. The panel selects which of the sometimes hundreds of proposed amendments will be considered by the entire House. It also limits the amount of time allocated for debate and the parliamentary procedures required to bring the final vote. Rules Committee membership skews heavily toward the majority party, and its members are handpicked by the speaker, giving him or her significant power over floor debate. The Rules Committee is known around the Hill as "the House's traffic cop," and it deserves more credit than it gets for keeping politicians from talking more than they have to.

With regards to our child labor bill, which is definitely not going to garner two-thirds support for a suspension of the rules, the Rules Committee might include an amendment allowing companies to force children who lose fingers to first seek redress through a mediator—as a nod to corporate donors hoping to avoid multimillion dollar lawsuits; or one providing tax credits to the manufacturer of ratty Dickensian sack coats—as a nod to the Ways and Means chairman who will be instrumental in a forthcoming tax bill and who is trying to keep a major textile manufacturer in his district from outsourcing; or one limiting redress with the National Labor Relations Board for children caught in Morbark 3036 industrial drum chippers—as a nod to Northwestern logging interests.

Debate will probably be limited.

Once the rules package is set and agreed upon by the full chamber, the House usually resolves itself into a "Committee of the Whole," an odd parliamentarian tool that turns the chamber into one large committee and requires only a hundred members to be present to quickly consider amendments with minimal debate and a simple majority vote. As arcane as this sounds, it's actually a fixture of contemporary House deliberations. The chair and ranking members of the committees that considered the bill typically are in charge of doling out speaking time for the amendment debate period.

Once the amendments have been considered, and members have said their two cents about job creation and the sergeant at arms has been instructed to remove the children in the gallery screaming about not having to work in iron foundries, the Committee on the Whole rises and reports the amendment package to the House. The Committee of the Whole then dissolves and the whole House votes on the amendment package. Per tradition, the House then considers a "motion to recommit," in which the minority party offers its alternative to the bill. Finally, the House votes on the bill. Unlike the Senate, where individual members signal their approval or disapproval to the clerk, House members have electronic key cards that they slide into a slot at the end of each row to vote.

It's a little wonky (OK, *a lot* wonky).

SENATE

The Senate majority leader runs the Senate floor, having first crack at being recognized by the Senate president and therefore controlling what bills are called up for consideration. However, his or her ability to control debate is considerably limited compared with the House speaker.

As in the House, bills passed out of committee are placed on the Senate's calendar, though this does not guarantee a bill will be considered. If the Senate majority leader chooses to bring up a bill, he or she could propose a *unanimous consent agreement,* which, like a House rules package, sets the debate and amendment parameters.[75]

---

[75] Unanimous consent agreements can also be invoked for any number of things, such as letting committees meet during a meeting of the whole Senate.

As the name suggests, a unanimous consent agreement requires, well, *unanimous consent* from the whole Senate. Anything more controversial than a bill urging America's troops to "Go get 'em, tiger" probably can't be considered under a unanimous consent agreement. Alternately, bills that have been worked out behind the scenes and approved by each caucus are sometimes considered under unanimous consent. Otherwise, the majority leader, or a member acting in their stead, offers a *motion to proceed* on a bill, requiring only a majority to pass.

A bill allowing America's youngest citizens to toil away in coal mines will probably not be subject to a unanimous consent agreement. So the Senate majority leader will instead propose a motion to proceed on the child labor bill. But we're forgetting one thing—cue the *Jaws* theme:

Duunnn dun
Duunnn dun
Dun dun dun dun dun dun dun dun DUN DUN DUN DUN
DUN DUN DUN DUN
DUNNNNN DUNNNNNNN

****THE FILIBUSTER****

Ahhhhhhh!

Senate procedure is primarily distinguished from that of the House by its lack of limits on debate and the number and types of amendments that can be offered. Any one senator can filibuster a bill at any time during its consideration—whether during a motion to proceed, a consideration of an amendment, or a final bill—by speaking and refusing to yield the floor during a debate. The "talking filibuster" of *Mr. Smith Goes to Washington* is rarely employed; rather the mere threat of a filibuster is enough to stall a bill. Senators will often put a "hold" on a bill, a note to leadership of their intention to filibuster a bill.

Absent the full support of the chamber through a unanimous

consent agreement, it takes a *cloture motion* to cut off debate and vote. Once a cloture motion is filed, debate continues for another two legislative days before the cloture vote occurs. It takes sixty senators, if all the seats are occupied, to end debate period on a particular question.

One of the features of the cloture process is that it makes it easier for the majority leader to limit the number of amendments considered in that period, a process known as "filling the tree." The tree is often filled to prevent members of the opposing party from offering amendments that might sink the legislation. If the cloture motion is agreed to, debate proceeds for another thirty hours and the matter is finally put to a vote.

George Washington famously told Thomas Jefferson that the Senate is the legislative saucer that cools the hot tea produced in the House. However, the sheer number of hurdles that the Senate must undergo to pass any even remotely contentious legislation has turned the Senate into the saucer in which the tea is placed, forgotten about, and then stumbled upon with disgust on Sunday night when the Senate is cleaning its apartment.

Filibusters have skyrocketed. Measured by the number of cloture motions filed to end debate, recent sessions of Congress have seen filibusters rise from roughly 40 percent of measures considered to about three-quarters in recent years. However, it's actually quite difficult to measure filibusters. Many holds aren't made public, and leaders will often not bring up a bill because of negotiations or even conversations in the halls of Congress that will never come to light.

Stage 4: Reconciliation or President's Signature

Though the Senate and House will sometimes vote to pass the other chamber's bills in their exact form and send them to the president, there are regularly differences between the Senate and House's version of the same bill. These differences can be resolved in one of three ways.

First, a chamber may take the other's bill, make changes to it, and send it back to the other chamber for its consideration. This often results in a kind of legislative ping-pong, in which both chambers send legislation back and forth with differing amendments, proverbially ripping off their shirts and asking the other chamber if they *wanna go.* In practice, this game of amendment chicken is resolved when party leaders convene to iron out any differences. It's rare that one chamber will, in a moment of collective humility, agree to the other chamber's bill for the greater good.

"The greater good." *That's rich.*

Secondly, the ping-pong may be avoided entirely if leaders from both chambers meet in private to hash out the differences in the bill and then bring that final bill to their chambers. Who exactly is involved in this process varies, as there are no official rules governing closed-door negotiations, though it almost always includes party leaders from both chambers and often the chair and ranking members of the committees that considered the bill. In these days of legislative gridlock, particularly around pressing budget matters, this part increasingly comprises the entirety of the legislative process

Then, finally, there are conference committees, officially sanctioned bicameral panels that hash out the differences in a bill. Conference committees are usually made up of relevant committee chairmen, ranking members, and other members who leadership thinks will not totally screw things up. At least one meeting of the panel must be public, unless both chambers agree to waive that requirement. After the committee has sorted out its differences, a conference report is submitted to both chambers for their approval. Like asking your girlfriend's parents for their daughter's hand in marriage, a conference committee is a nice gesture and a charming acknowledgment of traditional norms. However, like consulting one's putative in-laws, a conference committee can bring on more risk than is necessary.

Once the two chambers have passed the same bill, it is enrolled and sent to the president for his or her signature or veto. The commander in chief has ten days (not including Sunday—*what up, Jesus!*) to act on the bill, otherwise it becomes law (unless Congress is officially adjourned). If the president vetoes the bill, it is sent back to the chamber in which it originated. If two-thirds of the members of that chamber, and two-thirds of the other chamber, choose to override the veto, then the bill becomes law.

Once the bill is enacted, it is sent to the office of the federal registrar at the National Archives, assigned a public law number, and will spend the rest of its days looking with envy at the Constitution, the Articles of Confederation, the Bill of Rights, and all the other fancy bills that get to live in plexiglass display cases at the Archives.

Congratulations, our kids are now free to work.

One last thing, much fuss is made over the length of modern bills. The sight of a lawmaker, typically a "small government" conservative, standing beside a comically huge stack of paper while bemoaning the complexity of the law, is common. The 1913 bill establishing an income tax, for example, was a mere 14 pages while the Dodd-Frank financial reform bill of 2010 was a whopping 360,000 words, roughly three times the length of this book. There's no one explanation for the exponential growth of legislation. For one thing, the growth of government means legislators must consider the sweeping bureaucracy when drafting legislation. Partisanship means bills must be written to include countless clauses and considerations that please all parties involved. The declining number of bills passed by Congress and the molasses-slow way it works means each bill must contain more provisions. And, finally, America has become a more litigious place, and legal language must be thorough so as to be "airtight" (though in loophole crazy Washington, this should be taken with a grain of salt).

See also, *"Budget," "Hearing," "Legislative Glossary," "Lobbying," "Cash Committees," "Scoring," "Wonk"*

LEGISLATIVE GLOSSARY

Because C-SPAN is confusing. See "Legislation" for more legislative wonkery.

Act—Any piece of legislation—a bill, a joint resolution—that has passed both chambers of Congress. These days, it's hard for any proposed piece of legislation to reach Act status in one go, unless it's a nonbinding resolution honoring a bald eagle that is also a small-business-owning veteran.

Ad hoc committee—Literally meaning "for this" in Latin, an ad hoc committee is a congressional panel created to study a specific issue that is typically disbanded after it has fulfilled said purpose (i.e., the Select Committee on Homeland Security, which was established in 2002 to develop recommendations for the creation of a Homeland Security department).

Adjournment—Motion to end the day's business. Parliamentarian for *GTFO*.

Adjournment sine die—Motion to finish the business of an entire legislative session. Congress's way of yelling *"School's out!!!,"* throwing all its papers up in the air, rushing outside, and playing stickball. That is, unless you lost your reelection, in which case you skip the stickball and beeline for the nearest lobbying firm.

Amendment—A change to a bill that must be voted on before it becomes part of the larger measure. A really great way to kill said measure. See "Legislation."

Appeal—In the Senate, any member can appeal a ruling by the chair, at which point the whole body has to vote on its validity. This is the legislative equivalent of wasting time during a soccer match by faking an injury—you'll look like a tool and everyone will despise you for it.

Appropriation—Act that *allots* a specified amount of money to a federal agency. See "Budget."

Authorization—Act that *allows* for the creation and funding of a program or an agency. See "Budget."

Author—The legislator who introduces a bill, though he or she almost certainly didn't write the actual bill. That honor may well have gone to a lobbyist.

Calendar—The official listing of days a chamber will be in session, typically published by the number-two member of the majority party—the majority leader in the House and the Whip in the Senate—at the beginning of each legislative term. These schedules are only tentative and can change, particularly if either chamber needs more time to finish its work, which is almost always. Has more four-day weekends than Johnny Carson.

Chaplain—Clergyman each chamber appoints at the beginning of a legislative session to lead morning invocations and be their leading spiritual adviser. Every chaplain to date has been Christian, and only three Catholics have ever served in either chamber (Charles Constantine Pise served in 1832 and remains the only Catholic to ever serve as Senate chaplain). Guest chaplains are regularly invited, and often represent other faiths. A good chaplain must have the self-control not to call for Congress to burn in eternal hellfire, a rare ability among the citizenry.

Christmas tree—Bill that elicits a large number of amendments—legislative ornaments, if you will.

Clean bill—A bill reported out by a committee that has been repackaged to include all the amendments that the panel added to the original proposal. Bills finished undergoing committee consideration often look like the legislative equivalent of Keith Moon's hotel room. A clean bill allows the larger chamber to consider a measure in a more expeditious manner, rather than having to slog through each individual amendment.

Clerk/Secretary—Parliamentary geeks. Each chamber chooses a clerk (House) or secretary (Senate) at the beginning of each session to handle routine legislative business. The clerk/secretary receives and sends messages from and to the other chamber and the White House—news of a bill's passage, veto, and so forth—and also handles official paperwork like roll calls and official lists of members. During sessions, they handle questions of order from members, which are all but certain to occur given the complexity of parliamentary procedure. Both are responsible for handling the collection, storage, and distribution of lobbying disclosures. These poor souls have to watch Congress. Every day.

Closed session—Session of either chamber that is not open to the public, usually to consider matters of national security, though also when articles of impeachment are being debated. When Mitch McConnell lets loose and wears his "FBI—FEMALE BODY INSPECTOR" shirt.

Cloture—Motion in the Senate that cuts off debate (i.e., filibusters) and sets in motion a final vote on a bill. Source of untold frustration and decisions to give it all up for a better paying gig in the private sector. See "Legislation."

Companion bill—Bill that is similar or identical to one introduced in the other chamber. Two bills introduced simultaneously by a House and Senate member that contain identical language beefing up animal protection laws might be introduced as S. 32 Critter Protection and Security in the Senate and H. 543 Let's Keep Our Ferrets Safe in the House.

Concurrent resolution—See "Legislation."

Conference committee—See "Legislation."

Conference report—See "Legislation."

Congressional record—Transcription of all congressional activity in the two chambers and in committee. Remarks are often truncated, their full text submitted to the congressional record—a small mercy for the rest of us.

Controlled time—House agreement allocating a specified amount of time of debate to both parties (Senate debate is indefinite unless cloture is invoked). Designated members from both parties then divvy up speaking time for their members. Thus the "Yield the remainder of my time" you always hear on C-SPAN.

Earmark—See "Pork."

Ex officio—The status of a committee chair to participate in, but not vote on, bills up for consideration in their subcommittees. Literally "by virtue of one's status." Try sprinkling this one into your daily conversation. "Daaaaaaad, why are you reading my texts?" "Because I am your father, an ex officio a member of your text chain with Sophie and Suzanne."

Executive business—Senate business originating from the White House, namely treaties and nominations. That no spiteful majority leader has yet to rename this "the junk pile" is really astonishing.

Executive communication—Official notice from the White House, perhaps about a nomination, or a bill veto.

Filibuster—See "Legislation."

Filling the tree—Tactic by Senate majority leader to use all the opportunities to offer amendments to a bill, thereby depriving other members of the chance—much like decorating a legislative Christmas tree. If Senate majority leaders could dissuade other members from amending a bill by licking it, they would.

Floor—Term for the Senate and House chambers and any business that occurs in them. *Example:* "H. 523 Ronald, Please Stop Letting Your Doberman Pinscher Crap on My Lawn passed out of the House Judiciary Committee and was sent to the floor today."

Floor manager—"You want a bill?" every House and Senate leader in history has asked their members. "That's fine. Just be prepared to walk it, feed it, and care for it." The floor manager is assigned with overseeing floor activity for a specific bill. Managers are tasked with, among a million other responsibilities, handling conference committee negotiations and divvying up debate time on the floor.

Germane—Both a word on every stack of SAT vocabulary study cards gathering dust underneath the beds of America's high school juniors and also the rule that any amendment to a bill in the House must relate to the larger piece of legislation under consideration. Members hoping to attach their amendment to an economic stimulus package must be ready to defend the germaneness of naming a highway on-ramp after themselves to the nation's economic prosperity.

Hold—The ability of any senator to place an anonymous hold on a piece of legislation. Technically a hold is just a senator informing their leader that they intend to filibuster a piece of legislation. They say that the Senate is comprised of a hundred presidents-in-waiting. Nothing embodies that saying quite like the hold.

House calendar—A list of all bills in the lower chamber that do not involve revenue. Those hoping to learn when a Republican constitutional amendment outlawing baggy pants will come up for a vote should consult the House calendar.

Joint committee—A committee comprised of members of both chambers. Joint committees typically have all the force and effect of a strongly worded letter to an editor. Some joint committees are standing, meaning they exist from session to session, like the Joint Economic Committee (publishing economic reports), the Joint on the Library (overseeing the Library of Congress), and the Joint Committee on Printing (Congress's own Kinkos). Chairmanship of joint committees typically switches chambers between sessions.

Joint meeting or joint session—A meeting of both chambers of Congress. Such meetings tend to be for joint addresses of Congress, like the State of the Union and a speech by a visiting dignitary. A joint meeting is like a family reunion, especially when your uncle's family adopts a unanimous consent agreement to convene with your family at the All-Star Movies Resort at Walt Disney World.

Layover—Both what Hill schedulers desperately try to avoid when booking their bosses' travel and also the period after a bill has been reported out of committee and before it is presented on the chamber floor. Usually a layover period lasts one full legislative day and after the committee report has been made available for two calendar days.

Legislative day—Not necessarily a full rotation of the Earth on its axis. A legislative day consists of the period of time between a chamber being gaveled into session and its adjournment. Senate rules allow for the rules to be changed only on the first day of legislative business, meaning the first day of the Senate can stretch on for weeks as possible changes are considered and debated.

Markup—Term for a committee's preparation of legislation, including the offering of amendments and the chairman's staff director conferring with the oil lobbyist over the language.

Morning business—No, not *that* (get your mind out of the gutter). Morning business comprises the first two hours of the Senate's legislative day. This is dedicated to routine business like messages from the House and the president and announcement of a member's retirement. Such business is usually skipped by a unanimous consent agreement. Sometimes it isn't, and sometimes it takes place in the afternoon or evening. Congress is weird.

Party secretary—Sees everything. Hears everything. One of the most important officials in Congress who you'll never hear about. In the Senate, each party appoints a secretary to assist party leaders with floor activity and to coordinate with their Democratic or Republican counterpart. Senate secretaries tend to have considerable experience as political staffers in Congress. Would make for a great protagonist in a wonky political thriller.

Pocket veto—When the president vetoes a bill by not acting upon it within ten days of its passage. Congress must be out of session for a pocket veto to occur; otherwise, the neglected bill becomes law. Literal pockets rarely factor into things.

President pro tempore—Senator designated to handle the day-to-day business of the Senate in the vice president's absence. Traditionally, the Senate's president pro tempore is the longest-serving member of the majority party. The president pro tempore almost always designates a freshman member of their own party to preside over the Senate, except during landmark votes or ceremonial occasions. Within the Senate chamber, the president pro tempore is referred to "Mr. or Madame President," making it one of the only times many of the chamber's members will ever be referred to as such, much to their chagrin.

Presiding officer—The unlucky member, likely a freshman, who has been chosen to serve as the president pro tempore (Senate) or speaker pro tempore (House). The presiding officer is the member tasked with sitting up at their chamber's rostrum, looking bored, and conspicuously leaning over as the chamber's parliamentarian or other knowledgeable official whispers instructions.

Pro forma session—Congress's nanny cam, the pro forma session is a meeting of Congress that is gaveled into session despite both chambers being effectively on recess, the main function of which to prevent the president from making any recess appointments while Congress is away. Initiating a pro forma session isn't as simple as placing a pink teddy bear with a GoPro hidden in its torso on the Senate dais. The Constitution forbids the House or Senate from adjourning for more than three days without permission from the other chamber. If either chamber isn't controlled by the president's party, the likelihood of both chambers agreeing to a resolution of adjournment is slim-to-none. So every third day, a member from the House and Senate has to show up, gavel their chamber into session, join the handful of tourists and pages present in the Pledge of Allegiance, hear the clerk announce perfunctory business—the resignation of a member, the signing or vetoing of legislation by the president—and gavel the chamber out of session. If there is a bill that needs to be voted on—such as one that had been previously changed in an uncontroversial way—another member needs to be present to hold the floor and cast the perfunctory vote.

Question—A term for any measure up for consideration in the chamber. Has a polite ring to it, which makes even the most grave matter sound like seating arrangements.

Quorum—The minimum number of lawmakers required to be present to conduct the business of the chamber, typically a majority—218 in the House and 51 in the Senate (assuming there are no vacancies). This rule can be easily circumvented.

Quorum call—Technically a motion in both the House and Senate to get members to the chamber. In the House, a quorum call is usually initiated during a vote after a member makes a point of order that a quorum is not present and the absence of a quorum is established. A buzzer will ring throughout the House offices, alerting that they actually have to go do their jobs.

In the Senate, a quorum call is a reading of the roll to see if enough members are present to constitute a quorum. A senator will suggest the absence of a quorum, causing the clerk to call out each senator's name to ascertain whether they are present. The absence of a quorum in the upper chamber is usually suggested to delay the proceedings for any number of reasons (to bide time until a member scheduled to make an address arrives, etc.). The quorum call is read alphabetically, and for years this meant that the last thing C-SPAN viewers would hear from the Senate before the network cut audio from the floor was the clerk intoning the name of Hawaii's junior senator, Democrat Daniel Akaka. As the C-SPAN camera would pan out, the viewer would hear a pleasant, sing-song, half-whispered "*Mr. Akaka.*" *The New York Times*'s senior congressional correspondent Carl Hulse actually published an article in December 2012 about the pleasant ring of Akaka's surname.

Recess—Any substantial break in legislative activity. Congress cannot be in recess for longer than three days without both chambers reaching an agreement. When either chamber is controlled by the party not in the White House, Congress rarely enters into a formal recess as it would allow the president to circumvent the Senate and make a recess appointment.

Recognize—Move by the presiding member to allow a member to speak. Parliamentarian for "Yeah, sure, have at it."

Recommit—In the House, the losing side of a vote is usually afforded the right to vote to "recommit" a bill back to committee for further reconsideration. As always, "further consideration" is politicalese for "never speak of this again."

Reconciliation—See "Budget."

Reconsideration—Both the House and Senate allow for a member of the winning side of a vote to offer a motion to reconsider the bill. In the House, the speaker will offer up a motion of reconsideration, thereby preventing anyone else from doing so and effectively making the vote final.

Referral—After a bill is introduced, it is "referred" to the appropriate committee, which may or may not take it under consideration. A reminder that the committee chair cannot be sucked up to enough.

Rider—A nongermane amendment to a bill. Much more common in the Senate, where there is no rule governing how relevant an amendment must be to a piece of legislation.

Roll call—A vote where each member's vote is recorded, as opposed to a voice vote. The support of only a small fraction of lawmakers is required to force a roll call vote. The opposing party will often ask for a roll call vote on votes that may be politically embarrassing, so members hoping to quickly shuffle away after a quick voice vote on S. 65 Here's My Shotgun, Now Take Old Yeller Out Back and Do What Needs to Be Done have another think coming.

Rostrum—The tiered desks behind the well of the House and Senate chambers where the presiding officer and various parliamentary officials are seated.

Sergeant at arms—Head of security appointed by each chamber. Mostly responsible for removing hecklers, though the House's sergeant at arms gets to yell "MR. SPEAKER, THE PRESIDENT OF THE UNITED STATES" before the State of the Union. The sergeant at arms is empowered, at the direction of the chamber, to forcibly bring members to the chamber, as happened in 1988, when Senate majority leader Robert Byrd ordered the sergeant at arms to arrest absent senators, leading to Oregon Republican Robert Packwood being carried, feet first, into the chamber.

Session—The period when Congress meets to legislate. Each congressional term is comprised of two 1-year sessions.

Speaker pro tempore—Member of the House designated by leadership to preside over the House. Almost always a freshman member of the majority party, except in ceremonial occasions like the State of the Union, when the speaker presides, or when the experience of a more seasoned member is required.

Standing committee—A permanent committee dedicated to a specific issue area as opposed to an ad hoc committee, which is convened for a specific purpose and then disbanded. At the beginning of each Congress, the jurisdiction of each committee is laid out in the chamber's rules. The House rules for the 114th Congress, for example, describe the Agriculture Committee as having jurisdictions over "Agriculture generally." Got it.

Substitute amendment—Amendment that would completely replace the language of a proposed piece of legislation. This is

Congress realizing that, on second thought, it'll have the side of fries.

Supplemental appropriations—See "Budget."

Suspension of the rules—See "Legislation."

Unanimous consent—See "Legislation."

Veto—Presidential rejection of a bill.

Veto override—Act of overriding a president's veto, requiring two-thirds of both chambers to approve the override. Incredibly embarrassing for a president, falling somewhere between "biffing ceremonial first pitch" and "losing a war" in the spectrum of executive branch mortification.

Vice president—President of the Senate, occasionally recalled from touring Boys and Girls Clubs to break ties.

Voice vote—Vote where members are asked to register their support or opposition with an audible "yay" or "nay" (in the Senate), "aye" or "no" (in the House, even though recorded votes are referred to as "yays and nays"). The constitution actually calls for "yay" or "nay," but nobody puts the House in a corner. Because most successful voice votes tend to be unanimously supported, a more accurate expression might be the "yeah why nots and nays."

Yield—Act of granting another member time to speak. "Please" isn't the magic word in Congress, it's "yield."

Well—The open area between the chamber's rostrum and seating. Great for loitering.

See also, *"Budget," "Carveout," "Legislation," "Pork"*

LINE STANDERS

Individuals who are paid to wait in line for committee hearings, Supreme Court oral arguments, and other major Washington events with limited seating. For lobbyists, who want to hobnob with committee members and staffers mulling about during hearing breaks but don't want to waste time in line that could be spent meeting a client over Cobb salads, this is a highly valued service.

While the Supreme Court banned the practice in October 2015, it has flourished everywhere else. Missouri senator Claire McCaskill tried to ban it in 2007, but line standing is to Washington, D.C., what basket weaving is to South Carolina's low country, and that effort failed. *You* try telling Washington's lobbyists that they have to start slicing off hours of their days to stand in loafers or heels on marble flooring.

The new online "sharing economy" that has given us Uber and Airbnb has also produced sites like TaskRabbit, which can be used not just to get line standers for, say, an Armed Services Committee markup of a defense authorization bill, but also some of Washington's most popular restaurants. Rose's Luxury, one of D.C.'s hottest eateries and *Bon Appétit*'s "Best New Restaurant" of 2014, regularly features hours-long waits that are not irregularly endured by, you guessed it, line standers.

Many of D.C.'s bike messengers earn extra money through line standing, and the scene outside of austere hearing rooms before a major committee meeting is something to behold, with nicely dressed lobbyists, staffers, and other interested parties waiting alongside shaggy-looking men with messenger bags in spandex shorts. Many of the city's messenger companies also offer line-standing services, and one company touts itself as being "a leader in congressional line standing since 1985," which offers "high-quality standing services."

See also, *"Food," "Lobbyist," "Pork," "Washington, D.C."*

LISTSERV

An email mailing list and major source of Washington's inbox congestion, along with press releases from think tanks you've never heard of, reporters seeking quotes, and fundraising appeals "from" Paul Ryan with the subject line, "Hey."

Listservs abound in politics: there are journalist listservs, PR listservs, liberal listservs, economist listservs, blogger listservs, liberal economist blogger listservs—these things come in every shape and size. Some exist for reporters to share each other's "take" on a news item, others let activists hash out strategy, others feature spirited political debates between people from opposing parties, while others are simply ways for interns to find free booze. Many, if not most, members of these groups are "lurkers," people who rarely, if ever, chime in.

The most well-known D.C. listserv was now defunct JournoList, an email group started in 2007 by twenty-four-year-old *American Prospect* blogger Ezra Klein. The list was a veritable who's who of people who find sexual gratification in speculating about vice presidential picks and bemoaning the pitfalls of a chained consumer price index.

Several news outlets wrote about JournoList, but it wasn't until 2010 when conservative news site *The Daily Caller* published exchanges from it, featuring members making derogatory comments about conservatives and appearing to collude in its coverage of Barack Obama's presidential campaign, that it captured Washington's attention. *Washington Post* blogger Dave Weigel, who covered the conservative movement, was forced to resign over negative comments about the Tea Party.[76]

To many conservatives, JournoList confirmed their worst fears about the Great Liberal Media Conspiracy. It may not have *exactly* adhered to their vision of how that conspiracy bore out—hooded secret society members chanting in unison about single-payer health

[76] In one of history's most quintessentially Washington career arcs, Weigel quickly found a job at *Slate,* which at the time was a subsidiary of the Washington Post company. A few years later, after a stint at Bloomberg News, he landed back at *WaPo.*

care while encircling a sacrificial altar, atop which a bound-and-gagged teenage Christian rock concert attendee from exurban Columbus wiggled and grunted in bug-eyed fear—but these were definitely the lefty boogeymen and women of their nightmares.

To the list's defenders, the group was a natural extension of Washington's close-quarters social scene. A JournoList chain was not much different than a typical Washington party, whether at an ambassador's residence in Kalorama Heights filled with agency executives, TV news personalities, lobbying partners, and Supreme Court Justices, or at a groupshare rowhouse in Columbia Heights populated by young web journalists and political staffers. Washington types are going to rub shoulders and, quite often, speak with a candor that wouldn't be appropriate for a news article.

Perhaps the most legitimate knock against listservs like JournoList is that they accelerate and greatly magnify these interactions. Washington officials have always interacted behind closed doors; indeed, much of U.S. foreign policy was hashed out in the middle of the twentieth century over cocktails in Georgetown living rooms, but it wasn't like those partygoers could look down at their cell phones at any given moment and fire off an email about that day's vote.

However, time has shown that listservs might be as natural a Washington development as two journalists trading jokes about the Tea Party at a Halloween party. Klein ultimately shut down JournoList in 2010, but several different lists sprung up in its place, including one started by Weigel himself and another one that, in a very cheeky allusion to the JournoList controversy, called itself "Cabalist."

See also, *"Cards Against Humanity," "Digital," "Email," "Flack," "Hack," "Washington, D.C."*

LOBAEIST

Person who is both a professional contact and also *bae*—to use the kids' term for "significant other." Relationships between political counterparties, even those that present possible conflicts of interest, are natural by-products of Washington, a city founded for, and centered around, a single industry. High-profiles examples abound: veteran TV reporter Andrea Mitchell married Fed chair Alan Greenspan in 1997. White House Office of Budget and Management director Peter Orszag married *GMA Weekend* host Bianna Golodryga in 2010. White House press secretary Jay Carney married TV journalist Claire Shipman in 2001, when he was still a journalist with *Time* magazine. In 1998, an aspiring young reporter named Jake Tapper got a big break when he sold the *Washington City Paper* a story about his date with a White House intern by the name of Monica Lewinsky.[77]

There are countless other lobaeists who bridge the gap between newsrooms, the halls of Congress, administrations, and K Street. In 2015, *Politico* ran a piece detailing the relationship between Republican congressman and House Transportation and Infrastructure Committee chairman Bill Shuster and the top lobbyist for Airlines for America, the airline industry's top trade group. Not to be outdone, conservative magazine *National Review* ran a short item on its website detailing which of *Politico*'s reporters and editors were romantically linked to political operatives and lobbyists, including one of the article's authors, who was married to a lobbyist at DLA Piper: "[T]he Shuster story—particularly after all the steps the representative reportedly took to clear the relationship with House ethics officials—looks, on closer examination, a little bit dog-bites-man. And no one should know that better than Politico editors and reporters themselves." Perhaps as a gesture of intra-beltway comity, *National Review* quickly removed the story.

See also, *"Congressional Staff," "'Heads-up,'" "Lobbying"*

[77] Actual subhead: "Behind the tawdriest of headlines, there's a woman I wouldn't mind bringing home to mom."

LOBBYING

The practice, usually performed by lobbyists, of influencing government from the outside.

Lobbyists—from the greenroom-frequenting former senators all the way down to the mollusk-defending environmentalist—divide their days among meetings with members of Congress, administration officials, staffers, and other influencers and consulting with their own employers and political allies. Freelance lobbyists will also spend considerable time drumming up new business, conveying the urgency of a legislative situation to this or that corporation, trade group, and other would-be clients.

You don't need an MS in idle small talk to be a credentialed lobbyist—pretty much anyone can do it, and it's tremendously difficult to fail. Many, if not most, governmental offices accept meetings with interested constituencies,[78] and that is only compounded by an aversion among staffers to alienate lobbyists who might one day become partners in other legislative battles or quite possibly their employers. So as long you have the support of a semiorganized group of politically concerned citizens, a few talking points about jobs, and the phone number of an office secretary who can direct you to the relevant staffer, you can probably muster a few meetings. Most clients don't know this, and assume they're getting their money's worth when they're trotted out in front of some senator's legislative director or a deputy HHS administrator.

And even if a lobbyist fails to achieve their client's stated goals, so long as they can point to tangible efforts like meetings, public campaigning, or the insertion of language into bills, the oft-repeated refrain that "Washington is broken" will typically absolve them of guilt. *Hey, you tried! But . . . partisanship! And . . . filibusters! It's*

[78] That meeting might be with a low-level staffer, but it will still be held in a cool neoclassical building and the staffer will almost certainly exude importance by rudely checking their BlackBerry at frequent intervals.

hard out there! The moment Washington stops being "broken" is the moment lobbyists might have to break a sweat.

Even if it's difficult to fail at lobbying, some lobbyists are better than others. Influence peddling often happens below the radar, and the best lobbying often goes unseen. A decent lobbyist knows that loudly buttonholing a member of Congress during a fundraiser and bombarding them with platitudes—"This bill is really going to create jobs in your district, Senator, and I know the Urinal Cake Producers of America would greatly appreciate your support, if you know what I mean [*wink*] [*wink*] [*nudge*]"—won't get them anywhere, and could just as easily be forgotten by the lawmaker as it could offend their staff. Instead, a quiet word with the lawmaker's chief of staff or whoever is accompanying them about setting up a meeting might get them further.

And the best lobbying is also organic. A good lobbyist's Washington intelligence isn't cultivated by calling up acquaintances and demanding to know the skinny—though such occurrences are not unusual—but through the standard course of grabbing drinks with old friends, running into professional acquaintances in the halls of Congress, and bumping into a senior administration official as they pick up their kid from after-school sports practice at the Potomac School. When a politician is pitched, a good lobbyist will let their staff know ahead of time. When a direct appeal is necessary, a good lobbyist will choose their words carefully—"our client is concerned about toxic waste-dumping restrictions, can we get a heads-up if something develops on your end?" is far more effective than curtly demanding to know when the Keep Our Rivers Incandescent Act is being introduced.

But when we refer to *lobbying,* we aren't just referring to meetings or happenstance run-ins, but a litany of often highly coordinated plans that incorporate communications professionals, legal experts, and other secondary players.

To illustrate this, let's say you're a former legislative director for the Republican House majority leader, the number-two legislator in the lower chamber. Currently, you're a partner in the government relations team at the Washington offices of Wanker, Tool, and Douche. Word may reach you that the good people at Sweet and Succulent Produce International are worried about labor costs and are seeking to shrink their long-term capital outlays by implementing feudal-style employment practices—y'know, serfdom—at their sprawling farms in the Gulf, Pacific Northwest, and California. The CFO has run the numbers and concluded that binding, medieval-style work arrangements shackling people to the land for a lifetime of labor—their only compensation a miniscule fraction of the avocados they've picked with their leathery, weatherworn hands and any thought of escape squelched by the knowledge that armed contractors will hunt them down and drag them back to their corporate manor lord for harsh corporal punishment—would make Sweet and Succulent's next few 10-Ks pop.

However, the Debbie Downers in Sweet and Succulent's counsel office says such an arrangement is blatantly unconstitutional and would flout minimum-wage laws. Efforts at repealing such regulations at the state level have been a bust, and Sweet and Succulent is hoping to have more success at the federal level.

It won't be the most lucrative contract in history—this is clearly going to be a battle with labor and no Republican ever got rich convincing their fellow party members to hate unions. The fact is, the most lucrative lobbying contracts are usually the ones in which industries square off against one another—such as the 2011 battle over credit card swipe fees that pitted merchants (who hate them) against the financial industry (who loves them); or the 2015 debate over whether to reauthorize the Export-Import Bank, whose tariffs helped aerospace companies like Boeing but saddled airlines with higher costs. These battles don't usually create stark partisan divisions—legislative fights between moneyed interests often cause lawmakers to take sides with whichever one is a bigger employer or donor. As such, companies will pay more for lobbyists to help them make sense of the complicated legislative landscape and lobby those members who are caught in the crossfire and can't simply vote with their party.

What results is a lobbying arms race, but instead of increasingly complex nuclear delivery systems, the combatants' arsenal consists of wealthy men and women with $300 haircuts.

That said, Sweet and Succulent's money is still green, and even if it won't be your most lucrative contract, it definitely will make for a great case study on your website. And it actually isn't an open-and-shut issue. Your parliamentarian wonks will have to be brought in to draft legislative language that you can provide Hill staffers (this happens all the time), as will any members of your team with regulatory experience, and your constitutional lawyers will undoubtedly come in handy when the inevitable Supreme Court challenge comes to pass. The politics aren't that simple, either: some libertarian Republicans on the Hill aren't exactly gangbusters for the whole "indentured servitude" thing and some members in working-class swing districts might need a little push. Vulnerable Democrats looking to get in good with big business might be brought into the fold, too—a great way for your firm to increase its billing by bringing in some of your firm's Democrats.

Bipartisanship!

So your team will compile a pitch arguing that Sweet and Succulent's objective is not an open-and-shut case that your team is well positioned to handle. Like a politician soliciting donations by impressing upon their supporters how close the race is, how hard their opponents are fighting, and how they're uniquely suited to the job, a typical lobbying pitch—whether delivered over the phone, in an email, or in a meeting—will stress how essential their money is to tipping the balance.

So Sweet and Succulent signs with Wanker, Tool, and Douche. Fabulous!

Now come the ceremonial show-off meetings. To assuage any doubt Sweet and Succulent may have about your Washington bona fides, you'll immediately set up meetings with some of your most influential contacts. In your case, this will be the majority leader's office, where you previously worked before you "went downtown," as the saying goes. If you have contacts on committees that will be relevant to the serfdom bill, you'll also try to set up a show meeting or two with staffers from there as well. You just attended the AG Committee's staff director's wedding, so securing a meeting should be a cinch.

The staffers in the leader's office, most of whom you know well, will get what you're after and, being on the same career path as you, won't say no to the meetings. They'll know to nod understandingly as your client makes their case and airs their concerns and make sure to say how committed their boss is to the issue while more or less parroting exactly what the client just said. The truth is, your staffer buddies probably knew everything the Sweet and Succulent folks were going to say from the email you shot them beforehand, but you all know that this is just an exercise in making the client feel important. As most leadership offices are in the Capitol building—and not the less ornate congressional offices that flank it—the Sweet and Succulent folks will feel particularly special as they deliver their spiel in a room with high-vaulted ceilings, chandeliers, and paintings of dead white guys. Sufficiently impressed, the reps from Sweet and Succulent will conclude their fly-in feeling confident in your ability to press their case in Washington.

Before any of the real work can begin, you'll have to craft a potent political message, not just to sway public opinion, but to pitch lawmakers, who will need to be convinced that serfdom is in their political interest. Depending on the scope of your lobbying shop, you may have your own message experts, or you may have to outsource it to one of the countless political communications firms that exist in Washington and elsewhere. Whoever gets the assignment will conduct message testing, perhaps through polling or focus groups. In time, they'll discover that folks don't respond as well to the whole "lifetime of forced manual labor" thing and that images of scared runaway families being dragged out of hiding space beneath sympathizers' floorboards do not elicit strong feelings about Sweet and Succulent Produce International.

The messaging team will quickly realize they have an optics problem. So instead of focusing on the bad parts, the comms specialists will try to "refocus" the discussion. The naysayers are opposing *economic choice,* one of the most important freedoms Americans enjoy. Could Steve Jobs have created Apple if the big government sissies had forbidden him from working in his garage? Could Thomas Edison have invented the lightbulb, the phonograph, or the movie camera if these overregulation whiners were breathing down his neck about every last little safety infraction? Of course not! These would-be serfs, these smallfolk, these enterprising men and women of the land are writing their own economic story, but knee-jerk regulatory leftists would tell them that they don't know what's best for themselves and their families.

The real opponents of freedom are the enterprise-phobic nanny staters, not the opportunity-providing companies like Sweet and Succulent Produce International that drive the country's economic engine. And the jobs! While some of these naysayers are attacking an American's right to do an honest day's work, the Sweet and Succulent company is doing its utmost to create competitive servitude opportunities, ones that provide a wealth of benefits, such as energy-efficient hovels, short commute times, and semiseasonal harvest festivals with maypoles and several barrels of mead. And one cannot overstate the health benefits of fruit-based compensation. Y'know, what with all their antioxidants and fatty oils and the like. Even the leftists love that crap!

These messaging gurus also zero in on some of the folks who oppose your economic freedom agenda: radicals at the ACLU, *La Raza,* unions . . . Al Sharpton, for chrissake! The heuristics couldn't be more fabulous: a bunch of self-important radicals who elicit nothing but eye rolls from swing suburban districts bleating about the ills of serfdom. Soon, voters in the greater Columbus, Ohio, area will come to support these labor deregulations simply because they saw Michael Moore squawking *against* them on CNN. Your messaging gurus will conclude that this freedom-focused narrative polls much better than ones that harp on a few cases here and there of peasant mistreatment and revolts that are violently suppressed by the local sheriff.

Now that the messaging is hammered out, you'll need to get some facts to back it up.

You had urged Sweet and Succulent to contribute to the Constitution Foundation, a libertarian think tank. It's impossible to determine whether a think tank's position on an issue was directly or indirectly influenced by corporate contributions, but the fact is, this is a very common strategy that many Washington lobbyists urge their clients to adopt. So Sweet and Succulent's CEO mentions offhandedly, during a holiday gala for the Constitution Foundation and in the middle of a lengthy conversation about the benefits of serfdom, that he was strongly considering a donation.

[*Wink.*]

And wouldn't you know it, six months later, the Constitution Foundation published a white paper on the economic benefits of serfdom. Facts complete!

Public opinion isn't only shaped by full-page advertisements in trade publications (though you'll see to those) or talking heads who appear on cable news shows as "Republican strategists" despite representing a firm at the center of whatever issue is up for discussion (and if you're good enough on camera, you'll be one of them). It's also shaped by the news—the *actual news,* not news that, *after the break, will be discussing whether the War on Christmas is back* news, but *news* news. Reporters can be a lobbyist's best friend, no less a source of informational give-and-take as a staffer in a congressional or White House office. You might fire off a few emails with the white paper attached to reporters and bloggers for right-leaning outlets, perhaps after sending it around to acquaintances on the Hill. That way, when you send it along to the reporters, you can say that it's generating buzz on the Hill. Ginning up this kind of interest can engender a feedback loop, with lawmakers increasingly interested in issues that garner media attention and the media giving attention to issues that lawmakers are interested in.

With your messaging, facts, and favorable news coverage in hand, the time has come to lobby.

First, if you haven't already, you'll need to direct Sweet and Succulent executives to donate to the relevant lawmakers' campaigns: the chairmen who will manage the bill through committee (or committees, depending on how complex it is), the committee members whose votes will be crucial to its passage, any members you deem to be on the fence, and the congressional leaders who will manage the bill's consideration in the upper and lower chambers. The more money they're willing to cough up the better. Though there are contributions limits on traditional campaign entities, there are still ample ways to give, including maxing out a spouse's contributions, or donating additional money to a lawmaker's leadership PAC. Then there are super PACs and other political entities that are not subject to contribution limits. These groups can also receive donations from corporations, which Sweet and Succulent just happens to be.

A contribution doesn't guarantee a favorable outcome, but it certainly doesn't hurt, and it undoubtedly makes it harder for a lawmaker or their staff to ignore your entreaties. What *especially doesn't hurt* is a fundraiser, and at some point (or points) your firm and Sweet and Succulent will have to host fundraisers for some of the lawmakers you have in your sights. Though a collection of individual donations can resonate with a campaign, focusing all of those into a single event that is attended by the candidate themselves is a great way to telegraph to a lawmaker and their campaign the importance of an issue or industry. Even if the fundraiser doesn't yield much face time with the lawmaker, your point will very much be made. Washington's calendar is chock-full of fundraisers with names like "Oil and Gas Industry Lunch," "Railroad Breakfast," and "Auto Industry Meet and Greet." Why not have some "Produce Industry Luncheons"? At least it sounds mildly appetizing.

No one lobbyist can know every last Hill staffer, administration official, or regulator's top aide. At this stage, lobbyists will often cast a wide net, sending carefully worded solicitations to a large number of political staffers with the hopes that enough will take the bait and agree to meet. This can be difficult: while most politicos have familiarized themselves with the kabuki of pretending not to be lobbied while actually being lobbied, the lobbyist must stick to an oblique and polite script, so the staffer can save face and not feel as if they are kowtowing to the demands of a special interest. This way, the staffers can tell themselves that they are engaging a "stakeholder"—politicalese for "people who could make my boss's reelection a real pain"—about an important issue.

It's good to hold these introductory meetings as early in the process as possible, even before there's a bill that could be rallied around (although you will helpfully provide bill language drafted by your team). This will give you time to cultivate relationships with the relevant offices and staffers. The good lobbyists don't demand a meeting, but politely express their appreciation for the chance to discuss an issue of import to a key constituency; they don't blithely declare that the issue is open-and-shut, but attach an issue memo from a sympathetic think tank; they don't assume their boss will be on board, but mention an op-ed or floor speech they delivered that suggests a sympathetic view. Maintaining the kabuki is important, not just for decorum's sake, but also so the staffers can look at themselves in the mirror.[79]

After some weeks, months, or even years, after countless meetings and emails and advertisements in trade publications, after untold planted articles and op-eds, after endless committee wrangling, the bill finally comes up for a vote, is passed, and is signed by the president (in our imaginary world, the GOP controls everything for simplicity's sake).

However, the lobbyist's job doesn't end with the president's signa-

[79] Presumably a mirror fixed above a marble his-and-her bathroom sink that the staffers eventually install in the three-thousand-square-foot McLean home that they purchased with the salary from the job they'll eventually take at Wanker, Tool, and Douche.

ture. Despite the growing complexity of the bills that snake their way through Congress, the question of *how* a law is implemented is left to the relevant agencies and departments. A bill legalizing serfdom may become law, but some of the law's specifics—the minimum length of mead breaks, roughspun requirements, federally recognized harvest festivals—will be left to entities like the Departments of Labor and Agriculture. Lobbying disclosures regularly mention "implementation" as a reason for the lobbying and most major legislation is usually followed in the weeks and months after its passage by announcements from executive branch offices concerning the law's particulars. Truly, the job of lobbying is never really finished—something you'll surely remind the good people from Sweet and Succulent.

See also, *"Astroturfing," "Foreign Lobbying," "Fundraiser," "Legislation," "Lobbyist," "Pork"*

LOBBYIST

Individual who is employed to influence government officials on behalf of a specific organization, industry, corporation, or other entity.

Lobbyists have existed since the country's founding, and though the revolutionary period didn't feature any neatly furnished K Street offices with framed black-and-white photographs of bland urban scenery, the influence peddling was no less furious, though less widespread.

Consider William Hull, one of America's first "government relations" experts. In 1792, Hull, a former officer in the Continental Army, was contracted by Virginia's veterans to go to the capital at Philadelphia and press the newly formed Congress on providing the group back pay. Like so many of today's lobbyists, Hull formed a coalition—this one consisting of veterans groups—met with members of Congress, and dispatched letters to the nation's legislators. Hull's mission mostly failed—these things were harder without the benefit of Charlie Palmer Steak event catering—but that didn't stop him from making a pretty penny in the effort. About a hundred years before the literal revolving door was invented, Hull transitioned to government, ultimately becoming governor of the Michigan Territory. Like many revolving-door traversers, Hull ran afoul of the government, and was sentenced to be shot for how he handled the handover of Detroit to the British during the war of 1812. He ultimately received a pardon from President James Madison, who cited Hull's war service in his decision. It probably didn't hurt that Hull had a lot of contacts in government to make his case.

The scope of Washington lobbying has grown significantly since Hull's day. There are around 10,000 registered lobbyists operating in Washington, D.C., even more if you consider those operating on the margins of what constitutes influence peddling. Between 1996 and 2006 the number of entities with a Washington lobbyist shot from 6,681 to 13,776. Many of the nation's largest corporations will employ well over 100 lobbyists, both in-house and those retained for connections to specific lawmakers and expertise in different areas. Not quite an army, but definitely a healthy-sized company. We tend to think of lobbyists through the prism of the revolving door, though most begin their careers outside government. That said, the number of lobbyists with a professional background in the areas they're lobbying has increased dramatically in recent years.

Lobbying compensation varies: sometimes at generous, it's-the-property-taxes-that-really-make-owning-my-beach-house-a-chore levels; sometimes at even more generous, sure-I-guess-I-could-give-Netjets-a-try levels; and, on occasion, at meager my-Dodge-Neon-broke-down-and-I-missed-the-Save-the-Spotted-Wyoming-Prairie-Cat-Coalition-meeting levels. In 2014, the average pay for a Washington lobbyist, as estimated by the Sunlight Foundation, was $176,000, $2,000 more than a member of Congress.

Like Hollywood agents, and *Iron Chef* panelists, lobbyists are, in many ways, professional eaters—paid consumers of garden salads at Equinox, vodka tonics at the Hay-Adams, and coffee at the Hill's various latte-and-scone purveyors. A meal spent not catching up with a professional acquaintance is an opportunity lost. A lobbyist is just as liable to complain about obstinate freshman lawmakers as they are the jitteriness that arises from consuming four cups of coffee before noon. There may exist a conception about the high-flying lobbyist, awash in high-price alcohol, expensed dinners, and mountains upon mountains of cocaine. The first two may be true, and while there are well-documented examples of lobbyists enjoying a little *yayo* now and then, given the amount of caffeine coursing through a lobbyist's veins by 3:00 p.m., a line of nose candy would likely make for bad business, unless a potential client were looking for a government relations specialist able to punch a hole through a marble Corinthian column.

Despite the perception that lobbyists are all individuals of low moral standing and high credit rating, even the most humble, shrub-protecting, "Coexist" bumper-sticker-owning, used Prius–driving activist can, according to the federal government's definition, be a lobbyist. Legal definitions vary at the state and municipal level, but the Lobbying Disclosure Act of 1995 defines a federal lobbyist as:

> Any individual (1) who is either employed or retained by a client for financial or other compensation (2) whose services include more than one lobbying contact; and (3) whose lobbying activities constitute 20 percent or more of his or her services' time on behalf of that client during any three-month period.

A lobbyist is only as good as his or her contacts in government, and nowhere is that reflected more than on the "about us" pages in the websites of lobbying firms and corporations' government relations departments. This is where America's influence hunters display their professional accomplishments, proverbially beheaded, embalmed, and hung for all to see. Areas of expertise are all fine and good, but where that expertise was honed really matters. Not only are lobbying principals "former senior advisers" for this committee or that, but they are sometimes listed as an "*early* staffer" for a particular lawmaker, implying that they are more deeply connected to the office than their peers. A lot goes unsaid in these descriptions—"Had kind of an on-again-off-again thing with the legislative director, but they're still on good terms and their kids now both attend St. Albans"—but it's very much implied. Like many corporate bios, these will regularly include humanizing tidbits ("Between obtaining regulatory carveouts from the Food and Drug Administration for lab testing on puppies, Brent Hidewell loves deep-sea fishing").

That said, lobbyists—whether good, bad, or mediocre; whether issue crusaders or soulless for-hire power players—all fall into one of three categories.

Coalition

The coalition lobbyist represents umbrella groups, whose members typically pay dues. Lobbying coalitions can be collections of companies in a single industry, a confederation of corporations with a shared legislative goal, or a group of universities or municipal entities. As such, these lobbyists may not get into the legislative weeds the way a lobbyist for an individual company or organization may, but instead make sure that overarching agendas are pursued.

On the business side, the Association of Enterprising Employers, a group representing child labor employers, will keep its members abreast of political developments that affect all members—say legislative proposals forbidding gruel-based compensation or the automatic dismissal for children who lose three or more fingers fetching wrenches jammed between gears. Several dues-paying energy companies may advocate vociferously for the repeal of laws forbidding grinding up finger-poor children and compressing their tiny, tiny remains into fossil fuels, but the textile manufacturer members won't like what that would do to the child labor supply.

On the grassroots side, Americans for Mother Gaia will use its comparatively meager resources[80] to advocate for more muscular environmental regulations, but may not get too specific in its demands

---

[80] *"For the last time,* Oregonians for Climate Action, poetry is not a form of payment. . . ."

for a given bill. Californians for Environment Action Now may want a law calling for the destruction of ExxonMobil CEO's fleet of luxury yachts, while Californians for Environment Action Later may be content to key his Range Rover.

While coalition lobbyists aren't usually compensated in equity the way a law-firm partner might be, Washington's highest paid lobbyists often represent trade groups. The lobbyist for the Motion Picture Association of America—one of Washington's most plum gigs and currently held by former Connecticut senator Chris Dodd—earns anywhere from $2 to $3 million a year to rub shoulders with movie stars and urge members of Congress to crack down on intellectual piracy.

Reps for influential industries like pharmaceuticals, telecom, and health-care providers regularly pull in seven-figure salaries. In 2010, during the debate over Obamacare, former congressman Billy Tauzin was paid a whopping $11 million by PhRMA, the country's largest pharmaceutical trade group. That's not just wealth, that's Scrooge McDuck pool-filled-with-gold-coins-level rich.

Relations between coalition lobbyists and their constituent members can be complicated. Coalition lobbyists regularly complain of a perceived entitlement among members, who are said to regard their coalition lobbyists as employees, rather than a legislative partner. Members, meanwhile, sometimes find their coalition lobbyists hard to reach and deaf to their legislative concerns. Such tension is often the result of differing perceptions of what is considered significant. Three freshman members introducing the Creating Jobs Through Jobs Act may not make the Association of Enterprising Employers lobbyist's radar, as he or she knows the bill won't go up for a vote on the floor. However, a dues-paying member may be alarmed by a provision in the bill that requires child labor employers to pay for their workers' fingerless gloves. Such misunderstandings regularly end in snippy emails about how great it would be to get a heads-up about these things in the future.

The coalition lobbyist is often employed by a group with a banal or even deceptive name. A coalition representing payday lenders might call itself the Helping Hand Alliance—a benign-sounding name that can make one forget it exists to ensure that people are forced to sell their grandmothers' wedding rings to meet their 400-percent APR; a coalition of strip miners in West Virginia could call themselves Appalachian Growth; and a group of Christmas thieves chaired by the Grinch would be Americans for Sensible Holidays.

In-House

The in-house lobbyist is directly employed by individual organizations, unions, corporations, and other outfits who are either large enough to have their own legislative guru or for whom federal lobbying is central to their mission. The Minnesota Women's Health Network may want to see a federal law allowing birth control to be distributed at Scandinavian goods importers, but unless that is also on their fellow coalition members' agendas, it's unlikely that MWH be able to make its case unless it hires its own lobbyist. Similarly, Uncle Joe's Barn O' Stuff may be the Albuquerque area's second-largest locally owned retailer, but unless it can scrape together the cash for its own lobbyist, it will have to be content with crumbs from its coalition's table. Walmart's in-house government relations team, meanwhile, can focus its time and energy ensuring that the Department of Labor reclassifies its store greeters as livestock.

Many larger corporations will have their own public affairs websites, where they promote their agendas and weigh in on important votes. AT&T's "Public Policy" site, for example, features high-production videos touting how it's "betting big on America" through investment in broadband technologies. The site includes a blog widget, in which one can read "Thoughts on today's vote," an entry by the company's head lobbyist, former senior Reagan and George H. W. Bush official Jim Cicconi.

Like in-house counsel, in-house lobbying might not be as lucrative as making partner in a law firm's government relations operation or in a dedicated lobbying shop. That can depend on how much emphasis a corporation places on its Washington outreach. Some lobbyists can earn a spot in the C-suite and/or equity—Jim Cicconi is AT&T's "senior executive vice president—external and legislative affairs." Others are mere members of a larger counsel team. That said, the time an independent lobbyist would spend drumming up new business, a corporate lobbyist could spend having dinner with their family. Sure, the dinner table might not be made of the finest-imported mahogany, but life is all about trade-offs, y'know?

Freelance

A freelance lobbyist might work at a boutique firm or be a partner or associate at a law firm's government relations team, but does not exist to lobby on behalf of a single employer or trade group. Done right, there's good money in freelancing. From 1998 to 2015, the two largest lobbying contributors, the law firms of Patton Boggs and Akin Gump, distributed roughly $500 million *each* in contributions to candidates. Monthly retainers can run anywhere from four figures at smaller, boutique firms to upward of $50,000 at larger ones with research teams, paralegals, communications experts, and generally a wider range of services and contacts.

In addition to interfacing with clients and policymakers, the freelance lobbyist must spend a good chunk of their time seeking out new clients. Groups will often approach more well-established lobbyists with legislative and governmental concerns while greener ones must find new marks. Like any salesman, a good lobbying pitch will harp on how essential their lobbying will be for the client.

Freelance work can also be beneficial to a lobbyist's Rolodex. Whereas an in-house lobbyist might confine their business to interactions with the members, agency directors, and staff of specific agencies or committees, a freelance lobbyist likely has to cultivate relationships with representatives from a diversity of Washington agencies and committees.

See also, *"Food," "Foreign Lobbying," "Lobbying," "Pork," "Selling Out," "Transitioning"*

LONG RUMORED

Washingtonese for the "thing every reporter knows, but couldn't get three people on record about it." "Long rumored" is lazy news writing—"assumed," "suspected," "expected," and "anticipated" can also shoehorn an unconfirmed fact into an article without using the salacious and skepticism-inducing "rumored." Nonetheless, long rumoreds still crop up, even in prestigious publications. Long-rumored facts can be campaign speculation ("Long rumored to be contemplating a run, Mr. Webb is considered a long-shot to win the Democratic nomination."—*New York Times,* November, 20, 2014), sensitive matters of national security ("Foreign Minister Javad Zarif says it's time for Israel to follow suit and abandon its long-rumored nuclear arsenal."—*Politico,* July 31, 2015), and poorly kept secrets about a public figure's private life ("Tower has long been rumored to be a heavy drinker and womanizer, but the charge had not been leveled so publicly."—*Boston Globe,* February 3, 1989).

The apotheosis of a long-rumored Washington fact almost certainly goes to this 1998 *Boston Globe* article about the reported existence of a semen-stained dress belonging to former White House intern Monica Lewinsky and, in a way, to President Bill Clinton:

> The existence of the dress, which had been reported, then denied, then long rumored, took on renewed importance yesterday as the possible tie-breaking evidence in what many observers say will become a classic he said/she said showdown between Clinton and Lewinsky.

See also, *"Adultery," "Further Study," "Hack"*

LOOPHOLE

See, *"Carveout"*

M

MADAME TUSSAUD'S DISORDER

Madame Tussaud's Disorder, or MTD, is a condition where a politician, pundit, or journalist doesn't remove their TV makeup after a "hit," giving them the waxy, polyurethanic appearance of a Madame Tussaud's statue. Symptoms include, but are not limited to, a lofty sense of self-worth, a near-constant need to know if anyone picked up their "hit," and having the appearance of a walking, breathing cadaver.

See also, *"Booker," "Hit," "Greenroom,"* "Morning Joe"

MAIN STREET

Rhetorical symbol meant to evoke Rockwellian images of apron-wearing shopkeepers, old Chevy trucks with wooden flatbeds, laundry hung out to dry on clotheslines, Veterans' Day parades, and kids pushing hoops along the street with sticks. Never mind that the modern American main street is just as likely to have a payday loan center as it is a five-and-dime, or a run-down Dollar General as it is a family-run hardware store, or that it will just as likely be patrolled by meth-addled townies as by Sheriff Andy. Main Street remains Washington's favorite boulevard. Sure, there are plenty of other common street names, but nothing evokes America at its most small town, community-centric, "Come quick, Mr. Bixby! Trouble at the old mill!," quite like Main Street. Malcolm X Boulevard probably wouldn't test as well.

Main Street is usually referenced in conjunction with Wall Street, though it really is meant to contrast with urban areas in general, what with their glass monoliths that house godless money changers and soulless advertising executives who are removed, physically and spiritually, from the common sense and religiosity that define small-town life. The head of distressed assets at Goldman Sachs probably wouldn't know how to core an apple if his life depended on it.

You'd be hard-pressed to find a politician, talking head, lobbyist, or advocacy leader who hasn't appropriated Main Street at one point or another. "We must win it for Mr. and Mrs. Jones on Main Street," said House Speaker Nancy Pelosi in 2009 about the need for financial reform. In 2009, the National Association of Mutual Insurance Companies formed the Main Street America Coalition to lobby Washington on (or, really, *against*) financial reform. The Main Street Patent Coalition, a collection of national trade groups, launched in 2014 to advocate for stricter patent protections.

Very few of these bear much direct relationship to the problems and concerns associated with the Main Street of our collective imaginations. To date, there has not been a Main Street Alliance to Stop Windowsill Pie Thieves or Main Street Alliance to Retrieve Johnnie Manderson from the Well. Unfortunately, Lassie is not deeply sourced in the Beltway.

See also, *"Accents,"" American People," "America"*

MARK

See, *"American People," "Bundler," "Constituent," "Megadonor"*

MARYLAND

Land of crabs, Hons, and America's strangest accent. Also the state that surrounds most of Washington, D.C.

Washington and Maryland are virtually indistinguishable at their borders. "Suburban" Washington—Washington with yards—

radiates out from its urban center and begins well before its Maryland border. Maryland's border towns like Chevy Chase, Capitol Heights, and Takoma are mostly indistinguishable from their Washington neighbors, though the street signs are different and the roads slightly nicer. These are the types of neighborhoods that generations of first-year MFA writing candidates have described as "leafy" and "tree-lined," even though most neighborhoods tend to be lined with trees that have leaves.

Over the course of the twentieth century, Washington's racial divide spilled across its borders and the majority white and African American populations in Montgomery and Prince George's counties, respectively, reflect the urban flight that depleted the city of much-needed human and economic capital.

Montgomery County

One of the wealthiest counties in the country; the towns situated near Montgomery County's D.C. border have long served as bedroom communities for Washington's legislators, staffers, and bureaucrats. Its good schools, low crime, and comparatively cheaper real estate have made it a regular destination for upper-middle-class Washingtonians unable to cope with D.C.'s crime and lackluster schools (and high private school tuitions). Its strong ties to the federal government have reinforced its status as a liberal enclave.

It's also a boring enclave. Bethesda and Silver Spring's shopping districts feel like especially dull versions of the walkable "commercial promenades" you see in many cities. Luxury cars abound and well-to-do shoppers perambulate about recently constructed commercial "Main Streets" where they can peruse all the finest wares that L'Occitane, Cole Haan, and other upscale chains have to offer. Sure, there are Christmas lights strung across the street, and there might be a halfway decent French bistro here or there, and possibly someone busking outside the Apple Store, but . . . meh. These are effectively yuppie strip malls, providing deputy counsels for the Department of Transportation a highly manicured environment in which to purchase scented candles. Like Virginia, it's Montgomery's immigrant communities—who comprise roughly a third of the population—that are responsible for many of its more interesting cultural offerings.

Prince George's County

Washington, D.C., has the somewhat bittersweet distinction of not just experiencing white flight, but black flight, too. The downward spiral wrought by segregation, redlining, the War on Drugs, and all the other failures of twentieth-century urban policy also led to an exodus of the city's black middle class to the suburban environs of Prince George's County, Maryland, to the city's immediate east. It is the wealthiest African American majority county in the country, its economy buoyed by the well-paying and stable federal jobs both within its boundaries and across the border in the District and Virginia. It's also home to the University of Maryland, providing it with a built-in source of culture. "Prince George's County is more than a place to live," wrote Kevin Chappell for *Ebony* in 2006. "For the 500,000 or so Black county residents—many of whom are in occupations that range from doctors and lawyers to hotel owners and restaurateurs—it is home to a social, economic and political movement . . ." But P. G. County was not immune from the Great Recession's depredations. A year after *Ebony* published its piece, the economy crashed and foreclosures spiked to the highest levels in Maryland.

Many of the Washington area's predominantly black congregations still worship in District churches, despite mostly residing in the suburbs. Every Sunday, in mostly white neighborhoods like Georgetown, you'll still see throngs of black parishioners flocking to the churches their families have attended for generations. When developers reached an agreement in the late 2000s to construct a massive multiuse residential/commercial facility in Shaw, on the site of one of these historically black churches, it was also agreed that they would construct a replacement church in P. G. County, where most of the parishioners now lived. The old church's facade and spire is still extant, but it is now built into a block-large complex, complete with condos, a Giant supermarket, and Cambria Suites.

See also, *"Northern Virginia," "Washington, D.C."*

MASTER OF THE SENATE

Award-winning 2002 account of Lyndon Johnson's time in the U.S. Congress by historian Robert Caro; the third installment in the author's series of LBJ biographies. A sacred object among political bros, who uphold the history as a totem of yesteryear's overly masculine, zero-sum, back-slapping brand of politics that Johnson—and, by extension, said political bro—understood deeply. Like a lot of popular literature, the appeal of *Master* is as much about the content (which is truly impressive) as it is about letting people know that you've read it. The more dog-eared the copy of *Master* is on your desk, the better.

Put another way, *Master* is to wannabe political alpha males what *On the Road* is to moody college freshmen trying to let people know they're misunderstood, what *Infinite Jest* is to dudes trying to impress women on the subway, and what the Bible is to politicians. Interest in Caro and LBJ's take-no-prisoners brand of legislating was renewed by the 2012 publication of his fourth LBJ installment, *The Passage of Power,* which covered Johnson's ascension to the vice presidency and, ultimately, the presidency after President John F. Kennedy's assassination.

Inevitably, commentators draw comparisons, usually negative, between Johnson and the lacking tactical prowess of the present-day politician under discussion. "LBJ would never have taken this kind of crap from Democrats in Congress," the Bradley Whitford character Josh Lyman groused in an early episode of *The West Wing.* In August 2011, *Morning Joe* host Joe Scarborough lambasted President Barack Obama's leadership abilities. "A president that cannot control 45 backbenchers in the opposing party in the House of Representatives is too weak to be president of the United States," he ranted. "It is that simple. Lyndon Johnson would have eaten these people up for breakfast and spit them out before lunch."

Of course, both assessments are gross overstatements. Johnson enjoyed overwhelming majorities in both the House and Senate during his presidency—he could stand to lose some Democrats now and then—and also existed in an age of tremendous political flux defined by the kaleidoscopic politics of post–*Dred Scott* America that featured liberal and conservative members in both parties.

See also, *"Leaders (Senate),"* "Morning Joe," *"Whip"*

MEDIA MARKET

The area served by local news and radio networks. The media market in which a candidate runs strongly influences the amount of money he or she will need to raise to mount a successful campaign and how efficiently that money will be spent. The majority of the money a New Jersey gubernatorial campaign will spend on TV ads will be spent in the pricey media markets of New York and Philadelphia and will be wasted on viewers in Yonkers and Queens. This has contributed to very low turnover in the Garden State, where the price of mounting a challenge to an office holder can be prohibitively expensive. Similarly, Virginia candidates seeking to influence moderate suburban voters will waste a lot of their promises about fiscal austerity on liberal Washington, D.C., residents. However, states like Ohio with an abundance of medium-sized cities—it sports twelve media markets—allow campaigns to more ably target specific constituencies.

See also, *"Ad Buy," "Advertising," "Drivetime," "Finance"*

MEGADONOR

Breed of spectacularly wealthy political benefactor who, unbridled by the campaign contribution limits that once limited individuals from wielding too much direct influence, donates obscene amounts of money to a particular candidate or political organization. They're like modern Medicis, except instead of patronizing the age's leading artists they're patronizing the age's leading sociopaths.

For the time being, traditional campaign organizations like campaign committees and national parties are still subjected to contribution limits. However, the new campaign entities permitted in the post–*Citizens United* world like super PACs and political nonprofits (so-called dark money groups) allow individuals to single-handedly prop up a campaign, issue, or, in the case of the Koch brothers, Americans for Prosperity and the Tea Party.[81]

The amount that these guys (and, to date, they're all men, because why have a sports car when Newt Gingrich can be the Freudian expression of your phallus?) have dropped on political activity is astonishing. In 2012, businessman Foster Friess almost single-handedly propped up former Pennsylvania senator Rick Santorum's campaign for the Republican presidential nomination. In 2012, casino magnate Sheldon Adelson spent *at least* $100 million, first on Newt Gingrich and later on the GOP's eventual nominee, Mitt Romney. Overall, megadonors spent $2.5 billion on the 2012 campaign, surpassing the parties themselves, which spent a total of $1.6 billion. These amounts don't include any undisclosed donations to political nonprofits.

But megadonors have feelings, too. In 2015, when Donald Trump was leading the polls in the GOP presidential primary, some megadonors were disconcerted by the independence the billionaire real-estate developer and TV personality enjoyed thanks to his wealth. "This idea of 'I don't need to have any funding, I'll fund myself,' that scares the hell out of me," a befuddled Hubbard Broadcasting CEO Stanley Hubbard told *The Hill* in October 2015. "That's like a dictator. I think that any politician should have to answer to their constituents. . . . I don't think it's healthy to have somebody who doesn't answer to anybody."

See also, *"Adelson Primary," "Bundler," "Political Nonprofit," "Super PAC"*

[81] Though most of AFP's funds come from other donors, so they say, the Koch brothers have donated tens of millions of dollars to conservative and libertarian institutions like the Cato Institute and the Mercatus Center at George Mason University.

MEMBERS-ONLY ELEVATOR

Elevators in the Capitol complex that only elected officials are permitted to ride.[82] They were ostensibly created to reduce the time lawmakers needed to get from their offices to the House or Senate chamber for a vote. Today, they provide a respite for lawmakers who are pretending to talk on their cell phone to avoid reporters.

See also, *"Hideaway Office," "Office Space," "Senate Dining Room"*

MONUMENTS TO ME

Monuments to me are entities and programs named after the member of Congress chiefly responsible for their funding. Pop quiz: which of the below is fake?

a) Thad Cochran U.S. Bankruptcy Courthouse
b) James E. Clyburn Pedestrian Overpass
c) Mitch McConnell Distance Learning Center
d) Strom Thurmond Family and Fertility Clinic
e) Charles B. Rangel Center for Public Service[83]

Attempts to permanently curtail these Freudian expressions of power and virility have fallen flatter than a drunk off the James E. Clyburn Pedestrian Overpass. However, the decision by House Republicans in early 2011 to ban earmark spending has curtailed the pork that often results in monuments to me.[84] Though posturing against their continued existence makes for good politics, the out-

[82] To date, no one has tried to gain access to a members-only elevator by wearing a Members Only jacket, though we can't rule out that option.

[83] d)

[84] In 2009, Dave Obey, chairman of the Appropriations Committee and namesake of the $20 million David R. Obey Center for Health Sciences in Wausau, Wisconsin, tried to put the kibosh on the practice, prompting a heated exchange on the House floor with California congresswoman Maxine Waters, who was seeking funding for the Maxine Waters Employment Preparation Center in Los Angeles. Several bills have since been introduced to forbid "monuments to me," but none has become law.

right elimination of monuments to me rarely tops the list of parties' agendas for one obvious reason: the opportunity to remind voters of your legislative prowess by plopping an eponymous waste treatment facility in the middle of your district is too good to pass up.

The late Robert Byrd, who represented West Virginia in the Senate for over fifty years, deserves special mention for having procured over three dozen monuments to me, many of which he approved while chairing the Appropriations Committee.

An honorary mention goes to the late C. W. Bill Young. You may not know of C. W. Bill Young, the former chair of the House Appropriations Committee, but his former constituents in southeast Florida sure do. As pointed out by Jonathan Strong in a 2011 article for *The Daily Caller,* Young's constituents enjoy the benefits of the C. W. Bill Young Marine Science Complex, the C. W. Bill Young Drawbridge, the C. W. Bill Young Cell Transplantation Program, the C. W. Bill Young Center for Biodefense and Emerging Infectious Diseases, the C. W. Bill Young University Partnership Center, the C. W. Bill Young Armed Forces Reserve Center, the C. W. Bill Young Regional Reservoir, and the C. W. Bill Young Department of Defense Marrow Donor Program.

Hey, it beats a yard sign.

See also, *"Budget," "Legislation," "Lobbying," "Pork"*

MORNING JOE

MSNBC's politically focused morning show hosted by namesake Joe Scarborough and cohosts Mika Brzezinski and, previously, Willie Geist, defined by its breezy mix of political debate, informal VIP interviews, and lighthearted banter. The show's proposed title—"Middle-Aged White Guys in Tortoiseshell Glasses and Open-Collar Dress-Shirts Squabbling About Decorum in the Acela Quiet Car"—was scrapped in favor of the similarly literal but somewhat cleverer *Morning Joe*.

To the *Morning Joe* faithful, watching the show is like being a fly on the wall at the Delta departure lounge—the opportunity to listen in on the sage opinions of the jet-setting elite in a semiprofessional but nevertheless relaxed setting. To the show's detractors, it's like being a fly on the wall . . . *at the Delta departure lounge:* a group of expertly groomed and well-heeled professionals with too much regard for themselves—the types of people who smugly believe they have a firm grasp of the complexities of existence because they know the difference between revenue and EBITDA and one time read a will.i.am-penned op-ed about mosquito nets. What results is a sort of lazy centrism, a kind of feel-good establishmentarianism where the world would surely be a better place if our leaders listened to the hard-won knowledge of our swing-state senators and executives and simplified the tax code, did away with teacher tenure, and ran the government like a business.

One thing can be agreed upon: *Morning Joe* is an exemplar of brand building. Its ratings are lackluster at best; the program has not only ranked behind Fox News's morning program *Fox & Friends* in recent years, but it has also been trounced by less dominating networks like HLN and CNN. But so potent is the show's brand along the I-95 corridor that Starbucks not only sponsored the show, but released a line of coffee beans stamped with the *Morning Joe* logo. *General Hospital* may draw far more viewers, but it's unlikely we'll see a "Forbidden Passion in the Oncology Ward Blonde Roast" anytime soon.

That brand has been very much bolstered by Mike Allen, White House reporter for *Politico* and author of the widely read *Playbook* morning newsletter. Allen, a regular guest on the program, often highlights the show in his AM tip sheet. Nary a week—nay, a day—passes where the show is not referenced in one way or another. "MIKA BRZEZINSKI's opening question for the 'Morning Joe' roundtable: 'Romney won? . . . He was AGGRESSIVE'" cited Allen in the January 24, 2012, post-GOP debate edition. "JOE SCARBOROUGH SONG asks if there's 'Reason to Believe' decade after 9/11" read the boldface headline in the September 9, 2011 edition, drawing the reader's attention to a why-can't-we-all-just-get-along anthem released by the host (he fronted a band in his youth in Florida).

Morning Joe also features a stable of regular guests, many of whom are likely as familiar with the backseat of a Lincoln Town Car as they are their children's classrooms. Particular favorites are the media barons-cum-business people-cum-possible lobbyists who you can't exactly recall what it is they're doing now; people like Donny Deutsch, Tina Brown, and Harold Ford Jr.

One thing many of the guests share is a membership in the intellectual leisure class, the globe-trotting, business-friendly group of Very Important People accustomed to a certain level of living and whose understanding of the world's complexities has, quite frankly, been somewhat softened by the comfort of their station and the like-minded company they keep. Tom Brokaw, during a December 2012 *Meet the Press* discussion of the middle class, noted that "in large urban and suburban areas of America, $250,000 doesn't make you rich." Tennessee native Harold Ford Jr. was once asked—while he was mulling a primary challenge to New York senator Kirsten Gillibrand—whether he had ever visited Staten Island. "I landed there in the helicopter," he told *The New York Times* in a January 2010 interview, "so I can say yes."

The morning show, as it exists in the American cultural landscape, is both a stimulant and sedative. The show energizes the viewer as they prepare for their day, but in a manner that is defined by comfort and familiarity: a nice way for a host "family" to let the viewer know that their world is far less difficult and scary than it might seem. *Morning Joe* very much succeeds at providing the morning show experience to the early rising financial adviser, political operative, and other driven members of the burgher class. But instead of segments on five easy ways to create more closet space and familiar banter about getting the kids out the door, it's five easy ways to fix gridlock in Washington and back-and-forths about the difficulty of finding an Uber during rush hours—a way for their audience to feel a bit better about their existence and validated about their worldview.

That might be overthinking it. Like a lot of things in life, *Morning Joe* is a thing because it is a thing. Until that time that it stops being a thing, it will be a thing.

See also, *"Acela," "Booker," "Greenroom," "Intellectual Leisure Class"*

NETROOTS NATION

Annual series of sexual encounters interspersed with panels, political recriminations, and excessive self-affirmation. Started in 2006 as YearlyKos, a gathering put together by Daily Kos blogger Markos Moulitsas, Netroots Nation has become the year's foremost gathering of liberal politicians, progressive activists, left-leaning journalists, and other people who'd be perfectly fine slapping a trigger warning on *Bambi*. It's a can't-miss for America's bleeding hearts and a must-miss for people who would rather belly flop naked onto a bed of exasperated hedgehogs than attend a panel titled, "Who Leads Us? Tackling Structural Barriers to a Reflective Democracy."

As with any large gathering of a loosely defined political movement, Netroots Nation is an interesting cross section of the country's liberal political apparatus: earnest Midwestern do-gooders equipped with their nicest JanSport backpacks, twentysomething digital expert bros who hope their blazer/T-shirt combo will land them inside a woman, decreasingly youthful Gen Xers who mostly use Twitter to complain to airlines, and the liberal and liberal-leaning politicians who pretend not to be utterly annoyed by these people.

Like most conferences, Netroots plays host to headliners, panels, and smaller "breakoff" sessions. Some are genuinely useful: they help develop skills, make connections, and provide postgame analyses of elections. "Insanely Useful Tools You Can Use to Keep Track of Congress and State Lawmakers," "#EpicFail: A Look at GOTV Failures (So You Don't Repeat Them)," and "Problem, Platform, Program: Developing a Successful Campaign Strategy for Issue Advocacy" are among the panels featured during recent #NNs. Some other ones only drive America's left deeper into the intellectual muck of granular arguments that keep it from being able to put on a pair of jeans without wondering if they've assembled a broad enough pants coalition.

Though Netroots doesn't draw as many leading politicians as its conservative counterpart, CPAC, it does manage to sport at least a few A-list libs, whether in the guise of a few solidly blue state senators or a stray vice president who got lost finding the bathroom during a funeral. Its ability to draw major politicians has waned a bit in recent years, in part because it's hard to get a warm welcome at Netroots: attendees had to be reminded in 2008 not to be too icy to Nancy Pelosi for not bringing the Iraq War to a conclusion; in 2015, insurgent Democratic nominee Bernie Sanders was nearly booed offstage for not discussing matters of importance to minority communities. If *Bernie freaking Sanders, democratic freaking socialist from the freaking state of Vermont* can't get a warm welcome, it's hard to pitch a politician's team on having their boss endure the terrible visuals of being booed by their own base.

However, Netroots Nation does remain a potent force in Democratic politics and serves as something of a baptism by fire for those politicians who can't exist without the support (however grudgingly) of the base. For what it's worth, it didn't take long for Sanders to start incorporating those minority issues in his stump speech.

See also, *"Activist," "Astroturfing," "Digital," "Email," "Panels"*

NEW HAMPSHIRE PRIMARY

The country's second nominating contest and "first in the nation" primary, so-called because it's an actual primary, unlike Iowa, which, as was described in the entry on the Hawkeye contest, is a caucus—the rules of which are as easy to understand as a Japanese game show.

Like the Iowa Caucuses, the New Hampshire primary can make or break a presidential candidacy and one that declared and prospective presidential candidates make awkward excuses for visiting—"The minority leader is simply here to support his party's gubernatorial candidate and their Granite State–focused, jobs-creating agenda"; "There's nothing that New Mexico's junior senator loves more than the haddock chowder at the Old Salt Restaurant and Lamie's Inn"; "Nevada's governor is attending the annual meeting of the New Hampshire Podiatric Medical Association to . . . listen."

New Hampshire's primary dates back to the early twentieth century, but it was moved up ahead of the 1952 election, and Dwight Eisenhower's surprise win against Ohio senator Robert A. Taft established the primary as a crucial ingredient to winning the nomination. Though it was historically scheduled for the first Tuesday in March, other states' decisions to move their primary dates up forced New Hampshire's party officials to do the same, and it has been held, alternately, in January and February over the last few cycles.

In recent years, New Hampshire has become more of a politically distinct contest for Republicans than Democrats. While Dems do have New Hampshire–specific issues to contend with—specifically, *not* ethanol or embarrassing, corndog-based photos—New Hampshire's independent, low-tax, Live Free or Die streak makes it a much more alluring destination for more moderate and libertarian Republicans: John McCain upset the more traditionally conservative George W. Bush in the 2000 primary; libertarian-minded Ron Paul finished an impressive second in the 2012 primary; and his son, Kentucky senator Rand Paul, spent the lion's share of his early 2016 primary campaigning there, though he ultimately dropped out days before a likely embarrassing finish.

If the Democratic primary has become less differentiated from Iowa, the state's narrow demographics are to blame. While older white conservatives and libertarians remain major players in the Republican Party, the state's Democratic primary voters are not exactly representative of the national scene. Though the state has witnessed an influx of new residents, many from Massachusetts seeking retirement or the state's agreeable tax policies, the base could still be described as "white James Taylor fans in sweaters sipping hot toddies."

Indeed, despite former New Hampshire governor John Sununu's statement that "The people of Iowa pick corn, the people of New Hampshire pick presidents," the Granite State's primary hasn't always been an accurate predictor of electoral success. Hillary Clinton, John McCain, and Paul Tsongas are among the candidates who won the primary, but failed to ultimately secure their party's nomination. Also relegated to history's dustbin are other candidates who couldn't seal the deal after New Hampshire: there was Henry Cabot Lodge in 1964 and Pat Buchanan in 1996. And who can forget the generation-defining, youth-galvanizing political powerhouse that was Estes Kefauver? Oh, boy, those were some wild times on the campaign trail. Who among us doesn't know a Kefauver baby?

That said, you wouldn't want to bomb the New Hampshire primary, and beating expectations has breathed life into a number of struggling campaigns. Bill Clinton's surprise second-place showing in 1992 despite allegations of marital infidelity earned him the moniker "Comeback Kid." John McCain's path to his party's 2008 nomination began with a win in New Hampshire, prompting supporters at his victory rally to chant "Mac is back!" George H. W. Bush's 1988 campaign was revitalized after an Iowa whipping by Bob Dole by a strong primary, thanks in part to going on the offensive against his opponents but also to well-timed images of Bush manning snow-clearing equipment during a snowstorm.

New Hampshire can also be a momentum *killer*. In 1968, Michigan governor George Romney explained his support for the Vietnam War by saying he was "brainwashed" into doing so. George H. W. Bush's 1980 campaign was sunk after Bush stubbornly refused to participate in a debate. Ronald Reagan took the initiative, tussling with the debate's moderator, famously quipping (and misremembering his name), "I am paying for this microphone, Mr. Green" (it was Breen).

New Hampshire's also a great time to weep. In 1972, Maine senator and Democratic presidential candidate Edmund Muskie stood atop a flatbed truck parked in front of the *New Hampshire Union Leader*'s office and denounced the paper's publisher, William Loeb, as a "gutless coward."[85] Muskie took umbrage with Loeb's attacks on his wife and his move to publish a letter of dubious origin that claimed Muskie insulted Franco Americans—a not insignificant constituency in New Hampshire—for using the term "Canuck" during a campaign event in Florida.[86] It was reported that Muskie was so overcome with emotion that he shed a couple of tears. Muskie's people maintained that the water dripping down his face was melting snow, while press accounts maintained that he was, in fact, having a little cry. Remember that the next time you denounce the supposedly unprecedented vapidity of today's politics and media.

Thirty-six years later, Hillary Clinton—fresh off a bruising third-place finish in the 2008 Iowa Caucuses—choked up during a campaign stop in New Hampshire. Whereas Muskie's eyeborn droplets of woe came off as a manic extension of his frenzied state—also, *Franco Americans*? C'mon—Clinton's ocular salty discharge was seen as an earnest expression of a road-weary campaigner, a relatable instance of life's pressures weighing just a bit too heavily on her

[85] On the Senate floor, the term would be "friend."

[86] *Sacre bleu!*

shoulders. She went on to win the Granite State primary. Muskie's campaign was finished, though he took it in stride, later calling it "a watershed incident."

See also, *"Exploratory Committee," "Iowa Caucuses," "South Carolina Primary," "Super Tuesday"*

NEW YORK CITY

Source of money. Washington, D.C., has everything New York City has . . . but just one of each.

See also, *"America," "Maryland," "Northern Virginia," "Washington, D.C."*

NEWS CYCLE

Definitions vary, but traditionally, a news cycle was either the time that elapsed between a news organization's editions or, somewhat relatedly, the amount of time the public remained focused on a news story or stories. Before the Internet, news cycles could often last days or even weeks, bound by the daily deadlines of newspapers and evening news broadcasts and the weekly publications of magazines. Now, our news cycles blaze into the public's consciousness and promptly flicker out with atomic-like speed. Lawrence Livermore National Laboratory probably uses news cycles to precisely measure the degradation of magnetic fields.

See also, *"Bracketing," "Earned Media," "Winning"*

NORTHERN VIRGINIA

Virginia has long lived in the national psyche as a bastion of pastoral Southern gentility. The seat of the Confederacy is home to sprawling tobacco plantations, numerous Civil War battlefields, and the University of Virginia—one of America's foremost manufacturers of floppy-haired frat brothers named Caldwell. It was always among the more staid places in the South; proper men of Virginia wouldn't dare be caught "ramblin'" like some of their more French-influenced brothers in the Gulf. But increasingly, the Old Dominion is defined less by its legacy of aristocratic gentlemen farmers and far more by an untidier collection of immigrants, high-tech professionals, and young white-collar couples—Starbucks nonfat iced mochas in hand—scouring the epileptically luminous halls of a Bed Bath & Beyond for a new laundry hamper.

Over the last few decades, the growth of the federal government and its attendant industries has fueled a population boom in the Washington, D.C., metro area, much of it in the nearby Northern Virginia counties of Arlington, Alexandria, and Fairfax. As such, the state's political center of gravity has shifted from the more conservative and rural areas that make up most of the state to a comparatively tiny spit of land hugging the Potomac. The influx of Democratic voters to Northern Virginia—federal employees, young people, immigrants—has turned the state from a Republican stronghold to a bonafide swing state, with Barack Obama winning the state twice and sporting both a governor and two senators from the Democratic Party.

Virginia is by no means nirvana for NPR tote-bag-wielding lefties. The moment you cross the Potomac from Washington, D.C., to Virginia, you've crossed a threshold from a jurisdiction with one of the nation's strictest gun laws to one with one of the weakest. The coastal elite can easily forget with all of NoVA's modern urban flourishes—the organic grocery stores, the "walkability," the Ubers scurrying to and fro then that person standing next to them—at the Whole Foods could be legally packing heat.

NoVA

If this part of the D.C. area were a Roman province, its name would be Cheesecake Factorium.

The neighborhoods that sprung up around the Orange, Blue, Yellow, and Silver Lines look a lot like the "urban living" developments being constructed across much of the country's suburban areas—full-services condos with ample garage parking that cling to major road arteries and metro stations. Shirlington Village, for example, is centered around an ersatz urban downtown, complete with all the nitty-gritty features of big-city life such as a Hilton Garden Inn and a reflexology center.

Once the Metro crosses the Potomac into Northern Virginia, the hipster-heavy neo-speakeasies, fashionable boutiques, and charming, turn-of-the-century rowhouses give way to dime-a-dozen Irish pubs, J.Crews, and monolithic condo developments offering parking to all residents. The areas are effectively giant suburban halfway homes: eminently "livable" urban-style settings that provide the vehicular-based existence of the burbs without the crime, grime, or intellectual dissonance of the actual city. More often than not, condos in neighborhoods like Clarendon, Ballston, or Court House are mere holding pens for twentysomethings until they settle down in a more suburban setting.

Of course, the District of Columbia does not lack for reflexology centers, chain stores, or monolithic condo developments, nor are NoVA's metro corridors completely devoid of interesting cultural offerings. But the fact is, life in Northern Virginia's urban settings is significantly less compelling than the city. The only crews beefing in Northern Virginia are the warring yuppie couples vying for the last mid-century sectional sofa at CB2 before it goes on back order.

Outer Northern Virginia

While Northern Virginia's Metro corridors are arties of homogeny, its less accessible suburbs are home to the D.C. Metro area's more diverse populations, including large immigrant communities from Asia and Latin America. In fact, Asians and Hispanics make up 32 percent of the residents in Arlington, Fairfax, and Prince William counties. However, the skyrocketing real-estate values mean these groups are clustered mostly in those counties' less metro-friendly parts. That these communities can at times be invisible to the area's more wealthy and influential is a shame—both for the obvious, disenfranchising reasons and that they contain some of area's most interesting offerings.

See also, *"Buy This Missile," "Crystal City Restaurant," "Maryland," "Washington, D.C."*

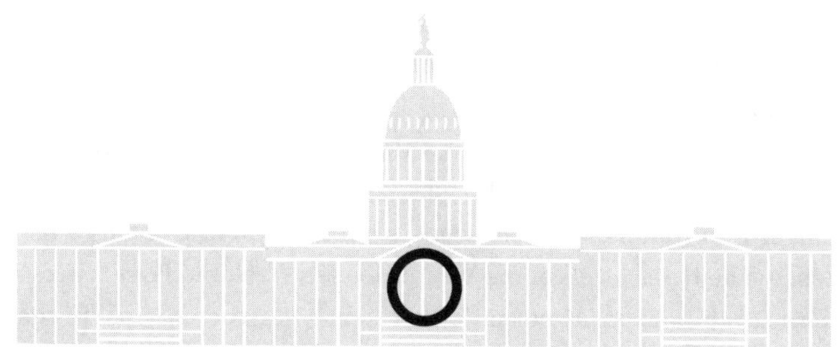

OCTOBER SURPRISE

An unforeseen development in the waning days of an election campaign, more often than not a presidential one. Also a great name for a thoroughbred, microbrew IPA, or a World War II bomber with a pinup painted on it.

October surprises more often than not are letdowns, evidenced most strongly by the fact that no one remembers them. Caspar Weinberger's indictment? Gennifer Flowers's *Playboy* interview? Osama bin Laden's preelection video message? Joe Biden's rare bird smuggling ring?[87] Most of these have faded into the recesses of the public's memory.

Ironically, the three most potent October surprises in recent memory didn't even occur in October. Republican congressman Mark Foley resigned on September 29, 2006, over allegations of sexual impropriety with House pages, a development that helped the Democrats retake Congress. The 2008 economic collapse that undid John McCain's campaign picked up steam in August and September. Mitt Romney's "47 Percent" comments were published by *Mother Jones* on September 17, 2012.

---

[87] OK, not that last one.

See also, *"Field," "Veepstakes"*

OFFICE SPACE

Place of business, site of refrigerator turf battles, home to bottomless anxiety over how to introduce oneself to colleagues who started six months ago, arena of idle small talk, thunderdome of unprofessional romantic come-ons.

Most White House employees don't work in the actual White House, and the mansion—the most familiar section with its iconic Corinthian columns and porticos—serves as the first family's residence. The three levels of the White House's West and East Wings—the little bits that jut out on either side—are the only parts that contain staff offices, including the Oval Office. Even then, only a few dozen administration officials are accorded the privilege of having a desk in the White House's historic confines, and most aren't accorded that much space. Like a pair of skinny jeans, it's a form over function thing: you want people to know that you're in a West Wing office, even if it's the kind of space a realtor would call "cozy."

The rest of the president's team—all 1,700 members of it—work primarily in two nearby buildings. Sitting beside the White House is the Eisenhower Executive Office Building, a grand, imperial-looking thing completed in 1888. Down the street on 15th and H streets is the New Executive Office Building, an uninviting mid-twentieth-century monstrosity that might easily be confused with a public housing project in Sarajevo if it didn't sit next to the Smithsonian's arts and crafts museum.[88]

Nowhere are workplace assignments more fraught than in the halls of Congress—some halls are more coveted than others. Even the largest office can be pretty cramped, with around seven hundred to eight hundred square feet for some ten Washington staffers. While the Senate's process is straightforward—senators choose

---

[88] Still, it would probably make Le Corbusier dry heave.

offices based on their seniority, new House members must assemble for a lottery drawing to determine the order.

There's nothing good about this process. On the Senate side, members can stay in their offices until a day before the next Congress begins, and elected members are often still working out of temporary offices months into their first term. Outgoing House members must relocate to basement cubicles so they can handle constituent services as their replacements move in. To behold Rayburn B337 is to witness Congress at its least ornate: an unapologetic cubicle farm that makes the epicenter of American democracy resemble a technical support center (it actually makes sense as junior House members are basically just Uncle Sam's customer service representatives—see the "Constituent Services" entry). Members are usually out of their offices by December 1, but there can be awkward run-ins as incoming members tour offices still inhabited by misty-eyed staffers and competing representatives-elect tour the same office, eyeing each other over like young house hunters sizing up each other's credit scores.

The most sought-after real estate in the Capitol is offices, well, *in the Capitol*. In Washington, all members of Congress are given office suites in the six House and Senate office buildings flanking the Capitol. Only members of leadership are given manned offices in their respective chambers. All senators are given hideaway offices, but only the most senior ones are provided ones that are anything to write home about. Nothing beats a good marble staircase or high-end wall sconce.

See also, *"Fundraiser," "Hideaway Office," "White House"*

P

PAC

Political action committee as defined by the FEC. PACs are your basic, plain-Jane political organizations and include campaign committees that candidates use to raise funds for their election campaign, fundraising entities for national party committees like the Democratic National Committee, Republican National Committee, the DCCC and NRCC, and outside groups like EMILY's List, which uses PACs to funnel money to female pro-choice candidates. Corporations and labor unions are also allowed to form their own PACs, which receive donations from their employees or members and can donate directly to campaign and party PACs. It's important to note that while all of these entities are PACs under the FEC's definition, when people refer to "PACs," they're typically referring to outside groups and not campaign committees, party committees, and other groups belonging to candidates or parties.

Indeed, the majority of PACs aren't actually tied to a campaign or political organization. These "connected PACs" are ones that were established by a specific union, corporation, or trade group and can only receive contributions from their employees or members. This "membership" loophole is why a great many political organizations actually call their donors "members."

However, with the advent of super PACs and dark money groups, many donors are shifting away from PAC contributions, especially when it comes to third-party organizations and unions. In the 2012 election cycle, the AFL-CIO's PAC raised a total of $316,000. Compare that with the union's Workers' Voice's super PAC, which, in the first quarter of 2012 *alone,* raised $5.4 million. Not a single donor to the group's PAC that cycle gave more than the $200 that triggers itemization for PACs. Compare that to the 2008 cycle, when AFL-CIO's PAC raised nearly $1.7 million.

PACs are still constrained by most of the rules governing campaign finance that existed prior to the *Citizens United* Supreme Court ruling that allowed unlimited corporate and union political contributions. PAC contribution limits vary depending on the type of PAC and are indexed to inflation and increase in odd-numbered years. The 2015–2016 limit on individual donations to campaign committees is $5,400 per candidate ($2,700 in the primary and $2,700 in the general election). In the 2016 cycle, individual contributions to political parties were $33,400.

However, even in this freewheeling age of super PACs and dark money groups, PACs are still the only political campaign organization that a candidate can use to directly advocate for their candidacy and fund basic, administrative expenses. For corporations, unions, and advocacy groups, PACs remain the only vehicles through which they can funnel money directly to candidate and party PACs.

See also, *"Finance," "Fundraiser," "Leadership PAC," "Political Nonprofit," "Super PAC"*

PANELS

Ubiquitous sight inside the Beltway. Navel gazing is one of D.C.'s most beloved pastimes, and it's no surprise that every week the city plays hosts to dozens—if not hundreds—of panels where its bottomless well of experts gather to impress each other. Truly, these things are no less common a sight in the nation's capital than black Lincoln Navigators with tinted windows.

Panelists pontificate on roundtables dedicated to the challenges of updating the tax code in the age of hashtags, they ponder the future of dog-grooming regulatory regimes at the Brookings Institution, and they convene at the National Press Club and discuss the challenges restless leg syndrome poses to think tanks in the post-MySpace environment. Most panel titles follow a similar blueprint, with a catchy statement or question followed by a description of the event—something along the lines of, "Righty Tighty, Lefty Loosey? Examining Knobs in the 21st Century" or "You Say, 'Potato,' I Say, 'Where's the Lactation Room?' Updating OSHA Regulations for Today's Working Parents."

Washington's rampant panel culture recalls Lake Wobegon, the fictional Minnesota town featured in Garrison Keillor's public radio program *A Prairie Home Companion*. In Washington, as in Keillor's imaginary hamlet, all the women are strong, all the men good-looking, all the children above average, and all the professionals invited to sit on panels about the future of technology and government.

A whole ecosystem has sprung up around Washington's love of panels. Conferences like Netroots Nation and the Conservative Political Action Conference play host to dozens of panels every year and groups like the New Organizing Institute more or less exist to train people by holding panels so their students can become politically adept enough to appear on panels of their own. Though this theory has not been confirmed, it's entirely possible that panels are just excuses for people to have photos of themselves taken while striking a thoughtful pose behind a folding table. Those things make for great Twitter bio photos, especially for people who don't have a TV appearance from which they can take a still from.

A parting query: if a game changer changes the game in the forest and no one hears someone discussing it on a *Politico* PRO-sponsored panel on what works in Washington, did the game really change?

See also, *"CPAC," "Expert," "Netroots Nation"*

PAYWALL JOURNALISM

Subscription-based news services providing members with up-to-the-minute updates on areas like transportation, energy, defense, health care, and IT policy that might not pique a general audience's interest, but is of tremendous importance to lobbyists, political staffers, and industry groups who may care quite a bit about an obscure fisheries amendment. The annual price tag for these services can run into the tens of thousands of dollars; they are being offered by an increasing number of news outlets, including *Politico,* Bloomberg, and *National Journal.*

For newsrooms, these services provide a much-needed cash infusion and allow it to fund other activities, to say nothing of jobs to journalists who are struggling to stay afloat in an otherwise contracting industry. *Politico*'s several-thousand-word piece on the history of Michael Dukakis's notorious tank photo op might make for a wonderful bit of political storytelling, but it's not necessarily going to lead the *Drudge Report.* The flip side is that limiting such hard-won information about the government to a handful of wealthy subscribers is not exactly in keeping with the spirit of a free and open press.

Moreover, these subscription offerings also serve to blur the lines between a newsroom's business and editorial sides. Newsroom advertising teams traditionally served as the point of contact for advertisers, insulating reporters and editors. Subscription services upend editorial's relationship to special interests. Not only are reporters for these paywall services actively tailoring their reporting to what clients might want to know, but some journalists on the editorial side are proactively engaged in courting them.

"Do you want to find out something that's really important in your universe now, or do you want to wait?" *Politico Pro* editor Tim Grieve told Nieman Journalism Lab, a news media industry site, in 2012. "For almost two years, I've started every day by reading Bloomberg Government," reads a testimonial from "Matt, lobbyist, healthcare industry," on the service's home page.

These appeals can be quite intimate, too, and can see journalists suddenly playing the role of lobbyist. "Margaret Carlson and Don Baptiste invite you to celebrate Bloomberg Government's New Lobbying Intelligence Suite," read a Paperless Post invite sent out to a number of potential clients in May 2015. Carlson, a veteran political journalist and commentator, is a columnist for Bloomberg View and Baptiste the head of Bloomberg Government. "I'm having a dinner for Don Baptiste, CEO of Bloomberg Government," read another invite from Carlson later that year to a senior Republican lobbyist with ties to GOP congressional leadership. "There's no program, just gathering together a group of people including Chris Dodd and Kirk Blalock." Dodd is a former Democratic senator from Connecticut and at the time was the senior lobbyist for the Motion Picture Association of America. Blalock is a GOP lobbyist who previously served in George W. Bush's public liaison office.

If nothing else, it's good source building.

***See also,** "Hack," "Lobbying," "Selling Out"*

PHOTO LINE

Godforsaken ritual where staffers, donors, reporters, and other White House visitors queue up for a photo and fifteen seconds of small talk with the president and first lady. Photo lines are a year-round phenomenon, springing up when victorious sports teams pay the commander in chief a visit, when groups of uniformed military officials tour the executive mansion, and during presidential meet-and-greets with lesser executive branch employees. Yet it's the holiday season when 1600 Pennsylvania Avenue is particularly lousy with photo lines. That's when the president and first spouse excuse themselves from their several dozen holiday parties to hold court in the State Dining Room to snap pictures with starstruck visitors—photos that will soon be splayed over social media and hung in personal studies.

Because everyone is important, everyone gets a White House holiday party: members of Congress, White House staffers, reporters, donors, the military, diplomats, dentists, guys named Rick—probably. This is precious time that the leader of the free world could be reading security briefs or building relationships with agency officials. Instead, he and his spouse are carted out for hours of grip and grinning—like mall Santas but with a better security detail and fewer sleeves crusted with children's snot.

It's almost enough to make you feel bad for the most powerful person in the world. Aides take women's purses in an attempt to thwart unplanned selfies, members of Congress buttonhole the commander in chief on all manner of issues ("You need to bomb the Iranian nuclear facilities," *The New York Times* reported former Republican representative Michele Bachmann telling Barack Obama during a 2014 photo line), befuddled reporters shed any semblance of impartial detachment, and political opponents who have publicly attacked the commander in chief's character sidle up for their very own presidential keepsake.

Death to the photo line.

See also, *"Access," "Bubble," "Hack," "Wall of Fame"*

PIVOT

Rhetorical stratagem used to shift a conversation, debate, interview, or other public dialogue to a topic that is more to the Pivoter's liking.

> *"Senator, your opponent in the presidential race, Governor Moistburn, says only one presidential debate is needed to air the issues. How do you respond?"*
>
> "You know, Janice, I want to talk about the issues as much as possible, that's why I've been traveling around our great country to talk about things I believe in, like the Support Our Heroes Act."
>
> *"Senator, your colleague this morning told a group of supporters that laws aimed at stopping elder abuse are, and I quote,*

> *'Destroying jobs and depriving our grandparents of character-building experiences.' What's your response?"*
>
> "You know, Janice, character *is* important, but the radical liberal left doesn't seem to agree. They oppose school prayer, they want to redefine traditional marriage, they won't support our troops. But I believe that we owe everything to our troops, and that's why I recently introduced the Support Our Heroes Act."
>
> *"Congressman, there are a growing number of calls for your resignation in the wake of photos emerging of you riding a tandem bicycle with your nineteen-year-old intern. Will you step down?"*
>
> "You know, Janice, there's one group of men and women with whom, proverbially speaking, I will never stop dressing up in matching seersucker suits and boater hats with, and that's our troops. And that's why I recently introduced the Support Our Heroes Act."

If it's not immediately apparent, all it takes to pivot is a vague sense of two things having some loose connection or overarching similarity. From there, you can transition to just about anything. Say you're a Republican running for office and wanted to bring up accusations that your opponent had sex with a moose, but some idiot reporter wanted to ask you why you opposed raising taxes on people making over $20 million a year. First, consider the similarities between the posed question and your talking point. To make it easier, here's a Venn diagram:

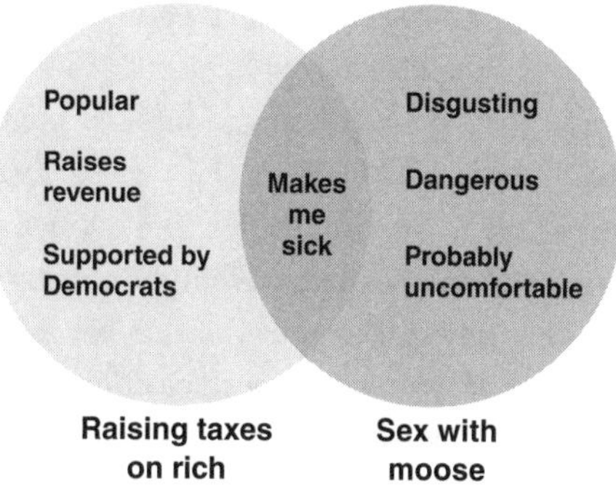

Then, have at it:

"You know, Janice, in America we reward hard work, and I, for one, am not about to start punishing people for their accomplishments by raising their taxes. It makes me sick, quite frankly, not unlike the recent allegations against my opponent, who defiled a moose."

See also, *"Flack," "Prebuttal," "Spin"*

POLITICAL NONPROFIT (DARK MONEY GROUPS)

Tax-exempt organization as defined under section 501(c) of the Internal Revenue Service code. These groups do not have to disclose their donors, thus the "dark money" moniker, whereas donors to super PACs who give $200 or more must have their names disclosed. The downside to these organizations, from the perspective of a wealthy donor or organization seeking to influence elections, is that only up to 50 percent of its activity can be directly in support of a candidate. The rest of its output can only be obliquely tied to an election, perhaps in the guise of "issue ads" that reflect negatively on a specific candidate.

"Political nonprofit" might evoke images of cat-sweater-clad-activist moms phone banking for a child car seat law, but political nonprofits are actually how oil and gas multinationals secretly fund TV advertisements warning that your congressman not only is destroying your job and tearing apart your community, but will probably line your house with asbestos as you sleep.

Some of today's most well-known outside political groups—including the Koch brothers' Americans for Prosperity and the Chamber of Commerce—are 501(c) groups. For the enterprising executive with a few million smackaroos lying around and who doesn't want a *New York Times* reporter staking out their driveway,[89] political nonprofits are an attractive way to influence elections. Instead of donating to, say, Union Busters Are People Too super PAC, the executive could give to Scabs Rising, Union Busters' affiliated 501(c) group.

The most onerous 501(c)s are the 501(c)(4)s, or "social welfare" groups, as they're officially known. These are entities which can engage in political activity so far as it doesn't constitute the bulk of their activity. If loophole jumping were an Olympic sport, "public welfare" groups would already be on a Wheaties box. What these groups, which include the aforementioned Americans for Prosperity and also Karl Rove's Crossroads GPS, consider to be "educational" *reallllllly* stretches pedagogical limits.

When you think of "public welfare" programming, you probably think of Ad Council spots urging you to not play chicken with oncoming trains or feed your babies arsenic because you've had a bad day. However, "public welfare," as many of these groups see it, is a very broad concept. "Tell [Democratic Arizona Congressman] Ron Barber 'Stop the reckless spending and fight for us!'" one ad, sponsored by Americans for Prosperity, "informed" viewers in 2014. Sure, the ad also "informed" viewers that Barber "voted three times to raise the debt ceiling and for more wasteful spending," but it doesn't exactly feel like Smokey the Bear's exhortation that only you can prevent forest fires.

Indeed, nonprofits, in theory, exist to support and "educate" the electorate. However, as the anti-Barber ad demonstrates, it's totally OK to educate the electorate about a lawmaker being a gigantic piece

[89] Well, *one* of their driveways.

of shit, but just so long as you don't tell the electorate to vote against said gigantic piece of shit. And lots of "social welfare" groups are "educating" the electorate about a great many gigantic pieces of shit. In the 2012 elections, conservative-leaning 501(c) groups spent *at least* $263 million while liberal-leaning ones spent $35 million. The final tallies for the 2016 elections will almost certainly dwarf those numbers numerous times over.

See also, *"Astroturfing," "Megadonor," "Super PAC"*

POOL REPORT

Chronicle of the president and vice president's hour-to-hour activities, documented by rotating members of the White House press corps—one from print, radio, and TV, each—that is distributed to members of the press. Of course, poolers aren't allowed to follow the president *everywhere* ("POTUS kissed FLOTUS and wished her good night. POTUS then yawned and added that he should get a boil checked out. POTUS rested head on pillow and lost consciousness shortly thereafter. We have a full lid."). Instead, they mostly serve to document a president's and vice president's arrival and departure from off-campus events and certain White House meetings, what is known in White House lingo as "public" events. When a "lid" is called, the president's press team is signaling to the pooler that POTUS has no more *public* events that day. Whether the president proceeds to play Settlers of Catan with the cabinet or, perhaps more likely, proceeds to the Situation Room to authorize an air strike, is outside the pooler's purview.

The pool report constitutes something of a compromise between the executive branch and the Fourth Estate. For the White House, it allows the president, to, say, go out to a local restaurant with his family and saves his press staff from having to deal with a logistical nightmare for such a mundane event. For the press, it solves a central conundrum of presidential coverage: it's something that should happen for transparency's sake, but it can be remarkably un-newsworthy most of the time and, as a result, unprofitable. And though some larger and wealthier news organizations can afford to follow the president around to the ends of the Earth, most would prefer to conserve their limited resources for other endeavors, and having to sacrifice a reporter's day every so often to relay that a president called a meeting "productive" is worth it.

The development of email has greatly opened up the process. Where once members of the White House press team would print out the reports and place them in the back of the briefing room, the reports are now emailed to thousands of recipients—recipients whose job is, in part, to shed light on the president's activity. In early 2015 Gawker began publishing every pool report on a section of its website. Much to the public's disappointment, the cache of reports wasn't nearly as exciting as one might have hoped ("See y'all at the coastal liberal media elite potluck tonight! Jon Meacham is bringing guac! Full lid.").

It's not a perfect system, by any means. For one thing, the White House Press Office sends out the report, making the government an intermediary in a process that is designed to keep it in check. In 2014, it was revealed that the White House asked that the content of several reports be changed. While the changes were minor—the contents of an unaired *Tonight Show* interview Barack Obama sat for, that First Lady Michelle Obama exercised, and that an unnamed intern fainted during an event—the power dynamic those changes represented was the chief concern. And though having a reporter near the president as often as possible serves the greater good, pool reports are as much about documenting the president as they are documenting the president's message, which is a focus-group tested synonym for "propaganda."

The pool report itself is one of the best, if not the best, microcosms for the press's relationship to the White House. Take the October 6, 2015, pool report from *The Daily Beast*'s Eleanor Clift,[90] describing

---

[90] Clift, a veteran reporter and pundit, was actually the pooler on duty in 1984 when President Ronald Reagan joked before recording a radio address, "My fellow Americans, I'm pleased to tell you today that I've signed legislation that will outlaw Russia forever. We begin bombing in five minutes."

President Obama's appearance after a meeting at the Agriculture Department to promote a Pacific Rim trade deal, the Trans Pacific Partnership, and to soothe representatives of the agriculture industry who were nervous about its provisions. It's a pretty good boilerplate pool report and very indicative of reporters' precarious relationship with the White House:

> Pool ushered in @ end of meeting @ Ag dept for preview of POTUS sales pitch on TPP that he says "creates a level playing field" for American businesses and families. Treaty took 5 years to negotiate and eliminates 18000 taxes and tariffs on American products. He cited three. Japan puts 38 percent on American beef before it reaches market. Malaysia adds 30 percent to American auto parts. Vietnam adds as much as 70 percent to American cars sold in Vietnam. Under the agreement all these fees will fall "most of them to zero." Potus said agreement has hiest [*sic*] labor and environmental standards and in the months ahead before it comes to a vote he will be talking abt it with the American people and with mayors and govs. "I suspect that misinformation will be propagated as there usually is with these deals" he said. "It will be an enormous achievement for us to have some 40 percent of the worlds [*sic*] economies operating under rules that don't hurt us." POTUS did not respond to 2 shouted questions. What about the air strike [*sic*] in Afghanistan? Is it a war crime? POTUS back @ White House 1 pm. Lunch lid til 230 with exception of briefing. Pls check quotes against transcript as always I will send list from White House of participants in Ag mtg in separate email.

1. Clift and the other poolers were not allowed into the closed-door meeting between President Obama and representatives of the agricultural industry, who were

P

nervous about a Pacific rim trade deal that Obama supported. Instead, the poolers were made to wait outside until its completion, at which point the president emerged and rattled off a series of talking points.

2. The stats Clift cited, minus those mentioned by the president specifically, were provided by the White House. But rather than being some kind of mindless administration mouthpiece, Clift was doing her job in relaying to the press whatever it was the White House was dishing out, leaving it up to the pool recipients to scrutinize it.

3. One of Clift's fellow poolers asked two questions about a U.S. air strike on an Afghan hospital that killed nineteen people several days prior, both of which were ignored. That short window was all the pool really had to ask the president a question. Such Qs are generally tolerated by the White House, but as the term "tolerate" suggests, it could very easily cut down on the president's "public availability" if those questions became too persistent, intrusive, or unwelcomed.

See also, *"Hack," "Hill Rags," "Photo Line," "Spin," "White House"*

PORK

Blanket term for legislative spending that is allocated to a legislator's district, possibly without any meaningful debate or oversight. Though once a staple of Washington's legislative give-and-take, congressional leaders have succumbed to political pressure over the practice and have adopted a decidedly kosher outlook on pork. People didn't like having their tax dollars used to fund museums dedicated to the Pacific Northwest's naval heritage, tree snake control in Guam, or the Montana Sheep Institute.[91]

Pork is a big source of confusion. Nowhere in the Constitution or in the rules of the Senate or House does the word "pork" appear—unless you count that Federalist paper in which John Jay outlined his patented recipe for a "bitchin', finger-lickin' BBQ sandy." Something is usually described as pork if it is clearly meant to benefit a single jurisdiction, if it circumvents the traditional debate process, or if it wasn't outlined in Congress's annual budget resolution or the president's budget proposal.

People tend to use the term *earmark* interchangeably with *pork*. However, an earmark is a distinct legislative tool that can be used in perfectly aboveboard ways while pork, as will be described below, can be created in a variety of ways. The Congressional Research Service defines an earmark as "provisions associated with legislation (appropriations or general legislation) that specify certain congressional spending priorities or in revenue bills that apply to a very limited number of individuals or entities."

As that definition notes, the main platform for pork earmarks—*the political potato bun, if you will*—has historically been the appropriations process. Every year, after the relevant congressional committees *authorize* the creation and continuation of the governmental entities and initiatives under their jurisdiction, the House and Senate appropriation committees convene to dole out money for these programs. This has historically been why spots on the Appropriations Committee were among the most coveted on Capitol Hill. Its members could dangle over their colleagues' heads the prospect of inserting politically enticing earmarks into appropriation bills. Inside the Beltway, the panel's members were known as the Cardinals, a reference to the Vatican's College of Cardinals.

After the GOP took control of the House of Representatives in

[91] All real things from 2010's appropriations process, the last one in which such proposals were permitted, as detailed in Citizens Against Government Waste's annual *Pig Book*.

2011, its leaders banned earmarks. Senate Democrats, faced with the prospect of their earmarks dying in the House and similar denunciations from President Obama, followed suit. This is largely why news stories about wasteful government pork have dissipated somewhat in recent years, replaced by more general bleats by fiscally conservative lawmakers about the size of government.

However, there are still opportunities for pork, though it's not quite the *pickin'* that it once was. In 2014, a bill breaking an impasse over raising the debt ceiling contained some glaring items, like $2.2 billion for a dam project in Senate Minority Leader Mitch McConnell's home state of Kentucky and a death grant of $174,000 to the late New Jersey senator Frank Lautenberg's widow (though a lovely gesture and a comparatively small sum by the standards of the federal government, Lautenberg had a net worth of $59 million). As *Politico*'s Austin Wright and Jeremy Herb reported in October 2015, lawmakers are also finding ways to include so-called "zombie earmarks" in appropriation bills. These provisions might not mention a specific municipality, organization, or other entity by name, but are written in such a way that will almost certainly result in the intended beneficiary receiving the appropriations. For example, a lawmaker might include a measure in a transportation appropriations bill that provides funds for a type of construction whose materials likely originate from a company in that lawmaker's district.

Arguments against pork are self-evident: it constitutes a wasteful allocation of taxpayer dollars, the manner in which it is snuck into larger pieces of legislation without any meaningful debate is decidedly undemocratic, and it contributes to a corrupt, logrolling legislative culture that is counter to the spirit of public service. And while some people argue that legislators were sent to Washington precisely to improve their constituencies with whatever tools were at their constitutional disposal, lawmakers traditionally don't get a fair shake when it comes to earmark dollars. Party leaders and, as referenced above, members of the appropriation committees have historically been the largest beneficiaries of pork. If the federal budget were a bar, and Congress's 535 members were all clamoring to get the bartenders' attentions, the members of the Appropriations Committee would be the hot ones in tight outfits showing a lot of skin, while the rest would be the cardigan-clad schlubs patiently holding out their credit cards and hoping to make eye contact.

West Virginia Democrat Robert Byrd and Alaska Republican Ted Stevens—longtime Senate appropriation chairs and neither of whom ever showed enough skin, frankly—were notorious for their flagrant abuse of their station to funnel dollars into their sparsely populated states. Arguably the most notorious example of pork in recent times was Stevens's $233 million earmark for a bridge connecting Alaskan backwaters Ketchikan and Gravina—you may know it as the "bridge to nowhere." West Virginia is basically one large holding pen for things named after Robert Byrd.

Pork's defenders, meanwhile, maintain that these earmarks are among the most effective bargaining tools that legislators have at their disposal. While earmarks can feel slimy, it's precisely that slime that helps grease Washington's skids. Congress, they note, will always be filled with people scrambling to get reelected, and while it's a nice thought that their better angels will prevail, the cold hard realities of electoral politics will usually win the day. Other carrots and sticks at leadership's disposal—CODELs, campaign dollars, introducing bills, plum committee assignments, or expulsions—simply aren't as potent.

And while earmarks were often portrayed, in campaign ads, in op-eds, and in stump speeches, as a major contributor to the deficit, the practice actually only comprises a relatively small amount of federal spending. In 2010, the last year that earmarks were permitted, Congress spent a total of $16.5 billion on them—a large number until you consider that it only accounts for .2 percent of the federal budget. If all the earmarks were rounded up into one large program called "The Government Not Shutting Down and/or Defaulting on

Its Debt, Thereby Ruining Our Economy and Decimating Your 401(k) Like a Clenched Fist Crushing a Dead Leaf Fund," people probably wouldn't mind as much.

See also *"Budget," "Legislation," "Lobbying," "Monuments to Me"*

PREBUTTAL

A preemptive statement, interview, or other "pre-response" to an anticipated event. A "prebuttal" is more or less just a stunt—a clever word for "speech" or "press release" or "two-minute hit on *The Situation Room.*"

There comes a point in every politico's existence when, in a moment of profound solitude, they gaze deeply into the void and realize that it's all just one big prebuttal, a never-ending, chicken-or-the-egg game of one-upmanship, prebut upon prebut, a permanent he-said-she-said imbroglio, destined to play out until the bright fire of our civilization is reduced to the faint glow of a few dying embers. Then the light goes green and they tell Wolf that they're glad to be here to talk about this latest Democratic attempt to shove big government down Americans' throats.

See also, *"Bracketing," "Hack," "News Cycle," "Spin"*

PRESS CONFERENCE

Event where lawmakers, candidates, or other VIPs field questions from the press, possibly in conjunction with a major event or announcement.

Answers to press conference questions will often elicit the same kind of practiced, banal statements that define political speeches. In that sense, a politician speaking to a scrum of reporters is not unlike a star athlete at a postgame press conference.

SPORTS	POLITICS
"We're going to take it one game at a time."	"I'm not going to be a rubber stamp for the party leadership."
"It's a game of inches."	"This bill isn't perfect, but it's a step in the right direction."
"I'm just happy to be here."	"I'm going to shake up Washington."
"I have the utmost respect for [my opponents]."	"My friend, the [senator/member] from [state]."
"He brought his 'A' game."	"I'd like to thank the [member] for all their hard work on this bill."
"It's do or die now."	"Now, more than ever, we need real leadership."
"I want to thank God for giving me this opportunity."	"I want to thank [fundraiser host] for having me today."
"They have to come together as a team."	"Members are urged to vote "YES/NO."

SPORTS	POLITICS
"We're going to go out there and give 110 percent."	**"I'm not afraid to break with my party."**
"I couldn't do it without the fans."	**"I can't do this without your support. Please click the link below and help me take back Washington."**

Congress is more or less one continual sports franchise media day, albeit one with more marble and fewer taciturn men with no necks. Members of Congress wander many of the same spaces as members of the press, meaning lawmakers have to be on constant guard for a disheveled-looking person in wrinkled khakis and ill-fitting blazer shoving a microphone in their face. That said, there are designated places for press events in the Capitol complex, including indoor ones, like the House and Senate radio and TV galleries and a number of smaller rooms in the basement, and outdoor ones sporting dramatic backdrops of the Capitol building, like the House Triangle and Senate Swamp. The Senate Swamp, despite its name, is actually just a patch of grass on the Senate side of the Capitol grounds. However, reporters will regularly receive notices from press secretaries that a politician will, without irony, be delivering their remarks in the swamp.

Woodrow Wilson was the first president to hold a press conference. Up until that point, most of a president's interactions with the press were informal and off the record. Teddy Roosevelt, for example, would regularly speak with reporters while getting his morning shave.[92] Wilson's first presser, perhaps a portent of things to come,

[92] Though no records exist of him chatting up a hack while wrestling a bear, it's not out of the question.

was something of a disaster. He had expected to greet each reporter individually, but was instead swarmed all at once. "I did not realize there were so many of you," a startled Wilson said according to *The Editor and Publisher and Journalist* (now better known as *Editor & Publisher*) in a March 22, 1913, article. "Your numbers force me to make a speech to you en masse instead of chatting with each of you, as I had hoped to do, and thus getting greater pleasure and personal acquaintance out of this meeting." He somehow won a second term.

That said, interactions between presidents and the press were far more cordial and obsequious than today. Franklin Roosevelt's marital indiscretions were well known, but seldom discussed by the press outside of private conversation. During a 1950 press conference, Harry Truman quipped about the rabid anticommunist crusader Senator Joseph McCarthy that "I think the greatest asset that the Kremlin has is Senator [Joseph] McCarthy." That sort of statement, which would have dominated the news cycle for at least several days if uttered in an environment like today's, was quickly scrubbed at the president's request after a reporter noted that the quote would make front page news. Instead, Truman was quoted as saying, "The greatest asset that the Kremlin has is the partisan attempt in the Senate to sabotage the bipartisan foreign policy of the United States."

President John F. Kennedy was the first commander in chief to hold a televised press conference, appearing on January 25, 1961, in the State Department's auditorium. Kennedy had already demonstrated his ability to thrive in a combative, back-and-forth televised setting during his 1960 presidential debate against Richard Nixon, who resembled a Muppet with a pituitary condition. After reading a short statement on a famine in the former Belgian Congo, the release of two American pilots from Soviet custody, and forthcoming nuclear negotiations, the thirty-fifth president fielded questions from reporters. Kennedy dispatched their questions with cool confidence, tackling questions about government transparency and controlled leaks to Soviet officials with considerable skill.

See also, *"Flack," "Hack," "Pivot," "Pool Report," "Spin"*

PRIMARY (VERB)

To mount a challenge to a sitting legislator in one's own party. The term "to primary" is often used in a speculative context and connotes a certain degree of hostility between the potential challenger and incumbent.

> *The senator's vote to curb coal emissions has members of his base fuming. The negative response, in blogs, online comment boards, and talk radio, was swift and unforgiving. "I hope someone primary's his ass," fumed one irate caller to Corndog and Butternuts in the Morning, a popular Knoxville-area talk radio program.*

> *The president's decision to table a bill on immigration reform drew criticism from his left flank. "Somebody might need to primary this guy," wrote left-leaning pundit Melanie Menendez-Rosenberg on her popular blog, Cöntemplative Revölutiön.*

See also, *"CPAC," "Freedom Caucus," "Netroots Nation," "RINO"*

PUNDIT

See, *"Expert," "Green Room," "Spin," "Spin Room," "Strategist"*

RACISM

Still very much a thing.

First, the numbers, and they're not great. Our government is pretty white. Partridge Family white. Step-dancing white. *Mentos commercial* white.[93]

The 114th Congress, which is in session until January 2017, is 83 percent white, per a January 2016 review by *The Washington Post*'s Philip Bump. As far as congressional discrepancies go, that ain't bad—the 2010 decennial census found the U.S.'s white population to be closer to 70 percent. However, just about everything else is another story. As of April 2016, the upper chamber is 94 percent white, with two black members, three Hispanic ones, and a single Asian American. Behind the scenes, the numbers are worse. According to one 2011 study by *National Journal,* 93 percent of the top aides on Capitol Hill were white. K Street and the Washington press corps don't fare much better, either.

Perhaps most alarmingly, only twelve of the top five hundred donors in the 2014 midterm election were nonwhite, according to a 2015 study by OpenSecrets.org, and none of them ranked in the top one hundred. Only one of those five hundred high rollers, investment executive Mellody Hobson, was an African American. Put another

[93] Little-known fact: budget impasses are often resolved by the House speaker popping a Mentos and then pointing the roll at an onlooker while flashing a big smile. Works like a charm.

way, well over *99 percent* of our country's biggest campaign contribution "gets" are not black. Even if African Americans were *over*represented in Congress, as long as their biggest benefactors don't share their community's agenda, those agendas will be *under*represented. There's a reason why you hear a lot more about "voter fraud" than inner-city asthma levels.

Yes, America elected its first black president in 2008, and that's just swell, but it's not hard to conclude from the language and policies tossed around Washington that a subenlightened view on race prevails, whether it's the not-so-subtle undertones of attacks on entitlement recipients, the hyperfocus on "voter fraud" in African American areas (though little-to-no such fraud exists), the regular denunciation of immigrants from Central and South America as criminals, or the near-constant suspicion that American Muslims are putative terrorists, even though nary a news cycle passes without some disgruntled white guy shooting up a movie theater.

There were Harry Reid's 2010 comments attributing Barack Obama's political success to being a "light-skinned black man . . . with no Negro dialect, unless he wanted to have one," or the headline on a Fox News website labeling Obama's August 2011 fiftieth birthday celebration a "hip hop barbecue" because some famous black people were in attendance, or Alaska congressman Don Young casually telling a KRBD interviewer in March 2013 "My father had a ranch; we used to have 50–60 wetbacks to pick tomatoes." Special recognition goes to conservative columnist Byron York, who took racist dehumanizing to a really special level in 2009 when, in a post for *The Washington Examiner,* he said Obama's "sky-high ratings among African-Americans make some of his positions appear a bit more popular overall than they actually are." He neglected to mention any kind of three-fifths rule in the crosstabs. If Congress had a spirit animal, it would be your Fox News–watching grandfather, or maybe your well-intentioned but aloof liberal grandchild who just wants to touch a black person's hair because it looks "cool."

Then there's Washington, D.C., itself, which is home to one of the country's largest African American populations. The city remains highly segregated, too, with stark contrasts between the city's whiter and wealthier parts in its northwest quadrant and around Capitol Hill, and its more underprivileged, and blacker, areas to the southeast of the Anacostia River and in parts of the northeast quadrant.

The sad fact is, Washington still has a hard time metabolizing an America that doesn't resemble a John Hughes film and isn't set to the pleasant cascades of Vanessa Carlton's "A Thousand Miles." Most demographic projections say white people will only be a plurality by 2050, so Washington had better get its act together, pronto.

See also, *"Sexism," "Voter Suppression," "Xenophobia"*

RAINMAKER

Well-connected individual who may or may not occupy a senior government position but nevertheless serves as a political fixer, headhunter, facilitator, gatekeeper, and/or doubles partner. More often than not, rainmakers are individuals who've attained their status through a relationship with a president, either personal or professional. These are the people who presidents don't just like, but *need.* These are the people with pantheonic Rolodexes; who do half their networking at Aetna board meetings; who know a great place in Davos that does the most *wonderful* tartiflette; who really wish Bono would lay off the cologne.

The rainmakers who serve in government often possess titles that belie their actual role of Washington whisperer. James Baker served, alternately, as chief of staff and in the cabinets of Ronald Reagan and George H. W. Bush; however, no person is actually qualified to be both secretary of treasury *and* state. That said, some people know the corridors of power like the back of their hand, and Baker was very much one of those people. Valerie Jarrett never once occupied the role of chief of staff, yet she served as the go-between for Barack Obama's professional and personal lives—nary a season passed without some insider White House report detailing the jealousy directed at Jarrett by some West Wing staffers.

Rainmakers are often called to serve on temporary entities like investigative panels, transition teams, and campaign boards. These jobs usually don't require the rainmaker to totally divest themselves of their other obligations. For example, when John Podesta served as Barack Obama's presidential transition chairman, he wasn't expected to conduct background searches on prospective agriculture secretaries, but instead tap into his network to hire the best people for the day-to-day grunt work. The Iraq Study Group was a veritable rainmaker supergroup, with rainmakers Jim Baker, Leon Panetta, and Vernon Jordan all serving on it. It's unclear whether they were tapped for their foreign policy chops or to advise other members on the merits of Turnbull and Asser oxfords.

When rainmakers aren't rainmaking, they are often cultivating their rainmaking prowess by serving on boards, receiving honorary degrees, and getting to know Tom Brokaw's grandchildren. There's a chicken-and-the-egg quality to a rainmaker's board service: they're on boards because they're connected to the world of politics, and they're connected to the world of politics because they're on boards.

See also, *"Access," "Intellectual Leisure Class," "Lobbying," "Selling Out," "White House Correspondents' Dinner"*

RED TAPE

See, *"Bureaucracy," "Executive Departments"*

REPUBLICAN STUDY COMMITTEE

The leading group of conservatives in the Republican House conference. When reporters and pundits refer to the GOP's congressional base, they're really referring to is the Republican Study Committee (RSC). Like a ruler-wielding nun at a school dance, the RSC primarily concerns itself with whether the hem of the GOP's proverbial skirt isn't too far from its knees—that is to say, whether the House GOP's agenda adheres to a conservative ideology. And like that nun, the RSC regularly makes sure that Congress is leaving some room for Jesus.

The RSC was originally founded in 1973 as a check on House Republican leadership, whom the founding members viewed as too moderate. As the party shifted rightward over the next forty years, the RSC became less a bloc and more of an extension of the House GOP apparatus, publishing a yearly budget alternative—more a right-wing wish list than a politically feasible piece of legislation—and fine-tuning the conference's policy positions. Today, a majority of House Republicans belong to the RSC, as do seven of the nine members of leadership, with groups like the Freedom Caucus increasingly playing an insurgent role.

See also, *"Caucus," "Country Club Republican," "Freedom Caucus," "RINO"*

RETIREMENT

Few politicians ever truly retire. Save for those beset by illness, old age, and infirmity, or those who are carted out of the Agriculture Committee on a stretcher, you're not liable to encounter many former officials who've totally forsworn life in government or public policy. Ex-presidents serve on boards, try to save Africa, work on their memoirs, and ponder whether the taupe carpeting in their presidential library's auditorium should be torn up and replaced with something livelier; governors termed out of office plot senate candidacies; and members of Congress voted out scoff at "cooling-off period" requirements as they take jobs as "strategic advisers" at lobbying firms.

One rule of thumb, particularly when it comes to members of Congress, is to pay absolutely zero attention to anything they say about their reason for retiring or their future plans as they near their final day in office—unless of course they're honest about their electoral prospects and/or taking a lobbying job. However, don't expect many aging lawmakers to deliver a retirement speech from a gazebo in a picturesque home state park and announce that they're looking forward to spending more time with the partners of Jones Day.

Lawmakers are loath to admit it, but the prospect of a crushing electoral defeat is often enough of a reason to announce retirement, especially for veteran members who would rather go out on a high note than face an embarrassing defeat. "I will be 68 years old at the end of this term, and it is time for me to say goodbye," South Dakota Democrat Tim Johnson said when announcing his retirement ahead of the 2014 midterms. What he didn't mention was how the political landscape had shifted since his last election in the Democratic wave year of 2008, with South Dakota moving increasingly to the right and his poll numbers looking increasingly anemic. Asked about it, Johnson simply replied, "I've never been beaten." Fair enough.

Then there are the farewell speeches: a member of Congress's final address on the chamber floor. These things are typically overflowing with a level of self-righteousness normally reserved for an Oberlin sit-in. "Our electoral system is a mess," Connecticut senator Chris Dodd said in his 2010 Senate farewell address, elaborating how "[p]owerful financial interests, free to throw money about with little transparency, have corrupted the basic principles underlying our representative democracy. And, as a result, our political system at the federal level is completely dysfunctional." Dodd, who later said he wouldn't take a lobbying job, ultimately took a million-dollar lobbying job with the Motion Picture Association of America, one of the most lucrative in Washington.

Exit interviews are also a popular choice for departing legislators. These are profiles of the politician where he or she can "open up" and speak candidly about what ails Washington without minding electoral politics.

In a 2010 interview with *The Washington Post,* Indiana senator Evan Bayh rhapsodized about a professional life not defined by the gridlock and dysfunction of the Senate. As Bayh put it, he wanted to "[be] in the classroom, leading a foundation, doing something where I could . . . come home some day and say, 'Dear, do you know what we got done today? I've got this really bright kid in my class, and do you know what he asked me, and here's what I told him, and I think I saw a little epiphany moment go off in his mind.' That'd make me feel pretty good. Doesn't happen too often here." Within a year he had joined the government relations team at McGuireWoods, was serving as an adviser to private equity giant Apollo Global Management, and was a contributor to Fox News. That said, there are probably plenty of bright kids working as analysts at Apollo Global Management.

"To be really honest, I think what I looked for most was a culture, [and] for me that was a bipartisan culture," former Arkansas senator Blanche Lincoln told *The Hill* in 2011 of her post-Congress plans. "I believed very strongly when I was in Congress in working in a bipartisan way." The remarkable thing wasn't that Lincoln ended up in the lobbying shop of Alston and Bird, but that she made these comments a month *after* joining the firm.

The most flagrant case might be former Montana senator Max Baucus. Baucus, a central-casting Washington type—he employed among the highest number of past and future lobbyists during his Senate tenure—was widely expected to stay in Washington after retiring the Senate. Imagine everyone's surprise, then, when, in a 2013 *Great Falls Tribune* op-ed announcing his retirement, he outlined his reasons for leaving Washington in a way that would make a rejected MFA candidate cringe.

> *This was not an easy decision, but the last few months I've felt the calling: It whispered to me among the elk resting in a meadow east of the Bridger Mountains.*
>
> *I heard it as thousands of snow geese flew over the Rocky Mountain Front. The pull came up from my soul like the ducks*

that rose in clouds from the winter wheat fields of Teton County at dusk.

Eight months later, Barack Obama tapped Baucus to be the ambassador to China. Soon Baucus's soul was being pulled by Baidu's CEO. That said, he still missed Montana. "If I had to pick only one thing, I have to say I miss the people of Montana," he told the *Great Falls Tribune* a few months later. Ever the consummate politician, Baucus added that he missed guns.

See also, *"Cooling-off Period," "Lobbying," "Selling Out," "Transitioning"*

REVOLVING DOOR

See, *"Selling Out"*

RINO

Acronym standing for Republican in Name Only and used derisively by the GOP's right flank to describe apostate members of their party. Though employed at various times throughout the twentieth century, it has most recently been adopted by Tea Party and other far-right Republican activists to describe members of their party who even remotely break with party orthodoxy.

Take South Carolina Tea Party activist Jan Williams's October 2015 statement to *The Washington Post* about Republican House Majority Kevin McCarthy's decision not to run for speaker. The sixty-nine-year-old told the paper, "The freedom groups have been sending out e-mails, telling us he's wrong for the job. I can't remember what the reasons were exactly, but I agreed with them. Plus, he's from California, and they're all RINO out there."[94]

A January 2015 study by the *Post* of public statements about GOP

[94] Bonus points for a jab at coastal elites!

members of Congress found that only 73 of the 243 Republicans in the upper and lower chambers had not, up to that point, been called a RINO.

Ideological discipline ain't easy. Just ask the former Republican legislator who, during a 1984 debate, offered up this whopper of a conservative gaffe: "I believe in the idea of amnesty."

That RINO was Ronald Reagan.

***See also,** "Country Club Republican," "Primary (Verb)," "Republican Study Committee"*

ROCK STARS

A-list pop artists and, in politics, bottomless wells of awkwardness. The images one conjures of Washington's relationship with America's musical royalty are mostly cringe-inducing: Richard Nixon's tête-à-tête with a bloated and disoriented Elvis in the Oval Office, Ronald and Nancy Reagan presenting Michael Jackson[95] an award for the positive message in "Beat It," and George W. Bush shimmying beside Ricky Martin during the forty-third president's first inauguration. The one possible exception might be John F. Kennedy's friendship with the Rat Pack, but that was the exception that proved the rule, and less than a decade later Spiro Agnew was threatening to hippie punch every last long-haired Jefferson Airplane fan while Nixon was commiserating with The King about how the Beatles fomented anti-American sentiment.

Democrats have typically enjoyed support from the bulk of the *Billboard* Top 100. Stars as varied as Aretha Franklin, R.E.M., John Mellencamp, and Lady Gaga have at one point or another lent their voices to Democratic candidates. The most well-documented star is almost certainly Bruce Springsteen, who clashed with Ronald Reagan

---

[95] Actual excerpt from the Gipper's remarks: "I hope you'll forgive me, but we have quite a few young folks in the White House who all wanted me to give you the same message. They said to tell Michael, 'Please give some TLC to the PYTs.' Now I know that sounds a little 'off the wall,' but you know what I mean." [Press conference where Reagan presented MJ with commendation]

over the fortieth president's attempted appropriation of "Born in the USA," Springsteen's anthem about the alienation experienced by America's Vietnam veterans. The Boss has since been a fixture on the campaign trail for Democrats.

There are a few heavy hitters on the GOP's otherwise thin bench. The party of Lincoln has traditionally enjoyed the support of many country music A-listers. The twenty-first century alone witnessed the "we'll put a boot in your ass / it's the American way" jingoism of Toby Keith's "Courtesy of the Red, White and Blue," and "Obamacare" jokes are now to the Country Music Awards what Jack Nicholson jokes are to the Oscars. Democratic attempts to appropriate Nashville have gone pear-shaped. In 2008, when Barack Obama exited the stage in Denver's Invesco Field to Brooks & Dunn's "Only in America," it felt strained—especially in conjunction with the ersatz Corinthian columns the convention organizers had erected behind the podium. The hokey stagecraft would've been better served by a rendition of "Fanfare for the Common Man" . . . with kazoos.

The GOP probably hit rock star rock bottom when the party's 2012 presidential nominee, former Massachusetts governor Mitt Romney, was joined at a campaign rally by country duo Big & Rich, Randy Owen of the country group Alabama, and—most disastrously—1980s cheesemonger Meat Loaf. As the group sang along to "America the Beautiful," the "Bat Out of Hell" singer upstaged them all by belting out the patriotic jingle with the voice-cracking atonality of a karaoke performance by your drunk father and the sweaty, eye-bulging appearance of someone experiencing a cardiac episode. It wasn't a James Brown, *bring-out-the-cape-I'm-done* kind of passion, it was a *we-have-EMTs-standing-by* kind of passion.

It's difficult to quantify how much rock star endorsements actually help a candidate. Even if someone were moved to vote for Mitt Romney because of Vanilla Ice's support for his jobs plan, it's unlikely they would ever dare *admit* that to a pollster. The likelier effect—and one that's even harder to quantify—is that these endorsements and concerts increase engagement with campaigns. Does an undecided voter go for Romney because Trace Adkins performed at a rally for the Massachusetts governor? No. Does that voter *attend* the rally because Trace Adkins will perform? Sure, why not.

One thing is for certain: rock stars are *great* fundraisers. Any time a headlining act comes to the D.C. area, members of Congress flock to the luxury boxes in the Verizon Center, Nationals Park, or any number of the region's high-capacity performance spaces. In 2015, when Taylor Swift came to town for a two-night stand at Nationals Park, no less than twenty-five members of Congress decamped to the ballpark to solicit contributions and awkwardly sway to high-production numbers about making out beneath bandstands. If you think the dads who chaperone their daughters to pop concerts seem out of place, try imagining Missouri congressman and Subcommittee on Communications and Technology member Billy Long getting down to "Shake It Off."

See also, *"Advertising," "Fundraiser," "Inauguration"*

"ROCK STARS"

A term of admiration that has been applied, at one point or another, to virtually every white-collar professional in the Washington, D.C., area. Unless Boz Scaggs has been loitering around the Commerce Department, or the nation's functionaries have taken to performing sold out gigs at the Cow Palace, it's unlikely that Washington is home to many individuals who could unironically pull off leather pants.

> *"You* have *to meet Tim, the head of digital outreach at MilkFart Strategies, he's a total rock star."*

> *"Ohmigod, I'm so excited for my coffee with Ashley—she handles social media for the Association of American Orthodontists. She is a total ROCK. STAR."*

"Bro, I think you'll really like Michael, he's a real rock star in the renewable ham space."

See also, *"CPAC," "Expert," "Netroots Nation," "Panels," "Rock Stars," "Wall of Fame"*

RUNNING OF THE INTERNS

Mad dash by network news interns to deliver hard copies of major Supreme Court rulings to their producers and on-air talent. The Supreme Court, which only recently modernized its media-relations strategy from one heavily reliant on town criers and a series of mountaintop signal fires, doesn't instantaneously post their rulings online. As such, news outlets have interns posted up by the high court's Public Information Office on the morning a major ruling is expected so they can rush it to their superiors the moment it's disseminated.

What results is a quarter-mile race (about four hundred meters) run by a group of twenty-year-olds in L.L.Bean and sneakers. Media outlets wouldn't dare have their on-air talent mess up their hair and makeup by running, and producers—being the types to sit around in control rooms—aren't exactly the most athletic individuals on God's green Earth. So the heavy burden of midwifing announcements of changes in American jurisprudence falls on a group of kids who would otherwise be fetching John King a chai tea.

The Supreme Court, which only recently allowed audio recordings of some of its deliberations to be publicized, is easily the country's most technologically hidebound branch of government. However, its approach to publicizing rulings is one of its least Luddite-ish practices: while the high court doesn't email the rulings to a press list—the way the White House distributes advance copies of speeches, for example—the delay between the distribution of the hard copies and the posting of the ruling online is only a matter of minutes. That might not seem like much of a delay, but a few minutes is a veritable epoch in news cycle time—*that's 50 Snapchats of a Congressman's testicles, for chrissake!*—so interns are tasked with doing work that might usually be performed by a spool of fiber optic cable.

The real catalyst behind these overeager communications and poli-sci majors' helter-skelter scramble is the media's unhealthy obsession with being first. The moment a news outlet can confirm a ruling, it doesn't just deliver the news on-air—it tweets out the ruling, it sends out text message and email alerts to its subscribers, all of which drives traffic both to its live programming and its website. Whoever sends their alerts first will get the most traffic. Plus the news provides the on-air talent *actual honest-to-god material* to chew over, rather than the endless speculation that filled the hours leading up to a ruling. Because every other outlet will be doing the same thing, it's of the utmost importance that a news org herds the news-hungry masses into its pen before someone rustles their livestock away.

Now one might wonder why the networks simply don't have the intern call their producer on the phone rather than sprint an Olympics-length relay to hand off the ruling. The thing is, the reporters and producers are Very Seasoned Journalists, some with legal backgrounds, and many of whom have years—sometimes decades—of experience under the belt. These are men and women who aren't going to hastily misread the ruling and botch the solemn duty of informing the public of changes to the U.S. Code.

Or not: in 2012, both CNN and Fox News incorrectly reported that the Supreme Court had struck down Obamacare's individual mandate, effectively stripping millions of Americans of health-care coverage and gutting President Barack Obama's signature domestic achievement. The mistake was quickly corrected and prompted a bit of soul searching among journalists for a few hours before the Next Thing came along.

Quite often, breaking news can be a sign of a reporter or reporting staff's vigilance, industriousness, or tenaciousness. Other times, it's a testament to intern Zach's hamstrings.

See also, *"Congressional Staff," "Federalist Society," "Judiciary"*

SCHUMWICH

Senator Chuck Schumer's (D-New York) favorite sandwich and the Elephant Man of lunch fare. A 2010 *New York Post* article called it "the most famous sandwich in New York politics." This franken-wich's ingredients, according to the *Post,* are, "roast beef, banana peppers, pickled jalapeños, extra onions, extra tomatoes, two layers of pickles, mayonnaise and mustard on hearty Italian bread." If sandwiches were people, this one would don a white mask, seclude itself in an underground lair, and channel all of its anger, disappointment, and unspeakable ennui into the organ, forever keeping its grotesque visage out of the public eye.

See also, *"Congressional Staff," "Food," "Jumbo Slice," "Senate Dining Room"*

SCORING

Act of tallying up a lawmaker's votes to assign them an overall grade on a specific issue or overall ideological purity. A politician's grade by an influential organization is often used as shorthand for their good standing with an interest group. As far as political messaging goes, the rating system is an incredibly potent political tool, partially due to of our society's visceral association of grades with achievement. A negative grade can also provide a political boost to lawmakers. "When we get a low rating from the ACLU we wear that as a badge of honor," a staffer for Republican Buck McKeon told the *Los Angeles Times* in the 1990s.

What results is a government filled with representatives who, if their grades are to be believed, have bipolar levels of commitment to competing issues. A hypothetical vote to increase taxes to pay for a children's health initiative may contribute to a lawmaker's 90 percent rating from the Children's Defense Fund but a 20 percent rating from the Chamber of Commerce. Similarly, women's health and reproductive rights organizations Planned Parenthood and NARAL Pro-Choice America regularly lambast conservative politicians for being "F on Women"[96] while antiabortion groups may denounce liberal members for being "zero on life."[97]

The growing partisan bent of many prominent organizations can lead to scoring of votes that have a tangential relationship to their core mission. Centrist Democrats were put in a bind when the NRA announced it would score a 2012 vote to hold Attorney General Eric Holder in contempt over his handling of "Fast and Furious," a botched weapons trafficking investigation. The vote ultimately fell on party lines, thus lowering Democrats' NRA rating, even those who may have voted against key measures like background checks and waiting periods.

And votes may not always be consistent across organizations. At one point during the 113th Congress, the Fort Wayne *Journal Gazette*'s Brian Francisco noted in a March 2014 article, Indiana Republican Marlin Stutzman sported a 100 percent rating from the Family Research Council, a 96 percent from the American Conservative Union, a 91 percent from Club for Growth, but only a 71 percent from conservative advocacy group FreedomWorks.

Within Congress, "scoring" can also refer to the budgetary cost assigned to a proposed piece of legislation by the Congressional

---

[96] Imagine ending a date with *that*.

[97] That could be a new tack for surgeons: "I'm sorry, ma'am, we did all we could but your husband he's . . . he's . . . *he's zero on life.*"

Budget Office. "Have you got the score yet?" is a common question on the Hill.

See also, *"Astroturfing," "Primary (Verb)," "RINO," "Tax Pledge"*

SCRUM

Crush of reporters, cameramen, and other members of the media who surround a politician to bombard him or her with questions and get on-record quotes and video. The word derives from a rugby term denoting the moment when players scramble around the ball in a dense mass. An alternate, less un-American term might be "media rat king."

Members of a scrum are basically journalistic street urchins, pleading for morsels from wealthier and more powerful people. Except instead of empty palms, the scrumee is likely extending an Olympus WS-600S recorder, and instead of a few coins from their pocket, the mark will toss off a few words about how hopeful they are that both sides will come to a compromise. Both the street urchin and the reporter are regularly threatened with violence and told to get a real job.

The size of a scrum usually corresponds to the relative importance or celebrity of the politician, though sometimes a backbencher will attract a large scrum if there is a dearth of more important lawmakers. Scrums can often be planned, like following a debate in a spin room or at a courthouse after a ruling is handed down. Some are spontaneous, as in the halls of Capitol Hill when lawmakers make their way to a vote. Scrums can also be avoided,[98] such as in the Senate and House, where lawmakers can enter through a number of peripheral doors if they wish to avoid the fourth estate. Scrums are fickle mistresses, and the hive mentality that may draw it to one lawmaker one moment may well draw it to another the next.

See also, *"Flack," "Hack," "Pool Report," "Spin"*

[98] If there is a universally acknowledged scrum rule, it's that you don't follow people into bathrooms, something which happens more regularly than journalists would like to admit.

SELLING OUT

Leaving a government office, advocacy job, or any position ostensibly aimed at improving the greater good for a more lucrative gig with a special interest. Like dislodging a booger and surreptitiously pasting it under your chair, there's a mix of shame and undeniable pleasure in selling out. Sure, you're no longer crusading for the greater good and are now contributing to an inefficient allocation of political resources in the hands of the powerful, but, *goddamn,* it'll be nice to finally upgrade your oven's range hood.

The numbers are quite . . . *dispiriting.* At least 427 former members of Congress were working on K Street as of September 2015, according to the Center of Responsive Politics, either as registered lobbyists who had outlasted their "cooling-off" period, or as "advisers" who hadn't. Thousands more former staffers operate in influence peddling, as well. In the first nine months of 2015 alone, nearly 400 congressional staffers departed the Hill for K Street. Thousands of the federal government's administrators depart for the private sector each year, helping lobbying firms, corporations, and other interested parties sort out regulations and the like. A 2014 study by the Sunlight Foundation found that a majority of the Washington lobbying industry's billion-dollar revenue comes from former government officials. It's a shame that pinstripe suits, monocles, and cigars have been out of political style since the Harding administration, because there are some fat-ass cats in Washington right now.

A natural outgrowth of selling out is the "revolving door," the phenomenon of staffers switching back and forth between government and the private sector. These days, it spins with such force that it's amazing Washington hasn't been decimated by decades of near-constant gale force winds. Few things have embodied the odiousness of this phenomenon quite like "revolving-door bonuses," payments made by corporations to employees who take government jobs. Numerous companies, particularly in the financial services sector, offer such payments. Barack Obama's treasury secretary, Jack Lew, had a clause in his Citigroup contract that allowed for a bonus if he left for government service. Lew later joined the Obama administration, rising to be his chief of staff and, ultimately, treasury secretary.

In 2015, the new House speaker, Paul Ryan, tapped David Hoppe, a veteran of Senate majority leader Trent Lott's office and then a lobbyist at Squire Patton Boggs alongside Lott, to be his chief of staff. "I told him this morning to tell Paul Ryan that I was happy for him and mad at him," Lott told *Politico*. "Happy because he got the perfect guy for that slot at this time and mad because we'll miss Dave." Maybe Hoppe whipped up the perfect boozy apple cider for the Squire Patton Boggs office holiday party, but it's pretty safe to assume Lott was not in the least bit mad. Rather, Lott was likely *fucking over the goddamn moon* that his colleague was going to be the most senior adviser to the most senior official in Congress and the de facto opposition leader to the president. Hoppe probably isn't turning down meetings with Squire Patton Boggs reps.

Democrats are no less guilty of such behavior. Numerous progressive or populist Dems have occasioned *say-it-ain't-so* moments by hopping to K Street. Former Democratic House leader Dick Gephardt, once a staunch ally of Democratic labor interests, turned heads after leaving Congress in 2005 when he began "advising" a number of corporate clients, including Goldman Sachs and Peabody Energy, the world's largest private coal company. Dave Obey, the forceful chair of the House Appropriations Committee, joined Gephardt's firm (slogan: "STRATEGY. ACCESS. RESULTS.") after he retired in 2011. Even Henry Waxman, the liberal crusader who manned the House Energy and Commerce Committee and who publicly declared his plan to not lobby following his 2015 retirement, ended up as an "adviser" at Waxman Strategies, a K Street consulting firm run by his son.

During Barack Obama's presidential campaign, the candidate, and later his transition team, made a considerable to-do about making the White House a lobbyist-free zone. True to his word, Obama signed an executive order on his second day in office mandating stricter regulations for the hiring of lobbyists, including prohibiting registered lobbyists from taking administration jobs, forbidding people from working on an issue that they lobbied on in the prior two years, and forbidding former White House officials from lobbying the administration. The move was by no means toothless, and the numbers of erstwhile lobbyists plummeted in comparison with previous administrations, while staffers were regularly recusing themselves from projects with potential conflicts of interest.

The rule was not perfect, and the administration had to issue waivers on more than a few occasions. Washington saw a dramatic drop in the number of registered lobbyists in Obama's first year in office, falling 14 percent from 2008 to 2014, all despite the growth of the influence industry. However, this decline was largely attributed to lobbyists deregistering for the purpose of avoiding the ban, many finding ways to justify spending less than 20 percent of their time lobbying—the threshold for registration. And this was to say nothing of instances like Lew, who was incentivized by a corporation to enter government, or other officials with strong connections to interested parties.

A misconception about selling out is that every last government official inside the Beltway is clamoring to Scrooge McDuck into a giant pool of gold coins; that each moment some Washingtonian is in the midst of a glamorous, 1980s-style "moving on up" montage set to Wham!, a luxurious smash cut of them shaking hands with a realtor in front of a "SOLD" sign, instructing movers where to hang a Basquiat, shaking hands with a Porsche salesman, clinking champagne flutes, and engaging in all manner of other glamorous activities that likely involve handshaking.

Yet only lawmakers and the most senior officials have the opportunity to cash out for multiples of their government salary. For mid-level employees, in particular those in the fast paced worlds of the White House and Congress, selling out is driven as much by a raise as it is not working eighty hours a week and being able to see one's children. The Congressional Management Foundation, a nonprofit focused on legislative management, has found that the typical Hill staffer makes 20 to 25 percent less than their private sector counterparts, by no means a small number, but not necessarily one that would cue George Michael. What's more, that number is heavily skewed by the exorbitant pay raises enjoyed by departing senior staffers. A White House press assistant might not necessarily land an $800K Edelman job the way a former press secretary might, nor a freshman member of Congress's legislative director a similarly lucrative gig at a lobbying shop. Not everyone can be the deputy treasury administrator who lands a compliance advisory gig at JPMorgan.

Many mid-level staffers who "go downtown" or pursue other private sector opportunities point out, not incorrectly, that they've sacrificed quite a bit by working five, ten, or fifteen years in government. They've still clocked in more public service than most of us and, in addition to the long hours and constant stress, many of these well-educated individuals will never be able to fully make up the earnings they lost by not working in the private sector. And Washington is not cheap, nor are its suburbs, with down payments on houses running into the hundreds of thousands of dollars and the cost of avoiding D.C.'s often subpar public schools through private or parochial education increasingly pricey. Add to this the graduate school debt that many staffers incur to credential themselves and suddenly a $70,000 salary, good money in most places, is insufficient. Even for staffers who would rather not sell their souls for an extra twelve grand a year and two more hours a day to see their kids, there are only so many well-paying gigs at campaign consulting firms, think tanks, and other more ethically palatable entities to go around. And *you* try making $45K a year working at a nonprofit advocacy org with two kids and law school debt.

See also, *"Cooling-off Period," "Lobbying," "Lobbyist," "Retirement," "Transitioning"*

SENATE

See, *"Budget," "Congressional Research Service," "Congressional Staff," "Hideaway Office," "Legislation," "Legislative Glossary," "Majority Leaders (Senate)," "Members-only Elevator," "Senate Dining Room," "Whip"*

SENATE DINING ROOM

The neglected dining room is a fixture of the American landscape—the comparatively ornate space where the family silver lies dormant, portraits of great grandparents hang unrevered, and china display cabinets sit dusty and unappreciated. It's where every attempt at family dinner night—those grand attempts at fostering intrafamilial comity—are crushed, dashed against the hard realities of the 24/7 workday, social media, Netflix, and the other responsibilities and distractions of our times. Only the occasional holiday or visitor will reactivate it.

In that sense, the Senate Dining Room is just like America's dining rooms. The two rooms that comprise the upper chamber's most prestigious canteen—one for senators, staff, and approved visitors and the other for senators only—were once scenes of boisterous ingesting, where senators of both parties kept their sharp elbows off the table and adhered to something approximating senatorial collegiality. In 1994, while Vermont senator Pat Leahy was dining with guests Jerry Garcia, Phil Lesh, and Mickey Hart of the Grateful Dead, he invited nonagenarian South Carolina senator Strom Thurmond over to his table for arguably the strangest meeting in the upper chamber's history. This isn't to say that partisan rancor never spoiled any lunches, or that the Senate Dining Room doesn't still play host to the occasional bipartisan tête-à-tête, but the undeniable fact is its rooms are decidedly emptier, evacuated by the same modern forces that transformed the American living room to an exhibit space for your dear departed nana's porcelain cat collection.

Most observers attribute the Dining Room's decline to the now-accepted practice among lawmakers of keeping their principal residence—and more importantly their families—in their home state. Most legislative weeks now only last three days, with lawmakers arriving Monday or Tuesday and beating a hasty retreat to Reagan National on Thursday or Friday. Like the rest of us, senators are too busy with work to cultivate many meaningful relationships over dinner. The time they do spend in Washington is a blur of votes, fundraisers, committee hearings, caucus lunches, and fundraisers. Did I say fundraisers? And when the honorable members do actually use the Dining Room, it's probably to entertain a guest. If it's not, and two or more senators do meet for a bite, there's a semi-decent chance they'll be glued to their phones, much like your twelve-year-old at family dinner.

However, unlike your family dinners—*I hope*—none of the prospective participants ever accused another one of undermining the American military to score cheap political points. Enduring a meal with someone who just challenged your patriotism on Fox News is not an easy thing to do.

"[The Dining Room] gave members a chance to be with each other without people handing them a piece of paper about what they needed to say or think about something," former Connecticut senator Chris Dodd, who was first elected to the upper chamber in 1980, reminisced to *The New York Times* in 2014. "It was a liberating space, and members need a liberating space where they can say what they think with their colleagues. I regret that it doesn't exist today."

It's a nice room—all high ceilings, chandeliers, and the like. But like the Old Senate Chamber—and your dining room—it's a lovely thing that exists mostly to impress out-of-towners.

See also, *"Food," "Fundraiser," "Members-only Elevator"*

SEX

See, *"Adultery,"* "Hustler," *"Lobaeist," "Sexism," "Skintern"*

SEXISM

Still very much a thing.

Well, it's been *worse,* sure: gone are the days when women's primary roles in Washington were as secretaries or the inheritors of late husbands' congressional seats. Washington has mostly shed the ethos behind male-only offices where party hotshots shook their tumblers, informing their assistants with the clinking of the ice cubes that they needed a refill. Things are better, to be sure, but Washington is still a man's world, sadly.

Actually, Washington is a freaking sausage factory. As of this book's publication, no woman has occupied the Oval Office. Men still hold over 80 percent of the seats in Congress and, as of early 2016, there was only one female committee chair (Michigan Republican Candice Miller was only appointed to that by GOP leadership after a considerable stink was made over the absence of chairwomen). A women's restroom near the House chamber wasn't opened until July 2011, a development only slightly worse than the Senate, where one opened in 1993 (it only contained two stalls and was expanded in 2013 after a number of senators complained of "traffic jams"). While there is near gender parity among Capitol Hill staffers, men still hold most of the top-ranking positions like chief of staff and communications director. On K Street, men still earn far more than women and the city's top lobbyists are still mostly dudes. The Washington press corps isn't much better, either, and women hold a scant number of leading editorial positions.

That said, the trend lines have been mostly moving in the right direction. The 114th Congress was the first to sport over a hundred female lawmakers, and considering just over three hundred women served in Congress between 1917 and 2014, it's certainly an impressive amount by historical standards. More and more women are occupying higher-ranking staff positions and a similar movement is afoot on K Street, where women are demonstrating that men aren't the only ones who can sell their souls.

Yet we're in the twenty-first bloody century, and the issues facing women in the political sphere remain widespread, often overlooked, and underreported. Such things don't just impact the people subjected to them, but also have a tremendous impact on policy and policymaking. Studies have shown women legislators to, on the whole, be more conciliatory. "[W]hile men may choose to obstruct and delay, women continue to strive to build coalitions and bring about new policies," so wrote one group of researchers in 2011 in the *American Journal of Political Science*. The fewer women in Congress, the fewer people there with firsthand knowledge of many of the issues facing their gender. If men could get pregnant, it's not a stretch to assume that there'd be fewer proposals mandating ultrasounds for people seeking abortions and more advertisements for Plan B featuring men surrounded by attractive women as they all pump their fists and take emergency contraceptives—all set to the twangy, rollicking sounds of Big & Rich.

What's more, a number of congressional offices bar women from being alone with their male bosses—whether in closed door meetings or driving around in a car—for fear of the rumor mill. As one staffer told *National Journal* for a May 2015 survey of the issue, these barriers means her boss, "never took a closed door meeting with me . . . [making] sensitive and strategic discussions extremely difficult."

Compounding matters, there's still a pervasive culture that often patronizes women as fashion obsessed, shrill, or otherwise less serious than men or incapable of handling the same pressures. First ladies are still expected to stay out of most policy matters and their comms teams usually tamp down their professional accomplishments—we heard a lot more about Michelle Obama's favorite recipes in *Good Housekeeping* than we did her experience as a lawyer and hospital administrator. On that same note, media profiles of female legislators disproportionately play up their home life, and the "work, kids, home—can she have it *all*?" refrain has become nearly as tiresome as 95 percent of the press corps' "quick takes" after a presidential debate. A 2013 *Today* show feature on new UN Ambassador Samantha Power featured a chyron that read, "POWER PLAYER: UN AMBASSADOR ON BALANCING DIPLOMATS AND DIAPERS." No one doubts the challenges of managing work and family, but it's a question that's rarely raised about male politicians. Plus the alliteration was godawful. "POWER PLAYER: UN AMBASSADOR ON KEEPING CONGOLESE WARLORDS FROM HACKING THEIR BLOOD RIVALS' HEADS OFF WITH MACHETES *AND* DROPPING HER DAUGHTER OFF AT TODDLER YOGA" would've been better.

Then there's just old school *sexism*. Not just cultural norms and professional disparities, but didactic, feel-copping, butt-leering, *hey-sweetie-why-don't-you-smile-more* sexism. There aren't many female professionals in D.C.—whether reporters, staffers, lobbyists, or even lawmakers—who haven't been personally subjected to this particularly vile stuff. It would be bad enough if Washington's women were only subjected to catcalls on the street or creepy come-ons over social media, but some of the most egregious trespasses originate from high-ranking officials and other professionals whom one might assume have had their baser impulses ironed out by the spotlight and twenty-first century norms of respect and decorum. Nope.

Perhaps the most well-known recent incidents were detailed by New York senator Kirsten Gillibrand in her 2013 memoir, *Off the Sidelines,* in which unnamed congressional colleagues told the lawmaker, "Good thing you're working out because you wouldn't want to get porky," "Don't lose too much weight now, I like my girls chubby," and "You know, Kirsten, you're even pretty when you're fat." Another well-known story on the Hill involved the late South Carolina senator Strom Thurmond groping his new colleague, Washington senator Patty Murray, while in an elevator. Staffers have recounted similar instances of Thurmond confusing female congressional colleagues with administrative staff and asking for drinks. Tales of members of

Congress requiring female staffers to wear skirts and stockings are only just now subsiding.

Such behavior by top officials is not uncommon, and you don't have to hang around in Washington too long to hear similar accounts from women. It might strike many readers as counterintuitive considering the relative paucity of harassment violations levied against D.C. movers and shakers. However, Washington is still a town run mostly by old men with tremendously outsized egos, and very few people want to be the person who is dragged into a very public scandal—plenty of examples were volunteered during research for this book, but none were given for attribution.

Even worse, such behavior can be so pervasive that many women have stopped even mentioning it.

See also, *"Racism," "Skintern," "Xenophobia"*

SHINY PARTY PEOPLE

The washed masses: the well-dressed, well-groomed, and utterly unimportant hordes who populate the city's society events. Whether it's a White House Correspondents' Dinner after-party, an embassy reception, or restaurant opening, Washington's positively lousy with people who carry the patina of too much wealth with not enough important people to impress with it. You probably couldn't pick them out of a lineup even after committing the last fifty years of *Roll Call* to memory.

It's a quirk of life in Washington that its high society is so untethered from its power base, especially when compared to other major cities—an ironic fact in a city known for its permanent political class. Compare that to New York City, whose multitude of power players regularly mingle—in the Hamptons, at the Met Gala, in the courtroom during Astor estate disputes, before the ritual human sacrifices at the Spence School's parents' night—with the socialites, professional philanthropists, and other folks for whom cotillions aren't total anachronisms. Yet Washington events are disproportionately filled with a kind of neatly dressed social ballast: the ambiguously thirty- or fortysomething in tailored business wear who "does some work for the government of Moldova" and whose age has been blurred by $300 haircuts and skin products is to the nation's capital what aspiring actor/model/songwriters are to Los Angeles.

Attend any even remotely fancy gathering in D.C., or browse the website of a society publication like *Washington Life,* and you're liable to encounter the faceless, exfoliated masses of McLean, Bethesda, and Georgetown, whose Botox-infused skin scintillates with a kind of radioactive glow. Not only is Washington's government apparatus large enough that it can support countless influencers outside of the federal sphere, but it also sports an even larger cast of peripheral hangers-on who still command impressive salaries. In many ways, D.C. is a table-scrap town: a $500,000 annual lobbying budget might not be a ton of money for a multinational corporation, but it only takes a handful of those corporations to make a lot of very random people in Washington very rich.

The Shiny Party People are the lobbyists you've never heard of with a number of senior-level contacts on the House Rules Committee; the PR professionals who've represented three of the last seven deputy Qatari ambassadors to the United States; the "strategists" whose client lists are something of a mystery but you're pretty sure you heard something about mining rights in Uzbekistan; the "D.C. fashion blogger" who somehow has enough money to appear on second-rate red carpets in Oscar de la Renta dresses, their arms firmly akimbo in the international "skinny arm" pose.

That said, D.C.'s social circuit isn't completely devoid of important or notable people: there will always be ambassadors, major real-estate developers, and power party hosts like Tammy Haddad. And it should be noted that these things aren't completely ignored by Washington's major power players. Top lobbyists can make appearances, as can TV news personalities and senators who barely pretend to live in their home state.[99]

[99] Shout out, Ed Markey!

However, there isn't as much meaningful cross-pollination between the powerful and the powdered as one might expect: most of the gala hoppers aren't likely to have the Senate majority leader on speed dial, and don't expect Belgium's ambassador extraordinary and plenipotentiary to the United States to be acting as a go-between for secret budget negotiations anytime soon.

The people closest to power—officials in the White House, Congress, and the other major organs of government—simply don't have much time to integrate themselves with the local gentry. Where once members of Congress settled down in the Washington area with their families, mingling with social big shots like Clark Gifford and Sally Quinn, a typical member of Congress, even a veteran one, now spends only a few days a week there, shuttling between votes, fundraisers, and committee hearings, leaving almost no time to, say, attend a charity gala at the Dumbarton House. Most senior staffers are too busy working seventy-hour weeks to even stay awake for these things.

And it's the Shiny Party Person's money that makes the contrast even more remarkable. In cities like New York and San Francisco, the most important and influential people tend to be among its wealthiest—the financiers, the tech moguls, the A-list actors, the power editors. But Washington's legislative elite are, by comparison, significantly less wealthy than many of the people clamoring for their favor. Members of Congress pull in over $170,000 a year and many senior staffers earn near that amount, but their salaries are eclipsed by that of even middling lobbyists, strategists, PR consultants, and other private sector types who exist to advance the agendas of their wealthy clients. Even government executives like the president, vice president, and the various cabinet and agency heads don't sport the impressive income of the K Street elite. Most government aides, meanwhile, are likely pulling in just enough to afford rent and booze.

The Washington elite are well-off, to be sure, and some sport dazzling levels of wealth, but extreme wealth is by no means a unifying characteristic of the city's top lawmakers. Many senior aides on the Hill still live in group houses. Vice President Joe Biden, despite being a heartbeat away from the presidency, sported a net worth of roughly $250,000 in 2015. Florida senator Marco Rubio had a negative net worth due to student loans and mortgages. John Boehner lived in a basement apartment, for chrissake.

And it's a catch-22 of Washington that the moment a person cashes out—enabling them to afford the nice suits and exquisite skin care and house in McLean and Tesla Model S and time to attend these parties—is the moment their value plummets. Suddenly, with only a few exceptions at the highest levels, the government refugee is just another chump in some backyard book party in Cleveland Park, waiting for the Senate majority whip to maybe make an appearance.

If there's a patron saint of the Shiny Party People, it'd probably be Michaele Salahi, the Washington-area reality TV star and self-described "socialite" and "model" who earned her fifteen minutes after crashing a state dinner with her then-husband, Tareq Salahi, for Indian prime minister Manmohan Singh. Salahi is a complete caricature of the dime-a-dozen Shiny Party Person: in addition to her appearance on *The Real Housewives of D.C.*, Salahi made false claims, about being a former Redskins cheerleader and Miss USA and ultimately divorced her husband, eventually marrying Journey guitarist Neal Schon in a pay-per-view ceremony. But there's something immediately recognizable in her moth-to-the-flame relationship with power, and the smoke and mirrors and makeup and gate crashing she employed to create the appearance of being connected.

Just another Washingtonian faced with a classic social conundrum: all dressed up with no one to buttonhole.

See also, *"Madame Tussaud's Disorder," "White House Correspondents' Dinner"*

SKINTERN

An attractive, female congressional intern who may or may not wear revealing outfits.

The term is troubling for a few reasons. One, it perpetuates Washington's often sexist reduction of women in the political sphere to objects and its unequal scrutiny of their appearance and outfits. The skintern phenomenon can subsequently lead to younger staffers, interns or not, being treated as if they are airheads or somehow undeserving of their job. As the blog Feministing put it, "All young women on Capitol Hill are 'Skinterns.'"

Two, the term only serves to perpetuate the phenomenon, not just of skinterns, but of the expectation that Washington women must go above and beyond the conventions governing appearance that men are subject to. Sure, some interns might be absentmindedly wearing revealing outfits because that's what they do in college (and that there is a whole 'nother can of skinworms), but others may feel they need to buy into a kind of coquettishness. This leads to a vicious blame cycle where many young women feel pressure to dress or behave a certain way and then shame is foisted upon them for their skinterniness ("We all remember what happened to Monica Lewinsky, who just wanted to be noticed," read the kicker of an ABC News piece on skinterns).

Finally, and perhaps most troublingly, skinterns are *real*. Not in the sense that there are attractive young Hill interns and so they should be termed thusly, but rather you can't spend a month in D.C. without hearing about someone hiring an intern, or even a higher-ranking staffer, at least in part, because of her looks. Though it takes a few rounds of bourbon and more than a dash of "between us guys" patriarchal camaraderie to dislodge such an admission, such admissions do happen and rumblings in congressional offices about intern hiring practices are not uncommon. That some offices almost exclusively hire *babes* for intern and administrative positions.

To conclude, Washington has problems.

See also, *"Congressional Staff," "Sexism," "Weight Loss"*

SMOKE-FILLED BACKROOM

See, *"Acela," "Capitol Hill Club"*

SOCIAL MEDIA

Internet-based communities that allow their members to share so-called "user-generated content," whether that content be a Valencia-filtered image of a cappuccino, hastily typed-out complaints about the weather, or a video of a chihuahua humping a yoga mat. The impact of social media on our politics—at risk of sounding like one of those fiftysomethings at South by Southwest who think they can get away with wearing hoodies and artificially worn Bad Brains concert tees because they use words like "ideate" and a few years back was mayor of Chez Panisse on Foursquare—cannot be overstated. Politicians are increasingly using these mediums to announce campaigns, make major personnel announcements, interact with the press, and quite often, like the rest of us, opine on whatever is happening on *Sunday Night Football.* A robust following on Twitter or Facebook can amplify the power of a politician or organization's endorsement and fundraising prowess.

All this from a medium best known for providing high school classmates you haven't spoken to in years a platform to constantly remind you about their improv shows and one for your cousins to share content from knock-off viral factories with names like BuzzNow and Viral Beat.

The resources that a politician or political organization devotes to social media depend largely on the scope of their operation. At the statewide or congressional level, social media accounts might be manned by a deputy communications director or press secretary, sometimes given the title of "Digital Director," meaning they are also tasked with making sure their website doesn't resemble the one you or your kids were visiting in 1998 to buy cargo pants. For larger organizations and endeavors, like the White House, a major union, or a presidential campaign, there can be a social media director, with a team of their own, reporting to the communications director.

A big hindrance to Washington's adoption of social media platforms has been Washington's tendency to double, triple, and quadruple-check things. A standard political operation might have a tweet, Instagram post, or other Web 2.0 dispatch checked by a communications director and maybe a chief of staff, but stories abound of offices requiring six or more people giving a tweet the greenlight. Horror stories like these are more common in organizationally complex and slow-moving operations like federal agencies. This can be especially irritating if the message you're trying to send is perfunctory ("Thanks for your support, Nancy!"), innocuous ("C-O-N-G-R-A-T-S to this year's national spelling bee champion!"), or particularly urgent ("shelter in place"). "One of the researchers wants you to change 'Donald Trump's dangerous immigration plan' to 'Donald Trump's misguided immigration plan'" is the sort of statement that sends countless politicos into frustration spirals every day.

The introduction of these platforms is perhaps nowhere more felt than in newsrooms, whose readership numbers are more and more being driven by referrals from Facebook, Twitter, and elsewhere. Relatively new organizations like BuzzFeed and your author's own *Huffington Post* invest considerable resources on fine-tuning the way their content is presented to these networks. A common refrain within news circles is that social media is rendering their home pages more and more obsolete. Newsrooms spent much of the 2000s and early 2010s fiddling with their headline wording to exploit Google's ever changing search engine algorithm (being the news organization whose article comes up when you Google "obama speech" remains a big get). Now they're exerting just as much, if not more, effort trying to game Facebook, Twitter, Instagram, Snapchat, and every other major content distributor.

In the world of political fundraising, email remains king, providing campaigns a direct way of appealing to donors time and again. However, social media has proven to boost those returns, both by helping campaigns cultivate voters' information (like email addresses) but also by facilitating direct donation through things like Facebook's "Donate" button. A Facebook study of the Georgia Democrat Michelle Nunn's 2014 Senate race and Colorado Democrat Mark Udall's Senate race, as reported by *The New York Times* in December 2014, found that Facebook had a very potent "spillover effect," meaning that while voters may not use the medium to make donations, it did lead them to spend more time visiting the candidate's websites and otherwise engaging with the campaign.

The rise of the latest must-have social network, Snapchat, is telling of just how fast the landscape can change. Originally known as a network in which adolescent boys would send possibly solicited pictures of their penises, Snapchat has become a preferred medium for broadcasting a more proverbial kind of dick: America's politicians.[100] Kentucky senator Rand Paul made a splash in reporting circles in 2014 when he joined and began responding directly—and in completely professional ways, one should add—to some reporters' Snapchat-based inquiries. Though Snapchat was founded in September 2011, politicians didn't really begin to adopt it in earnest until the 2016 election cycle. This was boosted by a crack team of political savvy developers and editorial staff that helped create everything from candidate-specific stamps that users could place on their images to curated images and videos of specific news events. In early 2016, Hillary Clinton's campaign handed over its Snapchat feed to Bill Clinton, who spent the day crisscrossing Iowa and making bland pronouncements about Hillary's fighting spirit.

There are countless other forms of social media: music app Spotify has publicized the playlists of members of Congress and campaigns have used online corkboard Pinterest to "pin" things that aren't photos of chevron-patterned throw pillows. These things don't always work out. In February 2016, it was reported that several female supporters of Bernie Sanders were suspended from dating app

[100] It's a pity Congressman Anthony Weiner had to leave Congress before Snapchat caught on.

Tinder for electioneering. It was not lost on people that the candidate's unofficial slogan, "Feel the Bern," probably wouldn't have made for appealing foreplay.

See also, *"Digital," "Finance," "Grassley's Twitter Account"*

SOUTH CAROLINA PRIMARY

Traditionally the last of the highly scrutinized early nominating contests, coming on the heels of the Iowa Caucuses and New Hampshire primary. A win in the South Carolina primary can serve as a frontrunner's knockout blow. South Carolina also tends to be the end of the line for candidates who struggled in Iowa and New Hampshire. After South Carolina, campaigns and the media fan out across the rest of the country, making it difficult to get back into contention with a single stroke.

The state usually plays a bigger role in the Republican primary, as the state's strong conservative bent can right the ship for front-running conservatives who sailed through Iowa but took on water in libertarian New Hampshire. Far-right candidates will often spend a disproportionate time campaigning in the state; we are talking about the state that sent Strom Thurmond to Congress for—give or take—50 gabillionty years. Tea Party–aligned Newt Gingrich briefly shot to front-runner status after a surprise South Carolina win in 2012 (it was the only time the victor of the South Carolina primary didn't win the GOP nomination). Conversely, John McCain's 2008 victory put the kibosh on conservative former Arkansas governor and pastor Mike Huckabee's campaign, which had prevailed in Iowa.

South Carolina's struggles with—well, let's just call it what it is—*racism* has resulted in some pretty ugly moments. In 2000, George W. Bush's campaign undertook a whisper campaign suggesting that John McCain's adopted Bangladeshi daughter was actually an African American child he fathered out of wedlock. McCain's relationship with Bush never really recovered. However, even McCain succumbed to the state's uglier pressures: He began curtailing some of his "straight talk" after conservatives responded negatively to his statement that the Confederate battle flag is a "symbol of racism and slavery."

Democrats—and the press, too—aren't immune from the state's racial politics. Despite African Americans comprising a large portion of the country's Democratic base, South Carolina's African American majority Democratic primary has led to commentators to regularly and unfairly dismiss victories in the state as *less than*. Jesse Jackson Jr.'s 1984 and 1988 victories in the state were largely written off by the press, who viewed a victory in a majority African American electorate small potatoes. After Barack Obama defeated Hillary Clinton in the 2008 primary, Bill Clinton tried to tamp down the Illinois senator's momentum by referencing Jackson's victories.

The politics of the state can make the ardors of Iowa and New Hampshire seem like a vacation. It's a lot easier to smile beside a prized heifer at an Iowa City–area farm than it is to flash thumbs-up in front of the Confederate battle flag.

See also, *"Constituent," "Iowa Caucuses" "New Hampshire Primary"*

SPEAKER OF THE HOUSE

Technically the *presiding officer* of the U.S. House of Representatives, but that makes the speaker sound like the person House members go to when they need a hole punch, and not the official who is unquestionably the most powerful official in the lower chamber. Not even the guy who schedules taco day in the House cafeterias can compare.

The speaker sets the agenda for the House, deciding which bills will come to a vote and how they will be considered. They also have close control over committee assignments, and the ability to strip a member of a plum committee job. Though many of these responsibilities are often delegated to the majority leader and majority whip, the speaker sets the overarching agenda and lets his deputies handle the particulars.

In his or her role as the highest-ranking member of the House, the speaker typically acts as the body's top representative when negotiating with the Senate and White House and when welcoming visiting dignitaries. In instances where the speaker and president are of different parties, the speaker has traditionally been the de facto leader of the opposition, and presidencies are often defined in part by a commander in chief's relationship with a House speaker, including, in more recent decades, Ronald Reagan and Tip O'Neill, Bill Clinton and Newt Gingrich, and Barack Obama and John Boehner. Some of these relationships are cordial and comparatively productive—as with O'Neill and Reagan—and others less so, as with Obama and Boehner.

The speaker manages floor proceedings largely through the Rules Committee, which is charged with establishing the rules and statutes of the chamber and setting debate parameters for individual bills, which includes the amount of time allowed for debate and the amendments that will be considered. Indeed, the panel is often gaveled into session at odd hours ahead of last-minute votes on pieces of legislation. It's often referred to as the "Speaker's Committee" and until the early twentieth century, it was actually chaired by the speaker himself. Whereas the party makeup of most committees is proportional to the party affiliation of the House as a whole, Rules Committee slots are disproportionately granted to the majority party so as to ensure its discipline in following through on the speaker's agenda. Today, the speaker maintains control of the panel by appointing his or her party's members on the panel, though those appointments must be approved by the House.

The speaker can exert his or her control over their members in nuanced and not easily detectable ways. During closed-door caucus meetings, a speaker might make casual mention of a member's good work on a certain issue. Given the power wielded by the speaker, such attaboys are strong messages to the other members that the namechecked lawmaker is someone with whom they can work and whose agenda won't be stonewalled by leadership.

The speaker's prominence makes them potent fundraisers, and members are often rewarded for good service with appearances by the speaker at their campaign functions. Speakers may be highly partisan and divisive public figures, so closely associated with a legislative body whose gridlock and rancor are deeply loathed by the public, but they're bloody ATMs when it comes to thirty-minute appearances at K Street fundraisers, signaling to donors that the beneficiary has access. In today's highly competitive campaign finance environment, much of a speaker's time when Congress is out of session is spent crisscrossing the country drumming up votes and money for their members.

A speaker has as many sticks as carrots, and they maintain their authority partially by punishing members who cross them. This can be accomplished by withholding the aforementioned attaboys or campaign appearances, or in more explicitly punitive ways, such as the stripping of committee assignments through his or her control of their party's steering committee. In both 2013 and 2015, John Boehner punished members of the House Republican Tea Party wing for voting against his reelection as speaker by removing them from key committees—including Kansas Republican Tim Huelskamp, who was removed from the Agriculture Committee in 2013, not exactly a great spot to be in if your Western Kansas district produces more corn than the Lifetime channel. "Because of some of the activities on the floor," Boehner said of two members removed from the Rules Committee in early 2015, "two of our members weren't put back on the committee immediately." Ice cold, man.

The speaker also is tasked with more administrative and mundane tasks. Most obviously are those associated with the speaker's role as the House's presiding officer. The speaker must personally open the House at least three days a week, where they march up to the dais and announce that "The House will be in order." Though it is the speaker's responsibility to preside over sessions of the House, that painfully dull responsibility (even members of

Congress think C-SPAN is boring) is usually delegated to speakers pro tempore, typically freshman members of the majority party who can a) learn the parliamentary ins-and-outs of the chamber and who b) are too junior to say no. The speaker is also responsible for housekeeping items like appointing the House's clerks and security officers.

The power of the speaker waxes and wanes with each congress and presidential administration. Despite belonging to the same party, Tip O'Neill never quite warmed to Jimmy Carter, whom O'Neill viewed as having a dangerously detached view of Congress. Dennis Hastert, meanwhile, not only happily played second fiddle to George W. Bush, but delegated a tremendous amount of authority to his whip, and later majority leader, Tom DeLay. And while John Boehner's hand was strengthened by the various tactics DeLay cultivated to maintain party discipline, he had a tremendously hard time keeping the sizable Tea Party–aligned wing of his conference in line.

A speaker's support can evaporate quickly. Newt Gingrich seemed nearly unstoppable when he was sworn in as speaker in 1995, the culmination of years of work cultivating a new generation of battle-hungry "movement" Republicans. Only four years later, however, Gingrich was out, forced to step down by an increasingly restless conference upset over a terrible showing in the midterms and Gingrich's souring public image over his heavy-handed approach to pursuing impeachment against Bill Clinton.

The speakership was established under Article I, Section 2 of the Constitution, which states, "The House of Representatives shall chuse their *Speaker* and other Officers." However, the document doesn't say the chamber has to *chuse* a member of the House, though to date the House has always . . . er . . . *chusen* someone from its own ranks. However, if they felt so inclined, America's representatives could elect Gallagher as speaker, and have each session gaveled into session by a mustachioed weirdo using a giant speaker's gavel to crush a watermelon—it'd be great television.

Unlike the explicitly partisan leadership positions, the speaker is elected by the entire House and custom dictates that the winner receive a majority of votes. Though multiple ballots are rare—the last disputed election occurred in 1923—the threat of a disputed election or, heaven forbid, a member of the opposite party being elected, is enough to shake up elections. In 1998, Newt Gingrich squelched a party coup by raising the specter of Democratic minority leader Dick Gephardt being elevated to the speakership. John Boehner stayed in the job longer than necessary in 2015 as his party struggled to find someone who could unite the party and not require Democratic support, ultimately settling on Budget Committee chairman and erstwhile vice presidential candidate Paul Ryan.

Today's speakership bears little resemblance to that of the early Republic, and the Founders likely envisioned the job as bearing some resemblance to speakers in the British parliamentary system, who serve a nonpartisan and clerical role. It wasn't until Henry Clay was elected speaker in 1811 that the speakership became an agenda-advancing partisan position. Clay used the parliamentarian tools at his disposal to help push the United States into the War of 1812 and elect John Quincy Adams president in 1824 after the disputed election was sent to the House.

The trappings of the job aren't that bad, either. In addition to a nice pay raise, roughly an extra $50,000 a year, the speaker enjoys the nicest office space on the House side of the U.S. Capitol, including access to the speaker's balcony, which overlooks the National Mall and is situated in the middle of the Capitol, providing striking symmetrical views of the Washington skyline. The speaker also enjoys the use of a personal jet—a post–9/11 security development owing to the increased security needs of the speaker. However, the perk came under scrutiny in the 2000s when Republican speaker Dennis Hastert and then Democratic speaker Nancy Pelosi came under fire for the practice. Her successor, Ohio Republican John Boehner, vowed to travel commercially.

One thing to keep in mind when dealing with speakers: more often than not, they like to drink. Harry Truman learned of Franklin Roosevelt's death while having a drink with House Speaker Sam Rayburn. Tip O'Neill's frosty relationship with Jimmy Carter was further cooled by Carter's decision to keep a dry White House—something that seriously rankled the vivacious Boston-born Irish Catholic. And John Boehner, whose father owned a bar and who famously liked to unwind with a cigarette and glass of red wine, was seriously put off by Barack Obama, whom he regarded as a teetotaling sissy. Boehner, as people near him tell it, knew his relationship with the commander in chief would not be a friendship for the ages when, during an early meeting over drinks at the White House, the president asked for a bottle of water.

See also, *"Leaders (House)," "Leaders (Senate)," "Whip"*

SPECIAL ORDER SPEECHES

Time designated at the end of a legislative day for House members to deliver thirty- to sixty-minute speeches on any matter of their choosing. Special order speeches these days are . . . ermmm . . . *special.*

Special order speeches were exploited in the 1980s and early 1990s by insurgent Republicans who used C-SPAN to launch coordinated broadsides against their Democratic opponents. The Republicans, who included future speakers Newt Gingrich and John Boehner, leveraged C-SPAN's policy of always broadcasting floor speeches, and the powerful image of a lawmaker delivering a stem-winder on the floor of the House. The practice so outraged Speaker Tip O'Neill that he demanded the cameras occasionally pan across the empty chamber to demonstrate that the lawmakers were not addressing a rapt audience of lawmakers but actually a mostly empty room.

These days, special order speeches are mostly used by members of little to no standing in the House. In 2014, Louie Gohmert, best known for his theory that pregnant terrorists were moving to the United States to birth wee little terrorist babies, clocked a total of twenty-nine hours of speaking time, the most in the House. Other leading bloviators included Iowa Republican Steve King, Texas Democrat Sheila Jackson Lee, and Texas Republican Ted Poe, who, rather endearingly, punctuates the end of his speeches with, "and that's the way it is." It's at these late hours when C-SPAN most closely resembles public access television: rambling, underwhelming programming, typically by fringe characters, that likely appeals to a microcosmically small audience. If a backbencher appeared in the well of the House one evening dressed in a muumuu and professing to offer moon-based healing therapies, it wouldn't be that much of a surprise.

Compare special order speeches to one-minutes, the sixty-second remarks that members deliver in quick succession before legislative business begins each day. These are usually coordinated by leadership and often focus on a single or small number of issues. If special order speeches are rambling email diatribes from your grandfather, then one-minutes are slightly more concise letters-to-the-editor: no less blustery and partisan, but significantly more contained.

The biggest victims of special order speeches are unquestionably the unlucky freshman members who are tapped to preside over the House during the late-night talkathons. In 2013, as Gohmert delivered one of his numerous ruminations on the evils of Obamacare, the camera suddenly panned up to the presiding member, North Carolina Republican George Holding, whose eyes were closed and whose head was resting in his hand. Let's give him the benefit of the doubt and assume he wasn't sleeping. Let's just say his patience yielded back the remainder of its time.

See also, *"Dear Colleague Letter," "Cloakroom," "Hearing," "Jackson Lee Jar," "Legislative Glossary," "Members-only Elevator"*

SPIN

A type of propaganda in which something is presented, or "spun," in a way that is in line with an agenda. However, a true spinner would bristle at their craft being referred to as propaganda—a spinner *tells stories*. And they're not "spinners," thank you very much. They're *storytellers*.

In politics, the same development can be spun in opposing ways, with people on opposite sides of an issue playing up certain bits, downplaying others, or outright misrepresenting the facts altogether. Turn on a cable news channel at almost any given moment and—assuming if you don't see a commercial for Life Alert or Goldline—you're likely to encounter a news panel comprised of a talking head from the left, one from the right, and a journalist or other nonpartisan contributor to balance things out.

The most flagrant venue for spin is the spin room, a designated room, typically set up after debates, where supporters of the participants stand around and wait for reporters to come up and ask them for their spin. Again, despite "spin room" being the accepted nomenclature, its participants would probably prefer that you don't solicit *spin,* but instead ask for their *take*.

The most regular catalyst of conflicting spin is the monthly jobs report from the Labor Department's Bureau of Labor Statistics. The report, which serves as something of a scorecard for sitting presidents, is usually presented as evidence of the administration's able economic stewardship or negligence, depending on who is doing the spinning. And given that the jobs report is a complex document rich with economic indicators, spinners are given ample opportunity to cherry-pick facts to their liking. Take, for example, the following excerpts from statements about the January 2015 jobs report, in which the economy added 257,000 nonfarm jobs but the unemployment rate rose from 5.6 percent to 5.7 percent as more people entered the workforce:

COMMERCE SECRETARY PENNY PRITZKER: "The January employment report shows that our economy is continuing to gain momentum in the new year. Today's jobs numbers were boosted by increases in the manufacturing sector, which created 877,000 jobs over the last 59 months."

HOUSE SPEAKER JOHN BOEHNER: "It's always good news that more Americans are finding work. That said, we know millions are still struggling and searching for a good job. That's why the House has already passed common-sense jobs bills to restore the 40-hour workweek, approve the Keystone XL pipeline, and rein in the overregulation that shackles small businesses."

The two statements were referencing the exact same report, yet their conclusions are miles apart. Reading Pritzker's statement, one might suspect that America is a land of robust prosperity—the type of place rife with hearty, plow-wielding farmers saluting passing newsboys with a wave of their straw hats, all while a French horn–heavy Aaron Copland number blares from an indeterminate location. Now 877,000 manufacturing jobs over 59 months comes to about 15,000 jobs a month, which may or may not be impressive for that sector, but definitely sounds a lot more impressive if combined into a six-figure number. Boehner's statement, meanwhile, is far more pessimistic. *Sure, some people found jobs, and that's great, but far too many Americans are still scavenging for scrap metal to reinforce their Mad Max–style roadblocks from President Obama's marauding groups of job-stealing jackboots.* He also uses the report as a way to "pivot" to his party's own agenda.

S

Massaging the truth can be difficult—knowing how much pressure to apply to reality's various muscles and tendons is important. To help you get started with your explorations of existence's elastic nature, here's a spin decision tree:

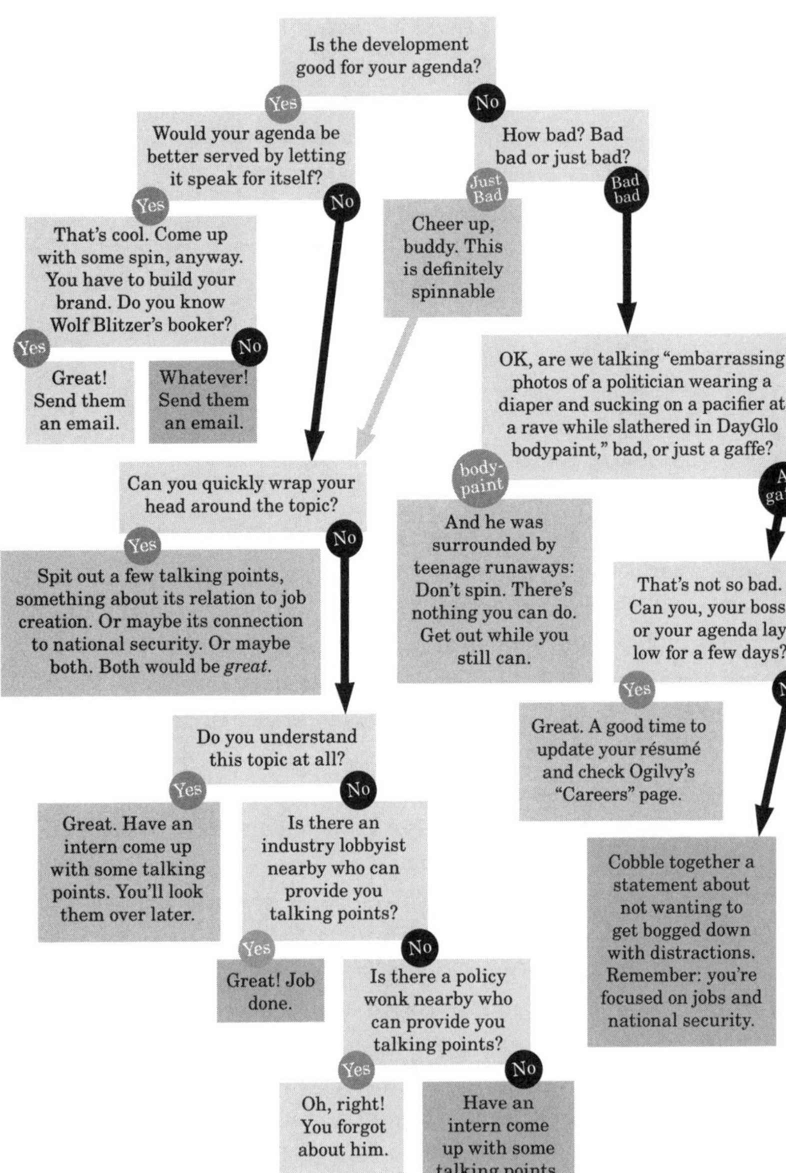

See also, *"Flack," "Hack," "Pivot," "Prebuttal," "Spin Room"*

SPIN ROOM

Space designated near debate sites for campaign surrogates and staffers to play up their candidate's performance. Basically political speed dating, except instead of one's counterpart droning on about their love of animals, it's a few canned sentences about a senator's commanding, issue-centric performance.

Typically, representatives will gather in a large room, their affiliation indicated by a sign or placard with their name and the candidate's name. Despite the advent of Twitter and the glut of instant analysis that bombards the public's consciousness likes flies to a pigeon carcass, the spin room remains very much alive, however superfluously, allowing reporters to feed at an opinion trough.

The first spin room was set up by Ronald Reagan's reelection campaign for rapid response to the fortieth president's debate with Walter Mondale. Aware that reporters had a tight deadline, Reagan spokesman Larry Speakes stood backstage by a handful of reporters watching the proceedings, feeding the journos quotes as the debate progressed. "It was a remarkable scene," the AP reported. "Not only because so many of these officials are difficult to reach on occasions, but also because when they are reached, most insist on speaking on background."

Adding to the general uselessness of the affair is that most of the points made by the participating spokespeople are the exact same—campaigns typically distribute talking points, both before the debate and as developments arise. While some spinners may be designated to discuss specific issue areas—foreign policy, the economy, etc.—the senior senator from North Carolina will just as likely have the deputy northeastern press secretary deliver a bland statement about the leadership that was on display. Though there's always a chance that a reporter might catch a spinner off guard, discipline is well maintained enough that the hack could have just as easily emailed the campaigns for a statement.

Spin rooms recall another practice made irrelevant by technology: class registration day. Washington is regularly compared to a school cafeteria—territorial, hostile to newcomers, and quick to expel those who mess with the order—but in the case of the spin room the closest cafeteria approximation might be the day when college cafeterias were filled with booths, each one detailing the curriculum of its class. In the spin room, campaign managers, top lawmakers, and other senior surrogates are the fun English lit survey course that doesn't have a final exam, while the dime-a-dozen "strategist" is the medieval history class enrolled in by everyone who slept late.

The thing is, once you've enrolled in medieval history, it's hard to get out of it. Reporters, on the other hand, regularly end interviews midsentence upon the arrival of a more headline-worthy spinner. Following the first major debate of the 2016 GOP presidential primary, members of Congress, top campaign advisers, and other spin room VIPs quickly saw the scrums of reporters encircling them disappear upon the arrival of human car dealership advertisement Donald Trump. Engaging in a bit of meta-spinning, Trump declared to the scrum, "According to what everyone was telling me, I won the debate."

See also, *"Flack," "Hack," "Pivot," "Prebuttal," "Spin"*

STATE OF THE UNION

The president's annual update to Congress about America's well-being and outlining of their agenda for the coming calendar year. Like a corporate employee filling out a company-mandated self-assessment, presidents rarely give themselves poor marks. There might be a stray three or four here or there to make things look semihonest; however, only a chump president would dare give himself a two or below, even on questions no one cares about like "How have you improved your team-building skills?," "How have you incorporated cutting-edge technology?," or "Foreign policy?"

These days, a State of the Union is mostly a laundry list of things Washington *won't* accomplish in the year ahead. According to a 2015 study by the Congressional Research Service, between 1965 to 2013, only 40 percent of State of the Union proposals have actually been enacted, a percentage that has only declined with today's increased partisanship. This isn't to say that the addresses have never portended major shifts in policy. In the twentieth century alone, FDR's "four freedoms" speech during his 1941 State of the Union bolstered the case for U.S. intervention in World War II; LBJ first laid the groundwork for his Great Society programs with his "War on Poverty" speech in 1964; and in 2002, George W. Bush foreshadowed the second war in Iraq with his now-famous "Axis of Evil" passage. But more often than not, especially in recent administrations, State of the Union addresses provide commanders in chief the opportunity to announce their most pie-in-the-sky goals, only to have a hostile Congress, unreceptive electorate, or other opposing force push it up against a wall, tie a bandage around its eyes, and mutter something about its everlasting soul. Some examples:

> *We will lay the foundation for our future capacity to meet America's energy needs from America's own resources.*
>
> —Richard Nixon (January 27, 1974)

> *The time has come to put the national interest above the special interests and to totally eliminate political action committees.*
>
> —George H. W. Bush (January 29, 1991)

> *By the year 2000, U.S. students must be first in the world in math and science achievement.*
>
> —George H. W. Bush (January 31, 1990)

Eliot Nelson

> *[A]nd that is why I have ordered the closing of the detention center at Guantanamo Bay.*
>
> —Barack Obama (February 24, 2009)

> *As they said in the film* Back to the Future, *"Where we're going, we don't need roads." . . . [W]e're going forward with research on a new Orient Express that could, by the end of the next decade, take off from Dulles Airport, accelerate up to 25 times the speed of sound, obtaining low Earth orbit, and fly into Tokyo in two hours.*
>
> —Ronald Reagan (February 4, 1986)

Thanks, Gipper.

The tenor of a State of the Union and the scope of its ambitions are very much tied to the year of a president's term. First-year speeches tend to be the loftiest, with the president emboldened by their electoral victory and flush with political capital. "If you work 40 hours a week and you've got a child in the house, you will no longer be in poverty," Bill Clinton predicted in 1993, yet only three years later, with his reelection looming and the midterm shellacking delivered to his party by the GOP in the rearview mirror, declared that "the era of big government is over." Indeed, addresses in election years tend to feature increased bipartisan appeals.

On the other end, a president's final State of the Union often consists of legacy burnishing—mentions of foreign policy goals, the ultimate legacy trophy, have been found to increase during second terms. In 2000, Bill Clinton, bruised from several years defined by scandal and impeachment proceedings, spent much of his speech touting his stewardship of the nation's economy. "We have built a new economy," he declared triumphantly. "Eight years ago, it was not so clear to most Americans there would be much to celebrate in the year 2000," he added, as if his point weren't clear enough. What policy proposals he did list were, as often as not, as humble as his reflections on his seven years in office were grandiose: expediting judicial appointments, funding waterways preservation in the Great Lakes, and increasing funding for English-language classes for immigrants.

Actually, those ESL immigrants might do well to watch some State of the Union addresses: linguistically, they're pretty dumb. A 2015 analysis by Vocativ of twentieth-century speeches, using the reading comprehension Flesch-Kincaid readability standard, found that the complexity of the vocabulary declined from college-level during Woodrow Wilson and Warren Harding's administrations to that of a passing ninth-grader. James Madison's 1809 address, by comparison, exhibited the lexicographic prowess of a PhD. By 2020, presidents will probably just opt to read passages from *A Day No Pigs Would Die*.

The Constitution mandates that the president "shall from time to time give to Congress information of the State of the Union and recommend to their Consideration such measures as he shall judge necessary and expedient." However, there's no prescribed way for POTUS to deliver said information. If the president were so inclined, he could give a PowerPoint presentation to a joint session of Congress, complete with little clip art images of the Capitol and the occasional embarrassing moment where the president turns on the projector too early and everyone sees his Internet Explorer browser opened up to BuzzFeed.

In fact, every president from Thomas Jefferson through William Howard Taft opted to stay home, and instead sent Congress a written status report. Jefferson maintained that an address to the Congress was too reminiscent of England's "speech from the throne," though some historians have speculated it was actually because he possessed the oratorical confidence of a pimply twelve-year-old delivering an English presentation about *A Day No Pigs Would Die*.

Though considering how much of a pain it was to schlep from the White House all the way down Pennsylvania Avenue in the dead of winter, it's not surprising that presidents stuck with Jefferson's approach—remind you, most of these guys were operating before the introduction of climate-controlled buggies. But the advent of radio and television turned the State of the Union into an opportunity for a nationwide address—something presidents found increasingly hard to pass up. Calvin Coolidge was the first president to deliver his address over the radio and Harry Truman the first to deliver a televised one. In 1981, Jimmy Carter became the last president to deliver a written report to Congress, and that was only because he was handing over the job to Ronald Reagan. So alluring is a nationwide address that ever since Reagan, presidents have opted to give a State of the Union–style address a month or so after their first inaugurations, with their predecessors foregoing the lame-duck-written update altogether.

George Washington's first State of the Union address was comparatively short, clocking in at 1,089 words, about a seventh the length of Barack Obama's average SOTU, and more or less the time a president typically needs to discuss how awesome America is. This was also probably for the best. "Among the many interesting objects which will engage your attention that of providing for the common defense will merit particular regard," Washington told the assembled members. "To be prepared for war is one of the most effectual means of preserving peace." Apparently no one figured out in 1790 that "The troops! . . . *Hooah!!!*" is a sufficient enough applause line.

The opposition response is a comparatively recent development. In 1966, Republican Senate majority leader Everett Dirksen and House minority leader Gerald Ford delivered remarks in the Old Senate Chamber in response to the president's State of the Union, remarks which were broadcasted five days after the president's address. Both parties experimented with different formats before settling on the current standard response. News conferences, town hall–style meetings with voters, and even a telethon-style call-in program to Democratic lawmakers were among the formats employed as response. In 1982 and 1985, Democrats broadcasted documentary-style responses, complete with terrible infomercial music, low-energy testimonials by "regular" Americans, and, in 1985, hosting duties by an up-and-coming politician: Arkansas governor Bill Clinton.

By the 1990s, both parties had settled on having one or two members deliver a brief response and by the mid-2000s, the standard practice was to give response duties to a rising star in the opposition party. Results have been mixed, with parties putting the ball in their own net seemingly more often than their opponent's. Kansas's Democratic governor Kathleen Sebelius's 2008 response to George W. Bush was widely seen as being more devoid of emotion than an Episcopalian wedding, while Louisiana governor Bobby Jindal came off as so aloof in his 2011 response to Barack Obama that many commentators compared him to Kenneth, the overly earnest hayseed page from *30 Rock*.

The increasing Balkanization of the parties has led to break-off responses in recent years. Rand Paul delivered his own response in 2015, while Utah senator Mike Lee delivered that year's "Tea Party response." In 2011, technical problems marred that year's "Tea Party response" in 2011 by Congresswoman Michele Bachmann.

The politics surrounding the White House's release of the speech are among the more ridiculous in Washington. Traditionally, the White House distributes excerpts several hours in advance for reporters to include in articles previewing the speech. Then, anywhere from ten minutes to an hour before the sergeant at arms announces the president, the White House sends an "embargoed" copy to several thousand reporters, staffers, lobbyists, and other D.C. types—"embargo" being an industry term for "if you publish this before the agreed-upon time, you'll be lucky to land an exclusive with the deputy vice groundskeeper for roses, lilacs, and petunias." For reporters, the advance copy allows them to get reaction from sources so that they can have their articles ready to go as soon as the speech is complete. Skirmishes regularly erupt on Twitter in the minutes before the embargo lifts, when someone inevitably publishes the speech or excerpts from it. In 2011, *National Journal* obtained a copy of the speech from a staffer on Capitol Hill and posted the speech on its website several hours before the address. The White House was outraged, while the publication maintained that because it received the speech from a non-White House source, it was not party to any embargo agreement. Asked about the leak, one miffed White House staffer snarked to Mediaite, "What's *National Journal*?"

In 2015, the White House, fed up with the precarious arrangement, decided to release the speech thirty minutes in advance on the publishing website Medium. "We posted the speech on @Medium bc the public should see it when press and Congress get it embargoed," White House chief digital officer Jason Goldman tweeted with as much self-satisfaction as if he had just disclosed the *Pentagon Papers*. "Changing a SOTU tradition forever."

State of the Union addresses are great times for members' inner fanboy and fangirl to come out. There is a dedicated cadre of members who arrive in the House chamber early on the day of the speech to grab aisle seats, both so they can shake the president's hand as he slowly moves to the dais and also to have that interaction broadcast before a national audience. The House sergeant at arms requires members to stay in their seats if they wish to hold on to them, so a member of Congress hoping to dispatch an intern to hold a good seat aisle would be SOL.

Members are often overcome with a similar frenzy during visits by foreign dignitaries. When Pope Francis visited Washington in September 2015, Speaker John Boehner was so concerned about members of the House playing grabass with His Holiness that he handpicked a group of reliably adult members to stand on the aisle and prevent especially touchy members from violating the holy person.

See also, *"Budget," "Inauguration," "Legislation"*

STRATEGIST

Washington for "unemployed."

OK, that's a little unfair. There are plenty of legitimately employed "strategists" in Washington—both full-time staff and consultants employed by campaigns, parties, and other political operations seeking outside help on everything from digital outreach to organizing ground operations. But there is an equal, if not greater, number who use the term as a kind of curriculum vitae flour to thicken up a meager résumé or to cover up their employer's politically unappetizing clients. The term "strategist" suggests the holder of that title regularly convenes to plot strategy with leading party leaders. If this were actually true, party strategy meetings would be as crowded as Unification Church weddings conducted by the Reverend Moon—strategists' numbers are positively legion.

These are the state directors for Hillary '08 who also served as a member of "Draft Wesley Clark" and on several congressional campaigns you probably don't remember; the associates for strategic communication firms who'd rather not play up their employer's connection to Kazakhstan's mineral industry; the officials who served in the final four months of the Clinton administration who've been dining out on it for years. At the end of the day, MSNBC's producers need to put *something* on the chyron.

A common tool for the strategist is to start his or her own communications firm. Martin Flopbaum's highest achievement may have been doing some polling for John Edwards in New Hampshire in 2004. But Martin Flopbaum, founder of Martin Flopbaum Communications? Now *there's* someone who can speak with an air of authority on *PoliticsNation with Al Sharpton*. All it takes is one or two contacts to throw them some token business and *boom*, you've got yourself a strategist.

A commonly used synonym is "operative."

See also, *"Expert," "Listserv," "Panels," "'Rock Star'"*

SUNDAY SHOWS

Sunday morning political interview programs broadcast by all the major networks and CNN. Where once the Sunday morning news shows—*Meet the Press, Face the Nation,* and *The Week*—were the go-to spots for commentary from A-list lawmakers, reporters, and pundits, the growth of 24/7 cable news and proliferation of online news outlets tailoring to every last constituency has stripped the programs of much of their luster. It's hard to justify the need to watch political programming on the one day of the week God mandated rest when you can watch the same people bloviate the other six days of the week. Sure, if it's Sunday, it's *Meet the Press,* but if it's Tuesday, it's *Anderson Cooper 360,* and Senator Lindsey Graham will just as likely appear on both to opine on America's foreign policy.

It would be unfair to say that the Sunday shows are completely irrelevant, however. Their legacy as the country's most prestigious political programming means politicians are still more likely to appear on them than on cable news during the workweek. An interview with the vice president remains a huge "get" for Greta Van Susteren, but it's par for the course for *Face the Nation.* Moreover, most news organizations—and a not insignificant number of politicians, lobbyists, and other interested parties—delegate staffers to watch all of the shows, in case a major figure makes a newsmaking pronouncement or slipup. However, ask any cub reporter or deputy press secretary whether they want to be up and ready at 9 a.m. on a Sunday to hear John McCain call the president weak and you'll likely elicit the same reply.

Indeed, the Sunday shows' tendency to invite on the same guests can reduce their luster. A show with high guest churn implies that it is something that newsmakers seek out—take *Charlie Rose,* for example—while mainstays suggest that they simply are seeking people who are "good television" or who have good relationships with the show's bookers.

In many ways this was the result of a feedback loop where the lawmakers would appear on the show to increase their Washington gravitas, and the more they appeared, the more their gravitas grew. As such, the Sunday shows would welcome them back more and more often. While this was all fine and good in the 1990s and early 2000s—when the shows could do no wrong—as the shows' shine began to dull, the repetitive nature of their booking started to feel a little stale. American University researchers found that between January 2009 and September 2014, John McCain appeared on one of the top five Sunday shows ninety-seven times, Lindsey Graham eighty-five times, David Axelrod eighty-three times, and Dick Durbin seventy-eight times.

It also doesn't help that the ascent of the 24/7 news cycle and Internet coincided with the departure of the hosts of *Meet the Press* and *Face the Nation*. Much in the way that Brokaw, Jennings, and Rather were so closely linked with their networks' evening news broadcasts, Tim Russert and Bob Schieffer had become closely associated with *Meet the Press* and *Face the Nation,* respectively.

Russert died suddenly in 2008, and while interim host Tom Brokaw helped sustain the gravitas to the show that Russert had built up—Russert was known as the mayor of official Washington—it proved too big a burden for the show's subsequent host, David Gregory, to support. Gregory was let go in 2014. Bob Schieffer, who had helmed *Face the Nation* since 1991, departed finally in 2015. The decline of ABC's *This Week* began far earlier. The show was hosted by capital-n-capital-m News Man David Brinkley from 1981 through 1996, and then cohosted by Sam Donaldson and Cokie Roberts until 2002. And while replacement George Stephanopoulos had a political pedigree like Russert's, he never possessed Russert's boisterous presence and his departure for *CBS This Morning* in 2010 and the *This Week*'s subsequent host shuffling, resulting finally in Stephanopoulos's return in 2012, didn't help its brand.

Then there's the matter of *actual diversity*. The Sunday shows remain very monochromatic affairs. Per the Census, white men make up 32 percent of the U.S. population, but made up anywhere between 55 and 67 percent of the guests on the top five morning shows in 2014, according to a study by Media Matters.

See also, *"Booker," "Greenroom," "Intellectual Leisure Class,"* "Morning Joe," *"Racism"*

SUPER PAC

Political organization that can raise unlimited funds from outside sources, including corporations, unions, and stupidly rich people, for the purposes of supporting a candidate, legislation, or other political cause. Super PACs grew out of the 2010 *SpeechNow.org v. FEC* ruling by the U.S. District Court for the District of Columbia. While the Supreme Court's *Citizens United* ruling earlier that year established that corporations and unions couldn't be limited in how much they could *spend* on electioneering, *SpeechNow.org* set the framework for political entities that could *raise* unlimited funds from those "liberated" corporations and unions. These "independent expenditure-only committees," as they're known by the FEC, quickly became known as "Super PACs." If a pre-*Citizens* and *SpeechNow.org* PAC is the rinky-dink Target-branded MasterCard in your wallet with the $5,000 monthly spending cap, then a super PAC is your friend's platinum AmEx that you just know is his father's, but he makes every effort to insist is not.

Total spending by super PACs in the 2012 election cycle came to over $600 million. The two largest ones, the Mitt Romney–supporting Restore Our Future and the Karl Rove–created American Crossroads raised, respectively, $153 million and $116 million. Priorities USA Action, which supported President Obama's reelection, raised $79 million. Despite fears after the *Citizens United* ruling that corporations would single-handedly bankroll campaigns, it's been individual donors responsible for the lion's share of super PAC funding. Of the top ten contributors to Restore Our Future, only two were companies, and the rest were individuals. Decide for yourself whether that is more or less terrifying.

To date, documented super PAC contributions from individuals have dwarfed those made by corporations and unions. This isn't to say that corporations and unions haven't been giving large sums, but due to lax disclosure rules, we may never fully know. In theory, Exxon could donate tens of millions of dollars to a political nonprofit, such as Karl Rove's Crossroads GPS, which does not have to disclose its donors. Crossroads GPS, in turn, donates those millions to its super PAC counterpart, American Crossroads. The donation would appear in American Crossroads filings as originating from Crossroads GPS. Alternately, a corporation could funnel money through an LLC to a super PAC.

FEC guidelines prohibit super PACs from directly coordinating with regular campaign PACs, but there are more holes in this stipulation than a backcountry "Stop" sign. A candidate can show up at a super PAC's fundraiser and deliver an address, but not violate any law so long as he or she leaves before discussions of fundraising or strategy are mentioned. Also, candidates and super PAC representatives are free to discuss strategy publicly, a stipulation that has been stretched so far it's a wonder that someone hasn't posted a photo of a manila envelope on Facebook with the caption, "Imma just leave the senator's forthcoming travel schedule riiiiiiiiight here."

That isn't far from the truth, sadly. In 2014, CNN reported that campaigns and super PACs and "dark money" political nonprofits were using Twitter accounts with little to no followers to "publicly broadcast" internal documents. One tweet read, "CA-40/43-44/49-44/44-50/36-44/49-10/16/14-52—>49/476-10s," which might seem like the type of thing your computer burps up when Windows crashes, but is actually polling data from California's 40th Congressional District. The sites were deleted within minutes of CNN contacting the National Republican Congressional Committee with questions.

A 2015 GOP primary ad run by Right to Rise, a super PAC supporting former Florida governor Jeb Bush's presidential run, perfectly exhibited the fine line that super PACs run in supporting candidates. In the ad, titled "Real Results," images of Bush mingling with supporters flash on the screen while a narrator tallies his accomplishments:

> *As governor, he helped create 1.3 million new jobs. He vetoed billions in government spending. He cut taxes $19 billion,*

> *balanced eight budgets and shrank state government. He took on unions, and won, with new accountability and over 200 new charter schools. The state was Florida. The governor was Jeb Bush. Proven conservative. Real results. Jeb. Right to Rise.*

The ad never once mentions that Jeb Bush is running for office, as that would suggest that Bush's campaign organization and Right to Rise are coordinating. Also, at the very end, Bush is seen addressing a large crowd behind a lectern. The front of the lectern appeared to be navy with a white border. However, as *The Washington Post*'s Dave Weigel noted, that navy bit was photoshopped in, as the lectern was actually fronted with a Jeb2016.com sign. Had the commercial featured that sign, it might have been considered an illegal bit of campaign/super PAC cross-pollination.

See also, *"527s," "Adelson Primary," "Bundler"* "Citizens United," *"Leadership PAC," "Megadonor," "PAC," "Political Nonprofit"*

SUPER TUESDAY

America primaries the way Homer Simpson eats: after a couple of restrained nibbles, it proceeds to gorge in a comic fit of rapid-fire grabbing and masticating. The *amuse bouche* of Iowa, New Hampshire, and South Carolina provokes America's appetite for representative government and it promptly indulges in a glut of democracy, a veritable horn o' plenty of nominating events.

The first Super Tuesday was held in 1988, with officials from Southern states in both parties seeking to nationalize their presidential candidate's agendas, as the focus on Iowa and New Hampshire had a tendency of making candidates for the most powerful office in the world sound like applicants for jobs at the Cedar Valley branch of the Iowa Farm Business Association. While Michael Dukakis and George H. W. Bush prevailed in that year's primaries—making it arguably the WASPiest, most Northeasterly general election in America's post-frock coat age—Arkansas's Bill Clinton leveraged its Southern focus in 1992 to help propel himself to his party's nomination.

Though Super Tuesday's Southern focus has waned somewhat, the jockeying around it has only grown more frenzied. In 2004, a "mini-Tuesday" occurred when a handful of Super Tuesday states seceded and moved their contests up. That year's regular Super Tuesday was known in some circles as "Super Tuesday II" (cue the movie trailer voice: "This March, Super Tuesday is *back,* and it's bigger, badder, and more participatory . . ."). Incensed at being second fiddle to the *first* Super Tuesday, the states in the *second* Super Tuesday then moved up their dates. In 2008, Americans were treated to "Super Duper Tuesday," so-called because it featured even *more* primaries than usual—each party hosted twenty-one contests that day, more than double the amount in 2004. That was scrapped in 2012, presumably because Wolf Blitzer's motherboard could only hold so much RAM. By 2016, the primaries had been distributed in such a way that networks and newspapers couldn't agree on which primary day constituted "Super Tuesday II."

Super Tuesday is often the last stand of second-place candidates—such as Republicans Steve Forbes and Pat Buchanan in 1996, Democrat Bill Bradley in 2000, and John Edwards in 2004. But the sheer volume of the day's primaries means a second-place candidate can win enough contests to blunt an opponent's momentum, too. In 2008, Hillary Clinton triumphed in delegate-rich states like New York and California, rewriting the narrative of Barack Obama's seeming divine coronation. George H. W. Bush came away from 1992's Super Tuesday with more delegates than his opponent, Pat Buchanan, but Buchanan's garnering of 35 percent of Super Tuesday votes took some of the wind out of Bush's sails.

See also, *"Constituent," "Iowa Caucuses," "New Hampshire Primary," "South Carolina Primary"*

TALKING POINTS

Concise, easily reprintable statements meant to be memorized and, more often than not, repeated ad nauseam.

Talking points are the foundation for all life in politics. Politicians lead talking-point-based lives the way organisms lead carbon-based existences. It's like the old saying about oxygen: you don't realize you need it until you're besieged in a post-debate spin room by a swarm of reporters asking you about a gaffe involving a country you've never heard of.

The oxygen thing is apt, though. Talking points swirl about the organs of government and media with the complexity and ubiquity of red blood cells delivering life-sustaining O2 to every nook and cranny in your liver. Practically everything that draws a breath in Washington is inundated with talking points, save for the president's dog and the flowers at the United States Botanic Garden. Actually, even the garden's notoriously stinky "corpse" flower is the subject of bullet-point-based email blasts from the Architect of the Capitol during its rare and unpredictable blooms.

Stone-faced White House press secretaries intone the same carefully crafted lines to ravenous members of the press corps, who hope to chip away at the spokesperson's defenses and dislodge some honesty by repeating the same question eight times. Members of Congress email out condensed explanations of thousand-page budgets, detailing the most politically resonant parts; advocacy organizations distribute talking points complete with eye-catching statistics; PR agents for political talk shows send bullet-pointed excerpts from marquee interviews. After referring reporters to the relevant agency, the White House Press Office arguably concerns itself the most with distilling the president's agenda and activity into word nuggets that could fit into a tweet. It generates sound bites for major policy announcements, mini-biographies of cabinet nominees, and serves up easily digestible facts about the elderberry compote topping the dessert at a state dinner (pun *entirely* intended).

Talking points aren't always presented publicly as such, if only because the term can be self-sabotaging. With that in mind, talking points are often packaged with all-caps statements like, "SET THE RECORD STRAIGHT," "BUSTING DEMOCRATIC MYTHS," or presented to reporters and interested parties as "some highlights" of an opposing politician's agenda. In late 2014, the Democratic National Committee launched YourRepublicanUncle.com, which provided young Democrats Thanksgiving table talking points. An increasingly common practice is for talking point memos to include a "sources" section at the bottom, imbuing them with a journalistic air.

In 2011, then-Secretary of State Hillary Clinton attended a sixty-fifth birthday party extravaganza for her husband at the Hollywood Bowl. Per the cache of personal emails released by her office, the then-Secretary of State was provided a list of talking points by her chief of staff in the event she encountered daytime talk host Ellen DeGeneres, who had been tapped to help promote global AIDS awareness. It was likely not the first time small-talk talking points were generated for a politician, but it was among the most notable.

The memo, "Talking Points for Secretary Clinton: Hollywood Bowl Party and Ellen DeGeneres," was hashed out ahead of time between Clinton's and DeGeneres's people. It went, per *Business Insider,* as follows:

- "I'm very excited about the possibility of your using your incredible platform to help us raise awareness about eliminating HIV/AIDS."

- "I'm giving a speech in two weeks where I'm going to call upon the world to join the U.S. in creating an AIDS Free Generation."

- "Thanks to the science, we are truly on the cusp of making this happen. And if you could help us raise awareness about this historic opportunity, it would be terrific."

Talking points go *way* back. In Deuteronomy 6, Moses relays God's Ten Commandments—God's own tl;dr Bible talking points—to his followers. He follows it up by discussing God's messaging strategy, which presumably had been hashed out with a real crack team from Ogilvy.

> These words, which I am commanding you today, shall be on your heart. And thou shalt teach them diligently unto thy children, and shalt talk of them when thou sittest in thine house, and when thou walkest by the way, and when thou liest down, and when thou risest up. And thou shalt bind them for a sign upon thine hand, and they shall be as frontlets between thine eyes. And thou shalt write them upon the posts of thy house, and on thy gates.

Great messaging advice from the Big Guy.

See also, *"Bubble," "Flack," "Spin"*

TAX PLEDGE

Pledge circulated by Americans for Tax Reform (ATR) that affirms the signatory will not move to raise taxes during their governmental tenure. Outside of 9/11, the 24/7 news cycle, and the ability to electronically transfer images of penises across the globe, few things have impacted federal policy quite like the "pledge" from Grover Norquist's antitax group.

The pledge was first introduced in 1986 to bolster Ronald Reagan's attempts at tax reform, and its popularity was bolstered by the Gipper's use of it as a talking point on the campaign trail. The pledge's promises are twofold, first that the *pledgee* will, "oppose any and all efforts to increase the marginal income tax rates for individuals and/or businesses" and that they will also "oppose any net reduction or elimination of deductions and credits, unless matched dollar for dollar by further reducing tax rates." Dozens of congressional Republicans and GOP candidates signed on to the pledge and by the time George H. W. Bush's reelection failed in part due to his "read my lips: no new taxes" flip-flop, signing the pledge had become an axiomatic truth of GOP politics with all but a handful of congressional Republicans adopting it.

Think of the pledge as the policy equivalent of when your spouse rolls over in bed and asks whether you'd still love them if they lost all their limbs. *Sure*, you say, *of course you would*. That's the expedient thing to do. If you said no, you'd probably be out on the street. Then, when the time comes that your spouse actually loses their extremities, reality sinks in and your earlier promise comes back to haunt you. This is what the tax pledge does to countless lawmakers who have signed it during their campaigns, not realizing the trouble it would cause down the line when they were in office and forced to deal with the realities of cutting an aide program to limbless spouses. The pledge has had the effect of making America's budgetary policy resemble a famous *South Park* scene where a group of underwear gnomes plotted to steal people's skivvies, settling upon a hilariously ill-planned strategy, "Phase 1: Collect Underpants | Phase 2: ??? | Phase 3: Profit."

Even the slightest attempt by signatories to break the pledge is met with swift disapproval from ATR and the GOP's right wing. These moments have a way of transforming Norquist from a wonky policy crusader to something more akin to a cult leader trying to bring their wayward thirty-second wife back into the fold. In 2012, when South Carolina Lindsey Graham suggested during budget negotiations that he'd be open to a tax hike, Norquist paid the Palmetto State lawmaker a visit to set him straight. "Every once in awhile you have somebody with an impure thought like Lindsey Graham," Norquist told *Washington Post*'s Dana Milbank after the meeting. Norquist triumphantly added that "Graham will never vote for a tax increase." These days, a person can visit Americans for Tax Reform's website to see which members of Congress have signed its pledge.

There are some exceptions. In 2011, Norquist told *The Washington Post* that allowing the sweeping tax cuts enacted during George W. Bush's administration to lapse would not count as a pledge violation. "There are certain things you could do technically and not violate the pledge but that the general public would clearly understand is a tax increase," he said on MSNBC that year.

See also, *"Primary (Verb)," "Republican Study Committee," "RINO," "Scoring"*

TEA PARTY

See, *"America," "CPAC," "Freedom Caucus," "Racism," "RINO," "Israel," "Xenophobia," "Budget"*

TRANSITIONING

A pleasant-sounding term used to describe politicos' job changes. Has the salubrious effect of making even the most ethically questionable career shifts sound as natural as the processional march of turtle hatchlings into the ocean. Each week, *Politico*'s tip sheets announce dozens of transitions, often in sections titled "Transitions." Some of these are benign—"DAN PFEIFFER (@Pfeiffer44) e-mails staff on his Communications reorg.: 'Kate Bedingfield will transition to one of the three new Associate Communications Directors positions'" read *Playbook* on April 12, 2011. Others, not so much. "TRANSITIONS: Billy Piper, personal chief of staff to Senate Republican Leader Mitch McConnell, will join Republican lobbying shop Fierce, Isakowitz and Blalock on Jan. 3 as a senior vice president" (*Playbook,* December 5, 2010). Spend enough time in Washington, and you start to get a feel for these things . . .

> **TRANSITION: "Timothy Honeybottom, legislative director for Senator Poppycock, will join Purple Strategies as Senior Vice President for Communications."**
>
> *Translation: "The Honeybottoms just applied their oldest child to Sidwell Friends."*
>
> **TRANSITION: "Amber Windpacker, Staff Director for Transportation Committee Chairman McNuts, is heading to the Alliance of Automobile Manufacturers."**
>
> *Translation: "Amber Windpacker's husband just took an advisory position on a presidential campaign and someone around here needs to pay the mortgage on their four-bedroom McLean house."*
>
> **TRANSITION: "Aloysius Lovecraft, Majority Leader Birdstink's Chief of Staff, will join CGA as President of their government affairs practice."**
>
> *Translation: "Aloysius Lovecraft is a greedy little miser."*

See also, *"Cooling-off Period," "Lobbyists," "Selling Out"*

TREE HUGGER

See, *"Activist"*

UNITED STATES

See, *"America"*

UNITED STATES NAVAL OBSERVATORY

Government agency tasked with providing accurate timing, positioning, and navigation data to the armed forces. Since 1974, the agency's northwest Washington observatory has served as the home of the vice president. That's right, the vice president lives in an observatory.

OK, he doesn't live *in* the observatory; he lives in a house on the observatory grounds—One Observatory Circle, to be exact. But isn't it fun to think of America's most legislatively impotent government official whiling away his days of political irrelevance by communing with the stars? It's hard to think of a government official whose existence more closely resembles that of a Roald Dahl protagonist—unless there's a senator no one knows about who lives in a lighthouse or a federal appellate judge made of taffy.

Until 1974, vice presidents were expected to find their own room and board in Washington—some found homes to rent or buy while others shacked up in hotels. One can only assume that Lyndon Johnson menacingly stared someone down until they gave him the keys to their home.[101] But with the growing complexity involved with keeping the vice president safe, it was decided that the job should come with its own permanent Washington address. One Observatory Circle, which at the time housed the head of Naval Operations, was chosen as an appropriate site for the veep, located as it was in the middle of a military installation and situated between Massachusetts and Wisconsin avenues, two of Washington's largest roadways.

The service most closely associated with the Naval Observatory is its Master Clock, which, through a series of precise radiological measurements, provides the time down to the 7×10^{-16} decimal point. Odd then, that the government's most efficient service is companioned to its most wasteful one: dial 202-762-1069 and you can hear long-dead actor Fred Covington, best known for his role as the auctioneer on *Roots,* tell you the time.

That said, it's still more useful than the vice president.

See also, *"Designated Survivor," "Legislative Glossary," "Veepstakes," "White House"*

[101] He actually upgraded from a modest home in Forest Hills to a mansion in the Spring Valley section of northwest Washington. No one was coerced, though good luck butting heads with LBJ at a neighborhood association meeting.

VANITY

See, *"'50 Most Beautiful,'" "Monuments to Me," "Panels," "'Rock Stars,'" "Wall of Fame"*

VEEPSTAKES

The quiet campaigning and media guessing game surrounding the selection of a party's presidential running mate. The veepstakes usually begins well before a presidential candidate has shored up a primary, either by focusing on politically appealing figures who aren't running for the nomination or on other candidates. The media is often overcome by the intense speculation of the veepstakes, and it has gotten the better of it on several occasions. A number of news outlets erroneously reported in 1980 that Ronald Reagan had tapped former president Gerald Ford as his running mate—a move that, in retrospect, seemed like a *House of Cards* story arc. In 2004, the *New York Post* ran a front-page headline declaring that John Kerry had selected House minority leader Dick Gephardt as his running mate. "KERRY'S CHOICE" it read (at least it didn't come up with a pun?).

A nominee's *actual* running mate selection process usually begins with the drawing up of a short list of possible candidates who are then vetted by campaign officials and party elders who are brought in to help conduct the search. In 2000, George W. Bush's selection czar, former White House chief of staff, secretary of defense, and

Wyoming congressman Dick Cheney, recommended himself, which was the most straight-up gangster thing he ever did . . . right up until that time he shot a guy in the face and the guy apologized to *him*.

Campaigns will usually leak a list of possible candidates. These lists are almost always filled with individuals who aren't seriously under consideration, but whose demographics—whether through their gender, race, religion, or other trait—gives the appearance of the campaign having a worldly and open-minded outlook.

Not surprisingly speculation usually centers around how a pick would *balance* a ticket. Sometimes, the person who placed second to the nominee in the primary will be considered as a good bet to unite the party (George H. W. Bush). An unconventional or dark horse choice will be seen as an attempt to infuse the campaign with new life (Sarah Palin, Paul Ryan) and an older or younger pick will be seen as a way of offsetting a perceived sense of inexperience or crustiness (Dick Cheney, Palin, Joe Biden). One consideration that has increasingly gone out of favor is the notion of a regionally balanced ticket. While Lyndon Johnson famously helped deliver the South to John F. Kennedy in 1960, John Edwards couldn't help John Kerry below the Mason-Dixon line in 2004 and Paul Ryan couldn't carry his home state of Wisconsin in 2012. Then again, Paul's running mate, Mitt Romney, couldn't even carry *his* home state of Massachusetts.

It is at this point of the public speculating that a political graybeard steps in and reminds everyone that the selection of a senior government official who will be a heartbeat away from the presidency is a serious exercise and that the president will choose someone with whom he or she is *comfortable*. With only a few exceptions, that second point has been universally true over the last few decades, but saying it out loud allows the talking head the opportunity to remind everyone that he or she is intimately familiar with how a president thinks. The host then thanks David Gergen and goes to commercial.

Surprise or "game changing" picks—to borrow the term used by Mike Allen in his July 13, 2012, edition of *Playbook* describing a possible Mitt Romney/Paul Ryan ticket—don't always pan out. Walter Mondale's selection of Geraldine Ferraro as his running mate, the first woman in history to be on a major party's ticket, was immediately regarded with tremendous excitement. However, polling soon showed that voters were underwhelmed by the choice, regarding it as overly calculating. "Chutzpah!" declared *Time* magazine's 2000 cover after Vice President Al Gore tapped Connecticut senator Joseph Lieberman to be the first Jewish member of a major party's presidential ticket. Lieberman, America soon found out, bore more than an uncanny resemblance to Droopy Dog in both appearance and temperament. John McCain's pick of Sarah Palin was seen as a masterstroke, and not long thereafter the Alaska governor was struggling to form coherent thoughts. And then there was George H. W. Bush's selection of Dan Quayle. *Yeah,* he won, buuuut, well, y'know . . . *Dan Quayle.*

While a possible pick has to let their willingness to be the number two known to campaign vetters, they remain frustratingly coy about their desire for the opportunity. Luckily, their noncommital statements can be translated thanks to this handy chart:

PHRASE	MEANING
"Right now, I'm just focused on serving my constituents."	**Pick me.**
"I'm happy with the job I have."	**Pick me.**
"I'll cross that bridge when I come to it."	**Pick me.**

PHRASE	MEANING
"I'm just focused on helping [nominee] win."	**Pick me.**
"I'm honored to be on the shortlist."	**Pick me.**
"I'm willing to do whatever I can to help our party take back/keep the White House."	**Sweet Jesus on the cross, *pick me.***

See also, *"United States Naval Observatory"*

VOTER SUPPRESSION

Disenfranchisement is nothing new, it's as central to our country as Pat Benatar's "Hit Me with Your Best Shot" is to car commercials; it was built into the Constitution and it's pretty much the oldest political development we have.

You probably know that only white male landowners participated in America's first quadrennial election in 1788—for some reason it was believed that people who burn easily, have testicles, and can't call a management company when their garbage disposal breaks down are ideally suited to chart history's course. This, however, wasn't great for turnout: roughly 1 percent of the country's population acted as presidential electors that year. A democracy isn't terribly robust if your get-out-the-vote strategy is, "Visit Bob."

A century's worth of constitutional amendments couldn't guarantee people not named Bradley the vote. Even after the Civil War and the 13th, 14th, and 15th Amendments, African Americans were still kept from the polls, a fact that magnified after Reconstruction ended in 1877. Poll taxes, grandfathering, gerrymandering, and literacy tests—not to mention outright intimidation and violence—were used well into the twentieth century to keep non-Bradleys from casting their ballots.

In the twentieth century, legislative and constitutional measures like the 17th Amendment mandating the direct election of senators, the 19th Amendment granting women the vote, the various civil rights acts, the Voting Rights Act, and the 24th Amendment outlawing poll taxes in federal elections, helped stem the tide of such antidemocratic efforts and boosted participation. Also helpful: realizing that being all hoity-toity about our democratic ideals while not letting massive chunks of the adult population vote is a total dick move.

Alas, that dickishness prevails, and is experiencing something of a renaissance. The conservative wave that swept the Republican Party into dozens of statehouses in 2010 meant some of the country's most reactionary officials would be tasked with the latest round of decennial gerrymandering. And *ooooh doggie,* did these new Republicans *Jackson Pollock* our congressional districts.[102] But not content with creating districts with shapes most immediately recognizable to a forensic team's blood-splatter expert, these legislatures began introducing a series of bills that would curtail access to the polls—specifically the access of traditionally Democratic constituencies like students and minorities.

Among the most heinous examples has been the effort to roll back early voting, which remains one of the most tried and true methods for increasing turnout. In a day and age when people are working longer hours while juggling the demands of work and family, finding the time to vote on a single day is kind of a big ask, even for the most engaged citizens—a late day at work, or a sick kid, or an illness of your own and you're SOL. Even more flagrant are attempts to undermine week-

[102] Barring a political cataclysm—like, say, Donald Trump—most observers expect the GOP to control the House of Representatives until 2023, at least.

end voting, which has historically helped drive up African American turnout, largely through church groups that drive "souls to the polls."

Similar attempts have been made to gut or block same-day and automatic voter registration. Add to all that efforts to limit voting by ex-convicts and the curtailing of voter drives, which studies have found boost African American and Hispanic turnout at twice the rate of white turnout and what you've got yourself is a big ol' shit sandwich with a hefty side of repression. Even when voters adjust to these changes, polling stations are often not equipped to handle the influx of voters who might not have voted on election day. Election day lines were so long in 2012 and 2014 that you'd think a new iPhone had been released.

The explanation for these efforts almost always has something to do with streamlining the process or, much more commonly, combating "voter fraud." Attempts to combat "voter fraud" have resulted in one of the most common forms of voter suppression: laws requiring people to show ID to vote. "The goal is to ensure the integrity of the election process and provide a common-sense means of combating voter fraud, and the perception of voter fraud," Ohio state representative Louis Blessing told *Governing* in June 2011 after the Buckeye State's lower house passed such a bill.

While ID laws might not seem terrible on the face of it, many vulnerable constituencies, including the elderly and the poor—not to mention students—don't necessarily have ready access to officially sanctioned identification. Plus there are all the people who don't have an ID on their person and for one reason or another cannot return to their polling place. You might think we're talking about a statistically insignificant number of people, but according to the Brennan Center of Justice at NYU, roughly 10 percent of the adult population does not have access to a valid, government-issued ID.

And here's the thing: the phenomenon of "voter fraud"—and, yes, you were correct to take note of the quotation marks—is complete and utter bunk. Did you notice how Representative Louis Blessing wanted to combat the *perception* of voter fraud? That probably wasn't accidental. Despite constant claims from GOP officials about ne'er-do-wells defiling our sacred democratic processes—actual incidents of voter fraud are quite rare. How rare, you ask? Well, to cite just one of the numerous reports debunking the "voter fraud" myth, of the billion-plus votes cast between 2000 and 2014, Loyola Law professor Justin Levitt tallied just thirty-one (*31*) incidents of genuine voter fraud. That's right, *31 cases*. On America's to-do list, voter fraud falls somewhere between "stopping shark attack victims from being struck by lightning" and "figuring out what to do with all the cool stuff from Al Capone's vault."

Like poll taxes, grandfathering, and other tactics, contemporary vote suppression does not *explicitly* block certain groups from the democratic process; indeed, it's difficult to divine whether a voter ID supporter does so out of racism, Machiavellian political calculations, genuine concern or—perhaps most likely, one suspects—a self-reinforcing and inscrutable mix of all three. However, the result from these laws is unmistakable: a decrease in the number of minorities and students at the polls. From 2011 through 2014, eighteen of the twenty-two state legislatures that passed such measures were entirely Republican controlled; around three-quarters of the states with the highest levels of African American and Hispanic turnout passed at least one and most of these states witnessed declines in minority and student participation from the previous midterm. One study following the 2014 midterms by the NAACP and Center for American Progress found that in states like Texas and North Carolina the number of people affected by these laws exceeded the victory margins of statewide races.

The Supreme Court has only made matters worse. Once upon a time, it was up to the Department of Justice to make sure these things didn't get too out of hand. The Voting Rights Act of 1965 empowered the Department of Justice to review any voting or districting changes from select areas—namely areas that rose against the Union, like grits, and have women who sardonically say, *oh, sweetie*. Some other areas, too, but mostly the ones with grits. However, in 2013, the high court gutted the Voting Rights Act and stripped the DOJ of much of its enforcement power. This had very real consequences.

In 2011, Texas's legislature, in the most Texas move ever, passed an incredibly inconsistent ID law, allowing concealed carry permits at polling stations but not state university IDs. That's right: Texas gun owners were implicitly encouraged to vote while Texas students were implicitly told to get back to their *high falutin' book learnin'*. The Department of Justice, using the powers granted to it by the VRA, rejected the proposal as discriminatory, but just hours after the Supreme Court gutted section five, the Texas government resumed its implementation. A federal appellate court had ruled it discriminatory in August 2015.

Everything's bigger in Texas, even the disenfranchisement.

See also, *"Field," "Gerrymandering," "Racism"*

WALL OF FAME

A lawmaker's photographs with VIPs, usually arrayed along a wall in their front office. The Wall of Fame's objective, of course, is to impress visitors, be they constituents, lobbyists, journalists, other legislators, or actual VIPs. While lawmakers typically offer numerous distractions to occupy a waiting visitor—such as a collection of newspapers and magazines neatly arranged atop a mahogany side table or a young, attractive staff assistant to ogle—the Wall of Fame really brings the room together.

Common subjects include presidents, foreign leaders, members of the military, activists, movie stars, pop singers, and athletes. Walls of Fame are also barometers of a lawmaker's political leanings. With which presidents are they photographed? Bill Clinton? Ronald Reagan? Which activists? Gloria Steinem? Phyllis Schlafly? Which celebrities? Paul Newman? That guy from that reality show who thinks gay people are responsible for higher gas prices?

A discerning visitor not only scrutinizes the photographs' subjects, but also how they are staged (or not). Here is the ranking of Wall of Fame photos, in ascending order of impressiveness and descending order of artifice:[103]

Posing: The ol' grip-and-grin. Possibly snapped after the lawmaker waited in line—say for a president during a White House holiday party. Don't make too much of these images; just because a politician was once backstage at a Fleetwood Mac reunion concert doesn't mean they've seen the inside of Stevie Nicks's sweat lodge.

Handshake with eye contact: You might not know that the VIP clasping the lawmaker's hand is Lithuania's foreign minister, but the ornate rococo furnishings in the photo's background suggest the lawmaker commands respect.

Conversation: At minimum, the lawmaker was able to occupy a VIP's attention for a short period of time. Bonus points if the VIP doesn't look bored.

Laughing: Lawmaker is on such comfortable terms with a VIP that the two are able to enjoy lighthearted moments. Bonus points if they're wearing tuxedos.

[103] This assumes the lawmaker is being photographed with a person. If you spot a photograph of your congressman talking to a ten-pound bass he bagged, consider finding a new congressman.

Huddling: The Cadillac of Wall of Fame poses. The huddle photo not only conveys a sense of intimacy between the lawmaker and VIP, but also the respect the VIP has for the lawmaker's opinions. Common huddle photos include, "looking out helicopter window while pointing," "hushed side conversation during committee hearing," and "hunched over chairs surrounded by binders." Oval Office photos are the most highly coveted, with "conversing beside fireplace with elbow perched atop mantle" and "seated in chair beside Resolute Desk" the straight and royal flushes, respectively, of Wall of Fame photos.

See also, *"Access," "Monuments to Me," "Rock Star"*

WAR

America's smoking habit: country's been trying to kick it for *years* but inevitably indulges, particularly in moments of stress. People warn America that it's a poorly considered practice that will lead to an early grave, but America never listens. It makes America feel *great,* or at least when it first happens. Usually makes it feel like death the next morning.

See also, *"America," "Buy This Missile," "Executive Departments," "Xenophobia"*

WASHINGTON, D.C.

Federal district home to Congress, the White House, the lion's share of federal agency headquarters, and summers that turn the city into such a hot, sweaty mess it makes you wonder if a municipality can suffer from a pituitary condition.

To use a classic—if overused—distinction, "Washington" could be said to be the federal capital, which is mostly situated downtown: the White House, the Capitol, and the Beaux Arts federal buildings circling the National Mall where cabinet agencies and other organs of government are headquartered. Also some Smithsonian museums where you can buy astronaut food and press your nose against a plexiglass display case and gawk at Alexander Hamilton's breeches. Outside of some of the grander federal buildings and museums, most of downtown Washington is defined by boxy, forgettable 1970s-style office buildings and the Starbucks, power restaurants, sandwich shops, and soup and salad-to-go chains that occupy their ground floors. If the producers of the next Batman film were looking for an anonymous city to destroy, downtown would be a great choice. If they actually wanted to destroy it, that would be fine, too.

Then there's *D.C.*, the city with some 600,000-plus residents and one of the country's more interesting—and frankly gorgeous—urban areas. The city with its beautiful residential neighborhoods defined by their iconic multicolored rowhouses, the city with a vibrant immigrant community, the city with storied alternative newspapers like the *Washington City Paper* and the LGBT-focused *Washington Blade,* the city with a proud musical history that has given rise to everything from Duke Ellington to hardcore punk pioneers Bad Brains and No Limit to Go-Go founding father Chuck Brown—all of whom benefited from the city's excellent offering of performance spaces.

Oh, yeah, and the city that was founded in a literal swamp and feels like Rodney Dangerfield's armpit in summer.

Even if D.C.'s cultural accomplishments have been somewhat few and far between, the city has begun to fill out culturally in recent years, witnessing an urban boom and subsequent explosion of new restaurants, galleries, shops, and bars, providing the capital with a cultural scene commensurate with its national standing. Like urban renewal and gentrification everywhere, this has been a mixed blessing.

Washington, D.C.'s official flag is modeled after George Washington's coat of arms, featuring three red stars atop four red-and-white bars. However, if D.C. had its own flag, each star would be replaced by the outline of an abandoned African American hair salon that some enterprising hipsters turned into a cramped bar or café called

"The Bun," "Blowout," or "Trim."[104] Indeed, the District of Columbia—the malarial swampland that our Founding Fathers thought would be a great place to stick a government[105]—has witnessed a startling, gentrification-fueled transformation over the last fifteen to twenty years. Edison bulbs and Mexican saint candles are no less a fixture of today's Washington than think tanks and marriages ruined by work commitments.

Much of this millennial-friendly gentrification has centered around the U Street and 14th Street corridors and in the Shaw and Logan Circle neighborhoods, which sit in the heart of D.C.'s urban core in its northwest quadrant. These areas were decimated, literally and economically, by the urban blight of the second half of the twentieth century. U Street was mostly destroyed by the riots following Dr. Martin Luther King Jr.'s assassination, and as the twentieth century came to a close, U, 14th, and Shaw were a bombed-out and crime-ridden shadow of their former selves, an especially tragic development, not just for the self-evident reasons, but because they were once one of America's most vibrant centers of African American achievement. Home to Howard University and known by some as "Black Broadway," U Street once contained a number of theaters, jazz clubs, and other cultural venues. Duke Ellington was raised only a couple of blocks from U Street's core and his first group, Duke's Serenaders, were a mainstay in the city's jazz scene. By 2000, there was only a handful of bright spots, like the performance venue 9:30 Club and Ben's Chili Bowl, a local institution serving half-smokes, a regional sausage variant comprised of a pork-beef blend.

Developers started to take note after the opening of the U Street metro stop in 1999. In recent years, the neighborhood's transformation resembled that witnessed in neighborhoods like Bedford Stuyvesant in Brooklyn and the Mission District in San Francisco,

[104] A tattoo of the D.C. flag is basically the capital's very own tribal tat.

[105] It's a long story, but attentive civics and history students might recall that Washington, D.C., is responsible for our national debt in more than one way. Also, Thomas Jefferson was a selfish dick.

with the opening of specialty coffee shops, wine bars, and other totems of gentrification. The area's development has achieved shameless levels of self-parody. Perhaps the most egregious examples are condos that have appropriated the area's storied past. Luxury residences like The Ellington and The Fitzgerald sport some of the most expensive rents in the city. These are the sort of condos with splashy websites that feature stock images of attractive young people flirting at bars with brightly colored drinks that no one actually buys and encourage prospective buyers and renters with vague pronouncements about the lifestyle such developments afford:

The Howerton: Modern Living, Classic Style

The Phlegm Lofts: The Time Is Now

The Mews at Fever Blister: Something for Everyone!

Given Howard University's proximity and consistent supply of middle-to-upper-class African Americans ensuring that there is at least a *modicum* of diversity in the neighborhood, there could certainly be *worse* places for condos named after black luminaries. However, every time you spy a white twentysomething emerging from the Ellington in a North Face fleece and Ray-Bans, a small part of you dies. Developers really have no shame.

The MLK: Live Your *Dream*

The Malcolm: X Marks the Spot!

OK, it's not *that* bad, but it's getting there. In 2014, the Central Union Mission on 14th Street, a homeless shelter that had served the neighborhood for thirty years, relocated to the Union Station area near the Capitol. The building was quickly gutted and filled with fifty luxury apartments and condos. Even the most unapologetic yuppies—

and your author, for full disclosure, is a yuppie asshole—let out a collective gag when the building's name was unveiled: The Mission. There are no plans to transform into condos the nearby Elizabeth Taylor Health Clinic, which served the city's sizable LGBT population through the AIDS epidemic and continues to treat the disproportionate number of Washingtonians with HIV/AIDS. The possibilities, as with the black figure–named condos, are similarly terrifying.

> *The Flats at The Elizabeth Taylor AIDS Clinic: Make the City Yours!*

While Capitol Hill teems with staffers, lobbyists, journalists, and other politicos after work—in staffer haunts like Hawk 'n' Dove and journo hangouts like the Tune Inn—things get pretty quiet by 10 p.m., even on weekends. If Logan, 14th Street, and U Street are defined by their ever increasing number of cutting-edge restaurants, then the Capitol area is defined by its ever-increasing number of thirty- and fortysomething professional couples with a baby bobbing up and down in a BabyBjörn.

D.C. achieves maximum sleepiness in its wealthier suburban areas nearer to the Maryland border. Neighborhoods like Chevy Chase, Tenleytown, Cleveland Park, and the Palisades, situated outside D.C.'s central urban core, are virtually indistinguishable from the suburban areas that make up the majority of the D.C. metropolitan area. These neighborhoods' proximity to D.C.'s downtown cultural, governmental, and business hubs makes them appealing places to live for many of the region's wealthier lobbyists, editors in chief, and other boldfaced names. A healthy portion of Washington's book parties, holiday shindigs, and other high falutin' gatherings occur in its wood-paneled living rooms and spacious lawns.

However, all this is moneyed D.C. The primarily white D.C. Washington is also home to a number of vibrant immigrant communities. The deposing of Ethiopian emperor Haile Selassie in a coup in 1974 prompted many of his supporters and others fleeing the violence that engulfed the country to emigrate from the country, many ending up in Washington, D.C.'s U Street and Shaw neighborhoods. Outside of the aforementioned half-smoke, the kitfo and tibs served up at many of the area's Ethiopian restaurants might be the closest thing D.C. has to regional specialties. Similarly, violence in Central America, particularly the Salvadoran civil war from the late 1970s to early 1990s, led to a mass migration to D.C., and Spanish-speaking populations still make up a sizable portion of the Columbia Heights and Mount Pleasant neighborhoods. But like many of the city's other working- and middle-class communities, many of these families have been forced by rising real-estate prices to relocate.

Washington's African American population has comprised a majority of the District's citizens since the 1960s yet it has regularly been its most disenfranchised, both through the legacy of America's institutionalized racism and because D.C.'s status as a District means the laws passed by its local government, which was only granted home rule since 1973, are still subject to congressional review.

Rock Creek Park, the sprawling, mostly untamed parkland that sits to the immediate west of 16th Street and juts into Maryland, has historically been the dividing line between the wealthier, white areas and poorer, black ones. However, the demographic shift back to the cities in recent decades has led to a gentrification bonanza, with once politically and economically forgotten areas like Petworth and Bloomingdale now bustling hubs of residential and commercial development. Not surprisingly, displacement is an issue and the phenomenon of predatory developers offering payments to longtime residents for well under the market price remains a sadly common thing.

D.C. remains an incredibly segregated city, if no longer by Jim Crow–era laws, then by the legacy of those policies and the hardship wrought by them. Some of Washington's neighborhoods east of Rock Creek Park and south of the Anacostia River are among the most crime ridden and downtrodden in the country. The AIDS rate among African Americans is at sub-Saharan African levels and one in seven homes struggles with food security, a number that rises when you limit your sample to D.C.'s less affluent areas. Many of the city's schools are struggling with a lack of teachers and basic supplies. According to a May 2015 report in *The Washington Post,* D.C.'s homeless population exceeds 10,000, and that's not counting individuals and families teetering on the edge of homelessness. Exacerbating that situation are the city's declining number of shelters and affordable housing units.

Development has been a mixed blessing for these communities. In the neighborhoods east of the Anacostia River, only six sitdown restaurants served 140,000 residents as of 2013, though many expect that number to grow as development finally reaches those communities. In 2008, a string of shootings in the Northeast Trinidad neighborhood led police to set up checkpoints on its perimeter. Only five years later, some rowhouses were on the market for nearly $1 million.

The city of Washington recalls the adage that America gets the government it deserves. In that sense, America also gets the capital city that it deserves: home to unprecedented urban renewal, struggling with Jim Crow's legacy, and home to one too many people in Warby Parker glasses.

See also, *"Maryland," "New York City," "Northern Virginia"*

WASHINGTON READ

The act of flipping straight to a book's index to see if one is mentioned and, if so, how often and in what capacity. The earliest known reference to "Washington Read" dates to a 1985 *Washington Post* write-up of a book party for Peter Goldman and Tony Fuller's *Quest for the Presidency, 1984*. "There was the usual jesting about the 'Washington read,'" wrote the *Post*'s Mary Battiata, "which consists of a flip through the index in search of one's name."

One day, index-browsing will be taken to its logical conclusion:

HERE LIES

NELSON, ELIOT, 39–41

BELOVED HUSBAND, 92–93

W

Eliot Nelson

CARING FATHER, 51–85

DEVOTED SON, 12–41

PUBLIC EXPOSURE ARREST, 43

See also, *"Bubble," "Expert," "Listserv," "Monuments to Me," "Wall of Fame"*

WEIGHT LOSS

A sign to the public and press that a rumored candidate is seriously considering a run. Candidates who are overweight[106] are often said to be politically vulnerable, though no one can really trace the source of these concerns. The media's obsession with a candidate's weight makes the collective body consciousness of a *Vogue* editorial meeting seem tame by comparison. This (almost) literal entrail reading is more likely an extension of America's body obsession than the electorate's genuine concern about a candidate's health.

"There are people who say you couldn't be president," Barbara Walters solemnly noted during a 2012 interview with Chris Christie, New Jersey's famously rotund governor. It was unclear who these "people" were. However, "there are people who say" strikes a more polite tone than *"Daaaamn, you fat."* Headline writers tend to take a cheekier approach in their assessment that pounds portend problems. "Weighty Issues Bedevil Campaigners," read the October 2011 headline in the Worcester *Telegram & Gazette.* "In a Year of Voter Unrest, Politicians Are Watching Waste and Waistlines," noted *The New York Times* in 2010. "HEY, POLITICIANS, PUT DOWN PORK, LEAD BY EXAMPLE" screamed the 2004 headline of a column by *Orlando Sentinel* columnist Mike Thomas, demanding that local lawmakers not only cut back on earmarks, but on their waistlines as well.

Christie, for what it's worth, actually did engage in some slimming down in advance of his ascent to the national spotlight, a

[106] Well, *seriously* overweight—fit politicians are themselves something of a novelty.

development that did not go unnoticed by America's puntastic press. "Governors Girth: Weight and See" published *Suburban Trends* of Morris, New Jersey in May 2013. "A BIG MOMENT NEARING FOR JERSEY'S GOV. CHRISTIE" blasted the *Pittsburgh Post-Gazette* in August 2012. And then there was the *Kansas City Star*'s May 2013 headline, "Christie Weight Loss Feeds Political Buzz."

There are plenty of arguments for why it's politically advantageous to drop some lbs. Lawmaking is not easy work, requiring long hours, physical stamina, and the ability to not drop dead from cardiac arrest while receiving a briefing in the Situation Room. And studies have demonstrated a psychological bias against overweight people, attributing their size to a perceived lack of will. But in the grand scheme of politics and all the issues and questions that bedevil legislators, a weight problem seems quaint compared to some of the serious problems that can sink a candidacy. And while excessive girth might bode ill for an aspiring actor or actress, a lawmaker's public battle with weight can just as easily engender sympathy from an electorate that is no stranger to such problems. It worked wonders for Oprah.

See also, *"Sexism," "Shiny Party People," "Skintern," "Veepstakes"*

WEST WEST WING

Area to the immediate west of the White House where staffers meet "off campus" with visitors, some of whom they don't want to appear in visitor logs—whether they be lobbyists, controversial figures, or Joe Biden's weed guy. One might assume that White House business occurs in the gilded environs of the West Wing, beneath the watchful eye of oil paintings of Benjamin Harrison and whatnot, but many meetings with non-principals are as likely to occur over a cup of joe at Peet's Coffee, a gourmet sandwich at Breadline, or, if the participants are particularly close, over an Ultimate Porker™ meat sub at the Jimmy John's on Pennsylvania Ave.

The White House is not legally required to disclose the names of its visitors or the purpose for their visits, a fact that was backed up by an appellate court ruling in 2013. However, in 2009 the Obama administration made a point of releasing its logs to the public in a grand show of transparency (only after it was taken to court over them). Like virtually every other presidential show of good governance, this one was riddled with holes. The White House's searchable database of the millions of entries in the logs is more incomplete that an NBA draftee's college degree. Many of the descriptions are incomplete and many scheduled visits that never occurred nonetheless appear in the logs. Then there's the distinct chance that the meeting didn't actually occur in the White House, but over a pizza sandwich at Potbelly. "A lot of them like lattes—that or a 'depth charge,' a coffee with a shot of espresso," a Caribou Coffee barista told *The New York Times* in 2010. "The caffeine rush—they need it."

See also, *"Food," "Lobbying," "Transitioning," "White House"*

THE WEST WING

NBC drama that ran from 1999 to 2006 and depicted a fictional Democratic president, Josiah Bartlet (Martin Sheen), and the frantic work of his senior staff. The program served as a shot of adrenaline to the political ambitions of countless millennials, sucked into the show's romantic portrayal of the nation's capital and the screwball cast of legislators, staffers, campaign operatives, and reporters who briskly walked-and-talked through its corridors of power. Just as *ER* piqued viewers' interest in medicine with its soapy dramatization of hospital life, *All the President's Men* bolstered applications to journalism school, and Dick Wolf reinforced New York's dangerous allure by convincing the world that Manhattan is entirely populated by bloodthirsty pedophiles, *The West Wing* remains our era's most resonant call to public service.

The West Wing of creator and lead writer Aaron Sorkin's imagination is inspiring: a wonderful (and wonderfully lit) world of whip-smart operators with razor-sharp tongues, a world where arguments sway, where oratory is as potent a legislative tool as a filibuster, where the census stirs passions with the same power as matters of war and peace, where presidents not only play the role of commander in chief, but SAT vocab cue card in chief, where Republicans aren't demonic obstructionists (most of the time) but fellow warriors in democracy's trenches, where K Street's revolving door is practically nonexistent and few problems can't be solved by a rousing soliloquy set to a soaring, string and French horn–heavy musical score. *The West Wing* stumbled after its fourth season when Sorkin left—more closely resembling *CSI: Interior Department* than the warmly intelligent show people had grown to love—but regained its footing by its seventh and final season with compelling turns by Alan Alda and Jimmy Smits as presidential candidates.

It's hard to overstate the Costco-sized plot of real estate *The West Wing* occupies in the consciousness of Washington's twenty- and thirtysomethings. Frayed DVD packages of the show sit stacked beside countless televisions in Washington group house living rooms and newly arrived interns compare one another to Josh (Bradley Whitford), Leo (John Spencer), Sam (Rob Lowe), CJ (Allison Janney), Toby (Richard Schiff), and Charlie (Dulé Hill) with the same vigor that wannabe ladies who lunch squabble over who is Samantha or Charlotte. For the lowly congressional legislative correspondent or think tank researcher whose days are defined by a drab monotony that is altogether absent from *The West Wing,* a dose of the show can help embolden them for the dreary work that lies ahead—like a deck officer's impassioned speech about the emperor to a fighter pilot readying to ram his fighter plane into a Cleveland-class light cruiser.

Washington has become a wildly popular setting for television shows over the last decade, many of which have achieved more, in one way or another, than *The West Wing.* D.C. has never looked sexier and sleeker than in Netflix's *House of Cards,* where Robin Wright's pixie cut is immaculate, Congress apparently has the money for Apple products, and kitchen splashbacks are always on point. Amazon's *Alpha House,* loosely based on the former roommate arrangements of senators Chuck Schumer, Dick Durbin, and Congressman George

Miller, is chock-full of D.C. flavor, thanks in no small part to the input of consulting producer Jonathan Alter, a veteran columnist, author, and TV pundit. *Veep,* starring Julia Louis-Dreyfus as an aloof vice president, captured many of the frumpy, socially inept ways of D.C.'s Beltway warriors, albeit in an exaggerated caricature. Amy Brookheimer (Anna Chlumsky) and Dan Egan (Reid Scott) remain the most accurate on-screen renderings of the types of thirty-five-year-olds mulling about 17th and Pennsylvania NW on any given work day—smart, attractive, and quite possibly on the spectrum. *Scandal* is just plain fun.

Yet nothing has burrowed itself so deeply into the hearts and minds of the next generation of Washington's elite quite like *The West Wing.* Binge sessions have served as a kind of televised Xanax for innumerable young politicos seeking an emotional salve, where sweatpants and a pint of Ben & Jerry's might otherwise do the trick. Its characters not only befriend each other, but the viewer, too, like in *Friends* or *Felicity,* but for people whose ambitions were wonkier than sitting around in a New York coffee shop in a loosely knit beret.

Just don't reference the show in a meeting. That'll earn you an eye roll.

See also, *"Cards Against Humanity," "Jumbo Slice," "White House"*

"WHAT DO YOU DO?"

Gauche party question that political Washingtonians never dare ask, lest they appear unduly ambitious or uninterested in their new acquaintance's nonprofessional life. Of course, the Washingtonians who tsk-tsks someone for asking the question are almost certainly themselves unduly ambitious and couldn't care less about a person's bocce ball league, CrossFit routine, or opinions about a YouTube video depicting a toddler trying to "swipe" a magazine. Asking a person about how they spend a majority of their waking hours isn't an inherently shallow line of inquiry, but in Washington, demonstrating one's work-life balance is a great way to make new friends—friends who could find you a better job.

Alternate conversation starters include:

"Where do you live?"	**Innocuous enough and great opportunity to publicly bemoan gentrification.**
"Where are you from?"	**Delicate question. Asking if a person is from Washington is to betray oneself as a complete noob, as most political Washingtonians rarely hail from D.C. originally. To ask where one is *originally* from conveys a kind of sleazy, Beltway-centric worldview. You might as well ask if they read that day's *Playbook*.**
"How do you know [party host]?"	**Backdoor into finding out what a person does, as they probably now or have previously worked with the host. Well done.**
"Do you like fun?"	**Who doesn't like fun?**

See also, *"'I'm sorry, (s)he's not in right now. Can I take a message?'" "Lobaeist," "Shiny Party People"*

WHIP

The leadership official tasked with keeping tabs on their caucus's votes and ensuring party discipline. The whip's responsibilities, both as a vote tallier and a senior party official, vary from chamber to chamber and congressional session to congressional session.

Before we continue, two quick answers:

1. The word comes from the British Parliament, which, in the late eighteenth century, started to cheekily compare their vote counters to the attendants on fox hunts tasked with "whipping in" the hounds. House Speaker Thomas Reed, Republican of Maine, borrowed the term in 1897 when he appointed the first whip, James A. Tawney of Minnesota. Jolly good.
2. No, do not address the whip as "Whip so-and-so." That's weird.
    a. Yes, some people do. It's weird.

Moving on.

The Senate's whips don't derive as much of their influence from their vote corralling, if only because it's much easier to keep track of dozens, rather than hundreds, of people. Their official title, assistant party leader, speaks to the leadership role they serve. Indeed, the politician most closely associated with vote whipping in the Senate, Lyndon Johnson, was his party's Senate whip for only two years, from 1951 to 1953. Whenever you see images of LBJ getting oppressively close to his colleagues, drenching them in his anger spittle, and haranguing them to vote one way or another, chances are he was his party's leader at the time.

House minority whips, being their party's second-in-command, usually play a larger role in strategy than majority whips. It's the House majority whips who spend the most time counting votes.

The whip goes about the business of vote tallying through use of a legislative buddy system. In the House, this "whip team" is made up of a chief deputy whip, who oversees a team of deputy whips, who themselves oversee a number of assistant whips and regional whips. These regional whips usually have deep connections to specific House factions, such as a state delegation or the Congressional Black Caucus. The distribution and makeup of this whip hierarchy is subject to change. In the 113th Congress of 2012–2014, the Democrats' whip operation had nine deputies. In the 2000s, House Republicans sported no less than sixteen deputy whips and sixty regional whips. In the 1980s, the Democratic whip operation nearly quadrupled in size. It's a lot of whipping, and it's hard to keep track.

A party only fires up its whipping operation for close votes—and these votes don't usually come up for a vote unless leadership has determined that there is sufficient support. That said, having a well-oiled whip operation[107] allows leadership to quickly ascertain where their caucus stands on a particular vote. Once a whip count is initiated, lower-ranking whips fan out to ask their colleagues whether they're a "yes," "leaning yes," "undecided," "leaning no," or "no." Anything south of a firm "yes" will usually instigate a conversation about what would turn that around. Members are expected to be honest about their intentions, or at least not misrepresent them entirely. A member who tells a whip they'll vote one way and then votes another will seriously piss off leadership. A good whip can nail down a vote tally in under thirty minutes, an impressive feat given the challenges posed in corralling members of Congress. Congress would be great at organizing snow day phone trees.

A somewhat scaled-down whip system exists in the Senate, with both parties sporting a handful of deputy whips. However, given the upper chamber's significantly smaller size, it bears much closer resemblance to an honest-to-God buddy system. Also it's the Senate, so members will probably spend several hours articulating their position in floor speeches.

In recent years, the House whip has gained prominence thanks to the Netflix program *House of Cards*. Its antihero, Frank Underwood,

[107] Heh.

begins the series as the Democratic House whip, using his position as the all-knowing vote tallier to manipulate his colleagues and ruthlessly climb his way up the Washington ladder. It goes without saying that the show dramatizes the intensity and tenor of a whip's day-to-day job. Still, it would be entertaining to have read reports of former Majority whip Jim Clyburn growling at union officials to proverbially get down on their knees and fellate him, as happened in one memorable *Cards* scene.

These days, actually, the whip is one of leadership's nice guys. Counterintuitively, it was Tom DeLay, the most sharp-elbowed whip in recent memory, who helped make that happen. DeLay, who served as chief vote tallier from 1995 to 2003 and who earned himself the nickname "The Hammer," patented many of the take-no-prisoners tactics that were later appropriated by speakers and minority leaders to keep their members in line. Those tactics included contribution quotas for the party's campaign committees, restricting votes for members' bills, and the granting and stripping of committee assignments. Now the whip gets to play good cop to their bosses' bad cop—a great development for a whip hoping to advance to party leader or speaker. *Look, I'm not the one who's going to strip you of your Financial Services spot. I'm just the messenger.*

Knowing where members stand is not only essential to pursuing an agenda, but also to avoiding political embarrassment. To employ a terrible, Frank Underwood-ish metaphor, "Vote whipping is a bit like filling out your dance card, you best know who y—-" Ah, never mind.

See also, *"Leaders (House)," "Leaders (Senate)," "Speaker of the House"*

WHITE HOUSE

Historical landmark presidential employees use to get laid and impress their families. Known for its all-white facade, if the White House were constructed today, people would probably assume it was some kind of Mormon temple.

"White House" is regularly employed as shorthand for all of the executive-level offices that assist the commander in chief in his duties, and sometimes it's used to describe the entire executive branch, as well. In addition to the offices under direct supervision of the Chief of Staff, the White House also works closely with nonpresidential entities like the Secret Service (a Homeland Security agency that protects the first and second families), the National Parks Service (which administers the White House grounds), and branches of the armed services that provide personnel and equipment such as Marine One.

To say that the org chart of the Executive Office of the President—the official name for what we think of as White House offices—is a *hot mess* would be an overstatement, but it's not exactly a model of managerial efficiency. However, the president's support offices can be divided into four main categories and a select group of them are included below:

Operational

The president doesn't plan his own visits to swing-state universities, his Raisin Bran doesn't serve itself, and former NBA star Alonzo Mourning doesn't spontaneously appear on a golf course for a leisurely nine holes with the leader of the free world. The work of getting the first family up and about and keeping the lights in the White House on is a herculean undertaking, one that can be no less logistically challenging than preparing for a State of the Union address.

The Office of the First Lady (they've all been ladies, so far) is a kind of mini White House within the White House. The first spouse sports her own political, communications, and logistics team, situated in the East Wing of the White House, on the other side of the Executive Mansion opposite the West Wing. While we may associate first ladies with *Today* show appearances and *People* magazine features on their secret zucchini bread recipe, most are given a policy portfolio—genuinely inoffensive pursuits like combatting illiteracy and helping veterans—and therefore need staff to execute their mission. The one office that is situated in the East Wing is the office of the social secretary, who plans White House events, handling the distribution of tickets to the

W

annual Easter egg roll, coordinating with the State Department ahead of state dinners, orchestrating the annual Christmas tree lighting, and soothing the egos of pissy donors who don't feel welcome enough in the president's home.

The White House chief of staff, at least titularly, is the president's most senior adviser, and oversees the White House's various offices. The head of White House staff helps hire employees; strategizes with the president's legislative, policy, and communications aides; and serves as the president's traffic cop, coordinating the offices, and acting as POTUS's gatekeeper and information conduit. To assist him (they've all been "he's" to date) in these duties, the chief of staff has his own staff, usually comprised of one or two deputies who assist in both political and operational matters and who are themselves supported by a small staff of assistants. Senior presidential advisers are often placed within the office of the chief of staff.

Managerial skills are a must, but political experience is even more crucial, as the traditional hierarchies of the private sector are often supplanted by a delicate ecosystem of egos and relationships. While chiefs of staff often pick much of the senior staff, a president typically installs several of his own people and chiefs of staff must accommodate such administrative anomalies. Such dynamics become even more complicated if a chief of staff joins midway through an administration. Many lower-level staffers will have a relationship with the president and enough of a preexisting celebrity or reputation that the traditional chain of command can be undermined. *You* try firing the president's friend.

Then there is a whole slew of offices concerned with making sure the president's office works. The Executive Residence office includes the White House curator, who manages the facility's decorations, the White House calligrapher, who handles official stationery, and the chief usher, who manages the chefs that serve the first family their meals, handles the White House's decorations, and shoos the first dog away when it tries to pee on a marble pedestal holding a bust of Martin Van Buren. The White House's schedulers and advance team work with their communications- and legislative-minded colleagues to plan out trips that sync with the president's agenda. They are the ones who decide which revitalizing mill town to visit and in which greasy spoon the president will be photographed biting into a hoagie.

Governance

These are the offices that work with Congress, the states, and the bureaucracy. The Office of Cabinet Affairs works to keep cabinet departments abreast of administration policy, keep tabs on policy implementation, and to ensure that the transportation secretary doesn't go off the reservation and starts tweeting about chemtrails.

The Office of Legislative Affairs works with Congress, finding allied members to introduce legislation, assessing the mood of the House and Senate, deciding which members need a call from POTUS, and promising moderate members things in exchange for not voting to completely undo the president's accomplishments. Legislative affairs liaisons are assigned a portfolio of congressional offices in both parties for which they will serve as the White House's point person. White House–Congressional relations can safely be assumed to be in the toilet when pieces appear in the press featuring lawmakers griping about not knowing who the office's director is.

The Office of Public Engagement and Intergovernmental Affairs coordinates with other government agencies—state and municipal—and also outside organizations and other "stakeholders." State of Connecticut needs help with its Medicare expansion? New York City's mayor wants to discuss coordinating antiterror efforts? A group of CEOs want to bend the president's ear about tax extenders? They got you. This is a great place to park a rainmaker, a power broker who is brought into the West Wing for their connections and experience in the corridors of power. A person with preexisting relationships with CEOs, celebrities, and prominent philanthropists will do well in this office.

The Office of the Vice President makes sure Joe Biden's brass knuckles are polished and readily accessible.

Policy

One of the most annoying things about being president is that you have to know things. This can seriously eat into time reading advance copies of the latest Divergent book, joyriding around Camp David in a golf cart, and having staring contests with oil portraits of William Henry Harrison in the Red Room. Luckily, the commander in chief has hundreds of employees at their disposal to remedy this.

The Council of Economic Advisers (CEA), made up of a chairman and two members, provides the commander in chief with advice on economic matters. The CEA employs dozens of economists and researchers who distill complex macroeconomic forecasts, shifts in international labor supply levels, waxing trade deficits, and intricate algorithmic measures of future lending rates into memos about jobs.

The Domestic Policy Council helps to formulate and refine the president's agenda that doesn't involve starting wars or secretly funneling arms to rebels. The council is comprised of numerous cabinet secretaries, senior presidential advisers, the vice president, and the heads of White House offices such as the Council of Economic Advisers.

The National Security Council (NSC), meanwhile, helps the president decide which wars to start and which rebels to ship Toyota pickups and shoulder-launched MAWs. The NSC consists of the president's national security adviser and most of the national security "principals" such as the secretary of defense and the director of national intelligence.

The Office of Management and Budget (OMB) helps the president assemble his yearly budget proposal. The OMB is the largest White House office, and, in addition to its work with the president, its employees coordinate with the executive branch's myriad agencies and departments to reconcile their needs with the president's vision and congressional processes. The moment the president offhandedly mentions the need for a new veterans hiring program, a thousand policy geeks' Saturdays are suddenly ruined.

To make sure the president isn't under threat of impeachment on any given day, there's the Office of the White House Counsel. The White House's top lawyer, known as the chief counsel, is assisted by a team of lawyers who help assess whether legislation squares with the Constitution, kicks a possible judicial nominee's tires, and whether a junior staffer's Kickstarter campaign for a line of Madeleine Albright–inspired brooches constitutes an ethics violation.

Communications

A number of White House offices sport their own communication aides, to say nothing of the hundreds of communication professionals who populate the federal government, the president's reelection campaign, or the president's party. However, press relations concerning the president's work, activity, and carefully staged attempts to seem normal by playing Wiffle ball on the South Lawn are handled by a dedicated communications team.

The Office of Communications is headed by the communications director, whose role oscillates between lead administration talking head and lead PR strategist. In addition to dealing with the press, he or she will develop an overarching messaging strategy that will complement the president's agenda, including deciding when and where the commander in chief will speak, coordinating with other White House offices, and identifying administration initiatives or proposals that should be promoted in the media. For example, a communications director may push to promote an Agriculture Department rural education initiative, as it fits in with a goal of casting the president as champion of the downtrodden, but play down an Interior Department initiative to thin Alaska's reindeer population, as it risks reigniting the War on Christmas. A team of communication researchers is on hand to assist the communications director—and to work with the other communications teams—in their work.

The White House press secretary reports to the communications director but is nevertheless the most public administration official after the first and second families, so closely are they associated with blue backdrops, a White House emblem, and calm referrals to the relevant agency. Press secretaries handle most high-level media correspondence for the commander in chief, save for the president's speeches, press conferences, and interviews. This includes on- and off-record interviews and the dissemination of press releases detailing presidential statements on news developments, nominations, and reactions to congressional activity. The press secretary also oversees a staff of deputy press secretaries, most of whom handle press during presidential trips and who are point people for specific types of media, including online, minority-centric, local, and foreign outlets. A slew of other staff members handle everything from credentialing reporters, shepherding them into and out of Oval Office press availabilities (or "avails"), and making sure radio and TV reporters have the necessary technical facilities.

A good press secretary not only serves as their president's go-between with the media, but also as the White House's chief hack whisperer. It might seem counterintuitive that an official typically known for their serial-killer-like equanimity and emotional distance would be such an excellent manager of relationships, but cultivating cordial relations with the press corps is essential for the press secretary, who has the unfortunate distinction of working only several dozen feet away from a group of people constantly trying to bend their ear and, more often than not, trip him or her up. Not only does this arrangement make it much more difficult for the press staff to remain cordial with reporters, but it makes it all the more essential.

White House press secretaries would probably make excellent middle school teachers.

A press secretary, tasked with the seemingly impossible job of interacting with the press without actually disclosing anything beyond administration talking points, must use a very meager toolbox to keep a rowdy press merely displeased (they'll never be happy) and not outright mutinous. This can include facilitating interviews with administration officials, having the president call on non-legacy news outlets during press conferences, and providing "controlled" leaks to select reporters. Lying is a *huge* no-no, and can irreparably damage a press secretary's relationship with reporters, who will likely be burned by publishing false information. This is a big reason why press secretaries, like most political communication aides, lean heavily on bland, specifics-light statements. "The president is committed to resolving this conflict," won't come back to bite a flack.

Nearly every president sports impressive academic credentials and most can extemporize in front of crowds without sounding like a Miss America contestant asked to solve world hunger. That said, a president doesn't have enough time in their day to draft his own 2,000-word remarks at the thirty-fourth annual At-Home Caregiver Society's "Golden Bed Pan" Awards. For that, the boss has a dedicated team of speechwriters who familiarize themselves with the commander in chief's speech patterns with such attentiveness that Daniel Day-Lewis would be impressed. The speechwriting team within the communications office is led by a director of speechwriting, who is the president's lead point person on public addresses and who is assisted by several deputies and a team of junior speechwriters and research assistants who double-check how to pronounce the Malaysian prime minister's name and make sure they get the correct tally of Taliban fighters a Medal of Honor recipient killed.

See also, *"Congressional Staff," "James S. Brady Press Briefing Room," "West West Wing,"* "The West Wing," *"White House Correspondents' Dinner," "United States Naval Observatory"*

WHITE HOUSE CORRESPONDENTS' DINNER

Annual black-tie gala hosted by the White House Correspondents' Association, featuring a keynote address by the president, the stylings of the evening's comedian emcee, and the hearty guffaws of the national security adviser as a *Saturday Night Live* cast member calls him a war criminal. The reception is the year's preeminent coming together of Hollywood's A-List and the people you see on CNN squawking about a senator's trustworthiness numbers. The dinner remains the highlight of D.C.'s social calendar, and an entire week of events has grown out of it, marked by dozens of welcome parties, pre-parties, pre-pre-parties, after-parties, and morning-after brunches.

Members of the press typically exhibit a blasé attitude toward the public figures they cover—one must if one's job involves shoving a recorder in public figures' faces and asking impertinent questions—however, the weekend is a flurry of gaped mouths, selfies, and other starstruck expressions by Washington's press corps, not to mention other Beltway denizens unaccustomed to such a glitzy displays of celebrity. It's become known as "nerd prom," not just for the socially challenged, erstwhile high school newspaper geeks who populate it, but for their fraught social interactions: their insecure huddling among friends, their jerky and uncoordinated dance moves, and their thinly veiled gawking at peers of higher social rank. Each news organization is accorded at least one table at the main dinner, and each typically invites a celebrity.

The dinner began in 1921 as a modest gathering of reporters in the Arlington Hotel just north of McPherson Square and in 1924 Calvin Coolidge became the first president to attend the festivities. The dinner is regularly, and not unjustifiably, criticized as an unseemly lovefest between the White House and the press corps meant to keep a professional distance from it. *The New York Times* has boycotted the event for some years, and the op-eds denouncing the event are as much a mark of the season as the dinner itself.

However, the celebrification of the event has had the curious effect of making the event less sleazy. For six decades after the first dinner, White House correspondents would invite administration officials as their guests, laugh side by side at emcee Bob Hope's japes, and ask about each other's families while picking at their butter-drenched halibut. That started to change in 1987 when *The Baltimore Sun*'s

Michael Kelly invited Fawn Hall, an attractive Defense Department secretary to Oliver North and subject of congressional scrutiny over her role in the Iran-Contra Affair. The attention garnered by Kelly's stunt prompted other news outlets to follow suit, and by 2000, administration officials were filming spoof videos with *The West Wing* cast for the event. Now, rather than engaging in ethically compromising beat sweetening, administration officials and reporters are spending as much time scanning the room for each other as they are scouting for the latest Bond starlet. And this is to say nothing of the hosts, whose material has gotten edgier in recent decades as event organizers have shown increasing preference for performers like Stephen Colbert and Wanda Sykes and less for yuk-yuk purveyors like Rich Little. In a given year, some of the most pointed comments made to a president's face in a televised setting are those made by a WHCD host.

The dinner itself, held in the Washington Hilton's capacious subterranean banquet hall, is a mostly dull affair, and if it weren't for the jokes or the *Dancing with the Stars* contestant seated beside you, there wouldn't be much differentiating it from the Southeastern Dermatology Association's Face Peeler of the Year banquet. While press coverage of the dinner focuses on the celebrities, the host's roasting of the political class, the president's jokes, and the first lady's dress, what it typically leaves out, understandably so, are the more everyday parts of the ceremony: the rote pageantry, the surf-and-turf menu, the presentation of lifetime honors, and scholarships.

It's the parties surrounding the dinner that define the weekend's revelry. Washington, with its imposing embassies, museums, and other large and resplendent facilities, likely has more party space per capita than any other U.S. city—that is, event spaces that aren't drab conference centers with stain-hiding carpet patterns that resemble a Smurf's vomit. No one person will attend every last party, but there's more than enough space for everyone—the dinner alone seats 2,500 people despite the WHCA having only some 250 active members. Each of these bacchanals provides a wonderful cross section of the powerful, not-so-powerful—the Republican "strategist," the senior White

House aide, the ruffled congressional hack, the intern or cub reporter who scored a ticket from their boss—all united in their desire to know what the star of *Fist Punch 3: The Bloodening* smells like.

That said, there is a definite pecking order to the parties and the challenges of scoring an invite increase proportionately to their prestige. While the parties vary year to year, and the degree to which celebrities and politicos embrace them depends on the fervor of that year's op-eds denouncing the correspondents' dinner, below is a totally unscientific ranking of the mainstay events.

1. Vanity Fair After-Party

Like the Oscars, *Vanity Fair* has a lock as the WHCD's most desirable after-party. It regularly features a glut of A-list celebrities, Hollywood moguls, media personalities, government principals, and even a stray supermodel or two. Typically held in the French ambassador's gorgeous Tudor-revival residence in the mansion-lined Kalorama Heights neighborhood, the power guests mingle beneath paintings on loan from the Louvre and Versailles. If ever the global elite were to decide to plant lizard people in the highest circles of government and culture, such a plot would probably be hatched at the *Vanity Fair* WHCD after-party—assuming Katie Couric, Ivanka Trump, Bradley Cooper, and John McCain could break the impasse over who gets to be the Illuminati's treasurer.

2. Tammy Haddad's Brunch

Haddad, a former cable news booker, used her deeply entrenched position in the intersection of politics and punditry to start an events company that hosts some of the year's more envy-inducing parties; her WHCD brunch is undoubtedly the crown jewel of her social calendar. While celebrities flock to the brunch—first started as a pre-dinner get-together in 1993 and more recently held as a morning-after brunch on Sunday—there's a slightly larger contingent of Washington types than at the *Vanity Fair* party. Matt Drudge! Tucker Carlson! Sally Quinn! Star of the forthcoming adaptation of the wildly popular

@BloodKnights: Adolescent Vampire Instagram Justice Crusaders novels! Undoubtedly the must-attend party for aspiring society types hoping to spy Eric Cantor and Lindsay Lohan sipping mimosas.

3. MSNBC After-Party

MSNBC's after-party in the Italian embassy usually serves as the go-to event for the politicians, staffers, reporters, pundits, and A–Z political guide authors who can't score an invite to the *Vanity Fair* party. It's often the second stop for celebrities with enough stamina left after the *Vanity Fair* event. MSNBC's second-fiddle status was underscored in 2015 when it was bumped to another location by *Vanity Fair* while the French ambassador's residence was being renovated. The boldfaced names are slightly less eye-catching, particularly in the beginning, when party headliners are still at the *Vanity Fair* soiree. For a number of years, early arrivers were treated to the sight of Rachel Maddow tending bar. This was a great opportunity to grab a beverage at the other drink stations that had been all but vacated by attendees hoping to be served a Jack and ginger by the popular cable news personality.

4. Washington Hilton Pre-parties

The Washington Hilton—the one where Ronald Reagan was shot by a Jodie Foster–obsessed John Hinckley Jr. in 1981—sports one of D.C.'s largest event spaces, and situated in its sprawling subterranean bowels are a number of conference and meeting rooms, including the main banquet hall where the dinner is held. These rooms are used as the sites for a number of pre-parties, including ones held by leading news outlets such as *The Washington Post* and Reuters. By virtue of their proximity to the evening's main event, these parties are popular destinations for the weekend's most well-known guests. However, given the sheer number of attendees, including the 2,500 banquet attendees and the hundreds of more people who only have tickets to the pre-parties, celebrity sighting can be hindered by the sheer mass of partygoers. However, a tenacious attendee still might get the chance to see Callista Gingrich's hair up close, or to spot celebrity chef José Andrés and the actress who plays Sansa on *Game of Thrones* trying on a virtual reality headset that allows the user to tour the Oval Office.

5. Everything Else

In any given year, there will be parties that deserve a spot on this list—*The New Yorker*'s welcome party and those thrown by *Politico* are several examples. However, for every *New Yorker* welcome party sporting a star-studded guest list, there are dozens, if not hundreds, of parties you'll never read about. These cater to possible Washington subsets: cocktail parties for conservatives, kickoff events for liberals, industry conferences for lobbyists, after-parties for Washington's fledgling tech scenesters to drink and ideate. There's the Rock the Vote party, the Mother Nature Network White House Correspondents' Jam, the Voto Latino party, the MPAA party, the Spotify party. These might attract the occasional movie star or administration official beholden to the party's host or target demo, but their sheer number has a tendency to dilute the guest list.

See also, *"Access," "Inauguration," "Shiny Party People"*

WINNING

To be victorious, not just in a debate, election, war, or other traditional power showdown, but in all manner of political and media endeavors. As the political arena has been increasingly portrayed as just that, the stage for a sporting event, the win/lose mentality has become increasingly prevalent in Washington. Interns have yet to "win" by retrieving giant cardboard coffee dispensers from Dunkin Donuts, but we're heading that way. Had John F. Kennedy delivered his "We choose to go to the moon" speech in today's climate, he probably would have vowed to "Win the cosmos."

The most quotidian form of D.C. "winning" is to win the morning, afternoon, or other segment of time with an announcement or piece of news that is expected to dominate the news cycle. Though actual, honest-to-god earnest mentions of "winning the morning" are few and far between, the concept is very much evident in the constant scuffling over who breaks news first, over whose press conference gets more coverage, and whose video goes viral. Even issues themselves have become things to be won or lost. "Tuesday's Planned Parenthood hearing shows why Republicans will lose on this issue" declared an October 2015 *Washington Post* headline about a congressional debate over Planned Parenthood funding, as if the legal status of a woman's uterus were something akin to a game of darts.

On April Fools' Day, 2009, *Politico*'s brass sent around a memo to its employees, saying that it was no longer content to merely "win the morning," but it now sought to "win the dawn." "Each of you should be focused on working your beats in order to file some kind of story that is ready for posting by no later than 6 a.m. each morning," wrote John Harris and Jim VandeHei. The memo was meant to be a joke, but many staffers took it seriously, and proceeded, bleary eyed and sleep deprived, to follow the memo's dictates.

During Barack Obama's 2012 State of the Union address, he repeated on twelve different occasions that it would be his administration's goal to "win the future." Though he was referencing a policy agenda, many observers felt he took the winning thing a bit too far, and the phrase sounded less like a goal of 4-percent GDP growth than a desire for the nation to triumph upon the Tron Game Grid. "[T]he line sounded more like the title of a self-help seminar, with Obama in the role of Tony Robbins," wrote *Slate*'s John Dickerson.

See also, *"Hill Rags,"* "Master of the Senate," *"Running of the Interns," "Spin"*

W

WONK

A person with a strong interest in, and knowledge of, policy. "Wonk" used to be a semi-pejorative term, a kind of Beltway version of calling someone Poindexter.[108] It derives from "wonky," which means broken, crooked, or in any way out of sorts. Tracing wonk's etymological evolution from "broken" to "policy nerd" isn't easy, but one suspects images of Buddy Holly glasses taped together at the bridge had something to do with it.

Writing in *The New Republic* in 1984, Sidney Blumenthal bemoaned Walter Mondale's "thralldom to the policy wonks and wise men of the Washington establishment."[109] Wonks were smart, but somewhat middling Beltway creatures, attested David Brooks in a 1990 piece on them. "He is good-looking, with his sandy brown hair and wire-rimmed glasses," Brooks wrote, "but he is not too good-looking."

The major break began in 1992, when Bill Clinton and Al Gore fashioned themselves as wonk candidates, steeped in policy and, along with Hillary Clinton, ready to overhaul the nation's health care. "Wonk If You Love Clinton," read one *Washington Post* headline. "Kennedys They're Not. The Torch Has Been Passed to a Nerd Frontier." "There's a new kind of creature running loose in America these days," wrote *St. Petersburg Times*'s Washington correspondent Jack Payton. "Some of you may have heard about it. It's called 'The Wonk.'"

But the wonkgates really opened in the 2000s, when Buddy Holly glasses were suddenly "in" and "nerd" and "geek" became cool, self-affirming things to be. *The Washington Post* launched its popular Wonkblog. American University started advertising for its poli-sci grad programs by assuring the perspective students that they would be transformed into wonks. "Is There a Wonk Bubble?" asked *Politico Magazine*.

"Wonk" hasn't achieved total vernacular parity with "nerd" or "geek." You're unlikely to encounter ditzy Arizona State freshmen professing their bookish love of policy the way they might, say, Harry

[108] With apologies to Reagan's national security adviser John Poindexter, Senator Miles Poindexter, and all the other notable Poindexters who have actually served in Washington.

[109] Thirty years later, Hillary Clinton would be accused, during the Benghazi investigation, of being enthralled by superwonk Sidney Blumenthal. Time is a flat circle.

Potter—"ohmigooooddd, i am *such* a wonk for occupational licensing issues."

American University even awards an annual "Wonk of the Year" award. And to give you a sense of how overused the term is, consider its 2015 recipient, that biggest wonk of them all . . . former first lady Laura Bush.

See also, *"Executive Departments," "Expert," "Strategist"*

WORLD'S GREATEST DELIBERATIVE BODY

See, *"Social Media"*

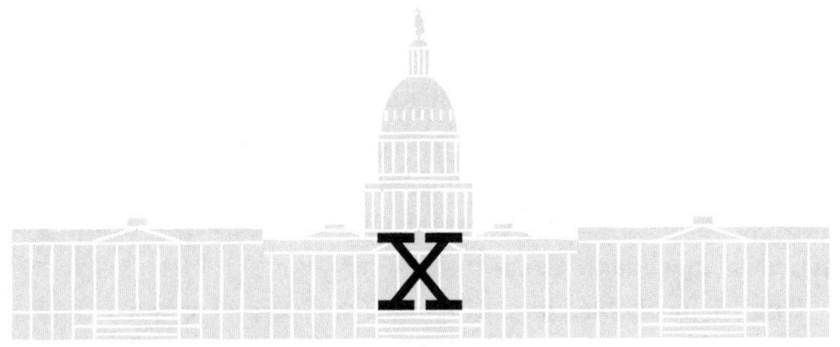

XENOPHOBIA

One of the country's most time-honored traditions, one that predates the current "border crisis," Japanese internment camps, Sacco and Vanzetti, Thomas Nast depictions of Irish immigrants as primates, and attempts to resettle freed slaves in Liberia because, hey, they have dark skin so anywhere in Africa should do the trick, right? And while America's immigration system has grown considerably more complex since the days of gap-toothed hayseeds on rocking chairs, cradling blunderbusses, and warning visitors that they best go back from where they came,[110] the spirit of those backwoods shut-ins is very much alive.

[110] It's actually surprising that one of those hayseeds was never nominated to be secretary of state. They were probably too busy hocking loogies into a nearby spittoon.

Today's political xenophobia is largely defined by unease with immigrants from Latin America and a particularly virulent strain of Islamophobia that emerged following 9/11. With respects to immigration, a June 2015 survey by Pew found that 41 percent of Americans felt that immigrants "take jobs, housing and health care." Anti-immigrant platforms have all but vanished from the Democratic party, thanks in no small part to unions eager to replenish their ranks with newly arrived blue-collar workers. It is, however, very much alive and well in the GOP. Donald Trump, during his timeshare presentation masquerading as a presidential campaign, worried aloud about the effects Mexican immigrants were having on American society. "They're taking our jobs. They're taking our manufacturing jobs. They're taking our money. They're killing us," he said.[111] In a July 2013 interview with Newsmax, Iowa congressman Steve King responded to a Democratic initiative to allow undocumented students a path to citizenship by worrying that for every aspiring student, "there's another 100 out there that weigh 130 pounds and they've got calves the size of cantaloupes because they're hauling 75 pounds of marijuana across the desert."

The Islamophobia emanating from the political sphere is no less virulent or downright ridiculous. Consider the rantings of House Republican Louie Gohmert, who claimed in a June 2010 speech on the House floor that pregnant women were being sent by terrorists to the United States so their children "could be raised and coddled as future terrorists"; or consider the numerous anti-Islamic "lectures" scheduled at Tea Party and far-right conventions by noted Islamophobe Pamela Geller; or consider the widespread anxiety in 2010 about the construction of a mosque near the ground zero site in downtown Manhattan. In an especially McCarthyesque example of other-phobia, New York congressman Peter King held a hearing in 2011 titled, "The Extent of Radicalization in the American Muslim Community and That Community's Response," which appeared to re-

[111] Mexican immigrants: not classy, apparently.

quire American Muslims to explain every last wrongdoing by a self-described Muslim. Presumably King doesn't want a Methodist family in suburban Cincinnati to explain that Christians are normal, peace-loving Americans every time some cult leader in the Adirondacks dons a flower crown and marries forty-three women because he thinks it's Christ's will.

Not that it's much consolation to the hundreds of thousands of recently deported undocumented immigrants or the Muslim American business owner who feels he has to festoon his shop with American flags, but hostility to non-WASPs by the ruling class is as common an American occurence as dancing football robots and AXE body spray.

Few groups have escaped it. Even WASPs were viewed with considerable hostility in early America. The first House speaker, Frederick Muhlenberg, himself the son of German immigrants, famously remarked, "the faster the Germans become Americans, the better it will be."[112] In an even more curious bit of self-loathing, Muhlenberg's father Henry (né Heinrich), widely regarded as the founder of American Lutheranism, publicly loathed the people he left behind. Germans, the elder Muhlenberg once said, would inundate the country with "unprecedented wickedness and crimes." Anti-German sentiment continued through the nineteenth century and well into the twentieth with the First and Second World Wars. The idea of pre-twentieth-century hostility to Germans might seem a little odd, but it really was a thing. Seriously, Benjamin Franklin *fucking hated* Germans. No joke.

That early anti-German animus paled beside the anti-immigration movement that sprung up in the nineteenth century, much of which was intertwined with anti-Catholic sentiment. Entities like the Know-Nothing Party existed, in part, to stem the tide of Irish and German immigration. Reading some of the anti-Catholic rhetoric of that age, one can't help but be struck by the similarity to today's hysteria surrounding the supposed goal of America's Muslims to

[112] There's a widely disseminated myth that a vote was held to make German the nation's official language. That's a load of *scheiße*.

impose sharia law. "These minions of the Pope are boldly insulting our Senators; reprimanding our Statesmen; propagating the adulterous union of Church and State; abusing with foul calumny all governments but Catholic, and spewing out the bitterest execrations on all Protestantism," one Texas newspaper published in 1855, as quoted in Richard Hofstadter's famous 1964 essay, "The Paranoid Style in American Politics."

It seems every new batch of immigrants to the United States is greeted with hostility and suspicion by their new peers, like some kind of societal frat initiation that goes too far to be considered a character-building experience. There was the Chinese Exclusion Act of 1882, which claimed that the thousands of Chinese who immigrated to the West and helped construct America's railroad system "endangers the good order of certain localities." There was the backlash to the wave of immigration around the turn of the twentieth century, with Americans complaining that the new immigrants from Central and Eastern Europe were stealing their jobs and, per popular eugenicist Madison Grant, weakening the American "stock."

The contemporary xenophobia that radiates out of Washington, D.C., is at odds with the city's cultural fabric. The Washington, D.C., metro area sports one of the country's largest immigrant constituencies, with large numbers of new arrivals from Latin America, Asia, and Africa settling in and around the District. The permanent diplomatic corps means there's a large base of exceptionally well-educated foreigners who are fixtures in the local social scene. Then there is the large foreign policy community, with its various think tanks and advocacy groups, populated by people who care passionately about the global community and who can't seem to stop raving about how great Beirut is.

You may spy a House member on the House floor delivering a stem-winder against the UN, unbridled immigration, and "creeping sharia," but the person who prepared their floor speech may well have enjoyed a great meal the night before at any one of D.C.'s countless immigrant-run restaurants, while the lawmaker's chief of staff may have spent the previous Saturday chaperoning his kids at the annual Around the World Embassy Tour, when D.C.'s embassies host cultural open houses. And, if the ethnic makeup of the yard crews working in the conservative enclave McLean is any indication, Washington Republicans don't *really* buy into all that deportation stuff. A shame for those hundreds of thousands of deportees, though.

See also, *"Racism," "Sexism"*

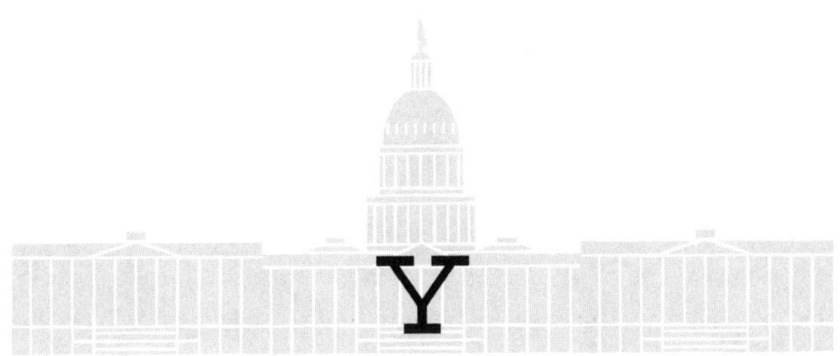

"Y'ALL"

See, *"Accents," "America," "Blue Dogs"*

"ZOOPHILIA"

See, *"Google Problem"*

SELECTED BIBLIOGRAPHY AND FURTHER READING

The Beltway Bible relied heavily on dozens of interviews I conducted in the year I spent drafting it, as well as countless more in the course of my time in Washington. In addition to the sources listed in the body of the text, I drew from the following works and resources, both directly and in helping to deepen my understanding of politics. All are recommended for anyone self-loathing enough to learn more about the issues introduced in *The Beltway Bible*.

CAMPAIGN FINANCE AND LOBBYING

The good people at the Sunlight Foundation do great work, cataloging political fundraisers, monitoring the revolving door, and making sense of the ever-changing and increasingly inscrutable world of campaign finance. They can be found at SunlightFoundation.com. Likewise, the Center for Responsive Politics and their OpenSecrets.org site are another go-to destination for campaign finance information and data. They have a number of great tools that allow users to easily sort through the political contributions of corporations, unions, and other outside actors (that is, the ones that we know about).

Ken Vogel is one of Washington's best investigative reporters and does great work chronicling the exploits of Washington's influence peddlers. His book, *Big Money: 2.5 Billion Dollars, One Suspicious Vehicle, and a Pimp—on the Trail of the Ultra-Rich Hijacking American Politics* is a must-read for anyone hoping to understand the bizarre, often shady world of campaign finance and the megadonors who've come to dominate it. Although it came out as I was finalizing this book, I've been enthralled (and perturbed) by Jane Mayer's *Dark Money: The Hidden History of the Billionaires Behind the Rise of the Radical Right.*

Even though he takes his eyewear cues from a 1970s West German playwright, Lawrence Lessig's *Republic, Lost: How Money Corrupts Congress—and a Plan to Stop It* is a great starting point for anyone hoping to get a sense of just how pervasive money has become in our politics. Similarly, and for those looking for something more provocative, Peter Schweizer's *Extortion: How Politicians Extract Your Money, Buy Votes, and Line Their Own Pockets* provides the best account of leadership PACs I've read to date and was referenced in writing in my entry on the subject.

Many of the tools that investigative reporters use are available to the public. Despite sounding quite dull, these websites can lead to some very juicy reading. The Senate and the House both have websites for searching lobbying disclosures, but I find the House one to be a bit easier to navigate—it can be found at disclosures.house.gov. Anyone wishing to research a foreign entity's lobbying activity should consult FARA.gov, the Department of Justice's website for Foreign Agents Registration Act filings. Campaign filings—declarations of candidacies, quarterly reports, and such—can be found on the Federal Election Commission's website at fec.gov/disclosure.shtml.

CONGRESS

The politico bros, whatever their faults, have it right: the first three installments of Robert Caro's *The Years of Lyndon Johnson* biographies—*The Path to Power, Means of Ascent,* and *Master of the Senate*—are brilliant. If you're looking for a more contemporary account, Robert G. Kaiser's *Act of Congress: How America's Essential Institution Works, and How It Doesn't,* provides an impressively detailed and up-close account of the 2009–2010 battle to pass Wall Street reform. Also tremendous is Robert Draper's *When the Tea Party Came to Town,* chronicling

Congress's chaotic year after the 2010 Tea Party wave. My *Huffington Post* colleagues Ryan Grim, Arthur Delaney, and Zach Carter wrote a number of excellent pieces earlier this decade about Congress and the corporate interests that heavily influence it. "The Cash Committee: How Wall Street Wins on the Hill," from March 2010, "Power Struggle: Inside the Battle for the Soul of the Democratic Party" from June 2010, and "Swiped: Banks, Merchants and Why Washington Doesn't Work for You" from April 2011 are all essential reading.

In addition to Robert V. Remini's fantastic *The House: The History of the House of Representatives,* which is cited in the "Inauguration" entry, I also relied on a tremendous history of the upper chamber, *The American Senate: An Insider's History* by Neil MacNeil and Richard A. Baker. Former Senate historian Donald A. Ritchie's *Press Gallery: Congress and the Washington Correspondents* is a concise history of Hill hacks, America's most permanently rumpled subgenus.

If you really want to nerd out over the people's branch, I suggest you head over to Congress.gov, where you can read the Congressional Record, scrutinize legislation, and follow the progress of the roughly two bills that actually go anywhere each session (OK, it's more than that). No entry in this book is more derivative than the "Legislative Glossary" entry, whose subjects were mostly culled from the one on Congress.gov (but didn't the jokes really *deepen* your understanding of adjournment sine die?). And then there's C-SPAN—sweet, sweet, C-SPAN. Visitors to C-SPAN.org can, after perusing over thirty-seven years of footage from both chambers and all of their committees (closed sessions notwithstanding), congratulate themselves on being such tremendous dorks. That said, you can also search for video by the content of their transcripts, which is [*presses bridge of glasses firmly against nose*] pretty cool!

ELECTIONS AND THE TRAIL

The campaign ticktock is a staple of political journalism, and nary a presidential election transpires without a healthy number of them hitting bookshelves. That said, Richard Ben Cramer's *What It Takes,* chronicling the 1988 presidential campaign, remains, in my mind (and many minds), the gold standard of deeply researched campaign reporting. Likewise, Timothy Crouse's *The Boys on the Bus* and Hunter S. Thompson's *Fear and Loathing on the Campaign Trail '72* provide vivid, genre-defining accounts of both campaign apparatuses and also the media that cover them.

If you're looking for a more recent account, I particularly enjoyed Jonathan Alter's *The Center Holds: Obama and His Enemies.* I'm indebted to Alter's hard-won examination of Obama's digital team and, more generally, the role of technology in his campaign. Beth Harpaz's *The Girls in the Van: Covering Hillary* is a wonderfully engrossing account of Hillary Clinton's 2000 Senate run. It provides a look at a down ballot campaign—albeit a highly scrutinized one—and a decidedly less male-centric update of Crouse's *The Boys on the Bus.* Though the print editions are still available for purchase, the AP recently released an updated version online. These days, no discussion of campaign books would be complete without mentioning John Heilemann and Mark Halperin's *Game Change* series, which at this point I'm pretty sure has its own clothing line and breakfast cereal. I for one am particularly excited for *Game Change 8: The More Things Game, the More They Change the Same.*

Ari Berman's *Give Us the Ballot* is the premier account of the contemporary effort to roll back voting access across the country. Berman's book, and his reporting for *The Nation,* are indispensable if you want to better understand modern disenfranchisement. Joseph Cummins's *Anything for A Vote: Dirty Tricks, Cheap Shots, and October Surprises in U.S. Presidential Campaigns* is a fun and breezy trip through 200-plus years of incredibly dumb presidential elections and was referenced with great amusement while drafting my entries on advertising and adultery. If you really want to get into the weeds of campaign knowledge, Michael McNamara's *The Political Campaign Desk Reference: A Guide for Campaign Managers and Candidates Running for Elected Office* and Sasha Issenberg's *The Victory Lab: The Secret Science of Winning Campaigns* provide in-depth and technical overviews of what makes successful field and digital teams.

Selected Bibliography and Further Reading

WASHINGTON: THE CITY

There are countless biographies, autobiographies, and tell-alls documenting the lives of the city's biggest movers and shakers, but if you're going to start anywhere, you might as well tackle the big one, Mark Leibovich's *This Town,* which gives the capital the anthropological treatment it so richly deserves—plus it reminded me about Ken Duberstein's ability to self-promote (due to time constraints, however, I sadly had to nix plans for an entry on political scrub time). Though *This Town* mostly leaves the Fourth Estate alone, you'd do well to check out the paper, "Did Twitter Kill the Boys on the Bus? Searching for a Better Way to Cover a Campaign," an examination of reporting life in the social media age by then-CNN reporter Peter Hamby. In a wonderful bit of poetry, Hamby, who wrote the paper while a Fellow at Harvard, is now the head of news at Snapchat.

If you want to get a sense of how Washington's close quarters can impact policy, 2014's *The Georgetown Set: Friends and Rivals in Cold War Washington* by Gregg Herken takes a careful look at, among other things, Henry Kissinger's social life. And if you're curious about the over 50 percent of Washingtonians who've likely never seen the inside of a Georgetown cocktail party, Harry Jaffe and Tom Sherwood's *Dream City: Race, Power, and the Decline of Washington D.C.* is a gripping history of Washington in the second half of the twentieth century, among the most tumultuous years endured by an American city at any point in the country's history.

I also have to make special mention of the late Marjorie Williams's *The Woman at the Washington Zoo: Writings on Politics, Family, and Fate.* Williams was among the most underappreciated political writers of recent decades and this collection of her work is one of my favorite books about Washington. My "Rainmaker" entry was inspired, in great part, by her profile of Vernon Jordan and drew from it.

Selected Bibliography and Further Reading

MISCELLANEOUS

I'm often asked about my news diet. In addition to excellent work being done by my coworkers at *The Huffington Post,* I also check the major "Hill rags" multiple times a day, including *Politico, The Hill,* and *Roll Call.* Other outlets doing great political work include *Mother Jones,* BuzzFeed, *The Guardian,* ProPublica, *Washington Monthly, Washingtonian, National Journal,* Yahoo! News, the *Washington City Paper, Vox,* Bloomberg, and *The New Republic,* to name a few. Then, of course, there are the journalistic mainstays like the wires, TV news networks, major regional publications, and legacy papers and magazines. I'd be lying if I said much of my news intake didn't originate from my Twitter feed. For all of its faults, it remains a great way to quickly learn what smart people are reading.

When I first told people about this project, many of them replied, "Oh, like William Safire's *Political Dictionary*?" Not quite, but if you're looking for a more lexicographic experience, the late *New York Times* columnist's reference is a must-have for the political junkie and anyone itching to know the political context of "mollycoddle."

I nearly went to law school, but I switched gears and chose the thriving worlds of news media and publishing, instead. As such, my understanding of our courts and the legal world has been greatly influenced by the SCOTUSblog, which remains the preeminent online source for all things legal and was a tremendous resource when drafting my entry on the judiciary. Also, Jeffrey Toobin's *The Nine: Inside the Secret World of the Supreme Court* provides an unmatched view of the High Court.

One of the most undervalued resources in the political world is the White House Transition Project, accessible on WhiteHouseTransitionProject.org. Founded in 1999 and run by Martha Joynt Kumar and Terry Sullivan, the project features White House org charts, essays by former administration officials on the challenges of governance and life inside the White House, and a treasure trove of other information that provided an excellent starting point in my research and interviews.

Though revered inside the Beltway (and the pages of this book), the

Congressional Research Service is also an underappreciated resource, in part because the goobers in Congress won't make its reports public. Luckily, *some* of the goobers in Congress regularly leak the reports, and there are a number of online resources to browse them. The Federation of American Scientists has compiled an extensive database at fas.org/sgp/crs and they are also available at CRSreports.com.

And, how could I forget? You should also subscribe to my newsletter, HuffPost Hill, a cheeky roundup of the day's political news. It has garnered a halfway respectable following in and outside the Beltway. Join the fun at huffingtonpost.com/newsletter/huffpost-hill. Or just Google it.

THIS IS YOUR FAULT

This could have been avoided, yet due to decades of reckless love and support by family, friends, and colleagues, I was not only emboldened by their unconditional dedication, but was moved to think this misguided endeavor was a good idea. These all-too-brief acknowledgments not only do a disservice to their impact on my life and the development of this book, but neglect the countless legislators, political staffers, reporters, lobbyists, activists, agency officials, and others whose knowledge has proved invaluable both for this endeavor and my day job.

Mom, Dad, and Andrea for a lifetime of love and support and not being too concerned when I opted against law school.

Meghan for her love, support, friendship, patience, editorial input, and patience. Did I say patience?

Ryan Grim, Nico Pitney, and Arianna Huffington for entrusting me with HuffPost Hill and to Arthur Delaney for helping make HPH what it is and for facilitating countless SANDs.

My *Huffington Post* colleagues past and present assisted me with this project and dozens more provided friendship and support, including Amanda Terkel, Sam Stein, Jen Bendery, Mike McAuliff, Elise Foley, Zach Carter, Ariel Edwards-Levy, Paul Blumenthal, Laura Bassett, Paige Lavender, Ryan Reilly, Jeff Young, Igor Bobic, Ashley Alman, Sujata Mitra, Matt Fuller, Jason Linkins, Christina Wilkie, and Lauren Weber.

Michael Flamini for taking a chance on this project. His editorial sensibility and tact are unparalleled and were employed to dazzling effect when telling me to tone down the toilet humor.

The entire St. Martin's team, including Vicki Lame, Gabrielle Gantz, Laura Clark, and Christine Catarino for being such pros and doing their utmost to make sure I don't completely embarrass myself.

Allison Hunter for playing both agent and therapist. I promise I won't bug you as much next time around.

Caitlin O'Shaughnessy, for midwifing the bejesus out of this project. Without her friendship and unrivaled publishing expertise, this book would just be an idea. Truly, this book is as much her fault as anyone's.

Howard Fineman and Mark Leibovich for providing valuable guidance on how one actually goes about writing a book and for talking me up at parties I'm not invited to. Their friendship never ceases to inspire me.

I kept returning time and again to a select group of individuals for contacts, brainstorming sessions, editorial input, and general assistance. They deserve special mention:

PSLGOPL and NIBS for, as always, being my go-to K Street sherpas.

Jim Manley for his A+flacking insights and unparalleled knowledge of Capitol Hill.

Josh Stewart and the entire Sunlight Foundation team for being on the side of the angels and helping me detangle campaign finance.

TJ Helmstetter and Mike Naple, whose friendship and insights into campaign life and countless other political nooks and crannies were both illuminating and essential.

And lastly, I couldn't have asked for better friends to gab about politics at Stoney's with than Alexa Combelic, Devon Kearns, Lennon Duggan, Dan Pollock, and Danielle Geanacopoulos.

Look what you all did.